The Gospel of Mary

Beyond a Gnostic and a Biblical
Mary Magdalene

Esther A. de Boer

T & T CLARK INTERNATIONAL
A Continuum imprint
LONDON • NEW YORK

Continuum
The Tower Building, 11 York Road, London SE1 7NX
15 East 26th Street, Suite 1703, New York, NY 10010

www.continuumbooks.com

First published in 2004 by T&T Clark, an imprint of Continuum, as *The Gospel of Mary: Beyond a Gnostic and a Biblical Mary Magdalene*.

British Library Cataloguing-in-Publication Data
A catalogue record for this book is available from the British Library

Library of Congress Cataloguing-in-Publication Data
A catalogue record for this book is available from the Library of Congress

Typeset by TMW Typesetting, Sheffield
Printed on acid-free paper in Great Britain by Cromwell Press, Trowbridge, Wiltshire

ISBN 0-8264-8001-2

CONTENTS

PREFACE

Although many copies of the Gospel of Mary may have been hidden, destroyed or just lost and forgotten, two tiny fragments in Greek and one copy in Coptic, containing about half of the Gospel, survived. For more than fifteen centuries this Coptic version was waiting to be found in a Christian cemetery in Egypt, well preserved by the dry Egyptian climate.

It was discovered in 1896 and published only in 1955, but no scholar of that time could have thought that it would arouse the interest it receives today. Like a little stone thrown into still water the Gospel of Mary initially had very little impact, but gradually interest in it spread wider and wider. Ever since Elaine Pagels mentioned it in her popular book *The Gnostic Gospels* and it was included in *The Nag Hammadi Library*, it has become known to a larger public. But, of even more consequence, the Gospel of Mary began to inspire writers of fiction, which resulted in a number of successful novels.

For instance, the Gospel of Mary inspired the internationally well-known Swedish author Marianne Fredriksson to write her novel *According to Mary Magdalene* (trans. Joanne Tate; Charlottesville, VA: Hampton Roads Publishing Company, 1999). It tells the story of how Jesus and Mary Magdalene met, and why she became his disciple. Years after his death Mary Magdalene comes to realize that Peter and Paul are altering Jesus' teaching to suit their own goals. In discussion with them and others she tries to recover his undistorted teaching herself, at the centre of which is Jesus' warning from the Gospel of Mary not to give rules or laws lest one become imprisoned by them. Gradually she begins to understand that her witness is of the utmost importance. After anonymously attending a Gnostic service, in which she hears the priest refer to her very words and actions just after Jesus' crucifixion, her husband Leonidas says to her:

'You've been drawn into a game which is far greater than we thought.'

'What game?'

'It's all about power, about the power the new church is to be based on.' (p. 167)

This power play is the subject of the international bestseller *The Da Vinci Code* by the American author Dan Brown (New York: Doubleday, 2003). Translated into numerous languages, this thriller about the secrets of the Grail kept readers in various countries in its grip.

In *The Da Vinci Code*, Dan Brown has his main characters suggest that the Roman Catholic Church should not have become the ascetic, male-centred and hierarchically structured organization it later turned out to be. In the book, Leonardo Da

Vinci is said to have possessed documents that would reveal this truth. The Grail specialist Sir Leigh Teabing points to Leonardo's painting of the Last Supper when explaining the hidden secrets in this work to the cryptologist Sophie Neveu. The painting shows the twelve apostles and Jesus sharing bread and wine shortly before his execution. According to Teabing, the figure at the side of Jesus would not have been meant to represent the apostle John, loved most by Jesus and always pictured in a feminine way, but the figure of a woman instead.

> 'Who is she?' Sophie asked.
>
> 'That, my dear,' Teabing replied, 'is Mary Magdalene.'
>
> Sophie turned. 'The prostitute?'
>
> Teabing drew a short breath, as if the word had injured him personally. 'Mary Magdalene was no such thing. That unfortunate misconception is the legacy of a smear campaign launched by the early Church. The Church needed to infame Mary Magdalene in order to cover up her dangerous secret – her role as the Holy Grail.' (p. 244)

Teabing also talks about the Mary who figures in the long lost Gnostic Gospels, especially drawing Sophie's attention to the Gospel of Mary, where Mary is called the disciple Jesus loved most:

> 'The woman they are speaking of,' Teabing explained, 'is Mary Magdalene. Peter is jealous of her.'
>
> 'Because Jesus preferred Mary?'
>
> 'Not only that. The stakes were far greater than mere affection. At this point in the gospels, Jesus suspects He will soon be captured and crucified. So He gives Mary Magdalene instructions on how to carry on His church after He is gone. As a result, Peter expresses his discontent over playing the second fiddle to a woman. I daresay Peter was something of a sexist.'
>
> Sophie was trying to keep up. 'This is *Saint* Peter. The rock on which Jesus built His Church.'
>
> 'The same, except for one catch. According to these unaltered gospels, it was not *Peter* to whom Christ gave directions with which to establish the Christian Church. It was *Mary Magdalene*.'
>
> Sophie looked at him. 'You're saying the Christian Church was to be carried on by a *woman*?'
>
> 'That was the plan. Jesus was the original feminist. He intended for the future of his Church to be in the hands of Mary Magdalene.' (pp. 247–48)

Although Teabing here specifically refers to the Gospel of Mary, Dan Brown, in contrast to the Gospel, limits the role of Mary Magdalene to her having a female body and being capable of bearing children. She is presented as the wife of Jesus and the mother of his child and remains a silent character. This role, according to Dan Brown's novel, is Mary Magdalene's chief contribution to the Christian belief. As such it is of great importance because it emphasizes Jesus' human nature and thus, in Brown's plot, threatens the Church's central belief in Jesus' divinity. In the Gospel of Mary, however, Jesus is called the Saviour, and Mary Magdalene is valued because of her penetrating teaching. Moreover, in the Gospel of Mary, Peter's attempt to limit Mary Magdalene to a woman's silent role is thoroughly criticized.

Of course both *The Da Vinci Code* and *According to Mary Magdalene* are works of fiction. Nonetheless, the success of these and other novels has made the Gospel of Mary known to an ever-growing public, and has stimulated a world-wide discussion about an alternative view of the beginnings of Christianity and the role of Mary Magdalene.

The present study introduces the scholarly debate about the meaning of the Gospel of Mary and questions the various views on the character and purpose of the Gospel. The study also investigates the Gospel's background, and the role and teaching of Mary Magdalene suggested by the Gospel.

It is thanks to Professor Riemer Roukema (Theological University of Kampen) that this study has been undertaken and completed. I am very grateful for his close involvement in the project and for his criticism and support during the research, writing and completion of the book. My sincere gratitude also goes to Dr Caroline Vander Stichele (University of Amsterdam) for her challenging comments on various drafts of the work. Paula Pumplin patiently read and reread all the drafts of the manuscript, and critically commented on my use of the English language. I could not have done without her, and wish to emphasize that any sins against the language that remain are mine.

Last, but certainly not least, I thank my husband Klaas Spoelstra and our children Maartje, Jan and Simon for their support. To them I dedicate this work.

Esther A. de Boer
Berg en Terblijt, The Netherlands
March 2005

ABBREVIATIONS

AB	Anchor Bible
ApocJohn	Apocryphon of John
1 ApocJas	First Apocalypse of James
ATR	*Anglican Theological Review*
BG	Berolinensis Gnosticus
BJS	Brown Judaic Studies
BTB	*Biblical Theology Bulletin*
BZ	*Biblische Zeitschrift*
BZNW	Beihefte zur *ZNW*
CBQ	*Catholic Biblical Quarterly*
CH	Corpus Hermeticum
ConBNT	Coniectanea Biblica, New Testament
DialSav	Dialogue of the Saviour
EKKNT	Evangelisch-Katholischer Kommentar zum Neuen Testament
EpAp	Epistula Apostolorum
EvT	*Evangelische Theologie*
ExpTim	*Expository Times*
GosMar	Gospel of Mary
GosPhil	Gospel of Philip
GosThom	Gospel of Thomas
GosTruth	Gospel of Truth
HeyJ	*Heythrop Journal*
HTKNT	Herders theologischer Kommentar zum Neuen Testament
HTR	*Harvard Theological Review*
JBL	*Journal of Biblical Literature*
JJS	*Journal of Jewish Studies*
JSNT	*Journal for the Study of the New Testament*
JSNTSup	*Journal for the Study of the New Testament*, Supplement Series
JTS	*Journal of Theological Studies*
LCL	Loeb Classical Library
NHC	Nag Hammadi Codices
NHMS	Nag Hammadi and Manichaean Studies
NHS	Nag Hammadi Studies
NovT	*Novum Testamentum*
NovTSup	*Novum Testamentum*, Supplements
NTS	*New Testament Studies*
P Oxy	Papyrus Oxyrhinchus
P Ryl	Papyrus Rylands
PS	Pistis Sophia
RNT	Regensburger Neues Testament
SJC	Sohpia of Jesus Christ
SVF	Stoicorum Veterum Fragmenta
TDNT	Gerhard Kittel and Gerhard Friedrich (eds.), *Theological Dictionary of*

Chapter 1

INTRODUCTION

The Gospel of Mary, the only known Gospel that is named after a woman, has aroused new interest in the figure of Mary Magdalene and the beginnings of Christianity. What was her impact and what was her message? What became of her and her ideas? These are questions which are raised not only by scholars but which also appeal to a larger public. Books about Mary Magdalene are popular. Marianne Fredriksson's novel, *According to Mary Magdalene*, for example, became a bestseller.[1] This novel tells the story of how Mary Magdalene comes to realize that Peter and Paul are altering Christ's teaching to suit their own goals and how she struggles to spread his undistorted teaching herself. In the introduction to the novel, Fredriksson explains that she decided to write this book after reading the Gospel of Mary. The present study examines the Gospel of Mary to discover what it reveals about Mary Magdalene and to determine the origin of this portrayal.

1. *Survey of Research*

1.1. *Saint Mary Magdalene*
In the Western tradition of the Church, Mary Magdalene is the sinful sister of Martha and Lazarus, who washed Jesus' feet with her tears and lovingly anointed them with precious oil. In return he absolved her of her seven deadly sins. As a result she became a serious devotee of his teaching. Her ardent love for him compelled her to go to his tomb to anoint his dead body. This made her the first witness of his resurrection. With Lazarus, Martha and others, she proclaimed the Gospel in France. She then withdrew to live the life of a hermit, as penance for her former sinful life.

Most modern exegetes consider Saint Mary Magdalene of the Western Church to be a product of the early Middle Ages when legends were used to supplement the biblical texts in order to provide exemplary and attractive models of faith. In the early Middle Ages, stories were drawn from several biblical narratives and texts from different Gospels were harmonized. Especially Peter Ketter in his study *The Magdalene Question*, published in 1935, has shown the harmonization of texts which is at the basis of the composite figure of Saint Mary Magdalene.[2] The

---

1. Fredriksson: 1999.
2. See also Sickenberger 1926 and Holzmeister 1922.

medieval story of Saint Mary Magdalene is based on a combination of the four
different New Testament Gospel narratives about a woman who anoints Jesus and
on the interpretation of demons as sins. The Gospel of John introduces Mary, the
sister of Martha, with the words 'who had anointed the Lord with ointment and
wiped his feet with her hair' (Jn 11.2).[3] In the Gospel of Luke it is 'a woman of the
city who was a sinner' who wipes Jesus' feet with her hair and anoints them (Lk.
7.37). Thus Martha's sister was identified with the anonymous sinner in Luke.
Directly following this narrative, Luke tells his readers of the women who followed
Jesus. The first one he mentions is Mary Magdalene from whom, as he says, 'seven
evil spirits had gone out' (Lk. 8.2). These seven evil spirits were interpreted as the
sins of the anonymous woman-sinner of the previous story.

Mary, the sinful sister of Martha and Lazarus, became Mary Magdalene. As
such she did not only anoint the feet of Jesus, but also his head just before the day
of his arrest (Mk 14.3-9; Mt. 26.6-13). When the disciples become angry about this
(Mt. 26.8), Jesus defends the equally unnamed woman, saying: 'I assure you that
wherever the gospel is preached all over the world, what she has done will be told
in memory of her' (Mk 14.9; Mt. 26.13).

Other stories of unnamed women were also drawn on. In Luke, Jesus says of the
anonymous woman-sinner that she 'loved much' (Lk. 7.47). This fits in well with
the narrative of the unnamed Samaritan woman in the Gospel of John who was said
to have had several husbands (Jn 4.18) and also with the anonymous adulterous
woman who was saved from stoning by Jesus (Jn 8.1-11). Thus Mary Magdalene
became the sexually promiscuous woman who inspired so many Christians
throughout the ages to care for prostitutes and for those who because of their weak
social position, succumbed to prostitution.[4] Even her name, 'Magdalene', became
the word with which to describe an adulterous woman or a woman prostitute.[5]

By anointing Jesus, Mary Magdalene did penance for her many sins. Her new
state of life was thought to be described in Lk. 10.38-42. In this narrative Mary,
Martha's sister, is sitting at the feet of Jesus, and is listening to what he has to say,
while Martha is busy serving the many guests. When she asks Jesus to let Mary
help her, he answers 'Mary has taken the good part and it will not be taken of her'
(Lk. 10.42). Thus Mary Magdalene became the symbol of the ascetic and contemplative life, and even of the Church itself.[6] Mary Magdalene's love for Jesus was
illustrated not only by the anointing scenes, but also by her presence at the crucifixion, and by her desire to anoint his dead body. As a result an ointment jar is one
of her main attributes in art.[7]

Old Testament texts were also drawn on,[8] such as the Song of Songs in which
the loving zeal of Mary Magdalene was believed to be described. As a symbol of

3.   Translation of biblical texts: Revised standard version.
4.   Haskins 1993: 170-75, 317-27.
5.   Haskins 1993: 176.
6.   Haskins 1993: 91-94.
7.   Anstett-Janssen 1974: VII, cols 516-41.
8.   For instance in liturgy. See Mary Magdalene's feast day in the Roman Missal and in the
Roman Breviary, both from before the Second Vatican Council.

the Church, Mary Magdalene became the Bride alongside the Bridegroom, one of the metaphors for Christ. In the same way she became the Queen alongside the King, for example in Psalm 45.

The composite Saint Mary Magdalene has become a popular subject in recent scholarly work. Many studies have been devoted to her and one may expect more to come. Studies have been published about the portrayal of Mary Magdalene throughout the centuries. In 1975 Marjorie Malvern wrote *Venus in Sackcloth. The Magdalen's Origins and Metamorphoses.* She reviews the biblical writings on Mary Magdalene, the Gnostic writings, the Church fathers, some plays of the Middle Ages and books and movies from the twentieth century. She includes art as well as literature. In 1993 Susan Haskins published *Mary Magdalen: Myth and Metaphor*, which also examines the portrayals of Mary Magdalene from the first-century four Gospels unto modern writers and artists, but in much more detail than the book by Malvern.[9] A similar procedure was followed by Ingrid Maisch, who in 1996 published *Maria Magdalena. Zwischen Verachtung und Verehrung.*

Each study describes the images of Mary Magdalene and, in addition, tries to evaluate them. According to Malvern, the metamorphoses of the composite Saint Mary Magdalene incorporate the remembrance of holy harlots and goddesses of love, wisdom and fertility. Malvern argues that the metamorphoses are mythical and reveal the need of a female counterpart next to the Jewish Christian male God.[10]

Haskins argues that Mary Magdalene's myth has changed Mary Magdalene into an effective weapon of the Church against the female sex. According to Haskins, in the figure of Saint Mary Magdalene the ascetic Church rejected sexuality with women as its embodiment. In her view, the biblical image of Mary Magdalene was deliberately adapted so that, instead of being a woman who proclaimed the Easter Gospel, she became a woman who served as a role model for a misogynistic Church.[11]

Maisch concludes that Mary Magdalene's metamorphoses reflect the masculine images of women: prostitute, wife, lover, ecstatic, saint. She argues that Mary Magdalene must be rediscovered as a biblical saint with modern virtues such as solidarity with the dying, compassion with the tortured, loyalty beyond death, courage, creativity and perseverance.[12]

Other studies show a fascination with the tradition of the composite Mary Magdalene and focus on her representations in art, in letters, in poetry, novels and plays, in mysticism and in esoteric traditions. In 1986 an exhibition in Florence was documented in an impressive catalogue with thorough articles. The same happened in 2002 in Ghent.[13] Two conferences devoted to Mary Magdalene were held

---

9. See also the chapters on Mary Magdalene in Warner 1985: 224-35 and Moltmann-Wendel 1980: 67-95.
10. Malvern 1975: 173-80.
11. Haskins 1993: 96-97.
12. Maisch 1996: 189-90.
13. Mosco 1986; Baert 2002.

in France in 1988 (Avignon) and in 1999 (Vézelay).[14] Margaret Starbird concentrated on esoteric traditions.[15]

Some books focus on the Middle Ages. Victor Saxer published an extensive study on the cult of Mary Magdalene in the Western Church from its origins up to the end of the Middle Ages.[16] Elisabeth Pinto-Mathieu studied Mary Magdalene in the literature of the Middle Ages; Marga Janssen studied her medieval representation in Western iconography; and Katherine Ludwig Jansen studied unpublished sermons of the Middle Ages.[17]

The latter, in the epilogue of her book, emphasizes the importance of the traditions about Saint Mary Magdalene. In her view, when returning to the biblical figure of Mary Magdalene, we not only gain 'historical' accuracy, but also lose much, for example Mary Magdalene's representation as a preacher and apostle of the apostles.[18]

In the tradition of the Eastern Church, Mary Magdalene and Mary the sister of Martha remained separate and each have their own feast day. In the Eastern tradition Mary Magdalene is not celebrated as the penitent sinner as in the Western tradition, but as 'ointment bearer' and as 'equal to an apostle'. Eva Synek studied the portrayal of Mary Magdalene in the Eastern tradition and concluded that a number of Church Fathers depict Mary Magdalene as a disciple and an apostle.[19]

In 1963 the Second Vatican Council of the Roman Catholic Church decided that the Calendar of Saints should be evaluated. Since then the calendar reads at Mary Magdalene's day, 22 July, that it 'celebrates only the one whom Christ appeared after the resurrection and in no sense the sister of St. Martha, or the woman who was a sinner and whose sins the Lord forgave'.[20] Officially the biblical Mary Magdalene has replaced the Saint. The composite figure of Mary Magdalene the Saint, however, has been extremely popular throughout the ages and still is today. The portrait of the composite Mary Magdalene is kept alive in places of pilgrimage, such as in Vézelay, where it is, oddly enough, officially acknowledged by local Roman Catholic authorities.[21]

1.2. *A Gnostic Mary Magdalene*

The present study is not about the traditions and origins of Saint Mary Magdalene, but belongs to the field of research on specific portrayals of Mary Magdalene in early Christianity. This study focuses on the portrayal of Mary Magdalene in the Gospel of Mary, in order to contribute to the scholarly debate on the Gnostic Mary Magdalene.

Beginning in the eighteenth century, papyrus codices have been found which are

14. Duperray 1989; Montandon 1999.
15. Starbird 1993.
16. Saxer 1959.
17. Pinto-Mathieu 1997; Anstett-Janssen 1961; Jansen 2000.
18. Jansen 2000: 336.
19. Synek 1995.
20. Calendarium Romanum Generale 1969: 97-98, 131.
21. Pierre-Marie 1995: 7-21.

believed to be among the Gnostic writings, in which a Mary occurs, who is commonly identified as Mary Magdalene.[22] In 1773 the Codex Askewianus was found, containing the writing Pistis Sophia. In 1896 the Papyrus Berolinensis, containing the Gospel of Mary, and in 1945 the Nag Hammadi Codices were found with the Gospel of Thomas, the Dialogue of the Saviour, the Gospel of Philip, the Sophia of Jesus Christ and the First Apocalypse of James. These writings are from the second and third centuries.[23]

In these writings Mary Magdalene is one of the disciples, learning from Jesus. She asks questions, she is spoken to and spoken of. Both in the Gospel of Thomas and in the Sophia of Jesus Christ she asks about the nature and purpose of discipleship.[24] In the Sophia of Jesus Christ she asks how the disciples can find knowledge.[25] In the Dialogue of the Saviour she is one of the three disciples (the other two are Matthew and Judas) who receive special instruction. She asks about the meaning of sorrow and joy.[26] She also asks her brothers where and how they will keep all the things that the Lord tells them.[27]

Furthermore, Mary Magdalene has a role as interpreter. She knows the Scripture and sayings of Jesus and discusses their meaning. In Pistis Sophia she quotes Isaiah and the Psalms. She memorizes what Jesus said and what Paul has written.[28] She also quotes sayings of Jesus in the Dialogue of the Saviour.[29] The author adds: 'She uttered this as a woman who knew the All'.[30] Mary Magdalene's insight is highly esteemed. In Pistis Sophia she is repeatedly praised by the Lord, because she phrases pertinent questions accurately and purposefully.[31] Her heart is said to be more attuned to the Kingdom of Heaven than those of any of her brothers.[32] In the Gospel of Philip and the Gospel of Mary the disciples state that the Lord loves her more than any of them.[33] In the Gospel of Philip she is said to be the constant companion to the Lord.[34]

The First Apocalypse of James relates that the Lord had twelve male and seven female disciples.[35] When James says of the female disciples, 'I am amazed how

---

22. Shoemaker 2001, for instance, defends the conjecture that the Gnostic Mary may be a composite figure, in which Mary Magdalene and Mary the mother of Jesus are merged. More about this in Chapter 2, section 1.6.

23. Other writings have been found too. For a survey of early Mary Magdalene texts (including the New Testament), see for instance Bovon 1984 and Atwood 1993. For a review of publications on early Mary Magdalene texts, see Thimmes 1998.

24. GosThom 21; SJC 114.8-12.

25. SJC 98.9-11.

26. DialSav 126.17-20.

27. DialSav 131.19-21.

28. PS 17-18; 60; 62; 113.

29. DialSav 139.8-11.

30. DialSav 139.11-13.

31. PS 25.

32. PS 17.

33. GosPhil 64.1-5; GosMar 18.14-15.

34. GosPhil 59.6-11.

35. 1 ApocJas 38.16-17; 42.20-24.

powerless vessels have become strong by a perception which is in them', the Lord instructs him to learn from them and he mentions a few names, including Mary Magdalene.[36] In both Pistis Sophia and the Gospel of Mary, Mary Magdalene shares her insights and teaches the disciples. For this she is praised, but also attacked. In some writings it is Peter in particular who shows hostility. In the Gospel of Thomas he says: 'Let Mary leave us, for women are not worthy of life' (GosThom 114). In the Gospel of Mary he argues: 'Surely he [the Lord] did not speak to a woman without our knowledge and not openly. Are we to turn and all listen to her? Has he chosen her above us?' (GosMar 17.16-23). And in Pistis Sophia he states: 'My Lord, we cannot tolerate this woman anymore: she does not allow any of us to say a word, whereas she speaks often' (PS 36).

The finding of the Gospel of Mary makes Mary Magdalene the only historical woman who has a Gospel to her name.[37] In the Gospel of Mary at least half of what has remained of the gospel is a revelation dialogue between Mary and the Lord, while in the other half she is one of the central figures. The Gospel of Mary is commonly studied as an important witness to the status of Mary Magdalene in early Gnostic circles. Antti Marjanen represents the general opinion when stating: 'A good indication of the esteem Mary Magdalene enjoyed among Gnostics is the fact that an entire Gnostic Christian gospel is written in her name'.[38]

1.3. *Various Opinions of the Gnostic Mary Magdalene*
As in the case of Saint Mary Magdalene, questions have been raised about where the Gnostic portrait of Mary Magdalene comes from and how it is to be evaluated.[39] In her book *The Gnostic Gospels* Elaine Pagels suggests that the Gnostic Mary Magdalene gives evidence of a debate about the position of women in the church in the second and third centuries. Mary Magdalene symbolizes the more unorthodox viewpoint on women, whereas Peter symbolizes the orthodox stand. Mary Magdalene is used by Gnostic authors to suggest that women's activity challenged the male leaders of the orthodox community.[40]

In contrast to this, Pheme Perkins in her book *The Gnostic Dialogue* argues that Mary Magdalene does not symbolize a debate about women leadership roles, but a debate about Gnostic insights. In her view, Mary Magdalene was used as a mediator of revelations because she was a figure closely associated with Jesus and one to whom esoteric tradition could be attached.[41]

According to Malvern, the Gnostic Mary deals not only with gnosis, but also

36. 1 ApocJas 38.15-23; 40.24-26. For this interpretation, see Marjanen 1996: 132-37.
37. There is also a Gospel of Eve (Schneemelcher 1990: 288-90). Some scholars, however, also deny that Mary Magdalene would have been a historical woman; cf. Bultmann 1961: 308. Heine 1989 convincingly argues against this conjecture.
38. Marjanen 1996: 94.
39. For a survey of the history of the scholarly work on the Gnostic Mary Magdalene, see Marjanen 1996: 6-20.
40. Pagels 1981: 76-81; see also Schmid 1990: 89.
41. Perkins 1980: 131-37, esp. 136 n. 10.

with 'the desire to link the Magdalen with Jesus'.[42] The Gnostic portrayal, in her view, corresponds especially with the resurrection story of the Gospel of John, which would evoke images of fertility goddesses, and encourages imaginations to go beyond the figure of the canonical Gospels.[43] As such both the Gnostic Mary Magdalene and the Saint 'reveal the efforts of early Christians to create a feminine counterpart for their man-God'.[44] Susanne Heine refers to Lk. 8.1-3 where, according to her, Mary Magdalene is presented as the closest companion to Jesus. She argues that Gnostic authors took Mary Magdalene to be the female counterpart of Christ in the Pleroma. Together with him she would be presented as an emanation of the highest God.[45]

Peter Brown, on the contrary, argues that Gnostic circles with their portrayal of Mary Magdalene valued the Mary Magdalene of the New Testament Gospels as 'an image of the sweet and irresistible absorption of the woman, the perpetual inferior other, into her guiding principle, the male'.[46] Haskins quotes Brown with approval.[47] In addition, Maisch points to Gnostic dualism and states that Mary Magdalene would have had her place in Gnostic circles at the cost of her femaleness.[48]

Others maintain that the Gnostic Mary Magdalene is not only an image but also has a solid historical core. Robert Price argues that the conflict in the Gnostic writings between Mary Magdalene and the male disciples reflects a first-century debate about Mary Magdalene being the apostle of a non-hierarchical, egalitarian Christianity. As a result, the biblical writers minimized her role.[49] Karen King concludes on the basis of the Gnostic writings that Mary Magdalene was a figure of apostolic importance and a prophetess, more important than her official portrait in the New Testament suggests. Mary Magdalene's absence, for instance from the Acts of the Apostles, in her view, is part of a strategy to exclude women from apostolic leadership roles.[50] In addition, Jane Schaberg sees evidence in the resurrection story of the Gospel of John that Mary Magdalene was regarded by some as a successor to Jesus, as Elisha was a successor to Elijah.[51]

1.4. *Different Gnostic Portrayals of Mary Magdalene*
The Finnish scholar Antti Marjanen was the first to go into detail with the study on the Gnostic Mary Magdalene. In his dissertation *The Woman Jesus Loved* published in 1996, he states that three aspects are not sufficiently dealt with in other studies about her.[52] First, one must consider the possibility that Mary Magdalene

42. Malvern 1975: 30.
43. Malvern 1975: 16-56.
44. Malvern 1975: 30.
45. Heine 1986: 139-42.
46. Brown 1989: 103-120 (113).
47. Haskins 1993: 54.
48. Maisch 1996: 36. See also Wisse 1988: 297-303 and Williams 1988.
49. Price 1990; see also Koivunen 1994: 210-11.
50. King 1998a: 39-40 and King 1998b: 21-41.
51. Schaberg 2002: 304-317.
52. Marjanen 1996: 28-29.

may have a different role in the various Gnostic writings. Secondly, her position must not be viewed in isolation, but must be dealt with in the context of what is related about the other disciples, especially the male ones. Thirdly, one must take into account that the positive characterizations of Mary Magdalene are 'accompanied by statements in which images of the feminine are used as negative symbols'.[53]

Marjanen shows that there are different Gnostic Mary Magdalene traditions.[54] He identifies several common features: Mary Magdalene is given a significant position among the followers of Jesus; she is introduced together with some of his best known disciples; and most of the texts portray her in the period after the resurrection. However, the differences Marjanen points out are significant.

According to Marjanen, in the Gospel of Thomas Mary Magdalene is a woman disciple who needs deeper understanding, whereas in the Sophia of Jesus Christ and the Dialogue of the Saviour she is the disciple who, together with two male disciples, receives special instruction on which the writings claim to build. In the Gospel of Mary and the Gospel of Philip, Mary Magdalene is singled out as the disciple most spiritually loved by Jesus, and is as such a model for the other disciples. In Pistis Sophia Mary Magdalene is comparably prominent, but, Marjanen argues, as in the Gospel of Philip, the proclamation of the Gospel is specifically entrusted to the male disciples. In the First Apocalypse of James, however, James is advised to turn to Mary Magdalene and three other female disciples to learn from them how to actually preach the Gospel.

Marjanen also points out that not only in the Gospel of Thomas, but also in the Dialogue of the Saviour, the Sophia of Jesus Christ, the First Apocalypse of James, and in his view in the Gospel of Mary as well, language is used that is male oriented and devalues women.[55] Last but not least, the conflict between Mary and Peter, which is generally interpreted as symbolizing a conflict between Gnostic and non-Gnostic orthodox Christians, in his view, must be limited to the Gospel of Mary only. In the Gospel of Philip the male disciples' envy does not turn into a conflict and in the Pistis Sophia Peter's ideas are as Gnostic as Mary's. In the Gospel of Thomas the debate concerns the position of women.[56]

Marjanen also goes into the question of the nature and the origin of the Gnostic Mary Magdalene traditions. According to him no literary dependence between the writings can be established. In his view two aspects are significant when looking for the roots of the Gnostic Mary Magdalene traditions. The testimony in the Gospels of Mark and John that Jesus after his resurrection appeared to Mary Magdalene would make Mary Magdalene 'an attractive figure for a Gnostic myth-making process'. [57] Secondly, the Gospel of Thomas, the Sophia of Jesus Christ and the Dialogue of the Saviour are in his view evidence that from the beginning of the second century Mary Magdalene emerged as a Gnostic disciple.

53. Marjanen 1996: 29.
54. Marjanen 1996: 216-25.
55. Marjanen 1996: 220-21.
56. Marjanen 1996: 222-23.
57. Marjanen 1996: 223.

1.5. *Gnostic Women Disciples*

The German scholar Silke Petersen also devoted her dissertation to the Gnostic Mary Magdalene, but in such a way that she focuses not just on her, but on all the women disciples in Gnostic writings, namely Mary Magdalene, Salome, Martha, Arsinoe, several unnamed women disciples (among them Jesus' seven women disciples) and Mary, the mother of Jesus. In 1999 her book was published under the title *'Zerstört die Werke der Weiblichkeit!' Maria Magdalena, Salome & andere Jüngerinnen Jesu in christlich-gnostischen Schriften.*

Petersen studies the role and position of women disciples in Gnostic writings. The fact that so many women disciples have a role in Christian Gnostic literature might lead one to conclude that they were quite important in Christian Gnostic circles. In Petersen's view, however, before concluding this, one should first compare this circumstance with the presence of male disciples in Gnostic writings and the references to women disciples in non-Gnostic texts. She concludes that for each Gnostic writing in which a woman has an important role there are two writings in which a man has such a position. At the same time, whereas in all the New Testament Gospels women play a role in the Easter story, there are several similar stories in Gnostic writings in which women play no role at all.[58]

Petersen focuses on the particular significance of women disciples in Christian Gnostic texts. How and why did the New Testament tradition of women disciples become part of these texts and what kind of Gnostic theology lies behind it? In the central part of her book Petersen examines in detail the women disciples' representation in the Gospel of Thomas, the Gospel of Philip, the Sophia of Jesus Christ, the Dialogue of the Saviour, the First Apocalypse of James and in the Gospel of Mary and Pistis Sophia, as well as in Patristic anti-Gnostic documents, and in Manichaean Psalms. In contrast to Marjanen who focuses on each separate writing, Petersen gives a cross-section and focuses on each of the women disciples.

The central part of her book is preceded by a section in which she introduces the different texts and critically re-examines the genre of the Gnostic dialogue. In the last part of the book the author identifies the one aspect of the Christian Gnostic texts in which women disciples appear to play a role in common: they all contain general comments on femininity and masculinity.[59] Petersen places these comments in the broader context of what is to be found on this subject in the literature of late antiquity.[60]

According to Petersen, the Christian texts of antiquity show a fatal alternative: either women become like men or, as women, they are to be submissive to men. Petersen argues that the superiority of mind (asexual and masculine) to body (sexual and feminine), which in her definition is fundamental to Gnostic thinking, is at the root of the Gnostic Christian discipleship of women. She concludes that women joined the Christian Gnostic community on the condition that they put aside their feminine nature and become male.[61]

58. Petersen 1999: 304-307.
59. Petersen 1999: 307-308.
60. Petersen 1999: 309-334.
61. Petersen 1999: 336-37.

Another German scholar, Erika Mohri, in her dissertation, *Maria Magdalena Frauen ub Evangelientexten des 1. bis 3 Jahrhundert*, published in 2000, argues that the changes in the portrayals of Mary Magdalene, not only in Gnostic, but also in other texts, reflecting the continuing discussion about the place of women in the communities and about the imagery of God and the world.[62] Mohri emphasizes that sexist imagery and self-confident women occur in the same texts. She explains this by arguing that through sexual asceticism women can escape matter and become equal to men. She suggests that sexual asceticism may have been experienced by women as a liberation from the burden of childbearing.[63] Moreover, Mohri argues that, in spite of its androcentrism, the androgynous Gnostic imagery of God opens up to women the possibility of experiencing themselves as close to the Divine.

2. The Present Research

2.1. Task

Two basic viewpoints can be distinguished in recent scholarly work: (1) Gnostic authors have constructed a Gnostic Mary Magdalene using the biblical portrait of her as a vehicle for Gnostic teaching, and, (2) biblical authors neglected the important role of Mary Magdalene, of which Gnostic authors preserved evidence. In addition, on the one hand the Gnostic Mary Magdalene is valued as a female apostolic leader, as an advocate of women and of egalitarian discipleship, and as a revealer of Gnostic insights. On the other hand, scholars point to the specific dualism, and the subsequently negative female imagery in Gnostic writings, and reject a positive evaluation of the Gnostic Mary Magdalene.

To be able to evaluate these different viewpoints on the Gnostic Mary Magdalene, the present study focuses on the Gospel of Mary, which is considered to be the most important early witness to the esteem of Mary Magdalene in Gnostic circles. We will investigate the following.

1. The dualism involved in the Gospel of Mary: is it a specific Gnostic dualism and does it contain a negative use of female imagery?
2. Mary's teaching in the Gospel of Mary: what is the specific content of her teaching?
3. The Gospel of Mary's view on Mary Magdalene: does this gospel advocate the apostolic leadership of women, an egalitarian discipleship and a non-hierarchical way of being the church?
4. The portrayals of Mary Magdalene in the New Testament Gospels: to what extent can the portrayal of Mary Magdalene in the Gospel of Mary, her relation to the Saviour, her position among the disciples, her function in the story, be understood from the New Testament Gospels?

By answering these questions I hope to contribute to the present debate about the Gnostic Mary Magdalene.

62. Mohri 2000: 374-77.
63. Mohri 2000: 219-28 in an excursus on the Gospel of the Egyptians.

2.2. *Approach*

Chapter 2 is an introduction to the Gospel of Mary. It will go into its three incomplete manuscripts, the provenance of the original document, its date and composition, the persons in the story and the identification of Mary as Mary Magdalene. This chapter also presents a translation of the nine pages from the Coptic manuscript, followed by a study of the meaning of the Gospel of Mary, and of the definition of the term 'Gnostic'.

Chapter 3 examines the purpose of and the dualism in the Gospel of Mary and the question whether it is to be seen as a Gnostic document. Chapter 4 focuses on the author's portrayal of Mary Magdalene in the Gospel of Mary. What is her relation to the Saviour, what is her position among the disciples and what is her function in the story? The author speaks from the viewpoint of Peter, of Andrew, of Levi, of the Saviour, and of Mary herself. Through the interaction of these views, through the extra knowledge and view of the narrator, through Mary's teaching and through certain indications in the text, we shall examine the development of the plot in which the author's view of Mary Magdalene becomes apparent.

To be able to investigate the origin of the portrayal of Mary Magdalene in the Gospel of Mary the next three chapters examine the New Testament Gospels, since they contain the earliest written material on Mary Magdalene. Chapter 5 studies the portrayal of Mary Magdalene in the Gospel of Mark. Almost at the end of the Gospel, Mark for the first time declares that a considerable number of women had been following Jesus. What to think of these women? What is their function in Mark's story? And what about Mary Magdalene in their midst? In order to answer these questions this chapter not only focuses on Mark, but also on the historical situation at the time. Chapter 6 investigates the Gospels of Matthew and Luke and Chapter 7 examines the Gospel of John.

Chapter 8 will evaluate the portrayals of Mary Magdalene in the Gospel of Mary and the New Testament Gospels. In conclusion, chapter 9 reflects on the questions raised in chapter 1.

Chapter 2

THE GOSPEL OF MARY

This chapter is an introduction to the Gospel of Mary. It will cover its three in-complete manuscripts, the provenance of the original document, its date and com-position, the persons in the story and the identification of Mary as Mary Magdalene. This chapter also presents a translation of the nine pages which survived in the Coptic manuscript, followed by a study of the meaning of the Gospel of Mary. It will investigate in what way the Gospel of Mary, although obviously different from the New Testament writings, contains similar themes. In addition, it will examine the reasons why the Gospel of Mary is considered to be a Gnostic writing and the debate about the definition of the term 'Gnostic'.

1. *Introduction*

1.1. *Three Incomplete Manuscripts*
The second-century Gospel of Mary is by far the most intriguing early text in which Mary Magdalene has a part, since this text portrays her speaking extensively about her knowledge and experience of the Lord. Three incomplete manuscripts of the Gospel of Mary have survived.[1] In 1896, C. Reinhardt discovered a fairly large fragment of a Coptic manuscript, which is now called the Berlin Codex, that con-tained four writings: the Gospel of Mary, the Apocryphon of John, the Sophia of Jesus Christ and the Act of Peter.[2] This Coptic manuscript dates from about the be-ginning of the fifth century, or the end of the fourth century and is written in the Sahidic dialect, which was generally used by the Egyptians at the time.[3] The codex was discovered, wrapped in feathers, in a niche in a wall at a Christian burial place near the ancient city of Panopolis, in Upper Egypt.[4]

---

1. For an introduction into the research on the Gospel of Mary see Tardieu and Dubois 1986: 99-107. Luttikhuizen (1986: 38-60), was the first to translate and publish the Gospel of Mary in Dutch with a short commentary. Photos of the manuscripts can be found in King 2003b: XI, 19-27, 91.

2. It is now in the Egyptology Department of the National Museum in Berlin under the name Papyrus Berolinensis 8502. It is also called Berolinensis Gnosticus. See for text and comment Till and Schenke 1972.

3. This is based on linguistic evidence and the form of the codex (Tardieu and Dubois 1986: 101).

4. Tardieu and Dubois 1986: 99-100.

From this manuscript it becomes clear that the Gospel of Mary contained nineteen pages, only nine of which (7.1–10.23, 15.1–19.5) have survived. The beginning of the Gospel and some of Mary's words are missing, but the end of the Gospel and the title are preserved. The manuscript is a Coptic translation of a Greek original. Two Greek papyrus fragments of the Gospel of Mary, both dating from the third century, were found near the ancient city of Oxyrhynchus, one of the principal Hellenized centres of Egypt. The first, P Ryl 463 discovered in 1938, which contains GosMar 17-19, dates from the beginning of the third century.[5] The second, POxy 3525 found in 1983, contains GosMar 9.1-10.[6] The Greek fragments were written by different hands and appear to be two separate later copies of the Greek original of the Gospel of Mary.[7]

In third-century Oxyrhynchus, Greeks from Macedonia and Persia formed the highest class.[8] There was also a Jewish quarter. At this time the economic situation was declining; Roman taxations were doubled and there was a great gap between rich and poor.[9] The first recorded persecution of Christians in Oxyrhynchus dates from about 250. At the beginning of the third century there were two churches and Christianity was widely flourishing.[10]

1.2. *Provenance*

The origin of the Gospel of Mary is unknown. Some argue, not very convincingly, that the Gospel was perhaps written in Egypt.[11] This suggestion is based on the Gnostic myth that, according to most exegetes, lies behind the text and on the fact that all three manuscripts of the Gospel of Mary were found in Egypt. The latter, however, is most probably due to the Egyptian climate.[12] Furthermore, the Gospel of Mary is first of all a Christian writing and all the early Christian and Jewish papyri which have been found in Oxyrhynchus originally came from outside Egypt. In addition to the Gospel of Mary, the following Christian texts dating from the first three centuries have been found there: the Gospel of John, the Gospel of Matthew, the Gospel of Thomas, the Letter from James, the Gospel of Luke, Paul's letter to the Romans, the Letter to the Hebrews and the Gospel of Peter.[13] None of these were written in Egypt. Why would the Gospel of Mary be the exception?

---

5. P Ryl 463; see Roberts 1938: 18-23.

6. P Oxy 3525; see Parsons 1983: 12-14. Lührmann (1988: 321-38) compares the two fragments. See also Mohri 2000: 261-65.

7. Roberts 1938: 20; Lührman 1988: 336; Marjanen 1996: 97.

8. MacLennon 1968: 13.

9. MacLennon (1968: 30), in his economic and social study of Oxyrhynchus, based on a large number of papyri which are testimonies of everyday life, concludes about the third century that 'the evidence as a whole presents a dreadful picture of unbroken trouble and exaction and depression, or ruthless profiteering and cynical violence'.

10. MacLennon 1968: 84-85.

11. Pasquier 1983: 13-14.

12. Petersen 1999: 57. Roberts (1979), on the basis of papyri, argues that early Christianity in Egypt was not, as some have suggested, specifically inclined to Gnosticism.

13. See van Haelst 1976: 409-410 and Grenfell and Hunt no. 80 1994, no. 84 1997, no. 85 1998, no. 86 1999.

The handwriting in the religious and philosophical papyri that have been found in Oxyrhynchus suggests that there were professional scribes and scriptoria in this town.[14] The papyri sent from abroad to be copied probably would have come via Alexandria, since the Oxhyrynchites had clear economic, cultural and personal links with this town. There is also written evidence that books were indeed acquired via Alexandria.[15] Judith Hartenstein suggests that the Gospel of Mary may have its origin in Syria, on the basis of the important role of Levi and the Syrian provenance of other writings in which Levi plays a role.[16] I suggest that the provenance of the Gospel of Mary may also have been in Asia Minor, because of similar imagery in the Pauline letters and in the Gospel of John. As we will see in Chapter 3, the context of the first recipients of the Gospel of Mary is probably one in which Stoic philosophy flourished.

1.3. *Date*

Various dates have been proposed for the Gospel of Mary. Some scholars argue that it dates from the beginning of the second century on the basis of the early second-century debates over women's leadership.[17] Others maintain that it dates from the middle or the second half of the second century because of the direct or indirect dependence of the Gospel of Mary on the New Testament Gospels[18] and because of the Gospel's closeness to Middle Platonist themes.[19] The end of the second century has also been put forward, because it allows the Gospel of Mary to be situated in the context of the School of Bardesanes and Aramaic philosophy.[20]

Since the Greek fragments found in Oxyrhynchus appear to be later copies of a Greek original of the Gospel of Mary and the original version probably came from outside Egypt, it should be dated some decades before the date of the oldest papyrus fragment, P Ryl 463: thus, some decades before the beginning of the third century. The possibility of an earlier date, however, must not be excluded, since, as I will show, the imagery of the Son of Man, who is in his disciples, and who made his disciples true Human Being, who are at the same time to clothe themselves with the perfect Human Being, is very close to the imagery of Christ in the Pauline letters.[21] The similarity of the Gospel of Mary to the New Testament Gospels could also be due to the fact that they are based on similar oral and/or written tradition.

1.4. *Composition*

Concerning the composition of the Gospel of Mary, Walter Till has suggested that the Gospel of Mary as we now know it is the result of a redaction, in which the original Gospel and a dialogue with the Saviour are rather clumsily put together.

---

14. Comfort 1992: 59-61.
15. Turner 1952.
16. Hartenstein 2000: 131-32.
17. King 1995: 628 and De Boer 1997: 76-79.
18. Marjanen 1996: 98.
19. Pasquier 1983: 3-4.
20. Tardieu 1984: 25.
21. See Chapter 3, section 3.1

According to him, the original Gospel of Mary begins at 10.1 of the Coptic manuscript.[22] His argument is that Mary does not occur in the first part of the manuscript. This is not convincing, however, since the first six pages of the Coptic manuscript are missing. Why would one assume that Mary is not present on these pages?

Furthermore, according to Till, GosMar 9.5–10.1 would form the link between the two original writings. Wilson, in his study of the New Testament references in the Gospel of Mary, supports this last thesis, since the New Testament allusions in his view are concentrated in the link between the two writings. However, he shows them to occur in 8.14-23, instead of 9.5–10.1.[23] Henri Puech argues that the Gospel of Mary must be a later redaction of two writings since it consists of two genres: a post-resurrection dialogue and an account of a vision. Like Till, he suggests that the work originally entitled the Gospel of Mary only fits the second part of the Coptic manuscript.[24]

Anne Pasquier offers a different view, according to which pages 9.21–17.9 (or up to 17.15) were not included in the original Gospel of Mary. Pasquier suggests this because of the strange way in which Peter contradicts himself in 10.1 and 17.18-22.[25] This may, however, also be a development of the plot.[26] In my view, there is no valid reason to assume that two different writings lie behind the Coptic Gospel of Mary, since, as will become clear, there is a unity in form and content throughout the Gospel as we have it.[27]

1.5. *Persons: Actors and Audience*

The first six pages of the Coptic manuscript of the Gospel of Mary are missing. On pp. 7 and 8 of the Gospel of Mary we suddenly enter into the end of a dialogue. We know nothing about the beginning of the dialogue. On p. 7 two questions are raised, one by Peter (7.10) and one by someone else (7.1) whose name is missing and was probably mentioned earlier.

Jesus apparently addresses more people than Peter alone, since he uses a plural when speaking to them (7.14-22; 8.5-9). In the course of the Gospel it becomes clear that in addition to Peter, Mary, Andrew and Levi are also present. It is possible that there are more brothers (9.14; 17.11; 18.2) present than the three mentioned. If we assume this to be the case, then Andrew and Peter in 17.10-22 speak to others in addition to Levi.

There might be also more sisters (10.1) present than Mary alone. If this is the case, then we can assume that the women Peter refers to in 10.1-3 are actually there. The Coptic word for 'brothers' CNHY in GosMar 9.14; 17.11 is the translation of ἀδελφοί (P Oxy 3525.9; P Ryl recto, 5-6). Whether this masculine plural includes women is not quite clear. Peter, indeed, addresses Mary as 'sister', CⲰNE,

---

22. Till and Schenke 1972: 26; see also Puech 1959: 253.
23. Wilson 1957: 236-43.
24. Puech 1959: 252-54.
25. Pasquier 1983: 7-10 and 96-101.
26. See Marjanen 1996: 104, who adds that he owes this suggestion to Prof. King. See also Chapter 4, section 3.3.
27. See also Tardieu 1984: 22-23; Luttikhuizen 1988: 158-68; King 1995: 626-27; Marjanen 1996: 100-104; Petersen 1999: 59, and Mohri 2000: 271-72.

but when Andrew in 17.10 turns to the brothers she is clearly not included. In 9.14
the narrator relates that she embraces her brothers, and thus places her over and
against them as a sister. This does, however, not necessarily mean that the word
'brothers' is meant exclusively. The rest of the women mentioned in 10.1-3 may
also be included.

  If they are, as in the Sophia of Jesus Christ, then they, as well as the brothers,
receive the teaching of the Saviour and the mission to proclaim the Gospel. They,
as well as the brothers, weep when he is gone and pose their desperate question.
They, as well as the brothers, are embraced by Mary and are encouraged by her
words. Peter and Andrew not only turn to the brothers in 17.10-22, but to their
sisters as well, but they do not take part in the discussion. Only Levi intervenes. If
women are mentioned on the first six missing pages as being present or as partici-
pants in the dialogue, on the extant pages, they have no active role whatsoever.

  However, it remains uncertain whether the word 'brothers' in the Gospel of
Mary is meant inclusively or not. As in the Dialogue of the Saviour it is also
possible that Mary is alone with her brothers. In the Gospel of Mary these brothers
may be limited to Peter, Andrew and Levi. This is as much as we can say. Only the
missing pages of the Gospel of Mary could really help to settle the question
whether there is an audience in the Gospel of Mary and whether this audience
consists of both men and women. Because of this uncertainty I translate CNHY as
'brothers (and sisters)'.

1.6. *Mary as Mary Magdalene*
Less than half of the Gospel of Mary has been preserved: ten of nineteen pages of
the Coptic manuscript are missing. The remaining pages always speak of Mary
(ΜΑΡΙ2ΑΜ) and do not specifically identify her. The Greek papyri fragments both
have Μαριάμμη. Perhaps the Mary meant is identified on the pages that are missing.

  Mary was a very common name in Palestine.[28] In the New Testament various
Marys occur: Mary the mother of Jesus,[29] Mary the mother of James and Josef,[30]
the other Mary,[31] Mary of James,[32] Mary the mother of Joses,[33] Mary the sister of
Martha,[34] Mary of Klopas,[35] Mary the mother of John Mark,[36] Mary in Rome[37]
and Mary of Magdala.[38] It is difficult to decide whether these names all refer to
different persons.[39] Their names are in Greek both written as Μαρία and Μαριάμ.
Which, if any, of these Marys is meant by Mary in the Gospel of Mary?

28. Ilan 1989: 191-92. See also Ilan 1995a: 53-55 and 174-75.
29. Mk 6.3; Mt. 1–2; 13.55-56; Lk. 1–2; Acts 1.14.
30. Mt. 27.56.
31. Mt. 28.1.
32. Mk 16.1; Lk. 24.10.
33. Mk 15.47.
34. Lk. 10.28-42; Jn 11; 12.1-11.
35. Jn 19.25.
36. Acts 12.12.
37. Rom. 16.6.
38. Mk 15.40, 47; 16.1, 9; Mt. 27.56-61; 28.1; Lk. 8.2; 24.10; Jn 19.25; 20.1-18.
39. See for instance Mayor 1906.

Most exegetes of the Gospel of Mary assume that Mary in the Gospel of Mary must be identified as Mary Magdalene.[40] An important argument is that the name of Jesus' mother in Coptic texts is spelled ΜΑΡΙΑ, whereas the name of Mary Magdalene is also spelled ΜΑΡΙΖΑΜ or ΜΑΡΙΖΑΜΜΗ. In addition, in the Greek texts of the Church Fathers Jesus' mother's name is usually spelled Μαρία and not Μαριάμμη as in the Greek papyri fragments of the Gospel of Mary.[41] Another important argument is one of characterization: only the traditions of Mary Magdalene would make her the one who could play all Mary's roles in the Gospel of Mary.[42] As King states: 'It was precisely the traditions of Mary as a woman, as an exemplary disciple, a witness to the ministry of Jesus, a visionary of the glorified Jesus, and someone traditionally in contest with Peter, that made her the only figure who could play all the roles required to convey the messages and meaning of the *Gospel of Mary*'.[43]

Other scholars suggest that Mary should be identified as Mary the mother of Jesus.[44] Luchessi mentions two arguments: the tradition that the risen Christ appeared to his mother and that his mother and the Twelve are interlocutors in post-resurrection dialogues.[45] Marjanen argues against these arguments: the tradition of the risen Christ appearing to his mother is a late one and only in the Questions of Bartholomew and Pistis Sophia Mary does the mother of Jesus participate in a post-resurrection dialogue.[46]

According to Stephen Shoemaker, the Gnostic Mary of the second and third century may be a composite figure, in which Mary Magdalene and Mary the mother of Jesus are merged.[47] Like Luchessi, he refers to the Syrian tradition of the risen Christ's first appearance to his mother. Unlike Marjanen, he insists that this tradition originates from the harmonization of the New Testament Gospels in Tatian's Diatesseron[48] and may be dated as early as the second century.[49]

Shoemaker also defends the conjecture that the Mary attacked by Peter in PS 36 and 72 must not be identified with Mary Magdalene, but with the mother of Jesus, because she is 'blessed among all women on earth' (PS 19) and 'blessed by all generations' (PS 56) which in Shoemaker's view would refer to Lukan 'epithets' of Jesus' mother.[50] However, could no other Marys be called blessed because the Gospel of Luke attributed blessedness to the mother of Jesus?[51] Moreover, the

40. Till and Schenke 1972: 26; Pasquier 1983; 23 note 75; Tardieu 1984: 20; King 1995: 601; Marjanen 1996: 94-95; Petersen 1999: 102; Hartenstein 2000: 130.
41. Marjanen 1996: 63-64.
42. King 2002.
43. King 2002: 74.
44. For instance Bauer 1909: 448; Heiler 1977: 101; Livingstone 1977: 325.
45. Lucchesi 1985: 366.
46. Marjanen 1996: 94-95 note 2.
47. Shoemaker 2001. See also Shoemaker 2002.
48. See also Baarda 1975: 254-57 and Murray 1975: 372-84.
49. Shoemaker 2001: 560-69. Marjanen (2002) goes into Shoemaker's arguments.
50. PS 19 – Lk. 1.42; PS 56 – Lk. 1.48. Shoemaker 2001: 572-73.
51. Luke already contradicts this: see Lk. 11.27-28 where a woman from the crowd exclaims to

disciples in Pistis Sophia are called 'blessed beyond all men' (PS 352).

The more general accepted interpretation is that the blessed Mary in Pistis Sophia is Mary Magdalene.[52] Ann Graham Brock thoroughly examines the unidentified Marys in Pistis Sophia and demonstrates that the texts show numerous distinguishing, identifying phrases such as 'the other one', 'the blessed one', and the 'pure spiritual one', helping the reader to identify Mary as Mary Magdalene. She concludes that 'in a volume that philosophically tends to negate the physical realm, Mary the Mother's status does not appear to be an especially high one'.[53]

In my view, the following considerations are convincing with regard to the identification of Mary in the Gospel of Mary as Mary Magdalene. In the Gospel of Mary it is Peter who is opposed to Mary's words, because she is a woman. Peter has the same role in the Gospel of Thomas and in Pistis Sophia.[54] In Pistis Sophia the Mary concerned is identified as Mary Magdalene.[55] Already the New Testament Gospels show a rivalry about Mary Magdalene and Peter and raise the question to whom the risen Christ appeared first: to Mary Magdalene or to Peter.[56] Furthermore, Levi in the Gospel of Mary states that the Saviour loved Mary 'more than us'. The disciples in the Gospel of Philip make a similar statement about Mary Magdalene.[57] In addition, in the Gospel of Mary, Mary is supposed to know more about the Saviour than the rest of her brothers and sisters. In the New Testament Gospels it is Mary Magdalene who knows more than the others. As we will see, the knowledge of Mary in the Gospel of Mary is especially close to the knowledge of Mary Magdalene in the Gospel of John.

2. *Translation of the Coptic Manuscript*

The translation presented in this section is of the Coptic text as given by Pasquier in her commentary, which is based on a thorough study of the original manuscript.[58] The words within square brackets are those which are difficult to read. The translation is literal in the sense that, if a Coptic word occurs more than once, I tried to translate it each time with the same English word. The words or phrases within brackets are not in the Coptic text. I added them to show my interpretation of the meaning of certain verses. The first pages, pp. 1-6, of the manuscript are missing.

Jesus 'Blessed is the womb that bore you, and the breasts that you suckled' and Jesus answers 'Indeed, blessed are those who hear the word of God and keep it'.

52. See also Marjanen 1996: 173-74, who argues that Mary the mother of Jesus in Pistis Sophia is always specifically introduced in a new passage.

53. Brock 2003: 47.

54. GosThom logion 114; PS 36 and 72.

55. Close to the discussion with Peter: PS 59 and 83.

56. Mk 16.9; Mt. 28.9; Jn 20.1-18 against Lk. 24.34.

57. GosPhil 63.30–64.9.

58. Pasquier 1983: 28-47. For the Greek text of P Oxy 3525 and P Ryl 463 with text-critical notes see Lührmann 1988: 324-25 and 328-30.

[7]
[...] will [matter] then (2) be [destroyed] or not? The Saviour said,
(3) 'All natural phenomena, all that has been moulded, all that has been brought
into being (4) exist in and with each other, (5) and will be unloosened again up to
(6) their own root, since the (7) Nature of matter is unloosened up to what belongs
to (8) her Nature alone. He who has ears (9) to hear, let him hear.

(10) Peter said to him, 'Since you have told (11) us everything,
tell us this also (12): What is the sin of the world?'

(13) The Saviour said, 'Sin does not exist, (14) but you are the ones who sin (15)
when you do things which are like the nature of (16) adultery: that is called sin.
(17) Because of this the Good One came (18) into your midst, to those who belong
to all natural phenomena, (19) in order to restore Nature up (20) to her Root. Then
he continued (21) and said, 'That is why you become sick and (22) die, for [...]

[8]
[He who] (2) understands, let him understand.

Matter [brought forth] (3) passion that, (4) since it proceeded from an opposite
nature, has no form. (5) From then on confusion exists (6) in the whole body. That
is why I said (7) to you, 'Be fully assured and (8) do not be persuaded (by what is
opposite to Nature), (9) since you are already persuaded (by the Good One) in the
presence of the various forms (10) of Nature. He who has ears (11) to hear, let him
hear'

(12) When the Blessed One had said this, (13) he embraced them all, saying,
(14) 'Peace be with you. My peace (15) bring her forth to you. Beware that (16)
no one leads you astray, saying, (17) 'Lo here!' or 'Lo (18) there!', for the Son of
Man (19) is within you. (20) Follow him. Those who seek him will (21) find him.
Go then and preach (22) the gospel of the kingdom. Do not

[9]
(1) 'lay down any rule other than (2) the one I appointed for you, and do not give
a law (3) like the lawgiver so that (4) you are not imprisoned by it'. (5) When he
had said this, he departed.

But they (6) were grieved and wept greatly, (7) saying, 'How shall we go (8) to
the nations and preach (9) the gospel of the kingdom of the Son (10) of Man? If
they did not (11) spare him, how will (12) they spare us?'

Then Mary (13) stood up, embraced them[59] all, (14) and said to her brothers
(and sisters), 'Do not (15) weep and do not grieve and do not be in (16) two
minds, for his grace will be (17) with you all and will shelter you. (18) Rather let
us (19) praise his greatness, because he (20) has prepared us.[60] He has made us
(true) Human Being'. When (21) Mary had said this, she turned their hearts (22) inward, to the Good One, and they began (23) to discuss the words of the [Saviour].[61]

[10]
(1) Peter said to Mary, 'Sister, (2) we know that the Saviour loved you (3) more

59. P Oxy 3525.9: embraced them and kissed them all...

60. P Oxy 3525.11-12: Rather, let us thank his greatness, because he has joined us together
and...

61. P Oxy 3525.13-14: After she had said this she turned their mind to the Good One and they
began to discuss the sayings of the Saviour.

than the rest of women.[62] (4) Tell us the words of the Saviour which you (5) remember, the things that you know (6) and we do not, nor have we heard them'. (7) Mary answered and said, (8) 'What is hidden from you I shall tell you'.[63] (9) And she began to say to them (10) these words: 'I', (11) she said, 'I have seen the Lord in a vision and I (12) said to him, 'Lord, I have seen you (13) today in a vision'. He answered, he (14) said to me, 'Blessed are you, because you are not wavering (15) when you see me. For where the mind is, (16) there is the treasure'. I said (17) to him, 'Lord, now, does he who sees (18) the vision see it with the soul (19) or with the spirit? The Saviour answered, he (20) said, 'He does not see with the soul (21) nor with the spirit, but with the mind which [is] (22) between the two that is [what] (23) sees the vision and that [...]'

[pp. 11-14 are missing]

[15]
(1) him and Desire said: (2) 'I did not see you, on your way downwards, (3) but now I see you, on your way (4) upwards. But how can you deceive me, when (5) you belong to me?' The Soul answered (6) and said, 'I have seen you. You did not see me (7) nor recognise me. I was (8) (like) a garment to you, and you did not know me'. (9) When she had said this, she went away rejoicing (10) loudly.

'Again she came to the (11) third Power, which is called (12) Ignorance. [She] (13) questioned the Soul, saying, (14) 'Where are you going? In (15) wickedness you were held prisoner. Yes, you were held prisoner. (16) Do not judge then!' And (17) the Soul said, 'Why do you judge (18) me when I do not judge you? I am taken prisoner (19) although I did not take prisoners. I am not recognized, (20) but I have recognized that the All is being unloosened, both the earthly

[16]
(1) 'and the heavenly things'. When the Soul (2) left the third Power powerless, (3) she went upwards and saw the fourth Power.

She took on seven (5) appearances. The first appearance (6) is Darkness, the second (7) Desire, the third (8) Ignorance, the fourth is the Jealousy of (9) Death, the fifth is the Kingdom of the Flesh, (10) the sixth is the Foolish Learning (11) of the Flesh, the seventh is the (12) Hot Tempered Wisdom. These are the seven (13) [power]s of Wrath. They ask (14) the Soul, 'Where do you come from, (15) you killer of people?', or, 'Where are you going, (16) you who leave places powerless?' The Soul answered, (17) she said, 'What imprisons me (18) is pierced. What turns me (19) is left powerless and my Desire (20) has been fulfilled, and Ignorance (21) has died. From a world I am unloosened

[17]
(1) 'through a world and from a (2) model through a model which is (3) from the side of Heaven. And the fetter of oblivion (4) is temporal. From this hour on, (5-6) at the time, of the decisive moment in the aeon, I shall receive the Rest in (7) Silence'. When Mary had said (8) this, she fell silent, since it was to this point that the Saviour (9) had spoken[64] to her.

---

62. P Oxy 3525.16: like no other woman.
63. P Oxy 3525.18: what is hidden from you and what I remember...
64. P Ryl 463 recto 5: had spoken.

(10) But Andrew answered and said to (11) the brothers (and sisters), 'Tell me, what do you say (12) about what she has spoken? (13) I at least do not believe that (14) the Saviour said this. For these teachings (15) seem to be according to another train of thought'. Peter answered (16) and spoke about (17) these same things, he (18) reflected about the Saviour: 'After all, he (19) did not speak with a woman apart (20) from us and not openly. (21) Are we to turn and all listen to her? 22 Has he chosen her above us?'

[18]
(1) Then Mary wept, she said to (2) Peter, 'My brother Peter, what are you (3) thinking? Do you suppose that I (4) devised this, alone, in my (5) heart, or that I am deceiving the Saviour?' (6) Levi answered, he said to Peter (7), 'Peter, you have always been (8) hot-tempered. Now I see you (9) arguing[65] with the woman as (10) these adversaries[66] do. If (11) the Saviour has made her worthy, who are you (12) indeed to reject[67] her? Surely, (13) the Saviour knows her (14) very well. That is why he loved her more (15) than us.[68] Rather let us be ashamed (16) and clothe ourselves with the perfect Human Being. (17) Let us bring him forth to us, as he (18) commanded us. Let us preach (19) the Gospel, without laying down (20) any other rule or law than (21) the one the Saviour said'.

[19]
When [(1) Levi had said] this, they began (2) to go forth [to] proclaim and to preach.[69]

(3) The Gospel
(4) according to
(5) Mary

3. *The Gospel of Mary and the New Testament Writings*

The Gospel of Mary is generally considered to contain Gnostic reinterpretations of themes that are known from the New Testament. In the commentaries on the Gospel of Mary many New Testament parallels are noted. As we will see, the Gospel of Mary also reminds one of Old Testament writings. In this section we will examine the Gospel of Mary as different from the New Testament Gospels and specify the similar themes in the New Testament and the Old Testament writings.

3.1. *A Different Gospel*
The Gospel of Mary is clearly different from the Gospels in the New Testament. Whereas the New Testament Gospels describe the work of Jesus in his earthly lifetime, the Gospel of Mary describes a post-resurrection dialogue which is rather philosophical.

65. P Ryl 463 verso 3: and now you discuss...
66. P Ryl 463 verso 4: like her adversary does.
67. P Ryl 463 verso 6: despise...
68. P Ryl 463 verso 6-7: since, surely, he loved her, because he knew her thoroughly.
69. P Ryl 463 verso 14-15: After he had said this, Levi departed and began to proclaim...

Post-resurrection dialogues with Jesus do occur in the New Testament, but they are not about notions such as matter and nature, let alone about the origin of a vision, the relation between soul, spirit and mind, and the dangers the soul has to conquer on its way to the eternal Rest. When Luke relates that Jesus appeared for forty days following his resurrection to the apostles he had chosen, speaking about the Kingdom of God, he only records one question and answer. The disciples ask whether Jesus will restore the kingdom to Israel in their time (Acts 1.3-8). The other post-resurrection dialogues in the New Testament Gospels are about opening the Scriptures (Lk. 24.27, 45) and the commission to preach repentance and forgiveness of sins (Lk. 24.47), to make disciples (Mt. 28.19) or to take care of the 'sheep' of the shepherd Jesus (Jn 21.14-17) and to be sent as Jesus was sent (Jn 20.19-23).

Perhaps the philosophical tone of the post-resurrection dialogue in the Gospel of Mary is closest to the dialogues of the earthly Jesus in the Gospel of John. These are about being born anew (Jn 3.1-21), about the spring of eternal water inside a person (Jn 4), about the Son and the Father (Jn 5), about the Bread of Life (Jn 6.35-59), about the resurrection (Jn 11.21-27), and the farewell dialogues about Jesus' way upwards, his glorification and the coming of the Spirit (Jn 13–17).

Another significant difference between the Gospel of Mary and the New Testament writings is that Mary Magdalene in the New Testament is clearly not singled out to speak about her knowledge and experience of the Lord. The Gospel of John is the exception with one line about her experience that she had seen the Lord and that he had told her about these things (Jn 20.18). Moreover, in the Gospels of the New Testament the disciples are nowhere portrayed as hesitating to preach the gospel. Only in the second ending of Mark they are portrayed weeping, but this is not because they are afraid to proclaim the gospel, but because they grieve about the death of their master (Mk 16.10).

3.2. *Familiar Themes*

Although the Gospel of Mary is different from the Gospels in the New Testament, at the same time, the Gospel of Mary is also strangely familiar. The reader who knows the Gospels of Mark, Matthew, Luke and John and who is also acquainted with the Pauline letters and other canonical letters, the Old Testament prophets and the Psalms will find many echoes of this literature in the Gospel of Mary.[70]

For instance, the strange philosophical remarks about matter and nature in GosMar 7.1-9 are embedded in two familiar metaphors. The metaphor of 'root' reminds one of New Testament parables about sowing and growing[71] and the metaphor of 'adultery' calls to mind the prophets Hosea, Jeremiah and Ezekiel who compare the bond between God and Israel to a marriage bond and describe the unfaithfulness and sin of Israel as adulterous behaviour.[72] The 'unloosening' (ⲃⲱⲗ

---

70. See, for New Testament echoes, Wilson 1956 / 57: 236-43; Evans *et al.* 1993: 415-20 and Petersen 1999: 59-61 and 139-53. I found some additional references and also looked at the Old Testament.

71. See Maurer 1977 about ῥίζα. The root is the life-sustaining force of the plant. See for the metaphor Mk 4.6, 17; Mt. 13.6, 21; Lk. 8.13; Eph. 3.17; Col. 2.7.

72. See Kühlewein 1984 about 'dzanah'. The Septuaginth mostly translates the Hebrew

єΒολ) of the cosmos is familiar too. It recalls the unloosening (Βωλ єΒολ)[73] of the elements and the heavens on the day of the Lord in the second letter of Peter (2 Pet. 3.10, 12). It also is reminiscent of the shaking of earth and heaven in Hebrews, in order that what cannot be shaken may remain. The author encourages the readers to be thankful that they have received a kingdom that cannot be shaken (Heb. 12.26-28). The unloosening of the cosmos also reminds one of Paul's letter to the Romans where he assures his readers that the creation will be set free (Βωλ єΒολ) from the servitude of corruption unto the freedom of the glory of the children of God (Rom. 8.21).

The 'sin of the world' in GosMar 7.12 reminds one of 'the Lamb of God, who takes away the sin of the world' in the Gospel of John (Jn 1.29, 35). The repeated encouragement to understand in GosMar 7.8-9; 8.1-2; 8.10-11 is similar to the encouragements in the Gospel of Mark, Matthew and Luke and in the Revelation of John.[74] The appeal not to be led astray reminds one of Jesus' admonitions of the coming persecutions in Matthew, Mark and Luke.[75]

The title, the 'Son of Man', recalls Jesus' self-designation in the New Testament Gospels.[76] The remark 'the Son of Man is within you (πετῆ2ογν)' in GosMar 8.18-19 especially reminds one of the references in the Gospel of John where the Son of Man who came out of heaven will go up to heaven (Jn 3.13; 6.62)[77]. The Johannine Son of Man, after being 'lifted up', which means being crucified and returned to the Father's presence in heaven, will, as the one who is thus glorified, live within (2Pλι ῆ2ητογ) his disciples (Jn 12.23; 17.5, 24-26).[78] This also reminds one of the way the Pauline letters speak of the crucified and resurrected

---

'dzanah' with the Greek πορνεύω or μοιχεύω. See for the metaphor Hos. 4.12; 9.1; Jer. 2.20; 3.1, 6, 8; Ezek. 16 and 23 and also Exod. 34.15; Deut. 31.16; Judges 2.17; 8.27, 33; Pss. 73.25-27; 106.34-39; 1 Chron. 5.25. The same metaphor is used in the New Testament; see Mk 8.38; Mt. 12.39; 16.4; Jas 4.4.

73. For the Coptic New Testament references see Horner 1969. For biblical texts in Coptic see also Schüssler 1995.

74. Mk 4.9; 7.16; Mt. 11.15; 13.9, 43; Lk. 8.8; 14.35; Revelation 2.7, 11, 17, 29; 3.6, 13, 22; 13.9.

75. Mk 13.5-6, 21; Mt. 24.4-5, 23; Lk. 21.8.

76. The Synoptic references, however, refer to the earthly activity of the Son of Man (Mk 2.10, 28; 10.45; Mt. 8.20; 9.6; 11.19; 12.8, 32; 13.37; 16.13; 18.11; 20.28; Lk. 5.24; 6.5, 22; 7.34; 9.58; 12.10; 19.10), his suffering (Mk 8.31, 38; 9.9, 12, 31; 10.33; 14.21, 41; Mt. 12.40; 17.9, 12, 22; 20.18; 26.2, 24, 45; Lk. 9.22, 26, 44; 11.30; 18.31; 22.22, 48; 24.7) and the future returning in judgment (Mk 13.26; 14.21, 62; Mt. 10.23; 13.41; 16.27, 28; 19.28; 24.27, 30, 37, 39, 44; 25.31; 26.64; Lk. 12.8, 40; 17.22, 24, 26, 30; 18.8; 21.27, 36; 22.69).

77. Son of Man passages in John: 1.51; 3.13, 14; 5.27; 6.27, 53, 62; 8.28; 9.35; 12.23, 34; 13.31. Compared to the Synoptics the most typical trait of the Johannine Son of Man theology is the notion that the Son of Man descended from heaven and is going to return; cf. Phil. 2.1-11. See Schnackenburg 1964-65: 123-37, who argues that this trait is due to the Jewish concept of Wisdom.

78. One could also think of Jn 6.53 'truly, truly, I say to you, unless you eat the flesh of the Son of Man and drink his blood, you have no life in you' and Jn 6.56 'he who eats my flesh and drinks my blood abides in me, and I in him', indicating the Eucharist (see Brown 1966: 284-85), but perhaps also relating to the Jewish Wisdom theology (Prov. 9.5-6).

Christ who lives within those (N̄2HTTHYTN̄) who believe in him.[79] In the letter to the Colossians this 'Christ in you' (N̄2HTTHYTN̄) is described as the word of God made fully known. It is the content of the mystery hidden for ages and generations but now made manifest to his saints (Col. 1.27).[80]

The appeal to follow the Son of Man and the promise that those who seek him will find him, remind one of the words of Jesus in John, where he says in three different places that he will go away and will be sought after.[81] He explains to the disciples that he is going to his Father, so that they will know the way and be able to follow him (Jn 14.19-23). Seeking and finding God is also a theme in the literature of the Old Testament.[82]

The danger of being imprisoned (ⲀⲘⲀ2ⲦⲈ) by laws and rules in GosMar 9.1-4 reminds one of Paul's words in his letter to the Romans about a law in his members that leads to sin and death, which imprisons (ⲀⲘⲀ2ⲦⲈ) the law of his mind that rejoices in the law of God (Rom. 7.6, 22-23). According to him, the law of the Spirit of life in Christ Jesus has set us free from the law of sin and death, in order that the law of God may be fulfilled through the strengthening of his Spirit which lives in us (Rom. 7.21–8.11). In the Gospel of Mary as we have it, it is not clear precisely what this one rule is that the Saviour gave. In the New Testament the whole law of God is fulfilled in one commandment: the commandment to love.[83] To this end Jesus' followers are freed from bondage to sin and law and are warned not to submit to any yoke of slavery again, for instance to circumcision or to specific feasts.[84]

The departure of the Saviour in GosMar 9.5 reminds one of his departure at the end of Luke (Lk. 24.50-51) and the beginning of Acts (Acts 1.9). It also reminds one of Jesus' farewell speech in the Gospel of John where he makes known his imminent departure. The disciples will be grieved, but Jesus encourages them to rejoice (Jn 14 and 16.16-23). In GosMar 9.12-20 it is Mary who has this role of encouragement. She says that he prepared (Ⲁ϶ⲤⲂ̄ⲦⲰⲦ) them and made them (true) Human Being (N̄ⲢⲰⲘⲈ) whereupon the disciples begin to study the words of the Saviour. This reminds one of the second letter to Timothy where the knowledge of Scripture enables one to be instructed for salvation through Jesus Christ, and results in a complete human being of God (ⲠⲢⲰⲘⲈ Ⲙ̄ⲠⲚⲞⲨⲦⲈ Ⲉ϶ⲬⲎⲔ ⲈⲂⲞⲖ), prepared (Ⲁ϶ⲤⲂ̄ⲦⲰⲦ) for every good work (2 Tim. 3.17).

When Levi later refers to Mary's words (GosMar 18.16) he encourages the

---

79. Gal. 2.20; 4.19; Rom. 8.10. See also Jn 14.20.

80. There is no significant difference between ⲠⲈⲦN̄2ⲞⲨⲚ and N̄2HTTHYTN̄. Various forms of 2ⲞⲨⲚ are used as inward experience opposed to outward appearance; see for instance Mk 7.21, 23; Mt. 7.15; 23.25, 27, 28; Lk. 11.40; Rom. 7.22 and 2 Cor. 4.16 in Horner 1969. This would also be the case in GosMar 8.15-20: the Lord is not here nor there (outward appearance), but inside (inward experience).

81. Jn 7.34, 36; 8.21; 13.33.

82. Deut. 4.29; 1 Chron. 28.9; 2 Chron. 15.2; Prov. 7.15; 8.17; Jer. 29.13. Cf. Mk 7.7-8 and Lk. 11.9-10.

83. See for instance Lev. 19.18; Mk 12.31; Mt. 22.39; Jn 13.34-35; Rom. 13.8-10; 1 Cor. 12.31–13.13; Jas 2.8.

84. For instance Jn 8.32-36; Gal. 4.9-11; 5.1-14; Rom. 6.18; 1 Pet. 2.16.

disciples to clothe themselves with the perfect Human Being (ⲠⲢⲰⲘⲈ ⲚⲦⲈⲗⲓⲟⲥ);
this reminds one of the letter to the Galatians where baptism is explained as 'clothing oneself with Christ' (Gal. 3.27). In the letters to the Ephesians and the Colossians
the readers are encouraged to clothe themselves with the new Human Being (Eph.
4.24; Col. 3.10). Earlier in the letter to the Ephesians one is encouraged to attain
the perfect Human Being (ⲠⲢⲰⲘⲈ ⲚⲦⲈⲗⲓⲟⲥ),[85] the measure of the stature of the
fullness (ϪⲰⲔ ⲈⲂⲟⲗ) of Christ (Eph. 4.13). In the letter to the Romans the readers
are encouraged to clothe themselves with the Lord Jesus Christ (Rom. 13.11).

The fear of the disciples to proclaim the gospel (GosMar 9.5-12) reminds one of
Jesus' predictions of future suffering in the New Testament Gospels.[86] In Matthew,
for instance, Jesus says to his disciples that he sends them out as sheep in the midst
of wolves (Mt. 10.16). Since a servant is not above his master and they call the
master of the house Beelzebul, how much more will they malign those of his
households? (Mt. 10.24) And he goes on to say: 'Do not fear those who kill the
body but cannot kill the soul; rather fear him who can destroy both soul and body
in hell' (Mt. 10.28).

The portrayal of Mary as knowing more than her fellow disciples (GosMar 10.4-
6) seems familiar too. In Matthew, Mary Magdalene and the other Mary are the
only ones who are told that the risen Christ will be seen in Galilee (Mt. 28.5-7). In
Mark, Mary Magdalene, Mary of James and Salome receive the same message and,
although the man in white says that Jesus told this to his disciples and Peter, the
remark that he will be seen in Galilee is not mentioned earlier.[87] In John, the
unique knowledge of Mary Magdalene consists of having seen the Lord and of
being told by him about his imminent ascension and about the new bond between
his Father and his disciples (Jn 20.17-18). In the Gospel of Mary her new knowledge consists of having seen the Lord in a vision and of being taught by him about
this and about the ascension of the soul (GosMar 10.9–17.9).

The word for vision in the Gospel of Mary is ⲌⲟⲢⲁⲘⲁ (ὅραμα) which occurs in
the Acts of the Apostles and in Matthew. Seeing visions seems quite common in
the New Testament writings. Peter has a vision about clean and unclean food (Acts
10.3, 17, 19). Stephen calls Moses' experience with the thorn bush a vision (Acts
7.31). Cornelius has a vision of an angel of God (Acts 10.3). Paul has a vision of a
man from Macedonia (Acts 16.9-10). There are also appearances of Jesus in a
vision. In Matthew, Jesus transfigures in his earthly lifetime on a mountain before
Peter, James and John. His face shines like the sun and his garments become white
as light. Peter, James and John are commanded to tell no one this vision until the
Son of Man is raised from the dead (Mt. 17.9). The other New Testament appearances of Jesus in visions are post-resurrectional. Thus he appears to Ananias and to
Paul (Acts 9.10; 18.9). All these visions include seeing and hearing and most of
them also questioning and answering.

85. In Nestle and Aland, the Greek of Ephesians does not read ἄνθρωπος as one would
expect, but instead ἀνήρ as a direct reference to the masculine υἱός τοῦ θεοῦ in the same verse.
86. Mk 13.9-13; Mt. 10.16-36; Lk. 21.12-19; Jn 16.1-4.
87. Mk 16.7. In Mk 14.28 Jesus only says that he will go before them to Galilee.

An equivalent word to ὅραμα is ὀπτασία (appearing). The vision of Zechariah in the temple is called an ὀπτασία (Lk. 1.22). In Acts Paul calls his meeting with Jesus on his way to Damascus an ὀπτασία (Acts 26.19), and the two going to Emmaus declare that the women at the tomb of Jesus, when they did not find his body, saw a vision (ὀπτασία) of angels (Lk. 24.23). Last but not least Paul, in his second letter to the Corinthians, relating his visions and revelations of the Lord (2 Cor. 12.7) tells about a person who was caught up into the third heaven and later into paradise, hearing things that cannot be told (2 Cor. 12.1-4). Paul adds that he does not know whether this experience was in the body or out of the body.

In the Gospel of Mary it is the soul which ascends. The personified soul declares that she first descended (GosMar 15.2-3). This reminds one of the descending and ascending of the Son of Man in John (Jn 3.13; 6.62), who will come again and take his disciples to himself (Jn 14.2-6; cf. 1 Thess. 4.16-17). It also reminds one of Eph. 4.8-9 where Jesus is said, after having descended, to have ascended, leading a host of captives. In Heb. 4.14 Jesus is called the Son of God who passed through the heavens, thus becoming a forerunner on the readers' behalf (Heb. 6.20). The powers which the soul has to conquer (GosMar 15.11; 16.4) remind one again of the letter to the Ephesians, according to which the principalities and powers in the heavenly places, because of Christ and through the church, will be made known with the manifold wisdom of God (Eph. 3.10).

The boldness of the soul's answers to the powers in the Gospel of Mary reminds one of the same letter when it says about the principalities of the heavenly places: 'in Christ Jesus our Lord we have boldness and confidence of access through our faith in him' (Eph. 3.11-12). The readers are encouraged to put on the armour of God:

> For we are not contending against flesh and blood, but against the principalities, against the powers, against the world rulers of this present darkness, against the spiritual hosts of wickedness in the heavenly places (Eph. 6.12).

The mind (ⲚⲞⲨⲤ; νοῦς) being described as a treasure (GosMar 10.15-16) reminds one of Paul's first letter to the Corinthians where he quotes Isaiah's question 'who has the mind (νοῦς) of the Lord that he may instruct him?' (Isa. 11.13). And he answers: but we have the mind (νοῦς) of Christ (1 Cor. 2.16). In his letter to the Romans the νοῦς is the inner Human being, which is able to distinguish between the good and the bad (Rom. 7.22-23). The νοῦς is able to honour the law of God, but is held prisoner by the flesh, causing death (Rom. 7.26). If the Spirit of God who raised Christ lives within one, this situation changes, enabling one to become free and alive (Rom. 7.24-25; 8.10-15). In the second letter to the Corinthians Paul calls the knowledge of God's glory in Jesus Christ, a treasure which we have in earthen vessels, referring to his hardships as an apostle (2 Cor. 4.6-11). He encourages his readers by saying that, although the outer human being is decaying, the inner one is renewed from day to day (2 Cor. 4.16). Furthermore he asks them to change themselves and to live their lives in accordance with their renewed νοῦς (Rom. 12.2). In the letter to the Ephesians this renewal through one's νοῦς is the same as clothing oneself with the new Human being (Eph. 4.23-24).

The fact that Mary is described as not wavering (ⲀⲦⲔⲒⲘ) when she sees the Lord in a vision (GosMar 10.13-15) reminds one of the Psalms, in which the righteous and those who trust in the Lord are described as those who will not waver.[88] In a sermon of Peter in Acts one of these psalms is quoted: 'I see the Lord always before me; because he is at my right hand I shall not be shaken' (Pss. 16.8). Seeing the Lord before him and not wavering is for Peter, quoting this Psalm, a situation full of hope and joy (Acts 2.25-28). In the second letter to the Thessalonians the readers are encouraged not to be moved (ⲔⲒⲘ) and not to be troubled and deceived by false teaching (2 Thess. 2.2).

Peter's statement that the Saviour would not speak to a woman concealed from the group of disciples (GosMar 17.8-20) reminds one of the disciples' marvel in John when they come to Jesus and find him talking with a woman (Jn 4.27). Peter's question whether they are all to listen to a woman (GosMar 17.21) reminds one of the apparent difficulties that men have with teaching women in various New Testament letters.[89]

What does it mean that the Gospel of Mary, although obviously different from the New Testament Gospels, contains so many themes and phrases that are similar to those which occur in the four New Testament ones, the Pauline letters, the Old Testament prophets and the Psalms?

4. *A Gnostic Text?*

According to most exegetes the Gospel of Mary belongs to the genre of the Gnostic dialogue.[90] If they do not all agree on the exact genre, they do agree that the Gospel of Mary is a Gnostic text.[91] This would account for both the differences and the similarities with the New Testament and Old Testament writings.

4.1. *The Genre of Gnostic Dialogue*
Pheme Perkins, on the basis of thirteen works,[92] concludes that a Gnostic dialogue consists of a revelation discourse framed by narrative elements. In the introduction

88. Pss. 15.5; 16.8; 17.5; 21.7; 26.1; 30.6; 36.11; 46.5; 62.2; 93.1; 96.10; 112.6; 125.1. See Budge 1898 (who holds the numbering of the Septuagint 14.5; 15.8 etc.).
89. 1 Cor. 14.34-36; 1 Tim. 2.9-15; 1 Pet. 3.1-7. See also 1 Cor. 11.1-3; Eph. 5.22-24; Col. 3.18.
90. Rudolf 1996: 108; Perkins 1980: 31; Pasquier 1983: 10-12; Marjanen 1996: 99.
91. The option of the Gnostic dialogue is criticized by Petersen (1999: 35-43, 49-55) and by Hartenstein (2000: 5-15). In their view the genre of the Gnostic dialogue is not clear enough. They opt for 'Erscheinungsdialog' (Petersen) or 'Dialogevangelium' (Hartenstein) and only include those dialogues in which the Saviour actually appears and disappears. This means that they also include the non-Gnostic Epistula Apostolorum. However, according to Hartenstein (2000: 254) this does not interfere with the 'relation' of the 'Dialogevangelien' to Gnostic teaching, since she labels the Epistula Apostolorum as anti-Gnostic. Petersen (1999: 40) simply states that the 'Erscheinungs-dialoge' are about Gnostic knowledge, although she includes the Epistula Apostolorum.
92. Perkins's research is based on the Prayer of the Apostle Paul; the Apocryphon of John; the Nature of the Archons; the Book of Tomas the Contender; the Sophia of Jesus Christ; the Dialogue of the Saviour; the First Apocalypse of James; the Acts of Peter and the Twelve Apostles; Apocalypse of Peter; Zostrianus; Letter of Peter to Philip; the Gospel of Mary; Pistis Sophia.

the narrator speaks in general terms about the place of revelation, the time and the recipients. The place is most often a mountain, for example the Mount of Olives; the time is usually after the resurrection and the recipients are in almost all cases names known from the New Testament. The Saviour appears to them at the moment when they are persecuted, proclaim the Gospel or reflect on Jesus' words. They are anxious, sorrowful and confused, or sunk in prayer. The Saviour introduces himself with 'I am' sayings, makes clear the purpose of his coming and rebukes the disciples for their unbelief.

Then follows the revelation discourse proper, through questions put by the disciples. The proclamation often consists of information about the origin of the cosmos, redemption and the true, this is Gnostic, teaching about baptism, the crucifixion and the interpretation of the scriptures, usually the New Testament ones. By far the majority of the revelation discourses concentrates on questions about redemption. At the end the disciples are given the task of handing on what they have been told to those who are worthy, or of protecting the revelation against those who dispute it. Their reaction is one of gratitude and joy.

The content of the Gnostic teaching consists of the belief that God is radically transcendent. The God who created the world, the Demiurge, is seen as a lower deity. The highest God has nothing to do with this world, except with human beings. They are bound to him in their deepest selves, but they have forgotten this. It is the task of the Saviour to remind the human beings of their bond with God and thus of their true identity. Moreover he has to overcome the demonic powers which keep human beings imprisoned in this cosmos. For a Gnostic believer, the complete realization of redemption consists in the return to God after death (the journey of the soul). Already in this life believers must strive to be free of matter and its passions by following an ascetic lifestyle.[93]

In Perkins's view the Gnostic dialogues must be seen in a polemical context. They were used as tools in missionary propaganda, containing the hermeneutic key to true Christianity.[94] They form an important part of the Gnostic debate with non-Gnostic, orthodox Christianity and handle in general three subjects: the nature of God, of salvation, and of authority. Perkins comments that the ideas about salvation and authority in Gnostic dialogues differ hardly, if at all, from the various Christian views of the second century, but they do differ in the third century and later. Salvation in the second-century sense is about Christ's victory over the demonic powers of death, which is manifested in the resurrection.[95] As to authority, in the second century, Gnostic as well as orthodox Christians adhere to the apostolic tradition. Gnosis in the second century is no secret teaching, but is viewed as Jesus' teaching to all the apostles and the true legacy of the Church.[96] However, as to the nature of God, the conviction that God is radically transcendent

---

93. Perkins 1980: 189.
94. Perkins 1980: 25, 73, 157-62.
95. Perkins 1980: 179-80.
96. Perkins 1980: 195-96.

and has nothing to do with the cosmos stands in strong contrast to the other views of the divine which are characteristic of the second century.[97]

4.2. *The Gospel of Mary as a Gnostic Dialogue*

If one considers the Gospel of Mary it appears at first to fit Perkins's description of the Gnostic dialogue remarkably well. The Gospel as we have it contains a revelation discourse between the disciples and the resurrected Lord; even two revelation discourses (GosMar 7.1–9.4 and 10.10–17.7), framed by narrative elements in GosMar 8.12–10.10 and 17.7–19.2. The recipients are known from the New Testament: Peter, Mary, Andrew and Levi. The Gospel of Mary deals with the nature of the cosmos (GosMar 7.1–8.6) and with redemption. New Testament Scriptures are interpreted (GosMar 8.14–9.4). The Saviour reminds the disciples of their true identity (GosMar 8.17-19); they are told of the lawgiver, who might be the Demiurge, keeping the soul imprisoned (GosMar 9.1-4), and Mary describes a journey of the soul (GosMar 15.1–17.7). The explanation that sin is adultery (GosMar 7.16) may refer to an ascetic lifestyle.[98] The adversaries in GosMar 18.10 may belong to a polemical context and refer to 'orthodox' Christians. These indications seem to be compelling evidence that the Gospel of Mary belongs to the genre of the Gnostic dialogue.

Although most of the exegetes of the Gospel of Mary differ in their specific comments, they agree in that the purpose of the Gospel of Mary is to reveal Gnostic insights. Till believes that the original Gospel of Mary begins in GosMar 10.1 where Peter asks her to relate the teaching which the Saviour has given only to her.[99] According to Till, the purpose of the Gospel of Mary is to depict Mary Magdalene, the first witness of the resurrection, as a proclaimer of Gnostic teaching, of which the ascent of the soul forms the central part.

Pasquier suggests that the dialogue between the Saviour and Mary about visions and the ascent of the soul (GosMar 9.21–17.9/15) does not belong to the original Gospel of Mary.[100] In her view Peter's comment in GosMar 17.16-22 is not about this account, but about Mary's words when she addresses the weeping disciples (GosMar 9.12-20). Peter objects, above all, to the word 'us' in the sentence 'He made us (true) Human Being' (GosMar 9.20). According to Peter, Mary is not a (true) Human Being but a woman. In Pasquier's view, Peter thus represents the orthodox thinking of the second century, that the appearances of the risen Christ to women did not in themselves give them the right to preach the message of the resurrection, far less exercise authority over the Christian community. By contrast, the Gospel of Mary allows the readers to hear an unorthodox voice. Peter is portrayed as an opponent. His view of women runs contrary to that of the Saviour. According to Pasquier, the Gospel of Mary shows that Mary can take preaching upon herself because only she has already really become (true) Human Being. She

---

97. Perkins 1980: 166-69.
98. According to Tardieu (1984: 226), adultery refers to the act of sexuality. See also Till and Schenke (1972: 27). Cf. Mohri 2000: 202-203 and Morard 2001: 155-71.
99. Till and Schenke 1972: 26. See also Wilson and MacRae 1979: 455.
100. Pasquier 1983: 7-10 and 96-101.

has achieved the Gnostic androgynous unity; her soul is reunited with its heavenly male element, showing the way back from the material world to the divine one.[101] According to Pasquier, the purpose of the Gospel of Mary is to use Gnostic arguments in the struggle against orthodoxy, which forbids women to exercise authority.[102]

According to Tardieu, the Gospel of Mary takes a stand in the debate about the role of Mary Magdalene. She is Jesus' substitute and his exegete. The Gospel of Mary, which Tardieu regards as a unity, serves as a simple and attractive introduction to the other works included in the Berlin Codex. In Tardieu's opinion the first six missing pages of the Gospel of Mary must have dealt with the Creator and his creation. In his interpretation there is a clear development in the Gospel of Mary, which offers a short survey of the essential doctrines of Gnosticism. The Gospel of Mary thus elaborates on the Creator and his creation, on sin and its consequences, on salvation through Gnosis and on the ascent of the soul after death.[103]

Hartenstein focuses on the two revelation dialogues and the discussions among the disciples. Whereas the dialogues contain knowledge about how to be saved, the discussions among the disciples deal with concrete questions about persecution and suffering, about the new teachings of Mary and about the possibility of a woman passing on divine revelation.[104] According to Hartenstein, the purpose of the Gospel of Mary is to strengthen the beliefs of the Christian Gnostic readers themselves.[105]

Thus, these exegetes, despite their differences, are all convinced that Gnosticism is at the centre of the Gospel of Mary. It is important to note, however, that, what Perkins describes as the most typically-second century Gnostic trait, the radical transcendence of God, seems to be missing in the Gospel of Mary. The Gospel of Mary as we have it contains no creation myth that portrays the creator as a lower deity (the Demiurge) and the creation as a fall.

4.3. *Debate*

In 1986 M. Tardieu and J.-D. Dubois in their *Introduction à la littérature gnostique* could still state about the Gospel of Mary: 'la nature gnostique du document n'a pas été contestée'.[106] In 1994 Karen King was the first to do this.[107] In her opinion, the Gospel of Mary provides no internal evidence to indicate that a fully developed Gnostic myth must be behind the text. Thus, according to her, the Gospel should be explicated in its own terms, without importing Gnostic myth. She adds: 'The reader will have to determine how successful that attempt has been'.[108]

101. Pasquier 1983: 15-17.
102. Pasquier 1983: 24-25.
103. Tardieu 1984: 20-25.
104. Hartenstein 2000: 132.
105. Hartenstein 2000: 134.
106. Tardieu and Dubois 1986: 107. Translation: the gnostic nature of this document has not been contradicted yet.
107. King 1995.
108. King 1995: 629 note 10.

In her commentary, King indeed proves that it is not necessary to import Gnostic myth. The question, however, still remains whether some internal elements should be called Gnostic. For instance, Marjanen, while acknowledging that the Gospel contains no creation myth or Demiurge, nevertheless emphasizes that both matter and the human body represent that which does not originate from the heavenly sphere, but which belongs to the realm of darkness, desire and ignorance, and, as such, originates from the world. Moreover, according to him, the ascent of the soul after death and beyond archontic powers has its closest parallels in Gnostic texts.[109] Petersen uses a similar argument. In her view the description of the ascent of the soul and the dissolution of matter are typical themes of a Gnostic theology.[110] Hartenstein emphasizes the use of Gnostic terminology and themes in the Gospel of Mary, such as, in her view, being ill, the Son of Man inside, to be made human, Mary not being shaken, silence and rest as purposes, the liberation of the fetter of sleep and the putting on of the perfect human being.[111] In my opinion, the only indication of a specifically 'Gnostic' context of the Gospel of Mary is the lawgiver, who might be the Demiurge, keeping mankind imprisoned in creation.[112]

No scholar really elaborates on the Gnostic character of the Gospel of Mary.[113] It seems as if the Gnostic character is taken for granted.[114] Perhaps this is due to the fact that the fifth-century Coptic version of the Gospel of Mary is part of the Berlin Codex, which also contains the Apocryphon of John and the Sophia of Jesus Christ, which are seen as typically Gnostic, as well as the non-Gnostic Act of Peter, which may allow a Gnostic allegorical interpretation.[115] Furthermore, at the beginning of the third century, Hippolytus relates that the Naasenes associate their Gnostic teaching with a Mariamme, which may be Mary Magdalene.[116] Moreover, the third-century Pistis Sophia, which is clearly Gnostic, assigns Mary Magdalene a major role.

We must remember, however, that the third-century Greek fragments of the Gospel of Mary from Oxyrhynchus were not found in a specific Gnostic context. In addition to the Gospel of Mary, the following texts dating from the first three

109. Marjanen 1996: 94 note 1 and p. 121.

110. Petersen 1999: 60, and 134 note 194.

111. Hartenstein 2000: 132-33. Hartenstein translates 'sleep' where others translate 'oblivion' (GosMar 17.3).

112. Basilides, according to Hippolytus's Refutation of all Heresies VII.24.4, calls the Gnostic Demiurge the Lawgiver.

113. Except Schröter 1999, who concludes that the Gospel of Mary belongs to the grey zone between Christianity and Gnosticism (178 note 2 and 186-87). See also Morard (2001: 160, 171) who situates the Gospel in the prophetic and ascetic movement of the early church.

114. See Till and Schenke 1972: 25; Wilson and MacRae 1979: 453; Pasquier 1983: 5; Perkins 1980: 133; Tardieu 1984: 22; Mohri 2000: 253.

115. For a Gnostic allegorical interpretation of the non-Gnostic Act of Peter, see Brashler and Parrott 1988: 529.

116. Hippolytus, Refutation of all Heresies V.7.1 and X.9.3. Some argue that this form of the name Mary mostly refers to Mary Magdalene; see for instance Marjanen 1996: 63-64. Petersen (1999: 157-62) argues for a clear connection between the Naasenes and the journey of the soul in the Gospel of Mary.

centuries were found in Oxyrhynchus: the Gospel of John, the Gospel of Matthew, the Gospel of Thomas, the letter from James, the Gospel of Luke, Paul's letter to the Romans, the Letter to the Hebrews and the Gospel of Peter.[117] These findings reflect a pluralistic Christian context, but not a specifically Gnostic one. This circumstance and the fact that the Coptic version of the Gospel of Mary appeared two centuries later in a Gnostic context seem to support King's suggestion that the Gospel of Mary was not originally Gnostic, but only later was read through Gnostic lenses, as were the letters of Paul and the Gospel of John.[118] But is this really true?

4.4. The Term 'Gnostic': Dualism in Creation as a Criterion
In the last decade a lively debate arose on the question of what the term 'Gnostic' should imply. This led Marjanen to a radical change of opinion on the Gnostic character of the Gospel of Mary. In an article subtitled 'Mary in the *So-Called* Gnostic Christian Texts' (italics are mine)[119] he explains:

> After finishing my own work on the so-called Gnostic Mary texts (Marjanen, *The Woman Jesus Loved*) I have redefined my conception of Gnosticism such that I no longer regard the *Gospel of Thomas*, the *Dialogue of the Savior*, and the *Gospel of Mary* as gnostic. Even if the anthropology and the soteriology of these writings correspond to that of Gnosticism (or Platonism) with the emphasis on the return of the preexistent soul to the realm of light as a sign of ultimate salvation, none of these writings contains the other central feature of Gnosticism. They do not contain the idea of a cosmic world created by an evil and/or ignorant demiurge.[120]

A crucial issue in determining the Gnostic character of a manuscript is the fact that so-called Gnostic writings include themes that occur throughout antiquity. If these themes occur in a certain text, but the creation myth and the Demiurge are missing, as in the Gospel of Mary, it is very difficult to decide whether they are meant in a specifically Gnostic way. The so-called 'Gnostic' elements mentioned by Marjanen (before his redefinition), Petersen and Hartenstein are widespread phenomena both in Jewish and Christian thought and in Greek philosophy. The ascent of the soul is a general theme in antiquity,[121] as is the theme of 'not wavering'.[122] A negative attitude towards matter,[123] the fetter of oblivion which imprisons people, and the need to be reminded of one's real nature belong to Platonic philosophy.[124] The Son of Man inside is found in the Gospel of John and the putting on of the perfect Human Being in the Pauline Letters.[125]

Last but not least, the 'lawgiver' (νομοθέτης) is a general term. In Jewish

---

117. See Van Haelst 1976: 409-410 and also Grenfell and Hunt no. 80 (1994), no. 84 (1997), no. 85 (1998), no. 86 (1999).
118. King 1995: 629 note 10.
119. Marjanen 2002.
120. Marjanen 2002: 32 note 3.
121. See for instance Culianu 1983.
122. See Williams 1985.
123. Especially in neo-Platonic philosophy; see Bormann 1972: 986.
124. See for instance Roukema 1999: 76-77.
125. Schröter 1999.

thought the word may apply to God, who for Gnostics would be the Demiurge, but it can also refer to Moses and the Rabbis. This is also the case in Christian terminology. The lawgiver stands for God or for Christ, but also for the church government. The lawgiver can also refer to the civil government of a city or a state.[126] As for being held prisoner by the law, this is an idea also expressed by Paul without assuming that there is a true God who is not the God of creation (Rom. 7.6).

In his book *Rethinking 'Gnosticism': An argument for Dismantling a Dubious Category*, Michael Allen Williams challenges scholars to abolish the term 'Gnostic' or at least to use the designation very cautiously and critically. He states that in antiquity there was no such thing as a clearly defined Gnostic religion; instead, the label 'Gnostic' is a modern way of categorizing certain late antique writings in order to understand them better. He warns against misunderstanding certain texts by assuming that they belong to a fixed 'Gnostic' religion, rather than allowing the texts to speak for themselves.

King concludes that Gnosticism is a blanket term that covers a lot of early Christian movements. She argues that the term only existed as a tool of orthodox identity formation, deriving from an early Christian discourse of orthodoxy and heresy which has now taken on an independent existence.[127] In her book *What is Gnosticism?* she shows that the early Christian polemicists' discourse of orthodoxy and heresy has been intertwined with twentieth-century scholarship on Gnosticism. This is an important insight, since, as she writes:

> At stake is not only the capacity to write a more accurate history of ancient Christianity in all its multiformity, but also our capacity to engage critically the ancient politics of religious difference rather than unwittingly reproduce its strategies and results.[128]

Instead of the term 'Gnostic', Williams coined a new term, which is more technical, namely 'Biblical demiurgical tradition'. He prefers this term because most Nag Hammadi Codices and related documents contain Jewish or Christian elements and start from a distinction between the highest God and the lower Demiurge of the world.[129] With this definition he is close to Perkins in that she too concluded that the radical transcendence of the Divine is the most common characteristic of the writings which she studied. King observes that the distinction of a true God and the creator God of Genesis is a popular choice to define Gnosticism.[130] However she does not agree, since she rejects typological methodology, because it does no justice to the fact that 'the so-called Gnostic works provide evidence of a wide variety of ethical orientations, theological and anthropological views, spiritual disciplines, and ritual practices confounding any attempt to develop

---

126. Lampe 1961: 919b. See also King 1995: 607. Hartenstein (2000: 145) suggests Jesus to be the lawgiver, because of the direct context. Jesus has given a law, his disciples should not give laws themselves.

127. King 2003a: 20-54.

128. King 2003a: 19.

129. Williams 1996: 263-66.

130. King 2003a: 226 and 335 note 21.

a single set of typological categories that will fit everything scholars have labeled Gnosticism'.[131]

If we, however, should decide to call the Gospel of Mary a Gnostic gospel, this would be a modern way of categorizing it as related to those Nag Hammadi Codices and other documents that start from a dualism in creation.[132] We do not presuppose a more or less clearly defined Gnostic movement and we only call the dualism in creation a criterion to call the Gospel 'Gnostic' as a modern way of categorizing it in order to understand it better.

The question is whether the Gospel of Mary as we have it gives internal clues that point to a dualism in creation. It seems that only the missing pages of the Gospel of Mary could really answer the question of whether the Gospel presupposes a dualism in creation or not, since in the Gospel as we have it no creation myth occurs.

We may, however, also examine the question from a different point of view: is there any internal evidence that the Gospel of Mary starts from another tradition? Petersen and Hartenstein agree with King that the ideas of the Gospel of Mary on p. 7 about matter and sin need not be read in a Gnostic context, but they are of the opinion that it could belong to a Gnostic context as well.[133] In contrast to Hartenstein, who argues that the Gospel of Mary gives no indications against a Gnostic reading, I believe it does.[134] The next chapter examines a new perspective on matter and Nature in the Gospel of Mary, which may point to a non-Gnostic context, in which Nature is a positive power directly stemming from the Divine.

131. King 2003a: 213.
132. See also Roukema 1999: 120-25. According to him Gnosis must be viewed as a radical form of the Hellenization, and especially Platonizing, of early Christianity (118-25). He refers to Harnack 1931: 250.
133. Petersen 1999: 134; Hartenstein 2000: 132; King 1995: 628.
134. Hartenstein 2000: 133.

Chapter 3

Character and Purpose of the Gospel of Mary

This chapter will investigate the themes of matter and Nature in the Gospel of Mary by comparing it to related ideas in Stoic philosophy. We will also study similar thoughts in the works of Philo of Alexandria. We will focus on the extant pages of the discourse between the Saviour and his disciples in the Gospel of Mary and more specifically on its traces of ideas on cosmology (GosMar 7-8). In addition, I will examine the themes of the other writings in the Berlin Codex and present my thoughts on the character and the purpose of the Gospel of Mary.

1. *Matter and Nature*

In the Gospel of Mary the way the words ϕΥϹΙϹ (nature) and ΠΑΘΟϹ (passion) are used and the way ϕΥϹΙϹ (nature) and 2ΥΛΗ (matter) are interrelated show an affinity with Stoic philosophy. Stoicism holds a monistic view of the origin of the world. In Stoic philosophy, matter is formed by Nature into a harmonious cosmos. One can either act according to Nature (κατὰ φύσιν) or against it (παρὰ φύσιν); to be guided by πάθος is clearly παρὰ φύσιν. The material world does not originate in the act of a lower God; the creation is a self-transformation of God. Nor do Stoics differentiate between a material and a spiritual world; according to Stoic philosophy everything that exists is basically material. The world originates from a state of pure fire in which God and the universe are coextensive. God as pure fire changes into hot air and condenses into moisture, which then changes into the four elements which constitute the cosmos: fire, air, water and earth.[1]

Obviously, the Gospel of Mary is not a Stoic document, since the 'body', which probably refers to the human as well as the cosmic body, is not in harmony but in confusion (GosMar 8.5-6). Moreover, the Gospel of Mary does not speak of one material world, but presupposes two worlds: one earthly and one heavenly (GosMar 16.21–17.3). However, although it is clear that the Gospel of Mary is not Stoic, Stoic philosophy can help to clarify some of its basic ideas.

Pasquier is the only other scholar who calls attention to the Stoic language in the Gospel of Mary.[2] She argues that Stoic categories are used in order to reveal Gnostic insights. In her view the Gospel of Mary characterizes Nature (GosMar

---

1. Long and Sedley 1987: I, 279.
2. Pasquier 1981: 390-404. See also Pasquier 1983: 48-56 and especially pp. 50 and 52.

7.17-22) and the nature of matter (GosMar 7.1-8) as two opposite natures. The disciples must choose Nature or perish with matter.

In Stoic philosophy, however, matter is only a thought-construct and does not exist in itself: Nature and matter are intertwined, Nature is material. The nature of matter in the Gospel of Mary, read within a Stoic context, is nothing but Nature itself. Another objection to Pasquier's thesis is her reading of GosMar 8.2-4, where she has added the word 'union'. Passion in her translation arises from 'une (union) contre nature' which she herself defines as a union between matter and Nature, whereas a more straightforward reading, as we will see, would be that matter has been acted upon by an opposite nature, just as in Stoic philosophy matter is formed by Nature. But the most important objection to her thesis is her interpretation of ΦΥϹΙϹ ΝΙΜ which occurs twice (GosMar 7.3 and 7.18). In the first occurrence (GosMar 7.3) Pasquier interprets the expression as the nature of matter. In the second (GosMar 7.18) this is interpreted as Nature.

On p. 7 of the Gospel of Mary we plunge into the end of a dialogue the beginning of which and its context we can only speculate about, since the first six pages of the Coptic manuscript are missing. The first question on p. 7 is about the destiny of matter (7.1-2): 'Will matter thus be destroyed or not?' (ΘΥΛΗ ϬΕ ΝΛΟΥⲰϬⲠ ⲬⲚ ⲘⲘⲞⲚ). The Saviour's answer in GosMar 7.3-4 is about all natural phenomena (ΦΥϹΙϹ ΝΙΜ), all that has been formed (ⲠⲖⲀⲤⲘⲀ ΝΙⲘ), and all that has been brought into being (ⲔⲦΙϹΙϹ ΝΙⲘ).

It is customary to interpret these words to refer to the material world in contrast to spiritual nature. The general opinion is that the Saviour's answer is about the fate of matter.[3] There is, however, one problem. When the words ΦΥϹΙϹ ΝΙⲘ occur again in GosMar 7.18-19, where the Saviour assures his disciples that the Good One came into their midst, 'to those who belong to ΦΥϹΙϹ ΝΙⲘ, in order to restore ΦΥϹΙϹ up to her Root', the same commentators who interpret the first ΦΥϹΙϹ ΝΙⲘ as referring to matter, interpret ΦΥϹΙϹ ΝΙⲘ the second time it occurs as referring to spiritual nature.[4]

Only Pasquier defends this inconsistent choice, arguing that the first ΦΥϹΙϹ ΝΙⲘ has to be interpreted in a material way, because the question is about matter alone, and because ⲠⲖⲀⲤⲘⲀ and ⲔⲦΙϹΙϹ also refer to the material world alone.[5] These two reasons, however, do not justify the contradictory interpretation. Clearly, the Saviour's answer to a question can be quite unexpected as can be seen on the same page, the second question being about the content of sin, where the Saviour answers that sin does not exist (GosMar 7.12-13). Furthermore the words πλάσμα and κτίσις do not need to refer to matter contrary to spiritual nature. They may also be meant in a Stoic way. In Stoic philosophy matter and spirit (or Nature) are intertwined, matter being passive. In a Stoic sense the words denote the forms God

---

3.   Till and Schenke 1972: 27; Pasquier 1981: 391-92 and 1983: 50; Tardieu 1984: 226; King 1995: 603.

4.   Till and Schenke 1972: 27 and 63; Tardieu 1984: 226; King 1995: 604. Pasquier (1981: 393) notes the antithesis between what she calls the first (material) and the second (pneumatic) nature; see also Pasquier 1983: 52-53.

5.   Pasquier 1983: 50 note 7.

or Nature made of substance. Interpreted this way ⲫⲨⲤⲓⲤ ⲚⲓⲘ in GosMar 7.3-4 as well as in 7.18-19 refers to all natural phenomena (all Nature) as an appearance of the Divine.

As in Stoic philosophy the Saviour in GosMar 7.3-4 does not seem to distinguish between material or spiritual realms in the cosmos, as does the disciple who limits his or her question to the fate of matter alone, thus suggesting that matter is the source of evil. The Saviour explains in GosMar 7.4-8 that all exists in and with each other (2ⲚⲚⲉⲨⲉⲢⲎⲨ [Ⲙ]ⲚⲚ̄Ⲙ̄ⲘⲀⲨ) and does not repeat the verb 'destroy' (ⲞⲨⲰ6ⲛ), which the disciple uses, but introduces the verb 'unloosen' (ⲃⲰⲗ ⲉⲃⲟⲗ). The answer of the Saviour is apparently unexpected in more than one way.

2. *Cosmology in the Gospel of Mary*

In this section we will examine Stoic thoughts on matter, Nature and the source of evil, because they can help us to understand the ideas of the Gospel of Mary on matter, Nature, an opposite nature and on the mixture of these. We will also turn to the exegete Philo of Alexandria (± 20BC–45CE), who makes use of dualistic (Platonic) as well as Stoic categories, as does the author of the Gospel of Mary, to express the deeper meaning of Jewish Scripture.[6] With the help of these two sources we will try to interpret GosMar 7.1–8.10 and investigate whether the Gospel of Mary is to be seen as a Gnostic text in the sense that its remarks on cosmology betray a dualism in creation.

2.1. *Stoic Philosophy on Matter, Nature and the Source of Evil*

2.1.1. *Mixture and the Stability of the Cosmos.* The idea that all things are mixed is an important part of Stoic physics. Diogenes Laertius says:

> The world is created when the substance is turned from fire through air into moisture; then the thicker parts of the moisture condense and end up as earth, but the finer parts are thoroughly rarefied, and when they have been thinned still further, they produce fire. Thereafter by mixture plants and elements and the other natural kinds are produced after these. (Diogenes Laertius, Lives of Eminent Philosophers 7.142)[7]

At the heart of the creation is God:

> God, intelligence, fate and Zeus are all one, and many other names are applied to him. In the beginning all by himself he turned the entire substance through air into water. Just as the sperm is enveloped in the seminal fluid, so God, who is the seminal principle in the world, stays behind as such in the moisture, making

---

6.   Morris (1987: 872), argues that Philo could be called a Platonist, but just as well a Stoic or a Pythagorean. This is why Dillon (1977: 139-83), calls him a Middle Platonist. Morris (1987: 873-80) emphasizes that Philo was first of all a Jew, since he regarded the Torah of Moses as the supreme authority. Furthermore, Philo does not present his thoughts systematically, but in conjunction with Old Testament texts. Thus in Morris's view he can better be called an exegete than a philosopher (p. 880). See for this view also Runia 1990: 189.

7.   Quoted in Long and Sedley 1987: I, 275.

matter serviceable to himself for the successive stages of creation (γένεσιν). He then creates first of all the four elements, fire, water, air, earth. (Diogenes Laertius, *Lives of Eminent Philosophers* 7.135-36)[8]

As such:

> They [the Stoics] say that god is mixed with matter, pervading all of it and so shaping it, structuring it, and making it into the world. (Alexander, *On Mixture* 225.1-2)[9]

Stoics referred to several types of mixtures as analogies from everyday life, through which they explained and confirmed their belief in the stability of the cosmos.[10] The Stoics maintained, for instance, that a single drop of wine, which spreads through the ocean, keeps its essential quality, since, if one puts an oiled sponge in a mixture of wine and water the two can be separated. As the drop of wine which spreads through the ocean, by keeping its essential quality, changes the whole substance, so does the pneumatic force pervade and influence all substance, thus holding the cosmos together and causing stability and harmony.[11] In Stoic philosophy matter is the substance of the cosmos. Everything is basically material, but matter never exists alone; it is always permeated by this pneumatic force, which is God himself. This pneumatic force is also called Nature, since in Stoicism God and the divinity of Nature are one and the same.[12]

2.1.2. *Nature and the Source of Evil.* Nature refers to the power or principle which shapes and creates all things, which unifies and gives coherence to the whole and the potential for growth. Nature is a fiery breath, self-moving and generative. Nature is necessity and destiny, God, providence, craftsperson and right reason.[13] Nature holds the cosmos together and is the source of stability and growth, the pure fire transformed in an active fiery breath: God himself, who is also called Logos, Pneuma, Zeus or other names.[14] As it was said:

> The Stoics made God out to be intelligent, a designing fire which methodically proceeds towards creation of the world (ἐπὶ γενέσει κόσμου), and encompasses all the seminal principles according to which everything comes about according to fate, and a breath pervading the whole world, which takes on different names owing to the alterations of the matter through which it passes. (Aetius, *Placita* 1.7.33)[15]

As Seneca says: 'What else is Nature than God and Divine Reason in the world and its parts?' (*De Beneficiis* IV.7.1). Nature is personified and called upon in a

---

8. Quoted in Long and Sedley 1987: I, 275
9. Quoted in Long and Sedley 1987: I, 273.
10. See Todd 1976: 36-49 and 70-72. See also Long and Sedley 1987: I, 273-74 and 294.
11. Long and Sedley 1987: I, 270-72.
12. Long 1974: 149.
13. SVF II 937, 549, 1211, 1132-3, 913, SVF I 158, 176 and SVF III 323. See Long 1974: 148.
14. Long 1974: 147-54. Stoics are, however, not to be seen as 'materialists'. Long argues that 'Stoics are better described as vitalists' (Long 1974: 154).
15. For the quotation see Long and Sedley 1987: I, 274.

religious way as the one ultimate deity, as Marcus Aurelius does, when he says: 'O Nature, from you is all, in you is all, to you all is related' (Meditations IV.23). Nature creates and arranges all for the good of the whole.[16]

How did the Stoics reconcile their thoughts about the cosmos being harmonious and all being arranged for the good of the whole, with the problem of the source of evil? In Stoic philosophy cosmic evil is seen as a misjudgment: as a human description of things necessary for the good on a universal scale.[17] Moral evil is also seen as a matter of misjudgment: of allowing oneself to be guided by powers of passion, rather than consciously subjecting them to reason, which results in the freedom to act in a morally good way.[18] The Stoics have an optimistic view on evil. Both cosmic and moral evil, according to the Stoics, are essentially misjudgments. Passion is an important cause of these misjudgments, but even passion is seen as a misjudgment itself. The origin of evil, in this Stoic concept, thus remains an embarrassing problem.[19]

2.1.3. *Passion and the Divine Within.* It should be noted that passion in Stoic philosophy is not to be confused with sexual desire. Passion is, instead, a general overpowering unhealthy state of mind. It is the source of all unhappiness, the four primary passions being appetite, pleasure, fear and distress.[20] These four primary passions should be understood in this way:

> under appetite: anger and its species…intense sexual desires, cravings and yearnings, love of pleasures and riches and honours, and the like. Under pleasure: rejoicing at others' misfortunes, self-gratification, trickery, and the like. Under fear: hesitancy, anguish, astonishment, shame, confusion, superstition, dread and terror. Under distress: malice, envy, jealousy, pity, grief, worry, sorrow, annoyance, mental pain, vexation. (Stobaeus, Anthologium 2.90.19–91.9)[21]

Allowing oneself to be guided by passion is acting contrary to nature (παρὰ φύσιν). In mainstream Stoic philosophy passion is a result of false judgments and 'a movement of soul which is irrational (ἄλογος) and contrary to nature (παρὰ φύσιν)'.[22] The Stoic Posidonius, however, ardently rejects the view that passion arises from false judgment. Instead, he argues that the soul itself exists of rational and irrational, animal-like faculties. The irrational faculties result in passions which in their turn cause false judgments.[23] Posidonius refers to a divine power within, a strength which enables one to choose daily for reason over passion. He says:

---

16. Long 1974: 148. Pohlenz (1948: 68) describes this as 'ein ganz neues Lebensgefühl'. Nature is no longer a mere mechanical force, but a living and leading deity, a shaping power in the cosmos as well as in human life: Zeus himself.
17. Long 1968: 332-33.
18. Long 1968: 337-41.
19. Kidd 1971: 206.
20. Long and Sedley 1987: I, 419-20.
21. As quoted by Long and Sedley 1987: I, 412.
22. Long and Sedley 1987: I, 410, quoting Stobaeus 288.8.
23. Kidd 1971: 207. See also Sandbach 1975: 135-36.

> The cause of the passions, that is a lack of harmony, and of the life of misery, lies in not following in everything the *daemon*[24] within, which is kin to the one who rules the whole world, but rather live in subjection to the worse and the brutish. (Galen, De placitis Hippocratis et Platonis 448.11-12)[25]

According to F.H. Sandbach, referring to Epictetus, Seneca and Marcus Aurelius, the Stoic discovery of God within is especially characteristic of Roman Stoics.[26] Epictetus, for instance, in an attempt to keep his listeners away from 'unclean thoughts and filthy actions' asks them:

> Why do you refuse to know whence you have come? When you eat will you not remember who it is that is eating and whom you are feeding? When you go to bed with a woman, who is doing that? When you mix in company, when you take exercise, when you engage in conversation? Don't you know that you are feeding God, exercising God? You carry God around with you, miserable creature, and do not know it. Do you think I mean some god outside you, a god made of silver or gold? No; you carry him within you, and do not perceive that you are defiling him with your unclean thoughts and filthy actions. In the presence of an image of God you would not dare to do any of those things you now do, but in the presence of God himself within you, who watches and hears all, are you not ashamed to entertain these thoughts and do these actions, insensible of your own nature and earning wrath of God? (Discourses II.8.11-14)[27]

Like the Roman Stoics and Posidonius, the Gospel of Mary also refers to a divine power within. The Gospel of Mary, however, contains a further explanation for the origin of passion. According to the Gospel of Mary the origin of passion does not lie in our animal-like nature, as Posidonius puts it, nor in our false judgments, as mainstream Stoic philosophy suggests. Instead, the Gospel of Mary introduces a new concept.

2.2. *The Gospel of Mary on Matter, Nature and an Opposite Nature*

2.2.1. *The Cosmos in Confusion*. In contrast to Stoic thought, the cosmos in the Gospel of Mary is not harmonious, but in confusion (8.5-6). The Saviour says:

```
2 [ΑΘ]ΥΛΗ [ΧΠ]Є ΟΥ
3 ΠΑΘΟС ЄΜΝΤΑϥ ΜΜΑΥ ΜΠЄΙΝЄ
4 ЄΛϕЄΙ ЄΒΟΛ 2Ν ΟΥΠΑΡΑϕΥСΙС ΤΟ
5 ΤЄ ϢΑΡЄΟΥΤΑΡΑΧΗ ϢϢΠЄ 2Μ
6 ΠСϢΜΑ ΤΗΡϥ ЄΤΒЄ ΠΑΙ ΑΙΧΟС ΝΗ
7 ΤΝ ΧЄ ϢϢΠЄ ЄΤЄΤΝΤΗΤ Ν2ΗΤ
8 ΑΥϢ ЄΤЄΤΝΤΟ ΝΝΑΤΤϢΤ ЄΤЄ
9 ΤΝΤΗΤ ΜЄΝ ΝΝΑ2ΡΜ ΠΙΝЄ ΠΙΝЄ
10 ΝΤЄϕΥСΙС[28]
```
(GosMar 8.1-10)

---

24. According to Sandbach (1975: 136 note 2), daemon in this quotation, which refers to the divine ruler of the world, is God himself.
25. As quoted by Kidd 1971: 209.
26. Sandbach 1975: 174.
27. Translation in Sandbach 1975: 167.
28. The Coptic text is quoted from Pasquier 1983: 32.

Matter [brought forth] (3) passion that, (4) since it proceeds from an opposite nature, has no form. (5) From then on confusion exists (6) in the whole body. That is why I said (7) to you, 'Be fully assured and (8) do not be persuaded (by what is opposite to Nature), (9) since you are already persuaded (by the Good One) in the presence of the various forms (10) of Nature.

The grammar in this passage is complicated, which allows for a number of different translations.[29] The question is to find a translation that makes sense in the direct context. The words between brackets render my interpretation. Four observations are important here. First, the passage 8.2-10 is an inclusion. In 8.1 the Saviour encourages those who can understand to understand and in 8.10-11 those who have ears to hear. Secondly, the inclusion consists of an encouragement by the Saviour not to be persuaded (8.6-10) which is preceded by the explanation on which this encouragement is based (8.2-6). This is clear from the words ⲈⲦⲂⲈ ⲠⲀⲒ (that is why) in GosMar 8.6. Thirdly, the word ⲈⲒⲚⲈ (form) occurs twice (8.3 and 8.9-10), and in both cases it is not directly clear what it means. Fourthly, the central word in the passage, ⲠⲀⲐⲞⲤ (passion), may be understood in various ways.

2.2.2. *The Meaning of* ⲠⲀⲐⲞⲤ. The word ⲠⲀⲐⲞⲤ (πάθος) may be translated as 'suffering', instead of 'passion'.[30] This would make sense, since in the previous verses the Saviour tells about the cause of sickness and death (GosMar 7.21-22).[31] When translating ⲠⲀⲐⲞⲤ as 'passion' this could be meant in the limited sense of sexual desire.[32] This would make sense, since in GosMar 7.16 the Saviour makes a statement about sin and adultery. This interpretation, however, would not be likely in the context of suffering of GosMar 7.21-22. Nevertheless, I translated ⲠⲀⲐⲞⲤ as 'passion', but in the Stoic sense of the word.

29. GosMar 8.7-10 has been translated in widely differing ways. The differences arise from the various grammatical possibilities, the different meanings of ⲦⲰⲦ ⲚⲊⲎⲦ and ⲦⲰⲦ as well as the attempted interpretation of the sentence as a whole. Till and Schenke (1972: 65) translate: 'Fasst Mut und, wenn ihr mutlos seid, habt doch Mut angesichts der verschiedenen Gestalten der φύσις'. Wilson and MacRae (1979: 459) follow this translation: 'Be of good courage, and if you are discouraged, be encouraged in the presence of the different forms of nature'. Pasquier (1983: 33) translates quite differently: 'Soyez obéissants et à la fois désobéissants pourvu que vous soyez obéissants envers chaque Image de la nature'. Tardieu (1984: 76) has: 'Soyez bien réglés! Et si vous êtes déréglés, réglez-vous donc par rapport aux différentes espèces de la nature'. King (1992: 362) has: 'Be content of heart. And do not conform (to the body), but form yourselves in the presence of that other image of nature'. Hartenstein and Petersen (1998: 759) have: 'Seid euch gewiss, und wenn ihr keine Gewissheit habt, seid gewiss angesichts der verschiedenen Gestalten der Natur!' My translation is: 'Be fully assured and do not be persuaded (by what is opposite to Nature), since you are already persuaded (by the Good One) in the presence of the various forms of Nature'. This translation makes a distinction between ⲦⲰⲦ ⲚⲊⲎⲦ (be fully assured, Crum 1939: 438a, πληροφορέω) and ⲦⲰⲦ (be persuaded, Crum 1939: 437a, πείθω). Because of the place of ⲀⲨⲞ I interpret ⲈⲦⲈⲦⲚⲞ like ⲈⲦⲈⲦⲚ̄ⲦⲎⲦ as a periphrastic imperative, belonging to ⲱⲱⲠⲈ. Because ⲀⲨⲞ does not occur a second time, I interpret the second ⲈⲦⲈⲦⲚ̄ⲦⲎⲦ as a circumstantial expression.

30. Bauer *et al.* 1988: 1220.

31. As I did earlier, see De Boer 1997: 82. King (1995: 605) uses both translations.

32. As do Till and Schenke 1972: 27 and Tardieu 1984: 226. According to them the Saviour in GosMar 7.13-16 identifies sinning as procreation.

According to Stoic philosophy:

> Proneness to sickness is a tendency towards passion, towards one of the functions
> contrary to nature, such as depression, irascibility, malevolence, quick temper and
> the like. Proneness to sickness also occurs in reference to other functions which
> are contrary to nature, such as theft, adultery and violence; hence people are called
> thieves, violators and adulterers. Sickness is an appetitive opinion which has
> flowed into a tenor and hardened, signifying a belief that what should not be
> pursued is intensely worth pursuing, such as the passion for women, wine and
> money. By antipathy the opposites of the sicknesses occur, such as loathing for
> women and wine, and misanthropy. (Stobaeus, Anthologium 2.93.1-13)[33]

This description of sickness as 'a tendency towards passion' and 'signifying a
belief that what should not be pursued is intensely worth pursuing' fits both the
context of sickness and death in GosMar 7.21-22 as well as the context of adultery
in GosMar 7.16, especially when interpreted metaphorically.[34] Thus the translation
of ΠΛΘΟΣ as passion in the Stoic sense of the word seems the best translation in the
context of GosMar 7-8.

According to most translations of GosMar 8.3 the Saviour declares about
passion 'that it has no equal' (ЄМN̄ТΛϥ ММΛY M̄ΠЄІNЄ).[35] A difficulty with this
translation is, that, although ЄІNЄ occurs again only a few verses later within the
same inclusion GosMar 8.2-11, it would have another meaning. The same exegetes
who translate ЄІNЄ in GosMar 8.3 as 'equal' translate ЄІNЄ in GosMar 8.9 as
'form': in their opinion ΠІNЄ ΠІNЄ N̄ТЄϕYСІС in GosMar 8.9-10 means 'forms of
Nature'. Another difficulty is that in the direct context it seems to make little sense
to state that passion has no equal. Passion having no equal can hardly be the
reassuring explanation which precedes the encouragement in GosMar 8.6-11.

Only Pasquier and King discuss the meaning of the passage as a whole. They
use 'image' in both instances.[36] By 'image' they mean the manifestation of the
truth in this world. They base their interpretation on the use of ТYΠΟС and 2ІΚШN
in the Gospel of Philip, where it says:

> Truth did not come into the world naked, but it came in types and images. The
> world will not receive truth in any other way. (GosPhil 67.9-11)[37]

---

33. Long and Sedley 1987: I, 418.

34. See for the metaphor Hos. 4.12; 9.1; Jer. 2.20; 3.1, 6, 8; Ezek. 16 and 23 and also Exod.
34.15; Deut. 31.16; Judges 2.17; 8.27, 33; Pss. 73, 25-27; 106.34-39; 1 Chron. 5.25. The same
metaphor is used in the New Testament; see Mk 8.38; Mt. 12.39; 16.4; Jas 4.4. Outside the biblical
scriptures, the use of 'adultery' in a metaphorical sense occurs for instance in the Exegesis of the
Soul (NHC II.6).

35. Till and Schenke 1972: 65; Wilson and MacRae 1979: 459; Hartenstein and Petersen 1998:
759. Tardieu (1984: 226) translates 'désordonée'.

36. Till and Schenke (1972: 25): Gestalten. Wilson and MacRae (1979: 459): forms.
Hartenstein and Petersen (1998: 759): Gestalten. Tardieu (1984: 76): espèces. Pasquier and King
are the exceptions. Pasquier (1983: 33) translates 'Image' in both instances and King (1992: 362)
'(true) image'.

37. Cf. GosPhil 84.20-21; see Pasquier 1983: 54 and King 1995: 605 and 629 note 11.

Pasquier adds that not having an Image as a result of passion is described in metaphorical language in Gnostic literature. In several Gnostic writings the fundamental passion of the Archonts or the lower powers is to possess the spiritual element of the world above, but no matter how hard they try they constantly fail.[38] However, is it justified to interpret ∈IN∈ in GosMar 8.2-11 as 'spiritual element' and use the 'types and images' of the Truth in the Gospel of Philip as a parallel? In our passage ∈IN∈ is specifically used in the context of Nature, which is not the case in the Gospel of Philip.

2.2.3. *The Meaning of Nature Having* ∈IN∈. The word ∈IN∈ basically means 'likeness' or 'aspect'.[39] The expression ΠIN∈ ΠIN∈ NT∈ϕYCIC does not occur in the other works of the Berlin Codex, nor in the Nag Hammadi Codices.[40] There are, however, parallel instances, which may shed light on its meaning. In the Paraphrase of Shem the expression N∈C∈IN∈ THPOY (all her 'aspects', NHC VII.45.30) refers to the earlier mentioned NMOPϕH NT∈ϕYCIC (the forms of Nature, NHC VII.45.15). In this context ∈IN∈ is a Coptic parallel to the Greek μορφή. A similar instance occurs in the Discourse on the Eighth and Ninth in a doxology on the Father, who is called 'the one whose will begets life for the "aspects" (NNIN∈) in every place; his Nature (ϕYCIC) gives form (MOPϕH) to substance' (NHC VI.55.30-32).

We should note that Nature in the Paraphrase of Shem, which is a Gnostic writing, is a burden. Every 'aspect' (∈IN∈) into which Nature has divided is 'a power of the chaotic fire which is the hylic seed' (NHC VII.11.1-4). One is to be freed from Nature and Nature is to be destroyed (NHC VII.48.9-24). Would this therefore be the case in the Gospel of Mary too? That Nature and its forms also occur in a positive context is clear from the Discourse of the Eighth and Ninth, which is a Hermetic writing.[41] In this writing the creation is lauded as the perfect deed of the perfect God. The Discourse of the Eighth and Ninth says:

> He is the one whose will begets life for the 'aspects' of every place; his Nature gives form to substance. He created everything. By him the souls of the [eighth and] the angels are moved [...] those that exist. His providence extends to everything [...] begets everything. He is the one who [...] the aeon among spirits. He created everything. He, who is self-contained cares for everything. He is perfect, the invisible God to whom one speaks in silence. (NHC VI.55.30–56.12)

---

38. Pasquier 1983: 55.

39. Crum 1939: 80b.

40. There is no complete concordance yet. I used the available volumes of the concordance, the Nag-Hammadi-Register of Siegert 1982, the indexes of the series of Bibliothèque Copte de Nag Hammadi and the indexes of the series of the Nag Hammadi and Manichaean Studies for the remaining writings.

41. Van den Broek 1996: 8. Van den Broek (1996: 1-21) examines the differences between Gnostic and Hermetic writings. He concludes that, whereas in Gnostic writings the cosmos is the bad product of an evil creator, in Hermetic writings the cosmos represents God's creative power. In Hermetic writings the Stoic doctrine that contemplation of the cosmos gives an impression of God himself 'became the core of a cosmic religiosity, which could lead to the mystical experience of falling together with the universe, that is to say with God himself' (Van den Broek 1996: 14).

The Discourse of the Eighth and Ninth and especially NHC VI.55.30-32 and 56.8-12 form the background of my translation of ΠΙΝΕ ΠΙΝΕ ΝΤΕϥΥϹΙϹ. I follow the exegetes who have 'forms of Nature', but in my view the expression must be understood in a context of creation in which substance is formed by the perfect invisible God, instead of in a context of creation as a fall.

2.2.4. *The Meaning of Passion Having no* ΕΙΝΕ.

Giving ΕΙΝΕ in GosMar 8.3 the same meaning as in 8.9-10, because they belong to the same inclusion, means that in my translation the Saviour declares that 'passion has no form' instead of 'passion has no equal', as most exegetes do. But what would this mean?

Again we must note that the expression ΟΥΠΑΘΟϹ ΕΜΝΤΑϥ ΜΜΑΥ ΜΠΕΙΝΕ does not occur in the Nag Hammadi Codices or elsewhere in the Berlin Codex. That something would have no ΕΙΝΕ occurs in Marsanes 17.7, but in such a fragmentary context that its meaning is not clear.[42] Furthermore, having no ΕΙΝΕ only occurs in the Berlin Codex in the Sophia of Jesus Christ. In BG 92.15 it is said that the highest God has no 'likeness' (ΜΝΤΑϥ ΕΙΝΕ), since he is inconceivable. It is clear that GosMar 8.2 must have quite another meaning since here passion and not the highest God lacks ΕΙΝΕ, a circumstance which furthermore, according to the direct context, should not cause awe, but encourage the disciples not to be persuaded by it (GosMar 8.7-10).

Stoic philosophy also has no parallel, since according to the Stoics only matter and reason (reason being the same as God and Nature) are without form (ἀμόρφους), meaning that they are ingenerated and indestructible, whereas the elements are endowed with form and pass away.[43] Passion being without form, and thus indestructible in this Stoic interpretation, would hardly encourage the disciples in the Gospel of Mary not to fear its strength.

Not having ΜΟΡϕΗ as something that is missing, however, occurs in the Apocryphon of John, where Sophia's product comes forth imperfect, 'not having form from her form' (ΕΜΝΤϥ ΜΟΡϕΗ 2Ν ΤΕϹΜΟΡϕΗ: NHC III.14.6-7).[44] It also occurs in the Paraphrase of Shem, where Nature originally is powerless 'since she did not have a form from the Darkness' (NHC VI.5.11). When ΜΟΡϕΗ is a parallel to ΕΙΝΕ passion having no form could thus mean that it is imperfect and powerless. It is, however, not likely that ΕΙΝΕ in GosMar 8.2-10 is the translation of μορφή, since ΜΟΡϕΗ as a Coptic rendering of the Greek μορφή occurs in GosMar 16.5-6.

Stoic philosophy distinguishes between what really exists and what exists only in one's mind. According to the Stoics, substance (οὐσία) manifests itself in forms and qualities. In this way substance really exists (κατὰ τὴν ὑπόστασιν), whereas matter (ὕλη) exists as a notion in one's mind.[45] Perhaps GosMar 8.2-4 recalls this

---

42. See Pearson 1981: 282-83: 'But it is necessary that a [...] does not have form' (ΜΝΤΕϥ ΕΙΝΕ).

43. Diogenes Laertius 7.134. See Long and Sedley I, 1987: 268.

44. See Wisse and Waldstein 1995: 60.

45. See Steinmetz 1994: 686. Dörrie 1976, in his monograph on ὑπόστασις concludes about the use of the word in Stoic philosophy: 'Es ist das substantielle konkrete Sein, das in der Mitte steht zwischen den nur aktuellen, aber zufälligen, und den nur gedanklichen Realitäten'. (p. 36).

Stoic theory about existence, and passion having no form means that it does not
really exist; it exists in our imagination. But here again the Greek ὑπόστασις
would have been rendered in Coptic by 2ΥΠΟCΤΑCΙC or translated as ΤΑΧΡΟ, and
not as ΕΙΝΕ.[46]

I suggest that we rely upon the translation of ΠΙΝΕ ΠΙΝΕ ΝΤΕΦΥCΙC in GosMar
8.9-10 as 'forms of Nature', referring to the creation of everything as in the Discourse of the Eighth and Ninth. Within a context of creation, passion having no
form in GosMar 8.2-4 means that its origin is not from God. It has no divine root.
As we already saw, the Stoics say passion is ἄλογος. It has nothing to do with
divine reason. Indeed, the Gospel of Mary directly explains this by stating that
passion's origin lies elsewhere.

2.2.5. Formless Passion and Forms of Nature. It seems most likely that ΕΙΝΕ in
GosMar 8.2-10 is the Coptic translation of the Greek εἶδος which means 'what is
seen': form, shape, class or kind.[47] Philo of Alexandria states that passion is
ἀνείδεος devoid of form (cf. GosMar 8.2).[48] In his allegorical exegesis of the story
of the tower of Babel (Gen. 11.1-9), Philo explains the meaning of passion being
formless in a metaphorical way. Because passion is formless, the work of the evil
brick makers results in sloppy clay rather than solid cement. Philo says:

> At present we have all the content of the soul in extricable confusion, so that no
> clear form of any particular kind is discernable. Our right course is to take passion
> and vice which at present is a substance devoid of form and quality and divide it
> by continuous analysis into the proper categories and the subdivisions in regular
> descending order till we reach the ultimate; thus we shall obtain both a clearer
> apprehension of them and that experienced use and enjoyment which is calculated
> to multiply our pleasure and delight. (On the Confusion of Tongues 84-85)[49]

But, Philo explains, this right course is not followed by minds that set themselves
up against God (88). Through reasoning designed to destroy righteousness and
virtue they shape passions and vices into bricks and thus build 'a city and a tower
which will serve for the hold of vice, as a citadel for a despot' (83).[50] They even

> violently forced their betters, the children of the race that has vision, to make
> bricks and build strong cities (Exod. 1.11) for the mind which thinks itself their
> sovereign. They wished in this way to shew that good is the slave of evil and
> passion stronger than the higher emotions, that prudence and every virtue are
> subject to folly and all vice, and thus must render obedience to every command of
> the despotic power. (On the Confusion of Tongues 91)[51]

46. See 2 Cor. 9.4 and 11.17. See also Heb. 1.3; 3.14; 11.1.
47. For ΕΙΝΕ as the Sahidic translation of εἶδος see for instance Lk. 9.29 (Crum 1939: 21a),
Exod. 24.10 and Isa. 53.2 (Crum 1939: 80b). For the meaning of εἶδος see Liddell and Scott 1968:
482.
48. ...and quality: ἀνείδεον τινα καὶ ἄποιον οὐσίαν (Philo, On the Confusion of Tongues
85). Pasquier mentions the reference to Philo in a note, but does not go into its meaning. See
Pasquier 1981: 399 note 37.
49. Colson and Whitaker 1958: IV, 55.
50. Colson and Whitaker 1958: IV, 55
51. Colson and Whitaker 1958: IV, 59.

There is, however, hope, since

> the Father of excellence in His loving-kindness will not suffer the platform to
> reach the condition of cement which defies dissolution, but makes the unsub-
> stantial result of their fluid industry to be but as sloppy clay. (On the Confusion of
> Tongues 103)[52]

Philo assures his readers that the freedom from the slavery of the despotic power of
the brick makers, the freedom which is really sure and stable, is to serve God.
Those who serve God are not supposed to do earthly things like the brick makers,
but

> in their thoughts to ascend to the heavenly height, setting before them Moses, the
> nature beloved of God, to lead them on the way. For then they shall behold the
> place, which is in fact the Word, where stands God. (On the Confusion of
> Tongues 95-96)[53]

These quotations show that Philo's allegorical exegesis of Gen. 11.1-9 has more
themes in common with the Gospel of Mary than the formlessness of passion
alone.

Although there are obvious differences, they share the theme of the ascension to
the heavenly height and of someone leading the way. They share the idea that there
is confusion, that dissolution or division is necessary, that there is a despotic power
who by false reasoning enslaves people, but that there is a God who prevents his
work from succeeding and there are people who have vision, trusting the 'eye of
understanding' rather than their bodily eyes (On the Confusion of Tongues 100).[54]

When we consider Philo's writings and search for the particular meaning of
ΠΙΝΕ ΠΙΝΕ ΝΤΕϤΥCΙC in a context of creation, translating ΕΙΝΕ as the Coptic
equivalent of the Greek εἶδος seems most likely too. Philo, in his exegesis on the
marked sheep of Jacob and the unmarked sheep of Laban (Gen. 30.25–31.21),
arguing that there are people who, like Laban, fashion material sovereignties as
Divine and do not take any trouble to know the moving Cause, declares:

> For the world has come into being, and assuredly it has done so under the hand of
> some Cause: and the Word...of Him who makes it is Himself the seal, by which
> each thing that exists received its shape (μεμόρφωται). Accordingly from the
> outset form (εἶδος) in perfection accompanies the things that come into being, for
> it is an impress and an image of the perfect Word. (On Flight and Finding 12)[55]

As in the quotation of the Discourse on the Eighth and Ninth, here again the words
μορφή and εἶδος are closely related. They both refer to the perfect forms of what
exists. This perfection comes from God himself: by his Word (Logos) according to
Philo and by his Nature according to the Discourse on the Eighth and Ninth.

52. Colson and Whitaker 1958: IV, 65.67.
53. Colson and Whitaker 1958: IV, 61.
54. Colson and Whitaker 1958: IV, 65.
55. For the translation and the Greek see Colson and Whitaker 1958: V, 16-17.

2.2.6. *The Origin of Passion*. Whereas Nature has forms, passion, according to the Gospel of Mary, has no form. The Saviour explains this by pointing to passion's origin. Up to now all commentaries insist that matter is the cause of passion.[56] In this reading of GosMar 8.2-4 ογπλρλφγсιс in 8.4, which can be translated as an adjective (something contrary to nature) as well as a noun (an opposite nature), explains the nature of θγλΗ (matter) in 8.2: since matter has brought forth passion, and passion proceeds from an opposite nature, matter and opposite nature are one and the same. And, indeed, in the Platonic dualistic view the material world is contrary to the spiritual world. In this view, whereas the union with the spiritual world brings forth the good, the union with the material world brings forth the bad.[57] In such an interpretation of GosMar 8.2-4, the disciples must be freed from their adulterous attachment to the material world (GosMar 7.13-16). But if this reading is correct, why is the Coptic so unclear? Why is the translator of the Greek version so hesitantly speaking of passion as proceeding from an opposite nature instead of clearly referring back to matter and state that passion proceeds from 'this opposite nature'? Or, even clearer, why does he or she not simply state that matter, because it is contrary to nature, brings forth passion?

GosMar 8.2-4 may also be read in quite another way: matter has not by itself alone caused passion, resulting in an unstable cosmos, but a combination of matter and an opposite nature are responsible. In this reading of GosMar 8.2-4 matter and an opposite nature are not one and the same, but 'an opposite nature' is a separate entity. This seems the most likely explanation for the fact that the translator speaks of passion which proceeded from an opposite nature instead of clearly defining matter as opposite to Nature.

In a metaphorical sense, matter is like a mother who has given birth (χπο) to a child called passion. Passion brings confusion in the whole body since the origin (ει εβολ 2Ν̄) of this product is 'an opposite nature', instead of Nature.[58] A parallel to passion having a 'mother' and an 'origin' is to be found in the Apocryphon of John, where passions (2Ν̄πλθος) come forth from the four chief demons (NHC II.18.14-20; IV.28.8-17). In NHC II.18.2-6 the mother of the demons is matter, while 'the origin of the demons which are in the whole body is determined to be four: heat, cold, wetness and dryness'. The background of this verse is Stoic philosophy in which these four qualities form the basis of the constitution of the cosmos. As we already noted in Stoic philosophy God is compared to a sperm. He is the seminal principle of the world, making matter serviceable to himself for the successive stages of creation.[59]

---

56. Till and Schenke 1972: 27; Pasquier 1983: 54; Tardieu 1984: 76 and 227; King 1992: 362; Marjanen 1996: 94 note 1; Hartenstein 2000: 129.

57. This view belongs to middle Platonic and especially neo-Platonic philosophers. Until Plato ὕλη (matter) has no abstract connotation: it simply means 'wood', 'material to build with'. Only with Aristotle does ὕλη become a philosophical term. See Bormann 1972: 977.

58. For χπο in the sense of 'giving birth' see Crum 1939: 779a. The male origin of a child is mostly described as ει εβολ 2Ν̄ †πι (coming out of the loins of; cf. Heb. 7.9). I thank Jan Helderman for this observation.

59. Note the ideas of Antiquity on procreation: 'the father was regarded as the sole cause of

I suggest that in the Gospel of Mary matter is acted upon by an opposite nature resulting in a confused and unstable cosmos, just as in Stoic philosophy matter is acted upon by Nature resulting in a harmonious and stable cosmos. Interpreted this way, the disciples in the Gospel of Mary are not to be freed from their adulterous attachment to the material world and to turn to the spiritual one, as is mostly suggested. On the contrary, the disciples, belonging to the one cosmos which is a mixture of Nature and matter, must be freed from the influence of 'an opposite nature'. This alternative reading considerably changes the view on matter, on sin and on salvation, which other interpreters of the Gospel of Mary hold. It is not the material world which is to be avoided, but the power of this 'opposite nature', which causes passion.

In the Gnostic writings of the Nag Hammadi Codices the expression 'opposite to nature' does not occur. This is not surprising since Nature itself is in Gnostic thought a negative power.[60] We should also note, that in Stoic philosophy with its monistic view, there is no cosmic power contrary to Nature.[61] Nature alone exists. In Stoic philosophy one can only act against Nature. Allowing oneself to be guided by passion is, for instance, acting contrary to nature (παρὰ φύσιν). Whereas in mainstream Stoic philosophy passion is a result of false judgments and 'a movement of soul which is irrational (ἄλογος) and contrary to nature (παρὰ φύσιν)',[62] the Gospel of Mary insists that there is a cosmic power contrary to Nature which, by acting upon matter, has produced passion.

Thus, the Gospel of Mary introduces a new concept, a cosmic power contrary to Nature, which, by infecting the harmonious mixture of Nature and matter, disturbs the original Stoic concept of cosmic harmony. According to the Gospel of Mary the ultimate cause of passion lies in this cosmic opposite nature. This power is the reason that confusion came into the whole body. The mixture mentioned in GosMar 7.4 apparently consists not only in a Stoic sense of Nature and matter, but of Nature and a power contrary to Nature, both acting upon matter.

The cosmic power contrary to Nature in the Gospel of Mary might perhaps be considered as an allusion to a Gnostic dualism in creation, since a similar distinction between Nature and an opposite nature is found in the Gnostic Apocryphon of John. In this writing, the Demiurge not only creates the material world, but also a counterfeit spirit (ἀντίμιμον πνεῦμα), which brings darkness and evil to oppose the Spirit of light from the divine Mother.[63] As we have seen, however,

---

generation, while the mother was thought to supply only a place for the embryo to grow in and obtain nourishment' (Runia 1983: 245).

60. In other writings of the Nag Hammadi Codices the word ΠΑΡΑΦΥϹΙϹ occurs. The tractate Asclepius uses ΕϨⲘΠΑΡΑΦΥϹΙϹ. The wicked angels in this writing teach 'things contrary to nature'. 'They lead into wicked things recklessly, as well as into atheism, wars and plundering. In those days the earth will not be stable' (NHC VI.73.5-13). This tractate is Hermetic; see section 3.2.2.3 note 41, above (King 2003a: 162). Marsanes mentions angels and says: 'some among them are polyphormous and contrary to nature' (NHC XI.25.6), but like Asclepius, this tractate also lacks a dualism in creation (see King 2003a: 193).

61. See Long 1968: 335-36.

62. Long and Sedley 1987: I, 410, quoting Stobaeus 2.88.8.

63. ApocJohn BG 56.4; 63.9; 67.15; 68.6, 18; 71.4; 74.8; 75.6, 9.

nothing in the Gospel of Mary refers to an evil Demiurge who creates the material world, but, on the contrary, the Gospel of Mary uses the positive Stoic concept of matter and Nature as the constitutive elements of the world and adds an opposite nature.

2.2.7. *Mixture, Creation and the Source of Evil.* A closer parallel to the cosmology in the Gospel of Mary may be found in Philo's works. Philo represents the Jewish view of the good God, who creates the world by means of his Word (cf. Gen. 1.1-31). Philo's Logos (Word) is not the same as the Platonic, let alone the Gnostic Demiurge. Like in Platonism, Philo's God does not enter in direct contact with matter, but he does not use a Demiurge to create the world. Instead, in Philo's works God employs his Logos (his Word), as an architect or as a cutter, to perform the task of creation according to his thoughts (the Platonic ideas).[64]

David Runia, who studied Philo's interpretation of Plato's Timaeus, concludes about Philo's concept of the Logos: 'Through the doctrine of the Logos God can be said to be immanent in the universe which he created without the affirmation of his transcendence put at risk'.[65] The same may apply to the more Stoic concept of Nature in the Gospel of Mary. By means of his Nature, God created the world and is thus present in the world and at the same time beyond it.

But what is, against this background, the meaning of this cosmic power opposite to Nature? Philo, when commenting on the Passover instructions and on the death of all the firstborn of the Egyptians, concentrates on the meaning of Exod. 12.23 that God will not let 'the destroyer enter your houses to strike'. He admonishes his readers that they are not to make God the cause of evil and describes the mixture of the cosmos as existing of two contrary powers. These are the salutary and beneficent power and the opposite one, the unbounded and the destructive.[66] According to Philo the heavens and the entire world have received this mixture. All that exists, however, is created in accordance with the better part of these, 'namely when the salutary and beneficent (power) brings to an end the unbounded and destructive nature'.[67] Philo then continues:

---

64. Runia 1983: 373-76.

65. Runia 1983: 375.

66. Runia (1983: 243) argues that the unbounded power must be identified as matter, since Philo describes matter as unbounded too. Matter, however, is not a power but a passive substance devoid of all quality (see for example On Flight and Finding 9). I agree instead with Marcus (1953: II, 32 note m) that the two opposing powers as Philo distinguishes them correspond to good and evil cosmic powers identified with good and bad angels (or demons). Philo adds that this view is also held by others. It is not clear which people Philo means, but it is known that the later middle Platonic philosopher Plutarch (ca. 50 to ca. 150 CE) also distinguishes between two antagonistic powers: one of them is beneficent and the other is the author of all opposite things. Van Kooten (2001: 117-21), in his study of the Pauline views on the cosmos, refers to Plutarch's On Isis and Osiris in which Osiris opposes the disorderly power, which mingles with the passive elements, and attaches himself to them (On Isis and Osiris/Moralia 369-73). A great difference with the Gospel of Mary, however, is that, according to Plutarch, Nature itself contains the creation and origin of evil as well as of good. See Dillon 1977: 202 and comments on 202-208.

67. Questions and Answers on Exod. I.23. Marcus 1953: II, 334.

Now, sometimes the evil becomes greater in this mixture, and hence (all creatures)
live in torment, harm, ignominy, contention, battle and bodily illness together with
all the other things in human life, as in the whole world, so in man. And this mixture is in both the wicked and the wise but not in the same way. For the souls of
the foolish have the unbounded and destructive rather than the powerful and salutary (power), and it is full of misery when it dwells with earthly creatures. But the
prudent and noble (soul) rather receives the powerful and salutary (power) and, on
the contrary, possessing in itself good fortune and happiness, being carried around
with the heaven because of kinship with it. Most excellently, therefore, does
(Scripture) say that He will not let 'the destroyer enter your houses to strike', and
this is what actually happens, for the force which is the cause of destruction
strives, as it were, to enter the soul, but is prevented by the divine beneficences
from striking (it), for these are salutary. (Questions and Answers on Exod. I.23)[68]

Apparently, according to Philo, the mixture of the two opposing powers within
humans is not ontologically fixed, but depends on behaviour. Thanks to the Divine,
in Philo's view, the prudent and noble soul receives the better power and is
protected against the destructive one.

Against this background, the Saviour's encouragement in the Gospel of Mary
not to be persuaded by what opposes Nature does not sound strange (GosMar 8.8).
In the end the salutary power is more powerful than the destructive one. Likewise
the Saviour's encouragement to be fully assured (GosMar 8.7) that his disciples
already are persuaded 'in the presence of the forms of Nature' (GosMar 8.9-10)
does not sound peculiar, when we recall Philo's view that, although the mixture of
the cosmos is a mixture of two opposing powers, all that exists is created in
accordance with the better part.

2.2.8. *Jesus' Parable of the Sower and his Enemy.* The existence of Nature and a
power opposite to Nature in the context of the agricultural references in GosMar 7
recalls Jesus' parable about a sower and his enemy (Mt. 13.24-30; GosThom
logion 57). In this parable Jesus compares the Kingdom of God to a person who
sowed good seed in his field, whose enemy then came and sowed weeds. When
they bring forth fruit, the servants of the householder ask him: Sir, did you not sow
good seed in your field? Where do the weeds come from? He answers that an
enemy has done this. Both the wheat and the weeds are allowed to remain until the
harvest, because if the weeds were immediately removed, the growing wheat
would be uprooted along with them.

As in Jesus' parable, destruction of matter in the Gospel of Mary is no solution,
since this would destroy both ογπαραφγсιϛ (an opposite nature) and φγсιϛ
(Nature). In GosMar 7.5-6 the mixture of things will, in the end, be unloosened
down to their own 'root' (ΝΟΥΝε). In the dry lands of the Mediterranean the root is
the life-sustaining force for plants which need to be deeply rooted to survive. As
such, 'root' symbolizes the life-sustaining force of the cosmos.[69] The Nature of

---

68. See for the translation Marcus 1953: II, 33-34. His translation of 'wicked man', 'wise man',
and 'foolish men' I changed to 'the wicked, 'the wise', and 'the foolish'.

69. Maurer 1977. See also Ménard 1972: 84. See for the metaphor Mk 4.6, 17; Mt. 13.6, 21;
Lk. 8.13; Eph. 3.17; Col. 2.7.

matter apparently belongs to this root, since, as the Saviour says, the Good One (ΠΑΓΑΘΟ) has come to restore Nature to its root (7.17-20).[70]

Again, the word 'root' could be interpreted in a Gnostic way. In the Gnostic Gospel of Truth, the Root is the Father, 'the one who has made them [the emanations] all grow up in himself. He assigned them their destinies' (GosTruth 41.14-28). According to the Gospel of Truth,

> This is the manner of those who possess (something) from above of the immensurable greatness, as they wait for the one alone and the perfect one, the one who is there for them. And they do not go down to Hades nor have they envy nor groaning nor death within them, but they rest in him who is at rest, not striving nor being twisted around the truth. But they themselves are the truth; and the Father is within them and they are in the Father, being perfect, being undivided in the truly good one, being in no way deficient in anything, but they are set at rest, refreshed in the Spirit. And they will heed their root. (GosTruth 42.12-34)[71]

Many themes in this quotation are also present in the Gospel of Mary,[72] with one important exception. Whereas in the Gnostic Gospel of Truth only those 'who possess something from above' have their root in the Father, in the Gospel of Mary Nature as a whole has its divine Root, as in the creation story of Genesis. This coincides with the fact that Jesus' parable of the weeds and the wheat also contains a reference to Genesis in that, among other things,[73] it parallels the belief that although originally the creation was good, some agent (in Gen. 3.1-19 it is the snake) corrupted it. In the Gospel of Mary this agent may be meant by ΟΥΠΑΡΑΦΥϹΙϹ.

We already saw that the cosmic power contrary to Nature is not a Stoic concept. The passages in which 'root' occurs (GosMar 7.3-8, 17-20) reveal a second important difference with Stoic philosophy. In the Gospel of Mary the Good One is apparently a power beyond Nature, since he has come to restore Nature to its divine Root. Thus, whereas in Stoic philosophy Nature and the Divine are one and the same, in the Gospel of Mary, Nature has a divine origin. The Good One is beyond Nature, capable of firmly restoring Nature, which has become mixed with a power opposite to Nature, to its divine Root again.

---

70. ΠΕ in ΠΑΓΑΘΟ may also be translated as a neuter, not referring to the Good One but to the good in general. Till and Schenke (1972: 63, 67); Wilson and MacRae (1979: 457, 461); King (1992: 361); Hartenstein and Petersen (1998: 759) all chose the neuter form. In GosMar 17.22 this indeed may be the case, since there ΠΕ is followed by the neuter form of the Greek adjective ΑΓΑΘΟΝ. See Marjanen 1996: 108-109, who argues that the Greek neuter forms of the adjectives in Coptic denotes non-humans. However, the form ἀγαθόν in the Greek original of GosMar 17.22 may have been used as the masculine adjective because of the preceding preposition. Indeed the Greek in P Oxy 3525.13 has ἐπ' ἀγαθόν. Since GosMar 7.17 has ΠΑΓΑΘΟ and not ΠΑΓΑΘΟΝ as the subject of the sentence, and since this subject is doing something, I translate the Good One, as do Pasquier (1983: 31 and 35), and Tardieu (1984: 76 and 77), instead of the good, as the other exegetes do.

71. Translated by Attridge and MacRae 1988: 51.

72. No envy nor groaning nor death cf. GosMar 7.19-22; rest cf. GosMar 17.4-7; being perfect cf. GosMar 18.6; being undivided cf. GosMar 8.7 and 9.15-16; the Father, the divine, within cf. GosMar 8.17-19; the good one cf. GosMar 7.17.

73. See the interpretation in Mt. 13.36-43.

But who is the Good One? The Good One in GosMar 7.17, who came into the midst of the disciples seems to be the Saviour himself who apparently is there in order to set them on the right path. The Good One in GosMar 9.22 to whom the disciples turn within their hearts seems to be identical with the Son of Man, since the Saviour in GosMar 8.19 assures the disciples that the Son of Man is within them. Both the Saviour and the Son of Man are references to Jesus in the New Testament writings, where Jesus is also above Nature.[74] In the New Testament Jesus is pictured in control of natural phenomena such as storms, sickness and death. He is pictured as vanishing and reappearing, as going through shut doors and even as the pre-existent Lord of the universe. It is this New Testament Saviour who in the Gospel of Mary has come to restore Nature to its divine Root.

As in Jesus' parable, where the weeds and the wheat are separated only at harvest time, in the Gospel of Mary only in the end ⲫⲨⲥⲓⲥ will be untangled from ⲞⲨⲠⲀⲢⲀⲫⲨⲥⲓⲥ (GosMar 7.1-9) and Nature will be restored to its Root. What happens to what opposes nature is not clear from the Gospel of Mary as we have it. Perhaps it vanishes, since, unlike the forms of Nature, it does not belong to Nature and only generates formless things. Until this eschatological moment, however, there is already a way to vanquish the grip of ⲞⲨⲠⲀⲢⲀⲫⲨⲥⲓⲥ which is a result of the coming and the work of the Good One. Even now the Good One has already begun to restore Nature to its divine Root (GosMar 7.10-22).

This is why in GosMar 8.5-14 the Saviour assures his disciples that they should not be persuaded to think that an opposite nature with its passion has any power over them. The disciples are to remind themselves that they belong to the forms of Nature and not to the formlessness of what opposes Nature. Thanks to the restoring work of the Saviour, the disciples are prepared to bring forth peace and harmony instead of confusion and passion.

3. *A Non-Gnostic Gospel of Mary in the Berlin Codex?*

According to King, although she insists that the Gospel of Mary itself is not Gnostic, the location of the Coptic version of the Gospel in the Berlin Codex is convincing evidence of a later Gnostic reading of the text.[75] Indeed, the idea that the Gospel of Mary is part of a Gnostic collection suggests that it circulated as a Gnostic text. But, even more so, assuming that the collector knew the pages of the Gospel of Mary that are now lost, should we not conclude that the Gospel of Mary was apparently intended to be read from a Gnostic perspective?

The Berlin Codex contains two writings that are clearly Gnostic, the Sophia of Jesus Christ and the Apocryphon of John. There is, however, apart from the Gospel of Mary, one writing which is non-Gnostic. Whereas most exegetes regard the Gospel of Mary as a Gnostic document, they agree in that the fourth writing of the

---

74. Pasquier (1983: 53, 56-57, 61-62 and 70) identifies the Good One, the Saviour and the Son of Man with the Gnostic Primordial Man. Tardieu (1984: 226) identifies him with Jesus bringing gnosis. Schröter (1999: 187) concludes that the Son of Man terminology in GosMar refers to becoming a true human being by following Jesus.

75. King 1995: 629 note 10.

Berlin Codex, the Act of Peter, is non-Gnostic. Exegetes have wondered why the collector of the Berlin Codex would have added the non-Gnostic Act of Peter to three Gnostic writings.[76]

3.1. *The Non-Gnostic Act of Peter*
In the Act of Peter, a crowd of sick people is brought to Peter on a Sunday, in order that they may be healed by him. One of the crowd challenges Peter to heal his own paralysed daughter. Peter does so and she walks, but immediately he orders her to go and sit down and she is an invalid again. Peter thereupon explains to the weeping crowd why his daughter is to remain an invalid.

It appears that a man named Ptolemy, who wanted to marry her, abducted her and was about to rape her, when she suddenly became paralysed. When he wept greatly over this, he became blind and received a vision in which a voice (obviously of Christ) said to him:

> Ptolemy, God did not give his vessels for corruption and pollution. But it was necessary for you, since you believed in me, that you not defile my virgin, whom you should have recognized as your sister, since I have become one Spirit for you both. (Act of Peter 137.1-11)[77]

He is told to arise and go to Peter, who cures him. After his death he gives his land to Peter's daughter and everything is subsequently given to the poor. Peter summarizes the meaning of the story in the statement that 'God watches over those who are his and he prepares what is good for each one' (Act of Peter 139.18–140.4).

Douglas Parrott suggests that the Act of Peter has been included in the Berlin Codex because the writing may be interpreted allegorically in a way that suits Gnostics. In Parrott's view Ptolemy symbolizes the soul who is attracted to the things of the world, which lead to ignorance and almost to his death. Only the light of knowledge rescues him and removes his blindness. The paralysis of Peter's daughter may be explained as the power of divine knowledge over the powers of this world and the daughter herself may represent the fallen Sophia.[78]

Tardieu also wondered why the non-Gnostic Act of Peter is part of the Berlin Codex. In his opinion there is a clear design behind the Berlin Codex as a whole. The book may be given the title 'De Fato', on fate.[79] According to Tardieu, the Gospel of Mary poses the problem of nature and destination and gives the Gnostic antidotes. It is an introduction to the Codex as a whole. The Apocryphon of John, as the dogmatic centre of the Berlin Codex, presents a tripartite theory on providence: transcendent, demiurgical and interiorized. The Sophia of Jesus Christ introduces the demiurgical rupture in the continuing development of the divine chains. The Act of Peter gives an edifying and simple story about the good actions of providence in human lives.

According to Tardieu, the Act of Peter has been added as an illustration of the

76. Brashler and Parrott 1979: 475-76.
77. Brashler and Parrott 1979: 487.
78. Brashler and Parrott 1979: 476.
79. Tardieu 1984: 17-19.

three Gnostic writings. Ptolemy recognizes Peter's daughter as his sister just as the disciples recognize Mary in the Gospel of Mary (GosMar 9.12–10.10). He has been caught by the drunkenness of darkness, which is his sexuality, and he has reached the union with himself (ApocJohn BG 59.20–60.16). He also testifies to his union with the Spirit (ApocJohn BG 64.13–66.13; SJC BG 121.13–123.1).[80]

3.2. *The Question of Evil*
Thus, both Parrott and Tardieu believe that the Act of Peter as a non-Gnostic writing fits the Gnostic design of the Berlin Codex. But what if the Gospel of Mary is a non-Gnostic writing too? This would mean that in the Berlin Codex two Gnostic and two non-Gnostic writings have been preserved together. The criterion of Gnosticism would not have determined which texts were included in the Berlin Codex but something else. One could object that the clear Gnostic character of two of the writings defines the character of the Berlin Codex as a whole, and that the Gospel of Mary and the Act of Peter in the Berlin Codex must be interpreted in a Gnostic context. If the latter is the case, King would be right. The Berlin Codex would then be proof that the Gospel of Mary, originally a non-Gnostic gospel, was later read through Gnostic lenses. But why should two writings out of four determine the character of the other two?

Indeed, the Apocryphon of John and the Sophia of Jesus Christ are very similar. The two other writings, however, the Gospel of Mary at the beginning of the Berlin Codex and the Act of Peter at the end, are also similar, but in quite another way. They both do not present a demiurgical tradition and contain more narrative elements than the other two writings. Furthermore they both are more concrete than the other two. In the Gospel of Mary the disciples worry about the suffering that is awaiting them when they go to proclaim the gospel. The Act of Peter deals with the question of why Peter's daughter has become and is to remain paralysed, whereas Peter cures so many others who are sick.

As I see it, it is not the question of fate in general, as Tardieu suggests is the main theme of these two writings, but the question of evil, which is central in the non-Gnostic Gospel of Mary and the non-Gnostic Act of Peter. How should the readers regard the suffering of disciples of the Lord? What are they to make of the suffering of the daughter of Peter?

In my view this theme is precisely what all four writings of the Berlin Codex have in common. They all give their own answer to the question of evil. The Apocryphon of John answers two basic questions: what is the origin of evil and how can we escape from this evil world to our heavenly home?[81] Christ appears to John, one of the sons of Zebedee, when he is doubting all he learned, after being mocked by a Pharisee in Jerusalem. In a long revelatory discourse John learns about the nature of true divinity, of the fall into creation and of the powers that control the cosmos. They invented the power of fate to enchain humanity in sin and ignorance and fear and hopelessness. With this knowledge people are able to resist the evil creator and to return to true divinity.

---

80. Tardieu 1984: 70-71.
81. Wisse and Waldstein 1988: 104.

The Sophia of Jesus Christ is about evil too. It also starts with a perplexed audience: the twelve male and seven female disciples. They want to know more about the underlying reality of the universe, about the evil power of the authorities and about everything the Saviour is doing. He tells them about the kingdom of the Son of Man and the divine aeons, the fall into creation and the bond of forgetfulness. The Saviour has escaped this bond and cut off the work of the powers. He encourages his disciples to break their yoke and gives them authority over all things 'as Sons of light that you might tread upon their power with your feet' (SJC BG 126.15). The Sophia of Jesus Christ ends with the disciples joyfully going to preach this gospel about the God who is above the universe.

I suggest that the four writings contained in the Berlin Codex do not deal with Gnosticism as such, but with the question of evil, providing answers from various perspectives. Thus the Berlin Codex is not a Gnostic codex, but a compilation of different views on evil.

3.3. *Other Themes in the Berlin Codex*
There are other important similarities, which hold the writings together. All of the writings are about life after and without the earthly Jesus. With respect to this the Berlin Codex maintains a kind of 'historical' order, which is parallel to the New Testament. In the Gospel of Mary, when the Lord is departing, Mary Magdalene is the central figure as she is in the New Testament Gospels. In the Apocryphon of John, John the son of Zebedee is apparently still in Jerusalem (as are all the disciples in Luke and Acts), whereas in the Sophia of Jesus Christ all the disciples, male and female, are gathered in Galilee, where Jesus asked them to go from Jerusalem in Mark and Matthew. The Act of Peter shows that the instruction to proclaim the gospel, which in all three writings is important, is indeed carried out. Furthermore, in each writing of the Berlin Codex Jesus' disciples are central figures, who cope with questions about his teaching. They all are helped by visions in which Christ appears and enlightens them. All the four writings deal with the difficulties which arise when proclaiming the gospel.

The Berlin Codex may have another theme as well. In the Gospel of Mary the integrity of Mary Magdalene's teaching is called into question by important disciples. The Gospel of Mary itself, at least on face value, leaves their attack unanswered. The other three writings, however, seem to support Mary's trustworthiness on this point.

In the Gospel of Mary, Andrew objects to Mary's teaching by stating:

> 'I at least do not believe that the Saviour said this. For, indeed, these teachings are according to another train of thought'. (GosMar 17.13-15)

Levi does not answer the question of Andrew. The question remains whether Andrew is in some way right that Mary's teaching differs from the teaching that the Saviour gave the others. The Apocryphon of John and the Sophia of Jesus Christ, however, show that Andrew is completely wrong. Not only Mary, but also John, the son of Zebedee and even the twelve male and seven female disciples as a group receive teaching about powers that try to keep the soul from its ascent to heaven.

In the Gospel of Mary Peter objects to Mary's teaching, saying:

> After all, he did not speak to a woman concealed to us and not openly. Are we to
> turn and all listen to her? Has he chosen her above us? (GosMar 17.18-22)

The Act of Peter, however, relates that Peter tells the crowd about Ptolemy's vision
in which Christ himself appeared to Ptolemy and declared that God's 'vessels' are
to be recognized as sisters 'since I have become one Spirit for you both'. Thus the
Act of Peter shows that Levi's answer to Peter in the Gospel of Mary 'if the
Saviour has made her worthy, who are you indeed to reject her' (GosMar 18.10-12)
is by no means only his own opinion. Christ himself gave a similar message to
Ptolemy in a vision. Indeed, both men and women have received the same Spirit of
Christ. Christ conveys this to Peter, by means of Ptolemy.

   Thus, the Berlin Codex cannot support the theory that the Gospel of Mary must
have been read as a Gnostic text by those early readers who knew the gospel in its
entirety. The Berlin Codex cannot be called a collection of Gnostic texts. There are
things other than Gnosticism that the four writings share. One of them may be that
later copyists of the Gospel of Mary felt the need to stress Mary's integrity more
evidently than the Gospel of Mary does itself.

4. *The Purpose of the Gospel of Mary*

4.1. *The Importance of Proclaiming the Gospel*
When King considers a non-Gnostic purpose of the Gospel of Mary, she focuses on
the structure of the Gospel of Mary as a series of dialogues and departures.[82] The
two main dialogues (GosMar 7.1–9.4 and 9.12–18.5) legitimate Mary's teaching
and her leadership role by placing her in a position parallel to that of the Saviour.
Because other dialogues are embedded within the second dialogue the reader is led
more deeply inward (cf. GosMar 9.20-23). In the second dialogue Mary tells of a
dialogue with the Lord of which other disciples know nothing (GosMar 10.12–
17.9). This dialogue contains a dialogue of the soul with the four Powers (GosMar
15.1–17.7). King concludes that 'both the content and the text's structure lead the
reader inward toward the identity, power and freedom of the true self, the soul set
free from the Powers of Matter and the fear of death'.[83] The Gospel of Mary, in her
view, is about inter-Christian controversies; about the reliability of the disciples'
witness, the validity of teachings given to the disciples through post-resurrection
revelation and vision, and the leadership of women.[84]

   The most important difference between King's views and mine is the fact that in
my opinion the soul is not to be freed from Powers of Matter, but from the power
of an opposite nature. Furthermore, I do not agree that the main purpose of the
Gospel of Mary is to lead the reader inward.

   In my opinion the main purpose of the Gospel of Mary is to encourage the

82. King 1995: 626-27.
83. King 1995: 627.
84. King 1995: 621.

disciples to go out and preach the gospel. The Gospel of Mary reveals its main purpose by its repetition of themes. The Saviour's instruction to the disciples to go and preach the gospel of the kingdom occurs twice (GosMar 8.21-22 and 18.17-21) and other parts of the Gospel are closely related to it. The Saviour's call to proclaim the gospel is embedded in a series of last exhortations, in which the disciples are urged to be convinced of their new identity and to seek and follow the Son of Man within them, bringing peace instead of confusion (GosMar 8.12–9.4). After the Saviour's departure the disciples weep because of his instruction to go and preach the gospel. The author of the Gospel of Mary places their grief right in the centre of the Gospel:

> How shall we go to the nations and preach the gospel of the kingdom of the Son of Man? If they did not spare him, how will they spare us? (GosMar 9.5-12)

Mary Magdalene, having encouraged them, turns their hearts inwards, whereupon the disciples begin to discuss the words of the Saviour, apparently as preparation for proclaiming the gospel (GosMar 9.12-23). This is what motivates Peter to ask Mary to tell them the things which the Saviour has told only to her (GosMar 10.1-6). Her answer takes the next eight pages (GosMar 10.7–17.6) which is clear from the author's remark in GosMar 17.7-9, when she falls silent: 'since it was to this point that the Saviour had spoken to her'.

Her words address the desperate question of the disciples. Mary, on the basis of her knowledge of the Saviour, assures the disciples that the soul will be able to conquer the powers which are contrary to Nature: darkness, desire, ignorance and wrath. These powers, which keep the soul from its heavenly rest, will be left powerless when the disciples use the insight and the new identity the Saviour has given them (GosMar 15.1–17.9).

When Peter and Andrew thereupon begin to dispute Mary's authority (GosMar 17.20-22), Levi does not only defend her trustworthiness, but he also compares Peter's conduct to the conduct of the adversaries of the soul. The powers attacking the soul are not only to be identified with the nations that will persecute the disciples. The powers are among and inside the disciples themselves. Levi concludes his speech by returning to the real issue at stake, the instruction of the Saviour to preach the gospel (GosMar 18.6-21). And, indeed, the Gospel of Mary concludes that 'they began to go forth and proclaim and to preach' (GosMar 19.2).

4.2. *Form and Content*

The Gospel of Mary, as we have it, consists of two main parts (GosMar 7.1–9.5 and 9.12–17.9) centred around the despairing and fundamental question of the disciples: what is the use of proclaiming the gospel when this only causes persecution and suffering? (GosMar 9.6-12). Both the Saviour (GosMar 7.1–9.5) and Mary (GosMar 9.12-17.9) insist that the gospel does not cause passion, but rather that which opposes Nature does. Instead, the proclamation of the gospel is necessary to enable people to hold on to Nature with its peace and harmony and to disarm the powers of passion. Then the soul will attain the rest of Nature's divine root.

But the Gospel of Mary in a third part (GosMar 17.10–19.2) also shows that passion rules not only those who persecute the disciples, but also the disciples themselves. This is clear from the reaction of Peter and Andrew, in which they attack Mary. The powers of passion are strong. They can get a grip on the disciples of the Lord, even when they are occupied with the things of the Lord, discussing among themselves the content of the gospel.

In the Gospel of Mary, the Saviour in his last exhortations warns against making rules and laws. The disciples will lose their freedom and be imprisoned by them. In Stoic philosophy, the divine law of Nature is contrasted with the laws made by human beings.[85] Epictetus said, for instance, when a man complained about the carelessness of his slave:

> Will you not endure your brother, who has Zeus as his forefather, who is as it were a son born of the same seed as you and begotten like you from above?... Do you not remember what you are and to whom you give orders? Your kin, your brothers in nature, the offspring of Zeus. 'But I have bought them, they have not bought me!' You see where you are looking – to the earth, to the pit, to these miserable laws made by corpses for corpses; you have no eyes for the divine law. (Discourses I.13.4-5)[86]

In the Gospel of Mary the one law which the Saviour gave is sufficient.[87] But Peter and Andrew do not heed this warning. They introduce two additional laws which reflect the male domination of the later church: in their view the brothers need not listen to a woman and only the knowledge and interpretation of the brothers should determine the validity of what is to be said about the Saviour. The Gospel of Mary, however, instead of submissively accepting these claims as coming from the divine law of Nature, resolutely banishes them to the world of what opposes Nature.

5. *Conclusion*

On the basis of the investigation in this Chapter I suggest that the Gospel of Mary should not be read as a specifically Gnostic text. It should, instead, be interpreted as a document belonging to a broader Christian context. Although many scholars regard the Gospel of Mary as a Gnostic text, the Gospel rather seems to start from a monistic, instead of a dualistic, view on creation, and its view on Nature and an opposite nature appears to be best understood in a context of Jewish, Christian and Stoic, rather than Gnostic, categories.

Stoic philosophy had a major impact on culture and society in the first and the second centuries. Every level of the population was deeply influenced by it,[88] and it also influenced the church. Before the early church begins to feel at home with Platonism in the third century, there is a period in the first and second centuries, from Clement of Rome to Clement of Alexandria, in which categories of Stoic

---

85. Pohlenz 1948: 133-39.

86. Translated by Sandbach 1975: 168.

87. It does not become clear what the content of this one law is. Perhaps the one law of love (Mk 12.31; Mt. 22.39; Jn 13.34-35; Rom. 13.8-10; 1 Cor. 12.31–13.13; Jas 2.8).

88. Pohlenz 1948: 363-66.

philosophy are favourably regarded as a means of explaining the gospel in the culture of the time.[89] The Gospel of Mary should perhaps be seen as a testimony of creative mission. The context of the recipients may have been one in which Stoic philosophy flourished. One may assume that the theologian behind the Gospel of Mary was acquainted with Hellenistic philosophy and with Philonic exegesis of Jewish Scripture.

The Gospel of Mary is close to the New Testament ones in that it intends to encourage the fearful disciples to be assured of the greatness of the Saviour, despite his suffering, and to go out and preach the gospel. In the Gospel of Mary the content of the gospel is the Kingdom of the Son of Man, who brings peace and restores all Nature unto its divine Root and enables his followers to conquer the cosmic power opposite to Nature and its grip through passion.

The next chapter focuses on Mary Magdalene in the Gospel of Mary: on her words, on the various views of her and on the author's portrayal of her. What is the view of the Gospel of Mary on Mary Magdalene's relation to the Saviour, her position among the disciples and her function in the story?

89. Spanneut 1957; see also Colish 1985.

Chapter 4

MARY MAGDALENE ACCORDING TO THE GOSPEL OF MARY

As I argued in Chapter 3, the author's main purpose with the Gospel of Mary is to encourage the readers to proclaim the gospel of the Kingdom of the Son of Man. To achieve this goal the author tells about a dialogue with the risen Saviour, about his departure and about the disciples' reaction to the Saviour's instruction to preach the gospel, thus showing its content and purpose.

That Mary Magdalene would be part of such a story is not wholly unexpected. But, that the author would give her such an active part, and describe her from so many different angles, even naming the Gospel after her, is extraordinary compared to other writings. The author speaks from the viewpoint of Peter, of Andrew, of Levi, of the Saviour, and of Mary herself. Through the interaction of these views, through the extra knowledge and view of the narrator, through Mary's teaching and through certain indications in the text, we shall examine the development of the story in which the author's view of Mary Magdalene becomes apparent.

In this chapter we will focus on the author's portrayal of Mary Magdalene. What is her relation to the Saviour, what is her position among the disciples and what is her function in the story?

1. Different Views of Mary

1.1. Peter, Andrew and Levi on Mary
Three of the brothers give their views of Mary: Peter, Andrew and Levi. They do not occur as a threesome in the New Testament Gospels. There we find Peter, James and John. The Gospel of Peter, however, does refer to them together, when, after Jesus' crucifixion, the disciples, full of sorrow, go each to their homes. Peter relates:

> Now it was on the final day of the Unleavened Bread; and many went out, returning to their homes since the feast was over. But we twelve disciples of the Lord were weeping and sorrowful; and each one, sorrowful of what had come to pass, departed to his home. But I, Simon Peter, and my brother Andrew having taken our nets, went off to the sea. And there was with us Levi of Alphaeus, whom the Lord... (Gospel of Peter 14.58-60)[1]

---

1.   Translated in Brown 1993: 1321.

That is the end of the fragment of the Gospel of Peter that has been discovered. In the complete version this part probably would continue with an appearance of the risen Christ and a dialogue with him. It would have been fascinating to compare this with what we find in the Gospel of Mary.

1.1.1. *Peter*. In the Gospel of Mary as we have it Peter speaks twice about Mary. The first time, after Mary has turned the weeping disciples' hearts inwards to the Good One and they begin to discuss the words of the Saviour, Peter says:

> Sister, we know that the Saviour loved you more than the rest of the women. Tell us the words of the Saviour which you remember, the things that you know and we do not, nor have we heard them. (GosMar 10.1-6)

We can make out from the initial 'sister' that Peter sees Mary as a fellow believer. They are brother and sister. They are equal in that they are both disciples of the Lord. But here the equality stops immediately. It appears to Peter that Mary occupies a special position: the Saviour loved her more than the other women. That is striking. Although Peter accepts Mary as a fellow disciple, he compares the Saviour's love for her not with that for the other disciples, but with that for the other women. Thus, for Peter, Mary is not a disciple in general, but, more specifically, a woman disciple. Among the women, she is special, in that the Saviour loved her more than the rest of the women.

It is not very clear what Peter means by 'love more'. It seems to be a spiritual loving, since his remark about 'loving more' leads Peter to ask Mary 'what you know and we do not'. Peter obviously assumes that because the Saviour loved her more than the rest of the women, Mary would know things that 'we', in any case we men, Peter included, but perhaps also women, do not know. It is striking that Peter invites Mary to reveal her knowledge: in all other writings where Mary and Peter appear together, Peter either does not speak to her or rebukes her.[2]

The second time that Peter reveals his view of Mary is in reaction to the words she has spoken on his invitation. After Andrew has asked the opinion of the others on Mary's words and has given his own, stating that they probably do not come from the Saviour, Peter continues thus:

> After all, he did not speak to a woman concealed to us and not openly. Are we to turn and all listen to her? Has he chosen her above us? (GosMar 17.18-22)

Apparently Peter agrees with Andrew. To Peter, although Mary has told the disciples that her words are from the Saviour, they are obviously not. His argument is gender related.

Here, to Peter, Mary is above all a woman. His earlier opinion of her as a fellow disciple and as a special woman among the other women is forgotten. Also his invitation to Mary to speak about things that he and the other men (and women) would not know are forgotten. Mary is a woman and as a woman she is subject to certain social limitations. First, the Saviour as a man would not have spoken to a

---

2.   See GosMar 17.16-23; GosThom 114; PS 36; cf. PS 72.

woman alone. Secondly, men are not to listen to a woman. Thirdly, the Saviour as a man would never have chosen a woman above men.

Thus, Peter's view of Mary is contradictory. Yes, she is a fellow disciple, yes she is special among the women disciples, yes she probably knows words of the Saviour that the men do not, yes he wants to hear about them and believes that the others should hear them too, but still that does not make Mary a man. She is a woman and as a woman she is a threat and inferior to men. As a woman the Saviour cannot have spoken to her alone; as a woman he and the others cannot listen to her; as a woman the Saviour cannot have placed her above the men.

1.1.2. *Andrew*. In the Gospel of Mary as we have it Andrew speaks once about Mary. He turns to the brothers (and sisters) to express his doubts about her teaching. He says:

> Tell me, what do you say about what she has spoken? I at least do not believe that the Saviour said this. For these teachings seem to be according to another train of thought. (GosMar 17.11-15)

Andrew does not believe that what Mary tells them is something she really heard from the Saviour. It is not clear whether he thinks that she is lying, or fantasizing, or wants to make herself seem important. It is, however, obvious that he does not find it necessary to discuss the matter directly with her. It is striking that he turns to the brothers (and sisters), instead of to Mary, and does not mention her name, but refers to her as 'she'. In contrast to Peter's arguments, however, Andrew's argument pertains to the content of what she has said. To him Mary's words do not seem to agree with what the disciples already know of the Saviour.

This raises the question of in what way Mary's teaching about the Saviour's words differs from the Saviour's teaching before his departure (GosMar 7 and 8). As we will see, Mary's teaching identifies the adversaries of the disciples, not as the nations, which the disciples fear, but as the powers of Darkness, Desire, Ignorance and Wrath, which the soul is able to conquer.[3] These powers issue from what is contrary to Nature, a category which the Saviour already introduced in GosMar 8.2-4. Mary, by revealing the Saviour's words she alone knows, defines what the cosmic confusion in GosMar 8.2-4 means to the individual disciple. In addition, Mary reveals that the knowledge of the All being unloosened (GosMar 7.1-8) liberates the soul from her adversaries, enabling her to go her way upwards to the Rest in Silence.

The reader realizes that, although Mary's teaching of the Saviour's words is new, it is not wholly new, since it explains what has been taught earlier by the Saviour to all the disciples.[4] Thus Andrew's argument against Mary's teaching that it does not agree with what the Saviour taught all the disciples is contradicted by the extant pages of the Saviour's teaching in the Gospel of Mary itself.

3.   See Chapter 4, section 2.3.
4.   Cf. King 1995: 614-15.

1.1.3. *Levi*

Levi reacts to Peter's objections. He says:

> Peter, you have always been hot-tempered. Now I see you arguing with the woman like these adversaries do. If the Saviour has made her worthy, who are you indeed to reject her? Surely, the Saviour knows her very well. That is why he loved her more than us. (GosMar 18.7-15)

In contrast to Andrew and to some degree also to Peter, Levi takes Mary's contribution quite seriously, since, according to Levi, Peter tries to stop Mary like the powers try to stop the soul on her way to the Rest in Silence. However, Levi also seems to share Peter's problems about Mary being a woman, although he calls Mary 'the woman'. According to Levi, the Saviour has made 'the woman' worthy. This means that Peter is not allowed to reject her. Unlike Peter, Levi can say, 'He loved her more than us', instead of 'than the rest of the women'. The reason he gives is: 'surely the Saviour knows her very well. That is why he loved her more than us'. As readers one might have expected him to say instead: that is why he told her more than us.

Like Peter, Levi also makes a connection between loving and knowing (GosMar 10.1-6), but Levi does not say that Mary knows more than the others. He concludes that the Saviour knows Mary 'very well'. Thus, to Levi, Mary is the woman who has been made worthy by the Saviour, but his exact view on her role of knowing more than the other disciples remains unclear, although he encourages the disciples to be ashamed, to put on the perfect Human Being and to refrain from making laws and rules when they preach the Gospel.

1.2. *Mary on Herself*

Four times in the Gospel of Mary as we have it we become a glimpse of Mary's view of herself. First of all we must note that when she speaks about the greatness of the Son of Man, she says: he has prepared us, he has made us Human Being (GosMar 9.21-22). She does not say: 'he has prepared you and made you Human Being', although the rest of her speech is clearly directed to the brothers (and sisters) as 'you' (GosMar 9.14-17). Apparently, she considers that she belongs to the circle of disciples. In her view, she, like them, has been made Human Being by the Son of Man. Like them, he has prepared her to preach the gospel of the Kingdom of the Son of Man.

When Peter thereupon asks Mary to relate what she knows and the brothers (and sisters) do not, Mary says without hesitation: 'What is hidden from you I shall tell you' (GosMar 10.8). She is evidently aware of the fact that she indeed knows things about the Saviour which the others do not know and with no holding back she is willing to share her knowledge.

Then she relates her story about having seen the Lord in a vision. She tells this simply and plain and without boasting,[5] but also without false modesty. She does not refrain from relating that the Saviour called her blessed: 'Blessed are you, because you are not wavering when you see me' (GosMar 10.14-15). She also does

---

5. Cf. 2 Cor. 12.1-7.

not conceal the fact that she is the one who started the dialogue, eager to know more.

The next time we hear anything about Mary's view of herself is when Andrew and Peter have cast doubt on the trustworthiness of her words. Weeping, she says to Peter:

> My brother Peter, what are you thinking? Do you suppose that I devised this, alone, in my heart, or that I am deceiving the Saviour? (GosMar 18.2-5)

Although Mary is crying, her answer to Peter is self-confident and to the point. In her reaction to Peter's struggle with her being a woman, she reminds him of his being a brother to her as a sister. Moreover, she shows Peter that if one takes his words to their logical conclusion it would mean that she knowingly deceived the Saviour.

1.3. *The Extra Knowledge and the View of the Narrator*
The narrator refers to Mary four times. Twice the remarks are about outward perception. When the disciples remain behind weeping after the departure of the Blessed One, the narrator relates: 'Then Mary stood up, embraced them all, and said…' (GosMar 9.12-13). And almost at the end of the Gospel, after the words of Andrew and Peter, the narrator says: 'Then Mary wept and said…' (GosMar 18.1).

The two other times that the narrator speaks of Mary are observations which reveal more about the narrator's view of her. When Mary has spoken to the weeping disciples the narrator remarks:

> When Mary had said this, she turned their hearts inwards to the Good One, and they began to discuss the words of the [Saviour]. (GosMar 9.20-23)

And when Mary has told her story about the Saviour, the narrator says:

> When Mary had said this, she fell silent, since[6] it was to this point that the Saviour had spoken to her. (GosMar 17.7-9)

In the first instance the narrator depicts Mary as having influence in a spiritual way. She apparently knows how to turn the hearts of the disciples inwards, so that they can reach the Good One. She is able to direct the attention of the disciples inwards, where the Son of Man is.

With the second instance the narrator bears witness that Mary is reliable. She hands on the words of the Saviour as he has spoken them to her. This last feature

---

6.   The Coptic text of BG1 reads ⲍⲱⲥⲧⲉ, whereas the Greek text of P Ryl 463, recto 4 reads ὡς. Lührmann (1988: 330), Petersen (1999: 156) and Mohri (2000: 260) both translate the Greek text with 'als ob': as if the Saviour spoke to this point. This raises the question, also from the narrator's point of view, whether what Mary relates actually comes from the Saviour. Mohri, Petersen and Lührmann give no reason for their particular translation. The other exegetes all translate both the Coptic and the Greek in the same sense, interpreting the silence of Mary as a silence on the part of the Saviour: Till and Schenke (1972: 75) translate 'so dass' (also), Pasquier (1983: 43) translates 'car'; Tardieu (1984: 80) translates 'puisque'; Marjanen (1996: 112) translates 'since', as do King (1992: 365) and Wilson and MacRae (1979: 467), Hartenstein (2000: 140) translates 'demnach'.

shows that the narrator is adopting a particular position. He or she knows more than the reader and is not a reporter trying to give a detached account of the discussion about Mary.

The narrator is on Mary's side. He or she is convinced of Mary's integrity and of her importance for the gospel message, since Mary remembers sayings of Jesus which the other disciples appear not to know. Moreover, according to the narrator, Mary has the gift of actually guiding the disciples' hearts to the Son of Man within them.

2. *Mary's Teaching*

The Gospel of Mary is the only early writing that has survived from antiquity in which Mary Magdalene teaches the disciples at length. When the Saviour has departed, after instructing his disciples to proclaim the gospel of the Kingdom of the Son of Man, she encourages the wavering disciples, reminding them of his greatness (GosMar 9.14-20). Then, at Peter's request, she describes the teaching that the Saviour has given to her alone. She talks about seeing the Lord in a vision, and about what he taught her, about stability and about the mind, when she asked about this phenomenon (GosMar 10.7-23). She speaks for eight pages, four of which are unfortunately missing. These missing pages were perhaps about the mind and the spirit, and about the mind and the soul. Mary concludes her teaching about the words of the Saviour by describing the soul's way upwards to the Rest in Silence (GosMar 15.1–17.7). In this section we focus on Mary's teaching in the Gospel of Mary.

2.1. *On the Greatness of the Son of Man*
The first time that Mary speaks is during a tense situation soon after the Saviour's farewell and mission charge. The disciples are very sad and cannot hold back their tears. They are afraid that in preaching the gospel they will call down upon themselves the same suffering that was inflicted on the Son of Man. They ask:

> How shall we go to the nations and preach the gospel of the kingdom of the Son of Man? If they did not spare him, how will they spare us? (GosMar 9.5-12)

Then Mary embraces the disciples and says:

> Do not weep and do not grieve and do not be in two minds, for his grace will be with you all and will shelter you. Rather let us praise his greatness, because he has prepared us.[7] He has made us (true) Human Being. (GosMar 9.14-20)

Mary puts the emphasis on praise instead of on sorrow and despair. In her eyes the suffering of the Son of Man is not the last word, but his greatness. This is a greatness which has been shown to the disciples themselves: the Son of Man has prepared them and made them (true) Human Being (ⲁϥⲥⲃ̄ⲧⲱⲧⲛ̄ ⲁϥⲁⲁⲛ ⲛ̄ⲣⲱⲙⲉ GosMar 9.19-20).

---

7. P Oxy 3525.11-12: 'Rather, let us thank his greatness, because he has joined us together and…'. See Chapter 4, section 2.1.3, below.

2.1.1. *On Suffering.* The question of the disciples about the suffering of the Son of Man shows that the Gospel of Mary does not hold the docetic opinion that the suffering of the Son of Man did not really happen to him.[8] Some exegetes believe that the fear of the disciples in GosMar 9.5-12 represents their misunderstanding of the Saviour's encouraging words before his departure.[9] There is, however, no indication of ignorance on their part, nor does Mary in the Gospel ridicule the fear of the disciples. In answering them, she does not try to deny the possibility of future suffering, but instead asks the disciples to look further than the suffering of the Son of Man and to see his greatness. She explains that their fear is caused by allowing their minds to be distracted from what the Son of Man has done to them.

To explain Mary's reaction to the disciples, Pasquier refers to a similar situation in the Letter of Peter to Philip, where the disciples ask themselves: 'If he, our Lord, suffered, then how much must we suffer?' (Letter of Peter to Philip 138.15-16).[10] Peter answers that it is necessary to suffer, because of 'our smallness' (Letter of Peter to Philip 138.18-20). A voice, apparently from the Risen One himself, affirms the necessity of suffering. Peter thereupon explains that, although Jesus was indeed crucified on a tree, buried in a tomb and rose from the dead, he is at the same time a stranger to this suffering. He only suffered 'in appearance'. The real suffering is caused by the 'transgression of the mother' (Letter of Peter to Philip 139.15-25). This answer presupposes the Gnostic Sophia myth, in which Sophia brings forth the Demiurge without the consent of the Father. This results in the creation and the actual suffering of the disciples. According to Pasquier, the Letter of Peter to Philip explains the situation of ignorance in which the disciples in the Gospel of Mary find themselves.[11]

The situation in the Letter of Peter to Philip, however, reveals more about Mary's answer by its differences than by its similarities. Mary in the Gospel of Mary says nothing about the necessity of suffering, as Peter does in the Letter of Peter to Philip, nor does her answer imply any kind of ignorance of the disciples, or anything that hints that the Saviour suffered only in appearance and that their own suffering has been caused by 'the mother'. She does not belittle the disciples. On the contrary she speaks of the greatness of the Son of Man.

2.1.2. *Who Is the Son of Man?* In the New Testament Gospels Jesus' greatness consists of his suffering, death and resurrection, of which Mary Magdalene is the key witness. In the Gospel of Mary, Mary describes the greatness of the Son of Man as an act of re-creation. When she describes the greatness of the Son of Man she says to her brothers (and sisters): 'He has prepared us. He has made us (true) Human Being' (GosMar 9.19-20). What can this mean?

Earlier the Saviour spoke about his work in connection with sin (GosMar 7.10-22). There is no sin, but there are people who sin by committing 'adultery', allow-

8.   See also Petersen 1999: 135 note 197.
9.   Pasquier 1983: 67; King 1995: 610; Marjanen 1996: 106-107; Hartenstein 2000: 146. Petersen (1999: 135) objects to this view.
10.   Pasquier 1983: 67.
11.   Pasquier 1983: 67-68.

ing themselves to be dragged along by the force of attraction exercised by that which is contrary to Nature. The Good One has come to restore Nature to its Root (GosMar 7.17-20). This adultery causes sickness and death (GosMar 7.20-22). However, the disciples, through the Son of Man within them, can bring forth his peace (GosMar 8.14-21).

Most likely Mary is referring to this teaching with her words 'he has made us (true) Human Being'. Being truly Human then consists of the indwelling of the Son of Man and this is seen as an act by the Son of Man: 'he has prepared us, he has made us (true) Human Being' (GosMar 9.19-20). Apparently the Good One has already restored the disciples to Nature's Root. They are already persuaded (GosMar 8.9-10). At the same time, this calls for activity on the part of the disciples. According to the Saviour, the Son of Man must be followed, sought after and found (GosMar 8.20-21). A similar activity is also referred to by Levi, when he says:

> Rather let us be ashamed and clothe ourselves with the perfect Human Being. Let us bring him forth as he commanded us. (GosMar 18.15-18)

King and Marjanen follow Pasquier when they state that the Son of Man is not Jesus, as one would expect from the New Testament Gospels, but the archetypal Man, the primordial Adam, who is the heavenly model of all humanity.[12] According to King and Marjanen, because this Son of Man is inside, salvation can only be found in discovering one's own true spiritual self.[13] Pasquier bases her view on the Gnostic writing Eugnostos, but we can also look at the Sophia of Jesus Christ, a Christian Gnostic rewriting of Eugnostos, in the Berlin Codex. In this writing the archetypal Man, the Son of Man and his Kingdom, is one of the Aeons of the Divine Pleroma, identified as Christ.[14] Pasquier states that this is in sharp contrast to the apocalyptic Son of Man in the New Testament Gospels.[15] In her view the Gospel of Mary unifies the presence now of the Kingdom of God (Lk. 17.21) with the future coming of the Son of Man (Lk. 17.24). This is also apparent from the fact that the disciples are asked to preach the gospel of the Kingdom of the Son of Man (GosMar 9.9-10).[16]

The title 'Son of Man' indeed reminds one of Jesus' self-designation in the Gospels of the New Testament. In the Synoptic Gospels, the Son of Man terminology not only refers to his future returning in judgment, as in Dan. 7.13-14, but also to his earthly activity, and to his suffering,[17] whereas in the Gospel of John the

---

12. King 1995: 606; Marjanen 1996: 108; Pasquier 1983: 61. See also Petersen 1999: 138 and Hartenstein 2000: 129 and 144.

13. King 1995: 607; Marjanen 1996: 108. King therefore does not translate Son of Man, but 'seed of true humanity'.

14. SJC BG 101.8-9. Hartenstein (2000: 129) refers to the Apocryphon of John (BG 47.14-15).

15. See also King (1995: 606) and Marjanen (1996: 108) who states that this is 'a clear Gnostic reinterpretation'.

16. Pasquier 1983: 62.

17. Earthly activity of the Son of Man (Mk 2.10, 28; 10.45; Mt. 8.20; 9.6; 11.19; 12.8, 32; 13.37; 16.13; 18.11; 20.28; Lk. 5.24; 6.5, 22; 7.34; 9.58; 12.10; 19.10), his suffering (Mk 8.31, 38; 9.9, 12, 31; 10.33; 14.21, 41; Mt. 12.40; 17.9, 12, 22; 20.18; 26.2, 24, 45; Lk. 9.22, 26, 44; 11.30;

most typical trait of the Son of Man is the notion that he descended from heaven and is going to return.[18] Furthermore, in the Synoptic Gospels Jesus indeed speaks of the Kingdom of God, but also of the Kingdom of the Son of Man (Mt. 13.41; 16.28). In addition, in the Gospel of John Jesus as the Son of Man speaks of 'My Kingdom' (Jn 18.36; cf. Jn 13.23-24).

Jens Schröter, who studied the Son of Man terminology in the Gospel of Mary with particular emphasis on its relation to the New Testament and other writings, also points out that the imagery in the Gospel of John is close to that in the Gospel of Mary.[19] According to Schröter, the Gospel of John emphasizes that in the Son of Man the relation between the heavenly and the earthly world is restored. In the Gospel of John Jesus compares the Son of Man to the ladder in Jacob's dream in Gen. 28.12-15, which rests on the ground, with its top reaching to heaven and the angels of God going up and down on it (Jn 1.51). Another important aspect, in Schröter's opinion, is that this relation, restored by Jesus, gives one 'life' through participation in the Son of Man's flesh and blood (Jn 6.53).[20]

Schröter suggests that the Johannine interpretation of the Son of Man illuminates the interpretations in Gnostic writings in which more emphasis is laid on the true self of human beings than on Jesus. In his view the Son of Man in the Gospel of Mary is similar to the one in the Gospel of John and should be interpreted in the context of the discipleship of Jesus, in which one attains true humanity (life). According to Schröter, the Gospel of Mary should thus be seen in the grey zone between Christianity and Gnosticism in that it is still familiar with the historic Jesus tradition, but is beginning to focus on knowledge of the true self in a more mythological and philosophical way.[21]

Following Schröter's lead I would argue that the Johannine Son of Man terminology is even closer to the Gospel of Mary than he suggests. Not only the relation of attaining true humanity and the work of the Son of Man can be found in the Gospel of John, as Schröter argues, but also the notion of having the Son of Man inside (GosMar 8.18-19). In Jn 17.26 Jesus says that he will be in his disciples. From the context it is clear that he will live within his disciples as the Son of Man being 'lifted up', which means being crucified and returned to the Father's presence in heaven, and thus glorified (Jn 12.23; 17.5, 24-25).[22] The Gospel of John shows that there were followers of Jesus who were convinced that the Son of Man inside was in fact the crucified and resurrected Lord, the one who had descended

---

18.31; 22.22, 48; 24.7) and the future returning in judgment (Mk 13.26; 14.21, 62; Mt. 10.23; 13.41; 16.27, 28; 19.28; 24.27, 30, 37, 39, 44; 25.31; 26.64; Lk. 12.8, 40; 17.22, 24, 26, 30; 18.8; 21.27, 36; 22.69).

18. Son of Man passages in John: 1.51; 3.13, 14; 5.27; 6.27, 53, 62; 8.28; 9.35; 12.23, 34; 13.31. Schnackenburg (1964–65: 123-37) argues that this Johanine trait of the descending and returning Son of Man is due to the Jewish concept of Wisdom.

19. Schröter 1999: 179-88.

20. Schröter 1999: 183.

21. Schröter 1999: 186-87.

22. This is in contrast to Pasquier who argues that having the Son of Man inside apparently means that the Son of Man in the Gospel of Mary has not descended, nor returned to Heaven, nor is dead, nor resurrected; see Pasquier 1983: 61.

from the Father and had returned. The same notion is to be found in Jn 6.56, where Jesus says 'he who eats my flesh and drinks my blood abides in me, and I in him'.[23]

The appeal to follow the Son of Man in the Gospel of Mary and the promise that those who seek him will find him (GosMar 8.20-21) recalls the Johannine Jesus in that he, at three different moments, declares that he will go away and will be sought after, but will not be found, except by his disciples.[24] He explains that he is going to his Father, that the disciples know the way and that they will be able to follow him (Jn 13.36; 14.4-8). When they keep his laws and love him, his Father and he will abide with them (Jn 14.19-23).

The most illuminating passages, however, are to be found in the Pauline letters. Paul does not speak of the Son of Man, but his use of the title Christ is similar to John's use of the Son of Man in that, to Paul, Christ is the one who came from heaven and is to return.[25] In the Pauline letters, not the Son of Man, but Christ is the title for the crucified and resurrected Jesus, who restores the relation between the heavenly and the earthly world.[26] Although Schröter mentions the correspondence between the Johannine Son of Man and the Christ of the New Testament Gospels, he does not deal with the Pauline Christ.[27] If we do, however, we find that Christ in oneself in the Pauline letters and the relation of this presence inside to his death and resurrection and to the Human Being imagery is strikingly close to the Gospel of Mary.

The Pauline letters speak of the crucified and resurrected Christ who lives within those who believe in him.[28] In the letter to the Colossians this 'Christ in you' is described as the word of God made fully known. It is the mystery hidden for ages and generations but now made manifest to his saints (Col. 1.27). At the same time the readers are encouraged to attain the perfect Human Being, the measure of the stature of the fullness of Christ (Eph. 4.13)[29] and to clothe oneself with the Lord Jesus Christ (Rom. 13.11). Baptism is explained as 'clothing oneself with Christ' (Gal. 3.27). In the letters to the Ephesians and the Colossians this clothing oneself with the crucified and resurrected Christ is imagined as putting off the old Human Being and clothing oneself with the new one (Eph. 4.22-24; Col. 3.9-10).

The imagery of the crucified and resurrected Christ being inside and at the same time outside like a garment (the new Human Being) in the Pauline letters, is parallel to the Son of Man being inside and to clothing oneself with the perfect

---

23. See also Jn 6.53 'truly, truly, I say to you, unless you eat the flesh of the Son of Man and drink his blood, you have no life in you', indicating the Eucharist (see Brown 1966: 284-85), but perhaps also relating to the Jewish Wisdom theology (Prov. 9.5-6).

24. Jn 7.34, 36; 8.21; 13.33.

25. See for instance Phil. 2.5-11.

26. See for instance 2 Cor. 5.14-19.

27. Schröter 1999: 184.

28. Gal. 2.20; 4.19; Rom. 8.10. See also Jn 14.20.

29. In Horner the Coptic text indeed translates ⲣⲱⲙⲉ in Eph. 4.13. In Nestle and Aland the Greek of Eph. 4.13 does not read ἄνθρωπος as one would expect from the other Pauline references and especially Eph. 4.24, but instead reads ἀνήρ as a direct reference to the masculine υἱός τοῦ θεοῦ in the same verse.

Human Being in the Gospel of Mary. The crucified and resurrected Christ in the Pauline letters as in the Gospel of Mary is a presence inside as well as a presence to be in. This is also the case in the Gospel of John, where instead of the imagery of a garment, the imagery of the vine is used, Jesus asking his disciples to abide in him as he will abide in them (Jn 15.4).[30]

Thus, on the basis of the similarity between the imagery in the Gospel of Mary and that in the Gospel of John and the Pauline letters, we may reasonably conclude that it is most likely that the Son of Man in the Gospel of Mary is not the primordial Man, but the crucified and resurrected Jesus.

2.1.3. *On Being Prepared and Made True Human Being.* Mary in GosMar 9.14-20 specifically states that the Son of Man has prepared his disciples and made them (true) Human Being. Where the Coptic text reads 'prepare' (ⲥⲟⲃⲧⲉ), the Greek text of P Oxy 3525 probably reads 'bind' (συναρτάω). According to Hartenstein and Petersen, this must be the better reading. They follow Lührmann, who suggests that the binding consists of uniting the male and female in man.[31] King thinks the binding refers to group unity.[32] The Coptic reading ⲥⲟⲃⲧⲉ, however, makes sense, in that it fits in the direct context. Mary assures her fearful brothers (and sisters) that the Son of Man, by making them true Human Being, has prepared them to go to the nations and preach the gospel. Parallel to this is 2 Tim. 3.17 where the perfect Human Being of God is 'prepared for every good work'.

The fact that Mary specifically uses the generic term ⲣⲱⲙⲉ (ἄνθρωπος in P Oxy 3525.12) and not the term denoting the male ϩⲟⲟⲩⲧ, as happens in the Gospel of Thomas (GosThom log. 114), does not necessarily mean that she is presenting an androgynous image.[33] It is too tenuous to come to this conclusion on the basis of this verse alone. We can only say that Mary does not speak in terms of male and female, as was customary in her time.[34] The word ⲣⲱⲙⲉ here denotes 'human being' and not 'man', or 'men'.[35]

The greatness of the Son of Man consists of an act of recreation. He has pre-

---

30. See also Jn 15.5-10 and cf. Jn 14.18-24.

31. Lührmann 1988: 332; Petersen 1999: 138; Hartenstein 2000: 147 note 115; Morard 2001: 157.

32. King 1995: 611. Marjanen (1996: 107) thinks both interpretations are possible.

33. As is defended by Pasquier 1983: 98-101; Lührmann 1988: 332; Petersen 1999: 138. Mohri 2001: 162-64.

34. Petersen 1999: 309-334. See also Mohri 2000: 282.

35. See also Lührmann 1988: 332; King 1995: 611; Petersen 1999: 137-38; Hartenstein 2000: 147-48. Wilson and MacRae (1979: 461) as well as Perkins (1980: 134) and Tardieu (1984: 231) overlook the difference with the Gospel of Thomas and refer to GosThom 114 to state that the phrase in GosMar 9.20 means that Mary has been made male. Pasquier (1983: 100-101) seems to use the French word 'Homme' in a generic way, since she translates GosThom 114 as becoming 'mâle' (King 1995: 629 note 13; Petersen 1999: 137 and Hartenstein 2000: 147 understand the French 'Homme' of Pasquier as a masculine word). However, Pasquier also asserts that the female element in the Gospel of Mary, as in the Gospel of Thomas, is weak and must be transformed. I agree with Lührmann (1988: 332) and King (1995: 611) that Mary's words do not refer to her now-reformed female defectiveness, but instead to her full humanity.

pared his disciples and made them (true) Human Being. The Letters to the Ephesians and Colossians assure their readers in a similar way: the new Human Being in which one is to clothe oneself is not to be made by oneself, but is already there, created after the likeness of God.[36] Paul compares Christ to Adam, Adam being the first earthly Human Being, and the Lord from heaven the second Human Being.[37] The first Adam was a living soul, the last was made a life-giving spirit (1 Cor. 15.45). According to the Pauline letters, as we have borne the image of the earthly, we shall also bear the image of the heavenly (1 Cor. 15.47-49). This will happen at 'the last trumpet' but even now anyone who is in Christ is a new creation.[38]

A close parallel to this being made a (true) Human Being is to be found in Philo's exegesis of the creation story. According to Philo, with Gen. 2.7 Moses means to say that God changed the earthly man from a dull and blind soul into a spiritual and truly living being by blowing the life-giving Spirit into his νοῦς.[39] To Philo the *nous*, which has God's *pneuma* in it, is the true Human Being in man.[40] In his view it is not the earthly man who is made after the image of God, but the true Human Being inside of him. The meaning of this is clear from his comment on the phrase 'Noah was a righteous human being' (Gen. 6.9). Philo says:

> We must not fail to note that in this passage he [Moses] gives the name of 'human being' (ἄνθρωπος) not according to the common form of speech, to the mortal animal endowed with reason, but to the one, who pre-eminently verifies[41] the name by having expelled from the soul the untamed and frantic passions and the truly beast-like vices. Here is a proof. After 'human being' he adds 'just', implying by the combination that the unjust is no human being, or more properly speaking a beast in human form, and that the follower after righteousness alone is human being. (On Abraham 32)[42]

Perhaps Philo's thoughts about the creation of the true Human Being in man are behind Mary's words in GosMar 9.14-20, especially since her next words are about the importance of the *nous* and state that the *nous* is between the *pneuma* and the soul (GosMar 10.19-23). This coincides with Philo's imagery of the soul who is guided and made alive by the *nous* which has God's *pneuma* blown into it.

With respect to the idea of the gospel of the Kingdom of the Son of Man in GosMar 9.9-10 it is interesting to note that Philo compares the true Human Being in man to a king. In his comment on Gen. 37.15 he says:

> The name which most correctly describes the real human being (ἄνθρωπος) and most thoroughly belongs to him is simply 'human being', the most proper title of

---

36. Eph. 4.24; Col. 3.10.

37. Rom. 5.14; 1 Cor. 15.22, 45.

38. 2 Cor. 5.17; Gal. 6.15.

39. Philo, Allegorical Interpretation I.31-32, 37-38. See Leisegang 1967: 87.

40. See Leisegang 1967: 85-88.

41. I changed Colson's translation, which unnecessarily has the androcentric 'but to the man who is man pre-eminently, who verifies' into 'to the one who pre-eminently verifies' (Colson and Whitaker 1959: VI, 21)

42. See Colson and Whitaker 1959: VI, 20-21. I have replaced Colson's 'man' with 'human being'.

a mind endowed with reason and articulate utterance. This 'human being', dwell-
ing in the soul of each of us, is discovered at one time as king and governor, at
another as judge and umpire of life's contests. Sometimes he assumes the part of
witness or accuser, and, all unseen, convicts us from within. (That the Worse is
Wont to Attack the Better 22-23)[43]

Philo also says that the task of the *nous*, the Human Being in man, is to bring 'the
disorder that prevailed in existing things as the result of mob-rule into the order of
regular government under a king'.[44] Below, we will see that Philo calls the ascent
of the soul the Kings' highway, a road of wisdom and virtue, that leads to stability
and knowledge of the King.

I suggest that Philo's thoughts are at the background of being prepared and made
(true) Human Being, but in a Pauline way: not referring to the creation of Adam,
but to the re-creation through Christ. This interpretation recalls the Johannine story
of the risen Jesus blowing the Spirit upon his disciples and sending them as he was
sent (Jn 20.21-23).

2.1.4. *Conclusion.* It is difficult to find anything like a 'doctrine' in the Gospel of
Mary as we have it. But we can say that we can discern a certain kind of argument.
Passion and confusion came into the created cosmos because of a power contrary
to Nature. Redemption consists in the fact that the Son of Man, the crucified and
resurrected Jesus, as God did when creating truly living beings, once again blows
the Spirit into the *nous*, the mind, which has the task of ordering the turbulence of
the soul. The Son of Man thus re-creates his followers into (true) Human Beings.
Through his living within them they are empowered to bring forth his peace instead
of passion and confusion which belong to the power contrary to Nature. They,
having been restored to Nature's Root by the Good One can indeed be 'fully
assured' (GosMar 8.7). Opposite nature has no power over them. They are thus
prepared to proclaim the gospel of the Kingdom of the Son of Man.

The weeping disciples, however, feel far from assured and prepared in this
moment of anxiety. Instead, in Mary's words, they are in 'two minds' (2ϨⲎⲦ ⲤⲚⲀⲨ
GosMar 9.15-16). On the basis of our interpretation of GosMar 7 and 8 we may
assume that this means that the disciples' minds are not only directed towards
Nature, but also towards what is contrary to Nature. What the Saviour warned
against is happening to the disciples. They are allowing themselves to become
'persuaded' (by what is contrary to Nature; GosMar 8.8). Their hearts are torn and
inwardly divided. They are confused by the suffering of the Son of Man and fear
their own. Mary instead calls on the disciples to remember and praise the Son of

43. See Colson and Whitaker 1958: II, 217-18. Again I have replaced Colson's 'man' with
'human being'.
44. On Flight and Finding 10. For the translation see Colson and Whitaker 1958: V, 15. Philo
also uses other images. For *nous* as father, see Allegorical Interpretation II.51 and III.84; for *nous*
as teacher, ibid. III,50; for *nous* as pilot, ibid. III.24, and That the Worse is Wont to Attack the
Better 53; for *nous* as origin of the, good see About the Sacrifices of Abel and Cain 54; for *nous* as
shepherd, see About Agriculture 48, 66; for *nous* as God, see Allegorical Interpretation I.40. See
Leisegang 1967: 139-40.

Man's greatness. She reminds them of his re-creating them into (true) Human Beings and thus of their being prepared.

2.2. *On Seeing the Lord, on Stability and on the Mind*

The second time that Mary speaks she is doing so at Peter's request. Mary has turned the hearts of the brothers (and sisters) inwards towards the Good One. They begin to discuss his words. Peter then asks Mary to relate those words of the Saviour which she knows and are still unknown to the others. She thereupon gives an account of a dialogue about the Saviour's teaching which she alone received from him. The occasion for this was that she had seen him in a vision and had told him about it. Only part of Mary's account in GosMar 10.7–17.10 has been preserved. The pages 11–14 are missing. In this section we first concentrate on GosMar 10.7-23.

> Mary answered and she said, 'What is hidden from you I shall tell you'.[45] And she began to say to them these words: 'I', she said, 'I have seen the Lord in a vision and I said to him, "Lord, I have seen you today in a vision". He answered, he said to me, "Blessed are you, because you are not wavering when you see me. For where the mind is, there is the treasure". I said to him, "Lord, now, does he who sees the vision see it with the soul or with the spirit?" The Saviour answered, he said, "He does not see with the soul nor with the spirit, but with the mind which [is] between the two that is [what] sees the vision and that [...]" (GosMar 10.7-23)

The situation recalls the beginning of the Gospel of Luke about the many reports that circulated in his day which were based on what had been told by those who witnessed everything from the beginning and who proclaimed the gospel (Lk. 1.1-2). The Apocryphon of James describes a situation similar to that in the Gospel of Mary: the twelve disciples sitting together to recall what the Saviour had said to each of them, whether in secret or openly. They try to arrange the various accounts into books (NHC I.2.7-15).

The precise situation in the Gospel of Mary is not that Peter assumes that there are words of the Saviour that some know and others do not, but that he specifically asks Mary to recall what she remembers. This is amazing, since in other instances where Peter speaks to or about Mary he rebukes her.[46] That Mary could have known things that the others do not also occurs in the New Testament Gospels. The Gospel of John is close to the Gospel of Mary in that the knowledge of Mary Magdalene consists of having seen the Lord and of having been told by him about his way upwards and about the new bond between his Father and his disciples (Jn 20.17-18). In the Gospel of Mary she first reminds the disciples of their new identity and then talks about having seen the Lord and about the way upwards of the soul.

2.2.1. *On Seeing the Lord in a Vision.*
Most exegetes believe that Mary in GosMar 10.7–17.10 recalls words of the Saviour which she received in a vision.[47] On the

---

45. P Oxy 3525.18: 'what is hidden from you and what I remember'.

46. See GosMar 17.16-23; GosThom 114; PS 36; cf. PS 72.

47. Till and Schenke 1972: 27; Pasquier 1983: 6; Tardieu 1984: 21; King 1995: 612; Marjanen 1996: 110-11; Petersen 1999: 153-54.

basis of this assumption, Marjanen concludes that Mary 'tries to show that the reception of divine revelation is not limited to repeating the old teachings of the Saviour but it means to be constantly looking for new ones, even in the form of visions'.[48] According to Marjanen, Mary's 'obvious purpose' is to encourage the disciples 'to seek new revelations of spiritual truths, i.e., the gnosis. By communicating her own vision she wants to lead them to a new way'.[49]

In Hartenstein's opinion, however, one should distinguish between Mary's vision of the Lord and her dialogue with him, since Mary clearly states that she has seen (ⲀⲒⲚⲀⲨ GosMar 10.10) the Lord in a vision and not that she sees him.[50] The dialogue with the Lord does not start with the phrase 'Lord, I see you now in a vision', but with the phrase 'Lord, I have seen you today in a vision'. Petersen objects to Hartenstein's view by pointing to the sentence with which Mary starts her story: 'I have seen the Lord in a vision and I said to him' (ⲀⲒⲚⲀⲨ…ⲀⲨⲰ ⲀⲈⲒⲬⲞⲞ⳹ … GosMar 10.10-12). According to Petersen this sentence, together with the Lord's words 'Blessed are you, because you are not wavering when you see me' (ⲈⲢⲈⲚⲀⲨ GosMar 10.14-15) points to the simultaneousness of the vision and the dialogue. In her view Mary in GosMar 10.12-13 should indeed have said 'Lord, I see you now in a vision', instead of 'Lord, I have seen you today in a vision', but according to Petersen the author choose not to present Mary saying this, but instead pictures her as using the perfect tense, as a reference to Jn 20.18 where Mary Magdalene 'told the disciples that she had seen the Lord and that he had spoken these things unto her'.[51]

The interpretation of Hartenstein seems the more logical one. When reading the text it seems most likely that Mary recalls a dialogue with the Saviour that she began by telling him that she saw him earlier in a vision. She clearly wants to know more about this phenomenon, since her first question is about what exactly sees the vision. However, if the exegetes are right who argue that the dialogue is part of the vision, I still do not agree with the conclusion of Marjanen, that Mary by pointing to her vision leads the disciples to a new way of knowledge. On the contrary, being taught by a vision is not something that is rare in Antiquity and in the New Testament writings learning through visions is quite a common phenomenon.

The word for vision that is used in the Gospel of Mary, ὅραμα, occurs in the Acts of the Apostles and in Matthew. Peter has a vision about clean and unclean food (Acts 10.17.19). Stephen calls Moses' experience with the thorn bush a vision (Acts 7.31). Cornelius has a vision of an angel of God (Acts 10.3). Paul has a vision of a man from Macedonia (Acts 16.9-10).

In the New Testament writings there are also appearances of Jesus in a vision (ὅραμα). In Matthew Jesus transfigures in his earthly lifetime on a mountain before Peter, James and John. His face shines like the sun and his garments become white as light. Peter, James and John are commanded to tell no one about this vision until the Son of Man is raised from the dead (Mt. 17.9). The other New

48. Marjanen 1996: 111; see also Pagels 1978: 422; Pasquier 1983: 6 and King 1995: 622.
49. Marjanen 1996: 111.
50. Hartenstein 2000: 130.
51. Petersen 1999: 153.

Testament appearances of Jesus in visions are post-resurrectional. Thus he appears to Ananias and to Paul (Acts 9.10; 18.9). In every case the 'seeing' of the vision and the words that go with it are taken very seriously by those who hear about it. No story about a vision has the connotation that something strange is happening.

As to why exactly Mary relates this dialogue with the Lord, Mary seems to make a connection with her encouragement of the disciples in GosMar 9.14-20, alluding to the themes of being in two minds and of having been made (true) Human Being, by recalling a dialogue in which 'not wavering' occurs and the treasure which is within the *nous*. If we are right and the dialogue that Mary starts with Jesus is not part of her vision, in the Gospel of Mary as we have it, the exact content of her vision remains obscure. On the missing pages Mary could have begun to tell about the content of her vision and the description of the way upwards of the soul may still have been part of it.

Hartenstein suggests that Mary in her vision has seen Jesus as Lord, that is, in his true nature, just as Peter, James and John saw Jesus in the Gospel of Matthew.[52] The words 'I have seen the Lord' from Mary's mouth suggest that she has seen the risen Jesus as in the Gospel of John, but in the Gospel of Mary all the disciples have already met and spoken with the risen Lord. If Mary indeed, now, recalls a vision of the Lord in his true, divine nature, as in the Gospel of Matthew, this fits in the context of Mary assuring the fearful disciples of the greatness of the Son of Man. Whereas they are confused by the suffering Son of Man, Mary assures them that she has seen him in his glorified state. This reminds one of Stephen, who, also in a context of expected suffering testifies: 'Behold, I see the heavens opened, and the Son of Man standing at the right hand of God' (Acts 7.56).

2.2.2. *On not Wavering when Seeing the Lord.* The fact that Mary is called not wavering (ⲀⲦⲔⲒⲘ) when she sees the Lord in her vision (GosMar 10.13-15) also supports the conclusion that the vision may have been about the glorified Lord. With most exegetes Mary being ⲀⲦⲔⲒⲘ is interpreted as a reference to her being a true Gnostic.[53] Mary would belong to the 'immovable race'. This expression occurs in two Gnostic writings contained in the Berlin Codex: the Apocryphon of John and the Sophia of Jesus Christ.[54] In the Gospel of Mary, however, nothing is said about Mary being part of a certain race. She is simply talking about her experience of seeing the Lord in a vision. King suggests that Mary's stability illustrates her advanced spiritual status, not assuming that Mary belongs to the Gnostic race, but because of her 'conformity to the unchanging and eternal spiritual world'.[55]

The fact that Mary does not waver during her vision of the Lord reminds one first of all of the Psalms, in which the righteous and those who keep to the Lord are

---

52. Mt. 17.9. Hartenstein 2000: 153-54.

53. Perkins 1980: 135; Tardieu 1984: 232; Petersen 1999: 154; Hartenstein 2000: 154.

54. BG 22.10-17; 64.17–65.3; 73.7-11; 75.15–76.1 and BG 87.8–88.10. The 'immovable race' also occurs in the Gospel of the Egyptians (NHC III.51.6-14; 59.12-15; 61.16-23 and parallels); in the Three Steles of Seth (NHC VII.5.118.10-13) and in Zostrianos (NHC VIII.1.51.15-16). See Williams 1985: 1-3.

55. King 1995: 612.

described as those who will not waver.[56] In a sermon in Acts, Peter quotes Ps. 16.8 (LXX 15.8) and says:

> I saw the Lord always before me;
> for he is at my right hand that I may not be shaken (μὴ σαλευθῶ; ⲚⲚⲀⲔⲓⲙ).
> Therefore my heart was glad, and my tongue rejoiced;
> moreover my flesh will dwell in hope.
> For thou wilt not abandon my soul to Hades,
> Nor let thy Holy One see corruption.
> Thou hast made known to me the ways of life:
> thou wilt make me full of gladness with thy presence. (Acts 2.25-28)

Seeing the Lord before him and keeping the Lord at his right hand cause Peter not to waver. Apparently this is an experience full of hope and joy. In the second letter to the Thessalonians, not to waver is equivalent to not to be troubled and deceived by false teaching (2 Thess. 2.2).

The Greek word ἀσάλευτος which was probably used for ⲀⲧⲔⲓⲙ in the original text of the Gospel of Mary is very evocative.[57] The verb σαλεύω is used for the restless tossing of ships in a stormy sea.[58] The same image occurs in the Letter of James for being in two minds (δίψυχος; Ⲛ2Ⲏⲧ ⲤⲚⲀⲨ). According to the letter, anyone who is in two minds and inwardly divided is like a wave driven and tossed by the wind (Jas 1.6-8).

In Mary's opinion the disciples, when they focus on the suffering of the Son of Man instead of on his greatness, are in two minds. Whereas they waver when considering the suffering of the Son of Man, Mary does not when seeing the Lord.

2.2.3. *Is Mary Spiritually More Advanced?* The image of tossing like ships in a stormy sea is also used by Philo when he says:

> The soul faints and loses all power through passion when it receives from the body the flood of tossing surge caused by the storm wind which sweeps down in its fury, driven on by unbridled appetite. (On the Preliminary Studies 60)[59]

Philo's use of the image is close to the Gospel of Mary, in that it refers to passion as the direct cause of the soul losing power (cf. GosMar 8.2-6).

To Philo, stability belongs to God and to those who draw near to God.[60] When, for instance, commenting on Abraham 'who is standing in front of God' (Gen. 18.22) Philo says:

> for when should we expect a mind to stand and no longer sway as on the balance save when it is opposite God, seeing and being seen. For it gets its equipoise from these two sources: from seeing, because when it sees the Incomparable it does not yield to the counter pull of things like itself; from being seen, because the mind

---

56. Pss. 15.5; 16.8; 17.5; 21.7; 26.1; 30.6; 36.11; 46.5; 62.2; 93.1; 96.10; 112.6; 125.1. See Budge 1898 (who holds the LXX numbering of the Psalms: 14.5; 15.8 etc.).
57. Williams 1985: 3.
58. Liddell and Scott 1968: 1581b.
59. Colson and Whitaker 1968: IV, 489.
60. Passcher 1931: 228-38; Williams 1985: 25-27 and 76.

which the Ruler judges worthy to come within His sight He claims for the solely best, that is for Himself. (On Dreams II.226-27).[61]

And commenting on Moses standing in front of God (Deut. 5.31) Philo continues: 'For that which draws near to God enters into affinity with what is and through that immutability becomes self-standing'.[62] In view of the Rest in Silence which the soul reaches after her ascent in GosMar 17.4-7, it is noteworthy that Philo defines this 'self-standing' as the mind which is at Rest:

> And when the mind is at Rest it recognizes clearly how great a blessing Rest is, and struck with wonder at its beauty, has the thought that it belongs either to God or to that form of being which is midway between mortal and immortal kind. (On Dreams II.228)[63]

Mary's stability is in contrast to the wavering of the disciples, when they focus on the suffering of the Son of Man, instead of on his greatness. Whereas Mary is called fortunate for not wavering, the disciples were weeping and in two minds. This difference may indicate Mary's advanced spiritual status. When Philo, for instance, describes Lot as irresolute, his mind set on the good as well as the bad, 'like a boat tossed by winds from opposite quarters',[64] he says that Lot suffers from a relapse 'carried off a prisoner of war by the enemies in the soul'[65]. Philo ascribes this to Lot's being at present 'a novice in the contemplation and study of things Divine'.[66]

The main objection, however, to Mary being more spiritually advanced and less affected by what is contrary to nature and its passion than the others, is the fact that not only the disciples give in to passion and become distressed, but in the course of the story Mary does so herself as well. The reaction of Andrew and Peter on her words causes her to weep like they did (GosMar 18.1). Perhaps, where the disciples are concerned, it is best to keep in mind Philo's comment on Abraham's momentary doubt, when hearing of the promise that he and his barren Sarah in their old age will receive a son. Philo says:

> Happy is he to whom it is granted to incline towards the better and more god-like part through most of his life. For it is impossible that it should be so with him throughout the whole length of life, since sometimes the opposing load of mortality throws its weight into the scales, and binding its time waits to find its chance in the miss-chances of reason and so prove too strong for him. (On the Change of Names 185)[67]

Philo assures his readers that being stable all the time is impossible, since this belongs to God alone, who is unmixed, whereas 'we are mixtures, with human and

61. Colson and Whitaker 1958: V, 545.
62. On Dreams II.228; Colson and Whitaker 1958: V, 545.
63. Colson and Whitaker 1958: V, 545.
64. On the Migration of Abraham 148; Colson and Whitaker 1958: IV, 217.
65. On the Migration of Abraham 150; Colson and Whitaker 1958: IV, 219.
66. On the Migration of Abraham 150; Colson and Whitaker 1958: IV, 219.
67. Colson and Whitaker 1958: V, 237.

divine blended in us'.[68] In the Gospel of Mary this is also the case. Whereas the disciples do not waver all the time, Mary is likewise not stable all the time.

2.2.4. *On the Soul, the Mind and the Spirit.* According to Philo, stability is one's richest possession. He states that 'so vast in its excess is the stability of the Deity that he imparts to chosen natures a share of his steadfastness to be their richest possession'.[69] In the Gospel of Mary the Saviour, in his teaching to Mary alone, reveals that the treasure of stability is within one's reach. When he tells Mary that he considers her fortunate for not wavering, he continues: 'For where the *nous* is, there is the treasure' (GosMar 10.15-16).[70] But what exactly is the *nous*?

The teaching Mary gives to the disciples in GosMar 10.11-23 is apparently centred around the *nous*, since in response to her question about what exactly sees the vision, the spirit or the soul, she says that the Lord replied:

> He does not see it with the soul nor with the spirit, but with the *nous* which is between the two... (GosMar 10.20-22)

Thus, the *nous*, which has 'the treasure' in it, is also the organ through which one sees the vision. Moreover, the place of the *nous* is disclosed to us: between the spirit and the soul.

To be able to really understand Mary's words, we must seek to comprehend Mary's question about the vision she saw: 'Lord, now, does he who sees the vision see it with the soul or with the Spirit?'(GosMar 10.18-19). Mary, apparently, before the Saviour instructed her about this, thought in the categories of soul and Spirit. In Stoicism the soul is the seat of perception by the senses. The divine Spirit is the immanent principle that holds the cosmos together, that gives the body life as breath, and human spirit, and that orders the turbulence of the soul.[71]

In this way of thinking there were two views about dreams.[72] One said that when the human spirit rested, the senses of the soul took over and produced ghostly images. The other said that the human spirit parted from the soul and now, detached from the confusing impressions of the soul, could converse freely with the spiritual and see the Divine.[73] On the basis of this we may suppose that Mary's question about precisely what sees the vision is the question of whether the vision comes from the divine Spirit or from the turbulence of her own soul.

The Saviour introduces a new category in answering Mary's question about soul and Spirit. One does not see the vision through the soul, nor through the spirit,

---

68. On the Change of Names 184; Colson and Whitaker 1958: V, 237.

69. On Dreams II.223; Colson and Whitaker 1958: V, 543.

70. This saying may also be a reinterpretation of Mt. 6.21 and Lk. 12.35-40, warning against greed and wealth: 'For, where your treasure is, there will be your heart', namely in heaven and not on earth. The inverted saying 'where the *nous* is, there is your treasure', however, is also known from other sources such as Clement of Alexandria. See Pasquier 1983: 101-104.

71. Pohlenz 1948: 81-88.

72. King (1998: 23 and 35 note 17) suggests that the vision came to Mary while sleeping.

73. The first view is for instance represented by Aristotle and the second by the Stoic Posidonius of Apameia. See Leisegang 1967: 176-78.

but through the *nous*. The place of the *nous* is in between the soul and the spirit. Now we no longer have 'soul and spirit', but 'soul, *nous*, spirit'. This means that, according to the Saviour, there is more to a human psyche than the turbulence of one's soul and the reception of divine revelation. Through the *nous*, which here because of its place between the soul and the spirit is a human category, one is able to actively draw near the divine. It also means that the Saviour creates an opposition. By separating the soul and the spirit, the Spirit has thus become a transcendent instead of an immanent divine category.

These three categories instead of two, together with the assurance that the *nous* is in between the soul and the spirit, once again recalls Philo's exegesis of Gen. 2.7: man is made a true living soul by the *nous* which has God's *pneuma* blown into it. The imagery of the *nous* with the life-giving *pneuma* in it also recalls the Pauline letters. To Paul, the *nous* is able to honour the law of God, but is held prisoner by the flesh, causing death (Rom. 7.26). If God's *pneuma* which raised Christ lives within one this situation changes, enabling one to become free and alive (Rom. 7.24-25; 8.10-15). He assures his readers that although the outer human being is decaying, the inner one, the *nous*, is renewed from day to day (2 Cor. 4.16; cf. Rom. 7.22-23).

To Paul the *nous* of a Christian is a renewed *nous*, because of God's *pneuma* that lives within it. In his first letter to the Corinthians Paul quotes Isaiah's question 'who has the *nous* of the Lord that he may instruct him?' (Isa. 11.13). And he answers: 'but we have the *nous* of Christ' (1 Cor. 2.16). In the letter to the Ephesians this renewal of the *nous* is the same as clothing oneself with the new Human Being (Eph. 4.23-24). Paul encourages his readers to actively change themselves and to really live in accordance with their renewed *nous* (Rom. 12.2).

Again, on the basis of similar imagery, I suggest that we may understand the *nous* in the Gospel of Mary, to be a renewed *nous* as in the Pauline letters: the *nous* of Christ, and in the case of the Gospel of Mary, the *nous* of the risen Son of Man. In the second letter to the Corinthians we even hear, in a context of suffering as in the Gospel of Mary, a faint allusion of a treasure being within the *nous*, when Paul, referring to his hardships as an apostle, calls the knowledge of God's glory in Jesus Christ, a treasure which we have in earthen vessels (2 Cor. 4.6-11).

2.2.5. *Conclusion.* The words of the Saviour, as yet unknown to the disciples, which Mary on Peter's request recalls in GosMar 10.7-23, help them to understand in a more profound way the teaching of the Saviour about the Son of Man being within, who is to be followed, sought after and found. Whereas the disciples think of the Son of Man as the one who suffered and fear their own suffering, Mary in GosMar 9.14-20 emphasizes his greatness, which prepared them and made them Human Being. Now, by recalling words of the Saviour that she knows and the others do not, she shows how they can conquer their wavering. The disciples do not depend on their souls' senses, nor do they need to wait for divine inspiration from outside. The Saviour has explained to Mary that there are not two categories, soul and spirit, but three. Their own souls' *nous* which has the spirit of the Son of Man blown into it enables them, first, to see the Lord's greatness; second, to become stable; and third, to experience bliss. Thus, 'where the *nous* is there is the treasure' (GosMar 10.15-16).

2.3. *On the Way Upwards to the Rest in Silence*

The dialogue on seeing the Lord, on stability and on the *nous*, ends abruptly (GosMar 10.23). Four pages of the dialogue of Mary with the Saviour are missing (GosMar 11-14). When we rejoin the story again in GosMar 15.1 we step into Mary's description of the way upwards of the soul to the Rest in Silence. The more the soul ascends, the more powerful the opposition becomes. Whereas at first individual powers want to restrain the Soul, the last power is sevenfold. In this section we concentrate on GosMar 15.1–17.7. The soul's road is barred by four powers. The first power is missing. The extant text starts on p. 15 with the second power:

> Desire said: 'I did not see you, on your way downwards, but now I see you, on your way upwards. But how can you deceive me, when you belong to me?' The Soul answered and said, 'I have seen you. You did not see me nor recognise me. I was (like) a garment to you, and you did not know me'. When she had said this, she went away rejoicing loudly. Again she came to the third Power, which is called Ignorance. [She] questioned the Soul, saying, 'Where are you going? In wickedness you were held prisoner. Yes, you were held prisoner. Do not judge then!' And the Soul said, 'Why do you judge me when I do not judge you? I am taken prisoner although I did not take prisoner. I am not recognized, but I have recognized that the All is being unloosened, both the earthly and the heavenly things. When the Soul left the third Power powerless, she went upwards and saw the fourth Power. She took on seven appearances. The first appearance is Darkness, the second Desire, the third Ignorance, the fourth is the Jealousy of Death, the fifth is the Kingdom of the Flesh, the sixth is the Foolish Learning of the Flesh, the seventh is the Hot Tempered Wisdom. These are the seven [power]s of Wrath. They ask the Soul, 'Where do you come from, you killer of people?', or, 'Where are you going, you who leave places powerless?' The Soul answered and said, 'What imprisons me is pierced. What turns me is left powerless and my Desire has been fulfilled, and Ignorance has died. From a world I am unloosened through a world and from a model through a model which is from the side of Heaven. And the fetter of oblivion is temporal. From this hour on, at the time of the decisive moment in the aeon, I shall receive the Rest in Silence'. (GosMar 15.1–17.7)

Although this part of the text only begins with the second power, by comparing it to the first three appearances of the fourth power, it is most likely that the first power was Darkness.[74] Thus, the soul's way upwards to heaven is hindered by Darkness, Desire, Ignorance, and Wrath; Wrath taking on seven appearances: Darkness, Desire, Ignorance, Jealousy of Death, Kingdom of the Flesh, Foolish Learning, and Hot Tempered Wisdom. These powers try to stop the soul from her ascent by arguments, but the soul is able to expose those as false. The four powers confront the soul with the fact that she belongs to them and is not to go elsewhere. The soul, basically by inverting their words, shows them to be above their claims

---

74. Pasquier 1983: 79.

and joyfully continues her way, which is not difficult, but light and playful.[75]

Given the structure of the Gospel of Mary, we can assume that the account of the soul is the answer to a question of Mary's. The specific question, however, is on one of the missing pages. This means that we can only speculate about the context in which the Saviour relates these things about the soul. It seems reasonable to assume that Mary has asked about the new category which the Saviour has given her and which he has placed between the soul and the spirit. The missing part of the work would then have been about the *nous* and the spirit, while the part that has been preserved is about the soul and the *nous*. Granted, the word *nous* does not appear in this section, but the answers that the soul gives to the powers bear witness to the knowledge of the soul's *nous*.[76]

But why would Mary recall words of the Saviour about the ascent of the soul at this very moment and what are they about?

2.3.1. A Post-Mortem Ascent Past Archontic Powers? Some exegetes assume that the ascent of the soul is an ascent after death.[77] In that case Mary would tell the disciples about it to reassure them about their fate even if 'the nations' (N̄2ЄΘNOC; τὰ ἔθνη)[78] do not spare them and put them to death as was the case with the Son of Man. According to Pasquier, however, the ascent symbolizes religious or psychic experience.[79]

According to Carsten Colpe who studied the general theme of the ascent of the soul, some ascents indeed describe one's fate after death, but other descriptions are about ascents while living and probably in ecstasy.[80] From what we are told by the Gospel of Mary, it is difficult to decide whether the soul's ascent is an ascent in the present or after death, since the beginning of the description of the way upwards of the soul is on the missing pages. Although we do know the final goal, the Rest in Silence, this is also of no help, because Rest may be experienced not only after death, but also now as a gift of grace.[81] We saw earlier that Philo calls the one who experiences stability 'the mind who is at Rest'.[82] This being at Rest is an experience in the present. According to Philo it is an experience of beauty which belongs to God or to 'that form of being which is midway between mortal and immortal kind'.[83]

We can only conclude that it is clear it is in the present that the soul in the Gospel of Mary encounters Darkness, Desire, Ignorance and Wrath. On the other hand

75. See Pasquier 1983: 86-93; King 1995: 613-14.
76. See also Perkins 1980: 134.
77. Till and Schenke 1972: 27-28; Tardieu 1984: 233; Marjanen 1996: 94 note 1. King (1995: 615) and Petersen (1999: 156) speak of the soul's liberation of the fetters of material existence.
78. For the Greek see P Oxy 3525.
79. Pasquier 1983: 22. She refers to Philo, Who is the Heir of Divine Things 81 (Colson and Whitaker 1958: IV, 323).
80. Colpe 1967: 439. See also Rudolph 1996: 244-55.
81. Helderman 1984: 25 and 338-42.
82. For Rest as stability and being near to God in Philo's thoughts, see Passcher 1931: 228-38 and Helderman 1984: 58-60.
83. Philo, On Dreams II.228; Colson and Whitaker 1958: V, 545.

it is also clear that the ultimate victory depends on a future action on the part of heaven, which, however, at the same time has already been started (GosMar 7.3-8 and 15.20–16.1).

Most exegetes of the Gospel of Mary consider the description of the ascent of the soul as typically Gnostic.[84] Most of them believe this, since they consider the ascent of the soul as a specific Gnostic phenomenon. Marjanen thinks that the ascent in the Gospel of Mary belongs to a Gnostic context, since 'the whole idea of the post-mortem ascent of the soul past archontic powers back to the realm of the light has its closest parallels in Gnostic texts'.[85] Colpe, however, has shown that the ascent of the soul is a widespread phenomenon and concludes that one should be very careful when deciding whether or not an ascent is to be called Gnostic.[86]

A moving account of an ascent to God which is hindered by adversaries is the vision of Vibia Perpetua from about 202 CE. She is a young Christian mother with an infant son still at the breast, who in prison awaits the probable sentence to be thrown before the wild beasts. Her account runs as follows:

> There was a bronze ladder of extraordinary height reaching up to heaven, but it was so narrow that only one person could ascend at a time. Every conceivable kind of iron weapon was attached to the sides of the ladder: swords, lances, hooks, and daggers. If anyone climbed up carelessly or without looking upwards, he/she would be mangled as the flesh adhered to the weapons. Crouching directly beneath the ladder was a monstrous dragon who threatened those climbing up and tried to frighten them from ascent. Saturus went up first. Because of his concern for us he had given himself up voluntarily after we had been arrested. He had been our source of strength but was not with us at the time of the arrest. When he reached the top of the ladder he turned to me and said, 'Perpetua, I'm waiting for you, but be careful not to be bitten by the dragon'. I told him that in the name of Jesus Christ the dragon could not harm me. At this the dragon slowly lowered its head as though afraid of me. Using its head as the first step, I began my ascent. (The Martyrdom of Perpetua 4)[87]

No one would call Perpetua a Gnostic or would identify the monstrous dragon as a Gnostic archon. In my opinion there is also no evidence that supports the interpretation that the powers in GosMar 15.1–16.13 should be identified with Gnostic archons. Assuming a Gnostic context, Till and others argue that the powers in

---

84. Till and Schenke 1972: 26; Tardieu 1984: 22; Marjanen 1996: 94; Petersen 1999: 60; Hartenstein 2000: 132-33.

85. Marjanen 1996: 94 note 1. On page 34 he refers to the First Apocalypse of James (NHC V.32.28-36), the Apocryphon of James (NHC I.8.35-36); the Apocalypse of Paul (NHC V.22.23–23.28). He also refers to the Second Book of Jeu (127.5–138.4) and Pistis Sophia (PS 286.9–291.23) and to descriptions of the Church fathers: Irenaus (Against the Heresies 1.21.5) and Epifanius (Panarion 26.13.2; 36.3.16). Marjanen also mentions the writing Poimandres (Corpus Hermeticum I.24-26), which is, however, not Gnostic, but Hermetic and which by Koivunen (1994: 235) is seen as the closest parallel to the Gospel of Mary. For the difference between Gnostic and Hermetic writings see Chapter 3, section 2.2.4 note 41.

86. Colpe 1967: 429-47. See for ascents in various contexts also Rudolph 1996: 244-55; Culianu 1983; Collins 1979; Dean Otting 1984; Himmelfarb 1993; Roukema 2003.

87. Translated by Rader 1981: 21.

GosMar 15.1–16.13 are the four powers of material creation, representing the four elements earth, water, air and fire.[88] Pasquier suggests that they are perhaps hypostases of Yaldabaoth, the Creator God in the Apocryphon of John.[89] According to Tardieu, the seven appearances of the fourth Power Wrath represent the passions of the God from the Bible.[90] King, however, simply speaks of the Powers of Matter, without identifying them with Gnostic archons.

As we saw earlier in Chapter 3, section 5 the Gospel of Mary is best understood from the Stoic perspective on matter, Nature and passion. It is important to note that the powers in GosMar 15.1–16.13 are vices. In Stoic philosophy vices such as darkness, desire, ignorance and wrath, belong to the life of passion contrary to Nature. I suggest that the four powers in the Gospel of Mary represent the influence of what is contrary to Nature, which according to the Saviour's teaching caused matter to bring forth passion (cf. GosMar 8.2-4).

2.3.2. *The Way to Rebirth and the Royal Road.* An interesting parallel to the ascent of the soul in the Gospel of Mary is the description of the way to rebirth in Tractate XIII of the Corpus Hermeticum. Hannelore Koivunen pointed to Tractate I (Poimandres) as a close parallel to the Gospel of Mary, but according to its description of the ascent, one simply gives one's vices to the heavenly spheres and there is no gaining victory over vices as in the Gospel of Mary.[91] In Tractate XIII, in the account that Hermes relates to his son Tat, the soul endures twelve senseless punishments of matter or of darkness:[92] ignorance, grief, incontinence, lust, injustice, greed, deceit, malice, treachery, anger, rashness, and wickedness (CH XIII.7).[93] The soul is able to overcome them by the ten spiritual Powers of the mercy of God. Knowledge of God drives away ignorance, knowledge of joy drives away grief, self-control drives away incontinence, steadfastness drives away lust, righteousness drives away injustice, generosity drives away greed, truth drives away deceit, the good drives away malice, and life and light conquer the remaining punishments of darkness: treachery, anger, rashness, and wickedness (CH XIII.8-9).[94]

Hermes calls this the process of 'regeneration' (παλιγγενεσία) and explains to Tat:

> By the arrival of the Decade,[95] child, the intellectual generation was put together.
> It drove out the Dodecade,[96] and we were deified by this generation. Therefore,

88. Till and Schenke (1972: 28 and 44) refer to the Apocryphon of John (BG 54.11–55.13), where the powers form the corpse of Adam from the four elements matter, darkness, desire and counterfeit spirit. See for the earthly elements also King 1995: 613. Petersen (1999: 156) calls the powers the earthly fetters.

89. Pasquier 1983: 21 and 84.

90. According to Tardieu (1984: 234 and 290-91), the Gospel of Mary would have inverted God's attributes mentioned in Exod. 20.5 and Isa. 33.22.

91. Poimandres, CH I.24-25.

92. Of matter: CH XIII.7; of darkness: CH XIII.11.

93. See for the Greek text and the translation Grese 1979: 12-15.

94. Grese 1979: 14-17.

95. The ten powers of God.

96. The twelve punishments.

whoever, through mercy, has obtained divine generation, after leaving behind bodily perception, knows himself to be composed from these powers and he rejoices. (CH XIII.10)[97]

This regeneration is called an intellectual perception and a true 'vision' (θέα CH XIII.3). The regenerated person is also described as being made 'steadfast' (ἀκλινής) by God, and thus to have come to be at Rest, which is called a blessing: not to be effected by the turbulence and confusion of the physical world (CH XIII.11, 20).[98] The beginning of the tractate states that it is about regeneration and the promise of silence (CH XIII.1). Similar notions occur in the Gospel of Mary: GosMar 10.13-14; 17.5; 8.5-6. It is also noteworthy that the producer of the regeneration is called: 'the Son of God, the one Human Being, by the will of God' (ὁ τοῦ θεοῦ παῖς, ἄνθρωπος εἷς, θελήματι θεοῦ CH XIII, 5).[99]

William Grese, who studied the meaning of this tractate and compared it to early Christian literature, points to Pauline baptismal terminology of putting off the old human being and clothing oneself with the new one, and dying and rising with Christ. Paul contrasts these two ways of life by means of lists of vices and virtues. Grese also refers to the Pauline terminology of being made a new creation.[100] Even more relevant is Grese's reference to the Letter to Titus in which the term παλιγγενεσία is used for baptism, which brings an end to the former sinful life and brings the gift of the Holy Spirit to make a new life possible (Titus 3.5). Furthermore, Grese points to the terminology of regeneration in the Gospel of John: of being born anew, thus becoming children of God (Jn 1.12-13). In the Gospel of John this is a change from bondage to release,[101] from darkness to light[102] and from death to life.[103] I would add that in the Gospel of John this way also includes the way upwards of the Son of Man himself, which is to be followed by his disciples, who are empowered to do this by the gift of the Holy Spirit.[104] On the basis of these parallels I suggest that Mary's teaching about the way upwards of the soul may be meant to illustrate what following the Son of Man, being made true Human Being, and living in accordance with one's renewed mind actually signifies.

By giving this account of the Saviour's teaching to her alone Mary also identifies the adversaries of the disciples. They are not the nations as the disciples assume, but they are certain powers. This recalls the Pauline statement that 'we are not contending against flesh and blood, but against the principalities, against the powers, against the world rulers of this present darkness, against the spiritual hosts of wickedness in the heavenly places' (Eph. 6.12). The readers of the Letter to the Ephesians are encouraged to put on the armour of God, which consists of truth,

---

97. See Grese 1979: 16-17.
98. For the text see Grese 1979: 16-17; 30-31. See also Grese's commentary on p. 136.
99. Grese 1979: 10.
100. Gal. 3.26-27; 6.15; Eph. 4.22–5.20; Col. 3.5-17; Rom. 6.3-11; 2 Cor. 5.17.
101. Jn 8.34; 12.31; 14.30; 8.31–32, 36.
102. Jn 3.19-21; 8.12; 12.46.
103. Jn 3.36; 4.14; 5.24; 6.47-51; 17.3.
104. Jn 13.36; 14.1-6; 16.5-11. Cf. 20.17, 21-22; 3.12-14; 13.1.

righteousness, the readiness to bring the gospel of peace, faith, salvation, and the word of God. These seven parts of the armour together seem to represent the manifold wisdom of God which will be made known to the principalities and powers in the heavenly places, because of Christ and through the church (Eph. 3.10). In consequence the readers are assured that 'in Christ Jesus our Lord we have boldness and confidence of access through our faith in him' (Eph. 3.11-12).

The powerful vices in the Gospel of Mary are conquered by the particular arguments of the soul. A parallel to this is found in Philo's writings. To Philo stability is experienced by drawing near to the Divine. Philo calls this an ascent of the soul on the royal road, leading towards the knowledge of the King.[105] Commenting on Num. 20.17, where Israel, on its way to the promised land of milk and honey, asks the king of Edom to be permitted to go through his land and promises not to pass through the fields but to go by the king's highway, Philo says:

> This road is, as I said by now, wisdom, by which alone suppliant souls can make their escape to the Uncreated. For we may well believe that he who walks unimpeded along the king's way will never flag or faint, till he comes into the presence of the king. (On the Unchangeableness of God 160)[106]

Philo says that the celestial and heavenly soul leaves the region of the earth, is drawn upwards and dwells with divine natures. It takes its fill of the vision of the incorruptible and genuine good and bids farewell to the good which is transient and spurious.[107]

In Philo's interpretation of Num. 20.17, where Edom refuses to allow Israel to pass through its land, Edom in his view means 'earthly' and Israel 'the one who sees God'.[108] Philo concludes that the earthly Edom, 'with its vices that war against us', purposes to bar the heavenly and royal road of virtue, but the divine reason on the other hand bars the road of Edom and its associates.[109] When Israel answers 'We will go by the mountain country' this means that they will 'examine each point by analysis and definition, and search out in everything its rationale, by which its essential nature is known'.[110] Philo does not here elaborate in what way Edom's vices war against Israel, but, as we already noted, Philo, in his exegesis of the tower of Babel, explains that minds, setting themselves up against God, use reasoning to build citadels of passions and vices, with the purpose to destroy righteousness and virtue.[111] They argue that good is the slave of evil, and passion stronger than the higher emotions, that prudence and virtue are subject to folly and vice, and thus must render obedience to every command of the despotic power.[112]

In a similar way the vices which war against the soul in the Gospel of Mary do

---

105. Pascher 1931: 10-23.
106. Colson and Whitaker 1960: III, 91.
107. On the Unchangeableness of God 151; Colson and Whitaker 1960: III, 87.
108. On the Unchangeableness of God 144; Colson and Whitaker 1960: III, 83.
109. On the Unchangeableness of God 164 and 180; Colson and Whitaker 1960: III, 91 and 99.
110. On the Unchangeableness of God 167; Colson and Whitaker 1960: III, 93.
111. On the Confusion of Tongues 86 and 101-102; Colson and Whitaker 1958: IV, 57 and 65.
112. On the Confusion of Tongues 91; Colson and Whitaker 1958: IV, 59.

so by emphasizing that the soul belongs to them instead of to the heavenly world. Their main question is paraphrased: where do you think you are going? Desire reminds the soul of the fact that she did not see her on her way downwards. How could she go upwards? The soul belongs to her. Ignorance reminds the soul of the fact that she is imprisoned by wickedness and thus not able to judge. Wrath with its seven appearances accuses the soul of being a killer of people and one who leaves places powerless. Perhaps the background of this accusation is the conviction that the soul is the life-giving centre of the body.

The soul's answer to Wrath summarizes the divine knowledge by which the soul overcomes the powers. Her Desire has been fulfilled, her Ignorance has died, what imprisons her is pierced (Darkness?) and what turned her is left powerless (Wrath?), since the soul has been freed from this world by a heavenly world. The soul argues that she indeed leaves places powerless as Wrath accuses her of, but these places are not the bodies: instead, she leaves Darkness, Desire, Ignorance, and Wrath itself powerless. Central to the soul's knowledge is the conviction that 'the All has been unloosened, both the earthly and the heavenly things': which is what the Saviour taught the disciples in GosMar 7.1-8. Freed from Darkness, Desire, Ignorance, and Wrath the soul can enter the Rest in Silence.

2.3.3. *The Figures Four and Seven.* Stoic philosophy was convinced of the in-escapable regularity by which all things run their course. The soul is determined by the body and by the natural surroundings in which it is born, as well as by the heavenly bodies. The whole cosmos and thus, in the view of the Stoics, also the body, consists of the four elements of earth, water, air and fire. In the cosmos the seven planets are made almost solely of fire. From the seven planets the soul receives its capacity for ordering, its five senses, and the growth which is necessary for the body. These are the seven parts of the soul.[113]

In the light of this it is striking that in Mary's account the Saviour uses the figures four and seven and arranges them in such a way that the fourth power, which is closest to heaven, has seven forms. The powers which, according to the Saviour, lay siege to the soul thus seem to be analogous to the elements which for the Stoics make the body and the cosmos what they are. However, it is not the material elements of the body that lay siege to the soul, but the powers of passion: not earth, but Darkness; not water, but Desire; not air, but Ignorance; not fire, but Wrath. Not the senses as such affect the soul, but Darkness, Desire, Ignorance, Jealousy of Death, Kingdom of the Flesh, Foolish Learning, and Hot Tempered Wisdom.

It seems likely that the Saviour in this way defines more closely what exactly the power contrary to Nature has caused by acting upon matter which thus has given birth to passion. The Saviour already told the disciples that this caused confusion in the whole body, which probably in a Stoic way is a metaphor for both the indi-vidual body and the body of the cosmos. But now Mary reveals that she has been told about what the confusion means for the individual. Apparently, the body,

---

113. Pohlenz 1948: 81-88, 217-18, 222-24.

being endowed with the natural elements of earth, water, air and fire with its seven parts for the soul, has come under the siege of the anti-natural vices of Darkness, Desire, Ignorance, and Wrath with its seven appearances. Redemption consists of being freed from the grip of these powers which are contrary to Nature. All Nature, however, in this case one's liberated soul, will be restored to its divine Root.

The figures four and seven in the ascent of the soul also stand for the liberation from the belief in one's bondage to the elements and planets. Not only Stoics believed that one's soul was determined by the elements and planets, but most of the ancient world. People believed the elements and planets to be gods and goddesses.[114] As Philo says:

> A great delusion has taken hold of the larger part of mankind in regard to a fact which properly should be established beyond all question in every mind to the exclusion of, or at least above, all others. For some have deified the four elements earth, water, air and fire, others the sun, moon, planets and fixed stars, others again the heaven by itself, others the whole world. But the highest and the most august, the Begetter, the Ruler of the great World-city, the Commander-in-Chief of the invincible host, the Pilot who ever steers all things in safety, Him they have hidden from sight by misleading titles assigned to objects of worship mentioned above. (On the Decalogue 52-53)[115]

Philo continues by mentioning the names: Kore, Demeter, Pluto, Poseidon, Hera, Hephaistus, Apollo, Artemis, Aphrodite, and Hermes. Elsewhere Philo assures his readers that they are but names for 'lifeless matter incapable of movement of itself and laid by the Artificer as a substratum for every kind of shape and quality'.[116] According to Paul, however, his readers were indeed in bondage to the elements of the world, like servants. But now the Spirit of the Son of God is in their hearts crying: Abba, Father. They now know God, and more than that, they are known by God, and are thus freed from their bondage.[117] To Paul, Christians are no longer subject to the elements, or to their ordinances.[118]

The Gospel of Mary emphasizes that not the four elements with the seven planets, nor the body with its senses, nor the (heathen) gods and goddesses with their ordinances, but the powers of passion, originating from what is opposite to Nature, keep the soul in bondage.

2.3.4. *Conclusion.* In Philo's comments we find themes related to those in the Gospel of Mary: seeing the Divine, stability, vices that try to stop the soul by reasoning and divine reason which enables the soul to continue on her way. In GosMar 10.10–17.7 the link is not made between these themes, but perhaps it occurred on the missing pages 11–14. In Philo's exegesis, however, the link is clear: whereas vices, by false reasoning, try to stop the soul from drawing near to

114. See Stricker (1990: 45-46) who refers to Philo and Paul.
115. Colson and Whitaker 1958: VII, 33.
116. On the Contemplative Life 3-4; Colson and Whitaker 1960: IX, 115.
117. Gal. 4.3-9.
118. Col. 2.20.

see the Divine and to experience stability, divine reason helps her to continue on her way and to reach her goal.

On the basis of the similarity of the related themes in Philo's comments and in the Gospel of Mary (as well as in part in CH XIII) I suggest that Mary recalls the themes of stability, the mind, and the ascent of the soul in GosMar 10.10–17.7 to reveal to the disciples the Saviour's teaching to her alone on what following the Son of Man, being made true Human Being, and living in accordance with one's renewed mind actually signifies. Mary identifies the adversaries as Darkness, Desire, Ignorance, and Wrath with its seven appearances and shows the wavering disciples the way stability can be obtained. On this way it is important to be able to distinguish false reasoning with the help of Divine reason. Divine reason consists of the conviction that the soul has been freed from this world by a heavenly world: the power opposite to Nature has been made powerless. This enables one to overcome the vices that try to keep the soul from drawing near to the Divine.

Mary, last but not least, through the words which the Saviour taught her, also shows that the soul's way to the Rest in Silence is not a road of suffering, but one of victory and joy. Her knowledge about this may already be behind her words in GosMar 9.14-20 where she encourages the weeping disciples to praise the greatness of the Son of Man, instead of to fear his suffering.

3. *The Author's Story of Mary Magdalene*

To the reader the story about Mary in the Gospel of Mary is complicated. Why does the author present so many different views of her? How do they relate to one other? What does it mean that the author or perhaps an early copyist gave the story the title the Gospel of Mary?

So far, we have studied the various views of Mary held by Peter, Andrew, Levi, the Saviour, and by Mary herself. We also studied the extra knowledge of the narrator and the narrator's view. Furthermore, we examined the meaning of Mary's teaching. In addition, we now turn to certain indications in the text and to the title in order to outline the development of the plot of the Gospel of Mary.

3.1. *Author's Indications in the Text*
The author is not only present as the narrator in the Gospel of Mary, but in the Gospel of Mary as a whole, since the author gave the Gospel of Mary its structure and perhaps also its title. In so doing the author gives the readers clues to understand the development of the story. In this section we will first examine Mary's role compared to the role of the Saviour. Then we turn to the themes of bringing forth either passion or peace and of making rules and laws. We will also go into the question of the identity of the adversaries and we conclude with the question of which actors in the story share the viewpoint of the author.

3.1.1. *Embracing, Being Blessed and Silent.* When looking at the structure of the Gospel of Mary the first thing that strikes the readers is the large role Mary has. The author allows her to speak from page 9 to page 17. If we assume that the post-

resurrection dialogue with the Saviour started earlier than page 7, for instance at the beginning of the missing pages of the Gospel of Mary or later, the author gives Mary as much or even more attention as he or she has given the Saviour. In this way the author encourages the readers to compare Mary to the Saviour and to question their relation. The author heightens the readers' curiosity by the different views of Peter, Andrew and Levi. According to Peter, the Saviour loved Mary more than the other women; according to Andrew, Mary is lying about the Saviour; and according to Levi, the Saviour knows Mary very well, he loved her more than all the others and he made her worthy. What is the author's view? By his or her choice of words the author gives the readers clues to answer this question.

When the Saviour departs, the author says that he embraces (ⲁϥⲁⲥⲡⲁⲍⲉ) the disciples.[119] The same is said of Mary. When she starts her teaching she also embraces (ⲁⲥⲁⲥⲡⲁⲍⲉ) the disciples.[120] By this, the author encourages the readers to believe that Mary in some way takes over the role of the Saviour. She seems to represent him. This belief is confirmed when the narrator in GosMar 17.8-9 assures the readers that Mary's teaching is a recapitulation of the teaching the Saviour gave to her.

Two other instances point to the conclusion that Mary represents the departed Saviour. First, the author not only calls the Saviour the Blessed One (ⲡⲘⲁⲕⲁⲣⲓ ⲟⲥ), but also assures the readers that the Saviour called Mary blessed (ⲚⲀⲓ Ⲁⲧⲉ).[121] Secondly, the author not only relates that Mary fell silent after her teaching about the soul having reached the Rest in Silence, but the author as the narrator also assures the readers that at this very point the Saviour had also fallen silent (GosMar 17.5-9).

3.1.2. *Bringing Forth Passion or Peace*. By using the verb ⲭⲡⲟ twice in crucial parts of the Saviour's teaching the author gives the readers another clue to understand the author's perspective in the Gospel of Mary. The Saviour explains in GosMar 8.2 that matter, being acted upon by an opposite nature, has given birth (ⲭⲡⲉ) to passion. He states further that this caused confusion in the whole body. When the Saviour departs in GosMar 8.14-15 he encourages the disciples to give birth (ⲭⲡⲟⲥ) to his peace and not to be led astray. The readers thus have a standard by which to judge the disciples' behaviour in the Gospel of Mary. Are they bringing forth passion or peace? When they bring forth passion they are apparently inspired by what is contrary to Nature. When they bring forth peace, they stay by the Saviour.

The disciples in GosMar 9.6-12 bring forth passion, which arises from their despair, which is a result of focusing on the suffering of the Son of Man. Mary brings forth peace, which is apparent from her calmness and her ability to encourage the disciples by focusing on the Son of Man's greatness (GosMar 9.14-20). The disciples, in reaction to Mary's words and behaviour, bring forth peace

---

119. GosMar 8.12-13.
120. GosMar 9.13.
121. GosMar 8.12 and GosMar 10.14. P Oxy 3525.20 reads μακάρια where the Coptic text of BG1 has ⲚⲀⲓ Ⲁⲧⲉ.

which results from their willingness to focus on the words of the Saviour instead of on the suffering Son of Man (GosMar 9.22). Mary again brings forth peace, which is manifest in her silence, after she teaches the disciples about how to reach stability (GosMar 17.7-9), but this silence is violently disturbed, since Andrew and Peter bring forth passion as a reaction to Mary's teaching, Andrew becoming distrustful and Peter becoming angry and confused (GosMar 17.15-22). Mary thereupon brings forth passion in her reaction to Peter: she starts to weep (GosMar 18.1). Levi, in contrast, brings forth peace, namely in the calm manner in which he corrects Peter and in his encouragement to return to the Saviour's instruction to proclaim the gospel (GosMar 18.8-21).

Thus Mary, when conveying her knowledge of the Saviour, and the disciples when focusing on the Saviour's teaching, plus Levi, when returning to the Saviour's teaching, stay close to the Saviour. The disciples, on the other hand, when they focus on the suffering of the Son of Man, and Peter and Andrew, when they attack Mary, and also Mary, when she allows herself to be touched by the implications of their attack, are under the influence of what is contrary to Nature.

3.1.3. *Making Rules and Laws.* By introducing the theme of making rules and laws, the author gives an extra clue to evaluate the behaviour of Peter and Andrew. The Saviour in the Gospel of Mary, before departing, warns the disciples against making rules and laws other than the one rule he has given to them (GosMar 8.22–9.4). This single unknown rule the Saviour gave in the Gospel of Mary may have alluded to the one law Jesus gave according to the New Testament writings: the law of love.

The reactions of Andrew and Peter show that they adhere to other rules as well. When Andrew asks the brothers (and sisters), what they think of his opinion that what Mary says does not come from the Saviour, he explains his view by stating that Mary's words seem to be according to another train of thought. Apparently, Andrew is of the opinion that he and the others share a sort of canon of teaching of the Saviour. Teaching that seems different is not to be viewed as coming from the Saviour. Thus, Andrew has a clear rule: only the teaching of the Saviour that the brothers (and sisters) hold as a canon determines the authenticity of what others add from their knowledge of the Saviour.

Peter, apparently, has rules about the roles of women and men. According to Peter, a man is not to listen to a woman, a man should not speak to a woman alone and a woman disciple is never above male disciples.

The Saviour in the Gospel of Mary, before he departs, warns the disciples that adhering rules other than the one he gave will imprison them. And indeed, Andrew and Peter, as a result of their extra rules, are no longer free to really listen to what the Saviour teaches them through Mary. They are no longer able to discuss the content of the Saviour's words, as they did before, but instead accuse Mary of falsehood.

3.1.4. *Being Like the Adversaries.* Levi, when rebuking Peter, compares his manner of arguing with 'the woman' to that of 'these adversaries' (ⲛⲓ ⲁⲛⲧ ⲓ ⲕⲉ ⲓ ⲙⲉⲛⲟⲥ).

According to Levi, Peter does not discuss (ⲚⲠⲣⲄⲨⲘⲚⲀⲌⲈ) the words of the Saviour as he did with his brothers (and sisters), their hearts having been turned inwards by Mary to the Good One. Instead, in Levi's view, with 'the woman' Peter discusses (ⲈⲔⲠⲣⲄⲨⲘⲚⲀⲌⲈ) as 'these adversaries' do.[122]

Who are these adversaries to whom Levi refers? Most exegetes, in a Gnostic interpretation of the text, suggest that 'these adversaries' are those who the Gospel of Mary is supposed to oppose, namely, orthodox Christians.[123] Peter and Andrew with their additional rules would represent the viewpoints of the catholic Church. The author, however, gives three clues as to the identity of the adversaries in the Gospel of Mary.

First, in the extant pages of the Gospel of Mary there are several opinions and attitudes the disciples must be on their guard against. GosMar 8.15-19 warns against people who want to lead the disciples astray, saying that the Son of Man is here or there. GosMar 8.22–9.4 warns against people who would give additional laws and rules. GosMar 9.7-12 mentions the 'nations' that did not spare the Son of Man and will consequently not spare the disciples. GosMar 15.1–17.7 describes the powers Darkness, Desire, Ignorance, and Wrath which try to keep the soul from her way upwards, and GosMar 17.10-22 portrays Andrew and Peter who try to prevent the other disciples from hearing words of the Saviour. The author in the Gospel of Mary thus presents a fivefold characterization of adversaries.

Secondly, when Levi corrects Peter he calls him hot-tempered (ⲚⲢⲈϥⲚⲞⲨⲞⲤ GosMar 18.7-8). This is the same word the author uses to describe the seventh power of Wrath: the hot-tempered Wisdom (ⲦⲤⲞⲫⲒⲀ ⲚⲢⲈϥⲚⲞⲨⲞⲤ GosMar 16.11-12). Thus the author encourages the reader to see something of this power in Peter.

Thirdly, the comparison Levi uses is unfinished and must be completed by the readers. With whom do 'these adversaries' argue, so that Peter's arguing with 'the woman' is compared to their behaviour? In the Gospel of Mary as we have it only Andrew and Peter and the powers Darkness, Desire, Ignorance and Wrath really argue in the sense that the author describes their arguments. Andrew and Peter argue about 'she' and 'a woman', while the Powers argue with the soul (ⲦⲈϥⲨⲬⲎ), which is a feminine word. In this way the author invites the readers to finish Levi's comparison as follows:

> Peter, you have always been hot-tempered.
> Now I see you arguing with the woman
> as these adversaries (do with the soul).

The author thus unmasks the adversaries through Levi's words. They are not those who lead the disciples astray, they are not the nations who did not spare the Son of Man and will not spare the disciples, they are not Andrew and Peter or others with their additional rules, but they are the powers of passion and of what is contrary to Nature in them and through them.[124]

---

122. Cf. GosMar 9.23 and 18.9-10. P Oxy 3525.13-14 and P Ryl 463, verso 3 have συνζητέω.

123. Pagels 1981: 77; Perkins 1980: 133; Pasquier 1983: 24; Quispel 1988: 81; Marjanen 1996: 221-23.

124. See also King 1995: 615, but in her view these powers are the Powers of Matter. Petersen

Also another important view becomes apparent. When Levi implicitly refers to the Powers that keep the soul from her way upwards as 'these adversaries', he apparently makes use of Mary's teaching. However, Levi does not explicitly acknowledge her teaching as coming from the Saviour. He says 'surely the Saviour knows her very well. That is why he loved her more than us' (GosMar 18.12-15). As readers one might have expected him to say instead: that is why he told her more than us. In contrast, Levi rejects Peter's reasoning by emphasizing the Saviour's love for 'the woman'.

3.1.5. *False Reasoning Versus Divine Reason.* The structure of the Gospel of Mary as we have it consists of dialogues. Throughout the Gospel certain reasoning is exposed as false. Additionally, the author, especially through the teaching about the way upwards of the soul, shows that it is of vital importance to expose false reasoning with the help of Divine reason, since this is the way the soul is liberated from the grip of the Powers and through which she reaches the Rest in Silence.

The Saviour in GosMar 7 exposes the disciples' reasoning about matter and sin as false. Mary in GosMar 9.18-20 shows that the reasoning of the disciples about the suffering Son of Man is false. The soul in GosMar 15.1–17.7 exposes the reasoning of the Powers as false. The narrator in GosMar 17.7-9 and Levi in GosMar 18.7-15 expose the reasoning of Peter and Andrew as false. But what about the reasoning of Levi? The author apparently leaves this question open, since no one in the text reacts on Levi's words.

How are the readers to evaluate Levi's view on Mary? In any case, Levi brings forth peace, appearing from his calmness and his encouragement to return to the Saviour's instruction. Levi also implicitly makes use of Mary's teaching which, according to the extra knowledge of the narrator, indeed derives from the Saviour. But what about Levi's referring to Mary as 'the woman', who has been 'made worthy' by the Saviour? What about the absence in Levi's correction of Peter of an explicit acknowledgment of Mary's teaching as coming from the Saviour? What about Levi's emphasis on the Saviour's love for 'the woman'?

It is difficult to answer these questions, but by using similar expressions the author invites the readers to compare Levi's words to Peter to Mary's words to the weeping disciples. Mary in GosMar 9.18 uses the phrase ΜΑΛΛΟΝ ΔЄ ΜΑΡΠ̄CΜΟΥ. Levi in GosMar 18.15 uses a similar expression: ΜΑΛΛΟΝ ΜΑΡΠ̄ΩΙΠЄ.

Mary says:

(1999: 167) argues that the Archons are meant and points to Authoritative Teaching (NHC VI.30.6, 27; 31.9), where the same figure is called ΔΙΑΒΟΛΟC and ΠΑΝΤΙΚЄΙΜЄΝΟC. Hartenstein (2000: 135) points to 1 Tim. 5.14, where also in the context of women's behaviour 'the adversary' is mentioned, which according to Hartenstein is an adversary from outside and according to Petersen (1999: 167) is the same as Satan in 1 Tim. 5.15. The parallel is interesting, since where the Gospel of Mary accuses Peter of being hot-tempered like the adversaries, instead in 1 Tim. 5.14 the women are called on to behave in a more womanly manner and thus not to occasion the reproaches of the adversary.

> Do not weep and do not grieve and do not be in two minds, for his grace will be with you all and will shelter you. *Rather let us praise* his greatness, because he has prepared us. He has made us (true) Human Being. (GosMar 9.18-20)

Levi says:

> Surely the Saviour knows her very well, that is why he loved her more than us. *Rather let us be ashamed* and clothe ourselves with the perfect Human Being. Let us bring him forth to us, as he commanded us. Let us preach the Gospel, without laying down any other rule or law than the one the Saviour said. (GosMar 18.12-21)

From the comparison it becomes clear, that, whereas Mary includes herself with her use of the word 'us', Levi excludes her. According to Mary, she obviously belongs to the 'us' who have been prepared to bring the Gospel and who have been made (true) Human Being: all disciples have been prepared and made (true) Human Being. In this sense all have been made 'worthy'.

According to Levi, Mary does not belong to the 'us' that should be ashamed, should clothe themselves with the perfect Human Being, and proclaim the Gospel. In Levi's view, Mary is a case apart, specifically having been made 'worthy'. It remains unclear what exactly Levi means by this. Has Mary especially been made worthy to teach the brothers, whereas the brothers (and sisters) would not need such worthiness? Why does Mary not need to clothe herself with the perfect Human Being as the brothers (and sisters)? Because she has done this already? Why does she not need to proclaim the Gospel as the brothers (and sisters)? Because she already has done so with her teaching to the disciples? Does Levi perhaps mean that the Saviour gave Mary, as a woman, a special warrant to teach the disciples, but did not authorize her to proclaim the Gospel to the nations as the male (and female) disciples are supposed to do?

One thing is clear: while unmasking Peter's reasoning, Levi, like Peter, assumes that Mary as 'the woman' is apart from 'us'. Mary's view of herself and the disciples is different. To her the 'us' includes her, and she as a woman is not a case apart.

Who is right: Mary or Levi? What is the view of the author? Levi's view is the end of the Gospel of Mary. Levi has the last word. This seems to leave the readers in uncertainty. There is, however, one indication yet to explore: the title.

3.2. *The Title*

It is not wholly true that the Gospel of Mary ends with the words of Levi. There is the reaction of the disciples. They indeed begin to proclaim the Gospel. Secondly, there is the title. The Gospel of Mary really ends with the title. This title has been preserved in the fifth-century Coptic text as well as in the third-century Greek text. On this basis we can safely assume that either the author him or herself added the title, or some very early copyist.

3.2.1. *A Gospel Named after a Woman.* We must note that the title of the Gospel of Mary is exceptional, since no other known Gospel from early Christianity is

named after a woman. The names which occur in Gospel titles refer to men: Mark, Matthew, Luke, John, Peter, the Twelve Apostles, Thomas, Philip, Matthias, Jude, James, Cerinth, Basilides, Marcion, Apelles, Bardesanes, and Mani.

To an orthodox audience it would have been offensive for a book to be ascribed to a woman. Several New Testament passages were quoted over and over again to explain that women were not allowed to have any authority over men.

In Ephesians, Colossians and 1 Peter, wives are encouraged to be submissive to their husbands, while the husbands are told to love their wives (Eph. 5.21-33; Col. 3.18-19; 1 Pet. 3.1-7). Paul, when demanding that women wear veils when praying or prophesying (1 Cor. 11.1-16), argues that the reason for this is that the head of every man is Christ, the head of a wife is her husband and the head of Christ is God. However, later in the argument he changes from wives to woman in general, referring to the creation: 'For man was not made from woman, but woman from man. Neither was man created for woman, but woman for man' (1 Cor. 11.8-9).

In addition, while 1 Pet. 3.1-7 refers to the submissiveness of Sarah to Abraham, in 1 Tim. 2.1-11 the creation analogy is used again: 'For Adam was formed first, then Eve', continuing thus 'and Adam was not deceived, but the woman was deceived and became a transgressor'. The author concludes that a woman has to learn with all submissiveness: 'I permit no woman to teach or to have authority over men: she is to keep silent'. This text and the possibly non-Pauline text in 1 Cor. 14.34-36 about women who are to keep silent in the assemblies[125] were in the centuries that followed quoted again and again to emphasize that women were not allowed to have authority over men.

In reference to women writing books and thus having authority over men, Schüssler Fiorenza cites the fourth-century Dialogue Between a Montanist and an Orthodox which, through means of a discussion between a Montanist and an orthodox Christian, shows their respective viewpoints.[126] The orthodox viewpoint may reflect a very early stand, since it corresponds to the arguments in the first-century letters, which claim that women are to be submissive to men.

The quotation from the Dialogue comments on women's authority, concentrating on those women who wrote books, like the second-century Montanist prophetesses Prisca and Maximilla.

> Orthodox: We do not reject the prophecies of women. Blessed Mary prophesied when she said: 'Henceforth all generations shall call me blessed'. And as you yourself say, Philip had daughters who prophesied and Mary, the sister of Aaron, prophesied. But we do not permit women to speak in the assemblies, nor to have authority over men, to the point of writing books in their own name: since, such is, indeed, the implication for them of praying with uncovered head (...) Wasn't Mary, the Mother of God, able to write books in her own name? To avoid dishonoring her head by placing herself above men, she did not do so.

125. Verses 33b-36 would have been added around the turn of the century. For extended text critical and literary arguments see Fee 1994: 272-81.

126. Schüssler Fiorenza 1983: 307-309. She uses the English translation of Gryson 1972: 129-31. The Greek text was first published by Ficker 1905.

> Montanist: Did you say that to pray or to prophesy with uncovered head implies not to write books?
> Orthodox: Perfectly.
> Montanist: When Blessed Mary says: 'Henceforth all generations shall call me blessed', does she or doesn't she speak freely and openly?
> Orthodox: Since the Gospel is not written in her name, she has a veil in the Evangelist.[127]

Would a Gospel then, primarily based on the authority of Mary Magdalene be acceptable? Later in the discussion the Montanist asks the crucial question:

> Montanist: Is it because they have written books that you do not receive Prisca and Maximilla?
> Orthodox: It is not *only* for this reason, but also because they were false prophetesses, following their guide Montanus.[128]

Schüssler Fiorenza also refers to the fourth-century Didymus the Blind who propounds a similar argument, likewise drawing heavily on the first-century letters:

> Scripture recognizes as prophetesses the four daughters of Philip, Deborah, Mary, the sister of Aaron, and Mary, the mother of God, who said, as recorded in the Gospel: 'Henceforth all women and all generations shall call me blessed'. But in Scripture there are no books written in their name. On the contrary, the Apostle says in First Timothy: 'I do not permit women to teach', and again in First Corinthians: 'Every woman who prays or prophesies with uncovered head dishonors her head'. He means that he does not permit a woman to write books impudently, on her own authority, nor to teach in the assemblies, because, by doing so, she offends her head, man: for 'the head of woman is man, and the head of man is Christ'. The reason for the silence imposed on women is obvious: woman's teaching in the beginning caused considerable havoc to the human race; for the apostle writes: 'It is not the man who was deceived, but the woman'. (On the Trinity 3.41.3)[129]

When Origen in the first half of the third century comments on the verse 'for it is shameful for a woman to speak in the community' from Paul's first letter to the Corinthians, he already draws on the same canonical examples of prophesying women, which the disciples of Prisca and Maximilla, he states, use as their argument. Origen argues that, when these biblical figures (the daughters of Philip, Deborah, Mary the sister of Aaron, Hulda, Anne the daughter of Phanuel) prophesied, they did not do so in public, since their prophesies are not recorded in Scripture. He refers to 1 Tim. 2.12 and Titus 2.3-5 concluding that a woman is to keep silent, 'even if she says admirable or holy things' and he continues 'however, it comes out of the mouth of a woman'.[130]

Tertullian, even after he became inclined to Montanism himself, quoted Paul's first letter to the Corinthians as fervently as he did before. Although in two cases he

---

127. Schüssler Fiorenza 1983: 308. Ficker 1905: 456-57.
128. Schüssler Fiorenza 1983: 309 (italics added by EAB). Ficker 1905: 458.
129. Schüssler Fiorenza 1983: 309. See also Gryson 1972: 130-31.
130. Gryson 1972: 56-57. See Jenkins 1909: 242.

cites the prophesies of Prisca and Maximilla he still argues that women are not allowed to speak in the assemblies, to teach, to baptize, to serve the eucharist, or to do any task that belongs to males. This, he adds, not only applies to married women, but to all women, including the unmarried.[131]

Thus, the second-century Prisca and Maximilla are not only discussed because of the content of their prophesies, but also because they as women prophesy in public and write books, and in doing so claim authority over men. Their authority is attacked with quotations from the first-century letters. It is striking that Clement of Alexandria, who clearly defends the equality of men and women, nevertheless, also does the same. According to him, although men and women have the same nature and are both capable of attaining self control and virtue, their physical differences lead to inequality. Quoting the first letter to the Corinthians, Ephesians and Colossians he argues that woman must submit to man.[132]

Apparently there were, already in the second century, Christians and Christian communities who would reject a Gospel written by a woman or which relied on the authority of a woman. The choice of the author or an early copyist to give the Gospel of Mary its name is thus not a neutral one. It acknowledges the unorthodox stand that a woman may have authority, including authority over men.

3.2.2. *The Impact of the Title.* We saw earlier that the narrator with his or her extra knowledge is not a neutral informer, but he or she is on Mary's side. He or she is convinced of Mary's integrity and of her importance for the Gospel message, since Mary remembers sayings of Jesus which the other disciples appear not to know and she teaches the disciples as she has been taught by the Saviour. Moreover, according to the narrator, Mary has the gift of actually turning the disciples' hearts to the Son of Man within them. In addition we saw that also the author takes a certain viewpoint: against Andrew and Peter and in favour of Mary and Levi.

By giving the writing the title 'Gospel of Mary', the author or early copyist supports the narrator's view and makes an even more radical choice. The title invites the readers to see not only Mary, but the whole writing in a certain light. The writing is not about questions of the disciples or discussions between them, about words of Mary or wisdom of Mary or about the Gospel of the Kingdom of the Son of Man. The writing is about the Gospel of Mary. This means that the teaching of Mary is central in the writing as a whole and that Mary's teaching about the Saviour is described as Gospel.

The title thus gives a vital clue to the readers: Mary's teaching is at the centre. When we return to the unanswered question of whether Mary or Levi is right, when they give opposite opinions on Mary as a woman belonging to the 'us' of the disciples, we can thus state that the Gospel of Mary shares Mary's viewpoint and not Levi's. Not only according to Mary, but also according to the one who gave the book its title, Mary belongs to the 'us' who have been prepared to bring the Gospel

---

131. Gryson 1972: 44. Tertullian, On Head-coverings for Unmarried Girls 9.1.
132. Roukema 1996: 163. Stromateis IV.58.2–60.3. Clement quotes 1 Cor. 11.3, 8, 11; Eph. 5.21-25, 28-29; Col. 3.18–4.1.

and who have been made (true) Human Being. Mary as 'the woman' has not specifically been made 'worthy' as Levi suggests. She simply belongs to the others: all have been prepared to proclaim the Gospel and have been made (true) Human Being.

3.3. *The Development of the Author's Story*
Because of the title it would not be surprising if the beginning of the Gospel of Mary originally also was about Mary Magdalene. The first pages of the Gospel of Mary could have been about Mary telling the disciples of Jesus' crucifixion, of his death and of her visit to Jesus' tomb, comparable to accounts in the New Testament Gospels. One could above all think of the Gospel of John in which Mary is said to have gone to the disciples to tell them that she had seen the Lord and what he had told her (Jn 20.18).

One could also think of the second-century Epistula Apostolorum, which, after describing several stories from Jesus' life, turns to his death and portrays Mary telling the disciples about his resurrection. When she is not believed, she returns to the Lord to tell him this. Then he sends Sarah. In the Coptic version these women are Martha and Mary. When the apostles still do not believe them, the Lord accompanies the women, whom the author calls 'Mary and her sisters' (EpAp 11.1), and rebukes the apostles (EpAp 9.4, 11-16). In this context a dialogue between the disciples and the Lord occurs, where various themes arise, such as the Lord's incarnation, his returning, the end of the world, the future of the disciples, the laws of the Lord, the instruction to proclaim the Gospel, the suffering of the disciples and their being uplifted with Jesus, to reach the final Rest.

In the Gospel of Mary the dialogue with the Saviour which starts somewhere before GosMar 7 may well have been situated in a similar situation as in the Epistula Apostolorum. The Saviour, on the missing pages at the beginning of the Gospel of Mary, perhaps appeared after Mary's testimony of the resurrection to affirm the reliability of her words and to go into certain themes. The difference with the Epistula Apostolorum is that the Gospel of Mary does not end with the Lord's departure, as does the Epistula Apostolorum (EpAp 51), but, after the Saviour's departure, continues the story and tells of the disciples' wavering reaction to the Saviour's instructions and of Mary's teaching.

In the Gospel of Mary the development of the story after the Saviour's departure is quite lively. The story not only gives the content of Mary's teaching, but also presents several different views of her. After her teaching on the greatness of the Son of Man, she turns the disciples' hearts inwards to the Son of Man in them. Thanks to Mary they begin to discuss the words of the Saviour, apparently with the aim of proclaiming the Gospel. It seems that initially only the men are doing this, since Peter asks Mary to join them, because in his view she is special among the women. According to Peter, the Saviour loved her more than the rest of the women.

The words of the Saviour, as yet unknown to the disciples, which Mary at Peter's request recalls, are meant to illustrate in a more profound way the teaching of the Saviour to all the disciples about the Son of Man being within, who is to be followed, sought after, and found. Whereas the disciples think of the Son of Man as the one who suffered and fear their own suffering, Mary first underlines his greatness, which has prepared them and made them (true) Human Being. Now, by recalling words of the Saviour that she knows and the others do not, she shows the way out of their wavering. The disciples do not depend on their soul's senses, nor do they need to wait for divine inspiration from outside. The Saviour has explained to Mary that there are not two categories, soul and spirit, but three. Their own soul's *nous* which has the spirit of the Son of Man blown into it enables them, first, to see the Lord's greatness; second, to become stable; and third, to experience bliss.

After the missing pages Mary tells the disciples what the Saviour taught her about the way through which stability can be achieved. By identifying false reasoning with the help of Divine reason the powers of passion, Darkness, Desire, Ignorance, and Wrath, the real adversaries – originating from what is opposite to Nature and keeping the soul in bondage – can be joyfully overcome. The author is clear that Mary's teaching about the words of the Saviour is what the Gospel is about. But still the Gospel does not end here. First the trustworthiness of Mary as a woman is put into doubt.

Andrew reacts quite bluntly to what 'she' says. Mary's words are simply not from the Saviour since they seem to be at odds with what the disciples already know. Peter becomes entangled in social rules about 'a woman' and men. Upon Mary's shocked reaction Levi tries to mediate but still excludes 'the woman' from the 'we' group of disciples. The Gospel of Mary ends here, which leaves the readers uncertain. Are Mary's words accepted? Is her teaching incorporated? The title shows that this is the case for the author or an early copyist. He or she wants the readers to accept Mary's teaching and to understand its importance. But Andrew, Peter, and even Levi seem to have decided to do without her. For them, the teaching Mary as a woman is a problem.

4. *The Author's Portrayal of Mary Magdalene*

In the Gospel of Mary the author tells a complicated story, in which the teaching of Mary is presented as well as several views of her. In this section we will go into the author's portrayal of Mary Magdalene. What is, according to the author, her relation to the Saviour, what is her position among the disciples and what is her function in the story?

4.1. *Mary Magdalene's Relation to Jesus*
Apparently, in the author's view, Mary is a disciple of Jesus, the Saviour, in the sense that she has been taught by him. She also has had access to teaching that the others have not had. She alone has been taught by the Saviour about the way through which stability can be experienced, about who the adversaries are on this way, and how to handle them.

In addition, she has been prepared by the Son of Man to proclaim the Gospel of his Kingdom and has been made (true) Human Being, like the other disciples. Furthermore, the author gives indications that Mary, in the author's view, after the

Saviour has departed, represents him. She is able to turn the disciples' hearts inwards to the Son of Man within.

The author also shows how the Saviour regards Mary. He calls her blessed, because she endeavours to live according to her renewed mind and is going the way upwards to the Divine. Mary's esteem for the Saviour appears from her eagerness to learn from him. She is not focused on his suffering, but on his greatness. She has seen him glorified in a vision.

4.2. *Mary Magdalene Among the Disciples*
In the author's view, Mary is a disciple among the disciples. After the crucifixion and the resurrection of the Son of Man, she is a special disciple, because she, after his departure, represents him and has a role in persuading the disciples to go and proclaim the Gospel of the Kingdom of the Son of Man.

The author shows that the position of Mary among the disciples is ambiguous. Her encouraging the weeping disciples is accepted by them and apparently arouses their curiosity to know more about her view of the Saviour. But when she talks more this is not accepted. It is difficult to understand precisely why this is the case. What exactly makes Andrew and Peter so angry, and why does Levi hesitate to plainly acknowledge that her teaching comes from the Saviour?

The author signals two related problems: the content of Mary's teaching and her being a woman. This generates a third problem: the relation between Mary and the Saviour. Would the Saviour as a man have taught Mary as a woman alone? Could she really know things that differ from what the others know?

The author presents three views of Mary among the disciples. First, Mary lies about the Saviour, since she tells things that seem to differ from those which the disciples already know. Moreover, the Saviour, as a man, would never have told her, as a woman, things that the male disciples would need to listen to. Secondly, Mary knows more than the other disciples, since the Saviour loved her more than the rest of the women. Thirdly, the Saviour has made Mary worthy, because he knows her thoroughly. That is why he loved her more than the others. Each of these three views is rejected by the author. Mary is not lying nor has she as 'the woman' specifically been made worthy, singled out by the Saviour because of his love and knowledge of her. In the view of the author, Mary is simply a disciple like the others, having been prepared and made (true) Human Being like them, although in this case knowing things that the others do not know and acting accordingly.

4.3. *Mary Magdalene's Function in the Story*
Mary Magdalene and her teaching are the subject of the story of the Gospel of Mary. That is why the author gives Mary Magdalene such a large and active role. As I suggested, the first missing pages of the Gospel of Mary may have contained Mary Magdalene's testimony of the death, burial and resurrection of the Lord, as in Matthew, Luke and John, the second ending of Mark, and the Epistula Apostolorum. When her testimony is not believed the Saviour himself appears to show that Mary has the authority to instruct the disciples and to summon them to proclaim the Gospel of the Kingdom of the Son of Man.

To the author, Mary's function in the story is crucial. This is evident from the fact that she is able to help the disciples to turn their hearts inwards, away from their being sadly focused on the suffering of the Son of Man, inflicted by 'the nations'. She points them to the joyous recognition of his greatness, which consists of his having prepared the disciples to preach the Gospel and of having made them (true) Human Being. In line with the Saviour's teaching to Mary alone, she also shows the identity of the real adversaries, the importance of the disciples' renewed minds, and the way through which stability can be experienced.

Although to the author Mary's teaching is crucial, the story makes clear that Andrew, Peter and Levi are of a different opinion, because Mary is not a man, but a woman. By the sudden and unexpected end of the Gospel of Mary the author, however, invites the readers to re-read the Gospel, to reconsider the function of Mary and to share the author's view.

Chapter 5

MARY MAGDALENE ACCORDING TO THE GOSPEL OF MARK

To be able to investigate the origin of the portrayal of Mary Magdalene in the Gospel of Mary, we now turn to the New Testament Gospels. The New Testament Gospels contain the earliest written material on Mary Magdalene. In each of the New Testament Gospels the general outline of the story of Mary Magdalene is similar: she is introduced rather abruptly and plays her part towards the end of their accounts in the events relating to the crucifixion of Jesus, his burial, and his resurrection.

Within this basic framework Mark, Matthew, Luke and John each appear to give Mary Magdalene a very different role. The following chapters identify their portrayals of Mary Magdalene. To be able to do this we will not only study the texts in which Mary Magdalene occurs, but also analyse the concepts of Markan, Matthean, Lukan and Johannine discipleship, their opinions of the Twelve, and their views on women.

1. *Mark's Introduction of Mary Magdalene*

Mark introduces the women followers of Jesus at the end of the Gospel, immediately after the death of Jesus. Mark relates:

> There were also women looking on from afar, among whom were Mary Magdalene and Mary the mother of James the younger and of Joses, and Salome, who, when he was in Galilee, followed him and ministered to him; and also many other women who came up with him to Jerusalem. (15.40-41)

Mark distinguishes between two groups of women: the first group is small and consists of women identified by name; the second larger group consists of many women who remain unnamed. Mark describes the small group as having been with Jesus longer, following him and ministering to him in Galilee. The larger group has decided at some point to go up with him to Jerusalem.[1]

Here, almost at the end of the Gospel, Mark for the first time declares that a considerable number of women had been following Jesus. What are we to think of these women? What is their function in Mark's story? And what about Mary Magdalene in their midst? To be able to answer these questions this chapter not

---

1. ἠκολούθουν and διηκόνουν: past continuous; συναναβᾶσαι ingressive aorist.

only focuses on Mark, but also on the historical situation at the time.

In her pioneering and influential work, *In Memory of Her: A Feminist Theological Reconstruction of Christian Origins*, Elisabeth Schüssler Fiorenza coined the phrase 'discipleship of equals'. In her view no distinction can be made between male and female disciples at the beginning of the Jesus movement. They were all disciples of one teacher, all brothers and sisters of Jesus. The gospel of the kingdom of God allowed no distinction. It was meant for everyone without exception.[2] Although Schüssler Fiorenza emphasized that her method of feminist historiography allows no conclusion with regard to historical 'reality', but rather generates a 'different historical imagination',[3] her reconstruction of discipleship as a 'discipleship of equals' challenges one to reflect on 'reality' again.[4] Especially because her insight into the use and the meaning of androcentric language provides a new perspective on the New Testament texts about the disciples. In *In Memory of Her* she says:

> A *historically adequate* translation must take into account the interpretative implications of androcentric language which functioned as inclusive language in a patriarchal culture. Such androcentric inclusive language mentions women only when their presence has become in any way a problem or when they are 'exceptional', but it does not mention women in so-called normal situations.[5]

Could it be historically adequate to imagine women and men when the word 'disciples' occurs in the New Testament, although the Synoptic Gospel writers allow the women followers of Jesus only to play a role at the end of their accounts?[6]

Two important arguments have been raised which seem to preclude the possibility that women could have been disciples. The first argument is the utter implausibility of the thought. Given the social status of women at that time, female discipleship would simply be inconceivable: it would not have been the custom for women and men to travel together and disciples of a rabbi normally would have been exclusively male since women were not to study Torah. If Jesus did have women disciples, why do the New Testament Gospels give no indication whatsoever of the scandal this must have caused? The second argument against the discipleship of women is that the New Testament Gospels do not record the call of a specific woman to be a disciple and that the disciples in general seem to be the male Twelve.[7]

In this chapter we will examine Mark's view on women and discipleship and go into the arguments and sources of scholars who investigate the historical situation and positions women held in Second Temple Jewish society and early Christianity. On the basis of this, and on the basis of the exegesis of Mark's story about the

---

2.   Schüssler Fiorenza 1983: 106-159.
3.   Schüssler Fiorenza 1992: 80-101, esp. 92
4.   See also De Boer 1997: 31-38.
5.   Schüssler Fiorenza 1983: 44.
6.   Mt. 27.55-28.10; Mk 15.40–16.11. Luke mentions the women in 8.1-3, but they also play their part at the end of his account in 23.49–24.11.
7.   E.g. Sanders 1993: 110; Schweizer 1982; Rengstorf 1977: 460-61.

women at the end of the Gospel, we will be able to conclude to the specific Markan portrayal of Mary Magdalene.

2. *Women and Discipleship in Mark*

2.1. *The Large Group of Women Followers*
Does Mark give any clue as to the position of the large group of women going up with Jesus to Jerusalem? They are not mentioned earlier, but is there any reference in Mark's story about the beginning of their going up with Jesus to Jerusalem? Are they perhaps somewhere implied?

The going up of the large group of women probably refers to the pilgrimage to Jerusalem for the sacred festival of Passover.[8] Some scholars suggest that the women follow Jesus in his pilgrimage to Jerusalem as his disciples, while others argue that they are mainly going as pilgrims themselves.[9] Mk 10.32 describes the going up of Jesus to Jerusalem, also mentioning 'those who follow'. Does Mark here allude to a large group of followers, among them perhaps the large group of women of 15.41? If so, one could conclude that Mark suggests that the large group of women in 15.41 followed Jesus as disciples, since following Jesus implies discipleship.[10]

Mk 10.32 is a peculiar verse:

> And they were on the road, going up to Jerusalem, and Jesus was walking ahead of them; and they were amazed, and those who followed were afraid. And taking the twelve again, he began to tell them what was to happen to him. (10.32)

'They' who are 'amazed' seem to be the disciples, who in 10.23-27 are also amazed by how hard Jesus says it is to enter the Kingdom of God, especially for the rich.[11] But who are 'those' in 10.32 who are 'afraid'? Some commentators indeed argue that Mark here alludes to the large group of women going up with him to Jerusalem.[12]

This might be possible, but the direct context seems to point to the Twelve, differentiating between the Twelve and the disciples in general.[13] Whereas the disciples, reacting to the departure of the pious rich man and to the saying of Jesus

---

8.   Cf. Lk. 2.42; Jn 2.13; 5.1; 7.8, 10, 14; 11.55. That women did participate in the annual pilgrimages (Passover, Shavuot and Sukkot) to Jerusalem is shown by Ilan 1995a: 179-80. See also Safrai 1991: 15-21.

9.   See for instance Schüssler Fiorenza (1983: 321), who calls them apostolic witnesses referring to Acts 13.31. For the other opinion see for instance Sanders 1993: 110.

10.   See Chapter 5, section 2.2.1.

11.   Both times ἐθαμβοῦντο (10.24, 32).

12.   For instance Pesch 1977: II, 148 and 508: those who are amazed are the disciples and those who follow are the Passover pilgrims including the women in 15.40-41. Gundry (1993: 569-71 and 573-74) suggests that both represent the people in general distinguishing between those in front of the train that accompanies Jesus to Jerusalem and those in the back. Lane (1974: 373 n. 60) suggests that there is only one group: the Twelve who are both amazed and afraid.

13.   See also Chapter 5, section 2.2.2.

about the camel going through the eye of a needle, ask themselves how anyone can possibly be saved (10.23-27), Peter, as a representative of the Twelve,[14] concludes that *they* are indeed followers of Jesus, having left everything behind (10.28), in contrast to the rich man in 10.17-22 and apparently also to the amazed disciples in 10.23-27.[15]

In 10.32b Jesus takes the Twelve aside to explain what will happen in Jerusalem. This suggests that in 10.32a Mark also may mean both groups describing the disciples as the ones who are amazed and the Twelve as 'those following'. The latter have just heard Jesus' enigmatic saying that 'many who are first will be last and many who are last will be first'. Indeed the Twelve are last now. Mark's mentioning that they are afraid suggests that this is why Jesus takes them apart to explain what will happen in Jerusalem.[16] In addition, he teaches them that their having left everything behind does not make them greater than anyone else. They are not to rule after his death, or exercise authority; they are to be servants and slaves, just as he will show himself to be in Jerusalem (10.35-45).

If the large group of women of 15.41 who came up with Jesus to Jerusalem would belong to the disciples who are amazed in 10.32a, then Mark implicitly portrays this large group of unnamed women in a discipleship context. In the Gospel of Mark, however, the group of disciples gathers in Jesus' house or in other houses.[17] It thus seems that the group is small.[18] Could Mark then intend the large group of women to be among them? I suggest that the large group of women who 'came up with him to Jerusalem' belong instead to the crowd (ὄχλος) that is with Jesus on his journey to Jerusalem from 10.1 onwards.[19]

If we are right about this, then Mark allows the readers to visualize the large group of women from 15.41 also among the crowd in 10.46, where they witness the blind beggar of Jericho regaining his sight. In addition, the readers can visualize them among the many at the entry into Jerusalem who lay down their garments on the road or spread branches which they had cut from the fields (11.8).

In both cases Mark allows the readers to imagine them speaking. The blind beggar, who is crying 'Jesus, Son of David, have mercy upon me', they order to be silent, but when Jesus tells them to call him they say: 'Take heart; rise, he is calling you' (10.49). At the entry into Jerusalem they cry out: 'Hosanna!' Blessed be he who comes in the name of the Lord! Blessed be the Kingdom of our father David that is coming! Hosanna in the highest!' (11.9-10).

14. Roloff 1965: 161-62. In Mark, Peter is mostly mentioned in the context of the Twelve (3.16; 11.21; 14.29; 14.54) or together with certain persons of the Twelve (1.16-20; 5.37; 9.2-5; 13.3; 14.33-37). He is always named first.

15. ἡμεῖς: 'we' with emphasis (10.28).

16. The earlier sayings about what will happen make no mention of Jerusalem and are directed to the disciples in general (8.31-33; 9.30-32).

17. Mk 7.17; 9.28, 33; 10.10; 14.14.

18. Large houses could be meant though. However, in Luke, where a large crowd of disciples is following Jesus (Lk. 6.17), they do not gather in houses. Instead, Jesus and the twelve apostles come together in a house, when they eat the Passover (Lk. 22.7-14), in contrast to Mark where Jesus and the Twelve join the (other) disciples to do so (Mk 12.12-17).

19. Jesus' journey to Jerusalem seems to start in 10.1.

In Jerusalem the readers may perhaps also visualize them among the crowd whom the chief priests, scribes and elders fear when they consider arresting Jesus (11.27; 12.12), the same crowd who, for the most part, are glad to hear Jesus teaching in the Temple (12.37). At this point, however, we should ask if it is historically correct to imagine women in the Temple. In the Outer Court yes, but in the Inner Court they were largely confined to a section called the Court of Women. Does this mean that men and women were strictly separated in the Inner Court, as in later times in the synagogue, where women were confined to the balcony?

The balcony for women in the synagogue is said to derive from a balcony in the Court of Women. Rabbinic literature reveals the reason for the construction of the balcony in the Temple: it was to enable men to dance in the Court of Women at the festival of Sukkoth without mixing with the dancing women. Thus, the Court of Women obviously allowed both men and women. Their contact with one another became a problem only when both groups were dancing. As Tal Ilan says: 'the Court of Women did not solely serve women, but marked the boundary beyond which women could not cross into the Temple if they had no sacrifices to offer'.[20]

We may, therefore, visualize both men and women listening to Jesus' teaching in the Temple, unless we assume that Jesus taught in the part of the Temple near the altar. This is, however, not likely since Mark emphasizes the fact that Jesus speaks in public (11.12, 38). Mark only once refers to a specific place in the Temple where Jesus teaches. It is opposite the treasury, where the crowd, both women and men, donated their money (12.41-44).

On these grounds we may conclude that the large group of women, being part of the crowd, was familiar with the teaching of Jesus in the Temple: the shocking parable of the tenants of the vineyard and Jesus' warning against the scribes. They also heard the questions from the official religious leaders and Jesus' answers to them: questions about Jesus' authority, about paying taxes, about the resurrection from death, about the most important commandment and about the Christ being the Son of David (11.27–13.1).

2.2. *The Small Group of Women Disciples*

But what about the small group of women in 15.40-41 whom Mark identifies by name, the ones who followed Jesus and ministered to him when he was in Galilee? It is not immediately clear whether Mark mentions three or four women, but in the flow of the story it seems more likely that there are four: Mary Magdalene, Mary of James, Mary of Joses, and Salome (15.40, 47; 16.1).[21] Is it Mark's

---

20. Ilan 1995a: 180 n. 7. For the discussion about the balcony, see Ilan 1995a: 180-81 and Safrai 1991: 69-76. See also Safrai (1991) for the active presence of women in the Temple. They prayed, they brought offerings, they donated, they completed nazirite vows, they belonged to the Temple congregation celebrating the annual festivals and partaking in daily service.

21. There is considerable argument about this, especially because in 6.3 a James and Joses (along with a Judas and a Simon) are said to be the brothers of Jesus. Mary, the mother of James and Joses in 15.40 could therefore be the mother of Jesus, which some find highly desirable. However, I opt for four women because the Gospel itself distinguishes between Mary she of Joses in 15.47 and Mary she of Jacob in 16.1. If this is taken seriously the four times that καὶ occurs in

intention that we imagine these four named women every time the following crowd is mentioned, as is the case with the large group of unnamed women? There seem to be major differences. The named women are apparently more closely related to Jesus than the larger group of women, having been with him longer, since Jesus' ministry started in Galilee (1.14). They are accustomed to following Jesus and to serving him.

2.2.1. *Following, Serving and Jewish Discipleship.* Some exegetes argue that following and serving, ἀκολουθέω and διακονέω, typically belong to Markan vocabulary and as a consequence are a result of Markan redaction.[22] Following and serving, however, are the main characteristics of Jewish discipleship.[23] The pupils of a rabbi were not supposed to learn only theoretically, but also to learn from daily life.[24] They were to follow their rabbi wherever he went and to serve (sjimesh) him.[25] The root of the verb διακονέω, which is the Greek equivalent of sjimesh, has the notion of being a 'go-between', of being sent out on errands, the dative designating the person authorizing the activity.[26] Philo describes the servant of Rebecca as a μαθητής (disciple) and Rebecca as the personification of the virtuous teacher. In the course of his explanation Rebecca as teacher appears to be a μαθητής of God.[27] Josephus calls Joshua a μαθητής of Moses, Elisha a μαθητής of Elijah and Baruch a μαθητής of Jeremiah.[28]

Mark relates that the disciples of Jesus did indeed follow him and serve him. Several times they arrange for a ship and serve as the crew (4.35; 5.21; 6.35 etc.),

15.40 must be interpreted as referring to four different persons. See also Pesch 1977: II, 505-507 and Melzer-Keller 1997: 49-52. Brown (1993: 1016, 1152-1154) argues for three women.

22.   For instance Fander 1992a: 167 n. 6 and Melzer-Keller 1997: 46-53.

23.   See the comments of Rengstorf 1976b: 153-54, esp. 154 n. 40 and Rengstorf 1977: 434-35. See also Strack and Billerbeck 1922: I, 527-29 and Davies 1964: 422-25 and 455-56. Collins (1990: 90), in his major philological study on 'diakonia', mentions this interpretation in his discussion of various modern authors on the early Christian notions of 'diakonia' (pp. 46-62). However, he does not evaluate the possibility of women as disciples and on p. 245 simply labels the women's ministry to Jesus as 'menial attendance of one kind or another'.

24.   For the classical Greek and Hellenistic background of the term μαθητής see Wilkins 1988: 11-42. The term was used with the general connotation of a 'learner', but in Hellenism most commonly designated the adherence to a great master.

25.   See Jastrow 1982: 1601-1602, who quotes Ketubot 96a: 'All manner of service that a slave must render to his master, a student must render to his teacher…'

26.   Karris (1994: 8-9), on the basis of Collins's study on 'diakonia', suggests that the women ministry to Jesus should be translated as 'going on mission for him', referring to Collins (1990: 222) where he writes about the 'diakonia' of Onesimus to Paul in Philemon 13 which in Collins's view would consist of 'more than (being) a butler for a gaoled apostle'. In the case of Onesimus in his role as 'diakonos' Collins refers to Tychicus 'who is sent to Colossae, Onesimus accompanying him, to inform the community there of Paul's affairs and to encourage their hearts (Col. 4:7-9)' (p. 222).

27.   Philo, On the Posterity and Exile of Cain 132 and 147. Philo does not literally call Rebecca a μαθητής as Wilkins (1988: 102) suggests, but Philo says she fetches her teaching from the wells of the Wisdom of God (On the Posterity and Exile of Cain 151).

28.   Josephus, Antiquities 8.354; 9.28-33. See Wilkins (1988: 92-125) for an extensive survey of the Jewish use of the word μαθητής.

they distribute food to the crowd (5.37), they find a donkey for Jesus to ride on (11.1-6) and they prepare the Passover meal (14.12-16). Jesus emphasizes the importance of service. The disciples are not to become masters, but to remain in service and even to serve all. To follow and to serve is clearly central to the Markan concept of discipleship (10.17-45).

Does all this mean that Mark in 15.40-41, by using the words following and serving when the named women are mentioned, and by stating that they had done so already in Galilee, encourages the reader to include Mary Magdalene, Mary of Joses, Mary of James and Salome every time we read the word 'disciples'? According to Luise Schottroff this is the case:

> Markus gibt hier zu erkennen, dass er bisher den in der Antike üblichen patri-archalischen Sprachgebrauch verwendet hat, in dem Frauen in Begriff mitein-geschlossen sind, die Männer bezeichnen.[29]

The question is, however, whether following and serving by *women* may be regarded as references to their discipleship. As Ricci rightly states:

> If the reality of being a disciple involved serving, the opposite was not necessarily true: that a servant had to be a disciple.[30]

The few exegetes who really address the status of the women[31] mainly focus on the exact nature of their service. They relate it to serving at table and preparing food and label it as specifically women's work. In this context they either conclude that the women were not disciples,[32] or they confine themselves to contrasting the roles of men and women disciples.[33] Others disagree with this and argue that the women's service must be seen in the broader light of the service Jesus demands of the Twelve (10.35-45), assuming that this does not necessarily include the preparation of food and serving at table.[34]

Within Jewish discipleship, however, serving at table and preparing food is not regarded specifically as women's work, or as unusual or unworthy, but simply as one aspect of the service of disciples to their rabbi, which is part of their discipleship. A fine example illustrating the worthiness of this kind of serving is the story about a great rabbi serving other rabbis, who dined with him. This indeed caused astonishment, but the discussion about it is thus concluded: 'God...spreads the table before all people, and should not Rabban Gamaliel therefore...stand and serve us?'[35]

29. Schottroff 1982: 3-4. Translation: Mark indicates here that he has until this point adhered to the patriarchal linguistic usage customary in antiquity, in which women are included in words that denote men.
30. Ricci 1994: 170.
31. See the survey of Ricci (1994: 29-50) about the research from 1860 onwards. For the most part, exegetes did not discuss the texts about the women followers of Jesus. See, for instance, also the bibliography 'One Hundred Years of Study on the Passion Narratives' by Garland 1984, which has entries on nearly everything, but the women at the crucifixion and the burial are decidedly absent.
32. E.g. Schweizer 1982: esp. 298-99 and Gerhardsson 1989: 219-20.
33. E.g. Witherington 1979: 243-47; 1990: 110-12 and Ernst 1981: 475-76.
34. Schottroff 1982: 11-12; Munro 1982: 232-34; Heine 1986: 68-70; Fander 1990: 145 and Melzer-Keller 1997: 53.
35. Qiddušin 32b; cf. Mekilta Exod. 18.2 as quoted by Beyer 1976: 83.

Mark's concept of discipleship conforms to the Jewish model of discipleship. The Gospel includes in a matter of fact way that Jesus' disciples prepare food and serve at table (5.37; 14.12-16). Thus, focusing on the exact nature of the service of the four named women in 15.40-41 does not really help to find an answer to the question of whether and how they were disciples. We conclude that the service as such, whatever its nature, belongs to the discipleship role of Jesus' male as well as female followers,[36] and that, therefore, Mark's portrayal of the four women as having been following and serving Jesus may indicate their discipleship role.

2.2.2. Markan Discipleship and the Twelve. Some exegetes would object that the disciples in Mark are obviously exclusively male, since they are the Twelve.[37] But is this really true? In the Gospel of Mark the disciples are always referred to in the plural, just as the disciples of John the Baptist and those of the Pharisees (2.18). Mark only once speaks of an individual disciple and even then uses the phrase 'one of his disciples' (13.1). Grammatically men as well as women may be meant by a masculine plural, but this would not be the case if Mark identified the disciples with the all-male Twelve.

The lack of a definite article with 'twelve' in 3.14, however, seems to suggest that Jesus summoned the Twelve out of a larger group he called to him. This may mean that he called more disciples than the Twelve alone.[38] The second time Mark mentions the Twelve this is confirmed: the Twelve are together with a number of other insiders. They are called the ones around him (οἱ περὶ αὐτόν) in 4.10 and together with the Twelve they are called his own disciples (τοῖς ἰδίοις μαθηταῖς) in 4.34. To these insiders Jesus explains everything that to outsiders is only in parables. The Twelve and those around Jesus thus receive the secret of the Kingdom of God from him (4.11).

It is also striking to note that Mark uses the word 'disciples' in a very special way, carefully avoiding identifying any specific individual as disciple. The Gospel never calls the Twelve 'the twelve disciples', nor is the word 'disciples' directly connected with the names of the Twelve, or with any name at all. At an interpretative level this, of course, does not mean that the Twelve are not disciples. Like the other disciples they learn from Jesus, but, unlike them, they do so with a special purpose: they are called apostles and sent by Jesus to preach and have authority to drive out demons (3.13-15; 6.7-13). The Twelve are also disciples, but the Markan disciples are not to be identified with the Twelve. The Twelve are a distinguishable group of specific individuals, as we suggested earlier when discussing 10.32,[39]

---

36. See also Gundry 1993: 167.

37. E.g. Sanders 1993: 110; Schweizer 1982 and Rengstorf 1977: 460-61.

38. See also Sanders (1993: 118-22, 291), who argues that Jesus used the number 'twelve' referring to the twelve tribes as a symbol of his mission and his hope. Roloff (1965: 145-50) considers the call of the Twelve not only as a symbolic act of representation but also as a demonstration of eschatological reality. See also Mt. 19.28 and Lk. 22.30.

39. See also 6.1//6.7; 6.30//6.35; 9.31//9.35; 14.16//14.17 and for instance Schüssler Fiorenza 1983: 319-20 and Gundry 1993: 167. Most scholars tend to identify the Twelve and the Markan disciples; see Wilkins 1988: 166. For various exegetes on the topic see Malbon 1986: 107 n. 9.

whereas the group of Markan disciples as a whole remains unspecified.

Mark, by always using the term 'disciple' as a male plural, which remains unspecified, opens up the possibility that both men and women are included. Mark indeed has no reference to women being personally called, but perhaps the Gospel wants us to visualize their call in 3.13 where the Gospel portrays Jesus on the mountain calling to himself whomever he wishes, before he appoints the Twelve.

However, it is clear that Jesus' invitation to follow him is not limited to specific persons and has nothing to do with a special personal call. The call to follow him is, on the contrary, all-inclusive, since he invites the crowds to follow him and, by the use of 'whoever', also includes even those who read or hear the Gospel.[40] Mark often sets the unspecified group of disciples over and against the unspecified crowd and frequently uses the word whoever or anyone.[41] According to Elizabeth Struthers Malbon, this is a compelling invitation to the readers to get into the story and to make the choice to follow Jesus: to be one with the crowd and to become one with the disciples.[42] Everyone is invited to follow Jesus as Mark relates:

> And calling to himself the multitude with his disciples, he said to them, 'If anyone wishes to follow me, let that one deny himself and take up his cross and follow me' (8.34).

Likewise Malbon concludes: 'Disciples, crowds, whoever – everyone is a potential follower. The demands of followership, however, make for a different actuality'.[43]

2.2.3. The Argument of Implausibility and Rabbinic Literature. In Mark the disciples are a relatively small group around Jesus who share in his life. They are in his house,[44] they eat with him,[45] they provide food,[46] they arrange for a ship and a colt,[47] they follow him,[48] they withdraw with him,[49] they ask him questions[50] and he asks questions of them.[51] Although Jesus' teaching is mostly in public, in the synagogue,[52] at the sea of Galilee,[53] in the villages,[54] on the road,[55] and in the

40. Malbon 1986: 105-110.
41. 3.7; 3.9; 4.1//4.34; 5.31; 6.45; 8.1; 10.46; 12.41//12.43; see also the useful appendix of Malbon 1986: 126-29.
42. Malbon (1986: 104-130) argues that Mark's use of the words 'disciples', 'crowds' and 'whoever' is complementary and opens up the followership of Jesus to the readers.
43. Malbon 1986: 110.
44. 7.17; 9.33; 10.10.
45. 2.15; 2.18; 2.23; 6.41; 7.2; 8.6; 14.14.
46. 2.23; 6.41; 8.6; 14.12; 14.16.
47. 3.9; 11.1-7.
48. 6.1.
49. 3.7; 8.10.
50. 5.31; 6.35; 7.17; 9.28; 10.10.
51. 8.4; 8.27, 29; 8.17, 21; 9.33.
52. 1.21; 1.39; 3.1; 6.2.
53. 4.1; 6.31.
54. 6.6b.
55. 10.1.

Temple,[56] his disciples also receive advanced teaching at his house or at someone else's house[57] or are taken aside on a journey.[58]

When one realizes how close the Markan Jesus is to his disciples, questions inevitably arise, which support the first argument we mentioned that has been raised against the discipleship of women: the utter implausibility of the thought. Does Mark really want us to visualize Jesus with men as well as women in the privacy of his house, teaching them as a rabbi would and answering their questions? Does Mark really want us to visualize women eating with him? Does Mark really want us to visualize Jesus in public, with male as well as female disciples? If so, why does Mark not once indicate that this would all be highly unusual?

In order to account for this, it is important to look at those texts in Mark where the Gospel specifically describes Jesus meeting women, namely, Peter's mother-in-law (1.29-31), the woman who suffered from severe bleeding and the daughter of Jairus (5.21-43), the Syro-Phoenician woman (7.24-30), the widow in the temple (12.41-44), and the woman at Bethany (14.42-47). In Mark's description of Jesus' encounters with these women Jesus touches them in the privacy of their houses (Peter's mother-in-law, the daughter of Jairus) and is touched by them in public (the bleeding woman and the woman at Bethany). Mark also relates that Jesus is convinced by and praises a woman who questions his negative attitude towards non-Jews (the Syro-Phoenician woman). Moreover, Jesus uses women as positive examples when teaching his disciples (the woman at Bethany and the widow in the temple). And last, but by no means least, he allows a woman to anoint his head in public and declares that her action is authentically prophetic, one which is to be remembered wherever the Gospel is preached throughout the world (14.8-9).[59]

It is noteworthy that in these texts nothing is said to imply that the attitudes of Jesus and of the women are strange or unusual with respect to gender norms. This may signify that, for Mark, these open attitudes were not strange or unusual at all.

At this point it is important to examine exactly what lies behind our conception of what is unusual. It is either a strongly rooted bias deeply internalized through art, literature and education, or it is based on sources of the time. The latter seems at first to be the case. Referring extensively to Rabbinic literature, Joachim Jeremias concludes that women were not supposed to go out of doors unless heavily

---

56. 11.15-17, 27; 12.35, 41.

57. 7.17; 9.28, 33; 10.10.

58. 4.33-34; 8.14-21; 8.27-33; 9.30-32; 9.23-27.

59. For the women in Mark see Fander 1990 and Fander 1992b: 413-32, Melzer-Keller 1997: 13-45, and D'Angelo 1999b: 138-44. Fander and Melzer-Keller argue that these five stories about women are at the centre of Markan theology: Peter's mother-in-law is an example of followership, the woman with the flow of blood recognizes Jesus' power and nature, the Syro-Phoenician understands Jesus' mission and identity, the poor widow serves as example of self-sacrifice and the anointing woman understands Jesus' destiny. D'Angelo draws attention to stereotypes of femininity, e.g. the malice of Herodias and the vulnerability of the widow. See the introduction of Dannemann 1996 for a survey of several feminist scholarly opinions on the women in Mark. Her study focuses on the Syro-Phoenician woman (7.24-30), Herodias and her daughter (6.17-29), and the female slave of the high priest (14.66-72). Dannemann argues that each story hides patriarchal supporting and patriarchal critical elements.

veiled, men were not to talk to women, women were to live in their own separate quarters, to obey their husbands or their male relatives and to devote their lives to housework rather than, like men, to religious life with its laws and the study of the Torah. Although in the country and in cases of poverty women would be allowed more freedom of movement, this, according to Jeremias, was the basic framework for women's lives.[60] Leonard Swidler, who also draws on Rabbinic literature, concludes,

> that in the formative period of Judaism the status of women was not one of equality with men, but rather, severe inferiority, and that even intense misogynism was not infrequently present.[61]

Both Jeremias's and Swidler's work has been heavily criticized, as has the use of Rabbinic literature as a source for the study of the lives of Jewish women. Rabbinic scholars have emphasized that Rabbinic literature is a literary source and that no history is to be found in it.[62] Feminist scholars have emphasized that Rabbinic literature is not about women, but about men's views on women and, as such, is mostly prescriptive rather than descriptive.[63] They have also shown that there is a tendency among (feminist) scholars to select Rabbinic sayings that are restrictive for women, declaring them to reflect the general Jewish attitude of the time.[64] If, however, Rabbinic literature cannot be used as a historical source, then which sources can be drawn on?

2.2.4. *Other Sources and Other Arguments.* On the basis of his research, Swidler suggests that Jesus must have been quite revolutionary in his attitude towards women, interpreting Jesus' attitude as liberational against the background of restrictive Jewish attitudes. The title of one of his articles became widely known: 'Jesus Was a Feminist'.[65] In contrast to this interpretation, Judith Plaskow argues that, because Jesus was a Jew, his open attitude towards women actually represents a possibility within early Judaism, rather than a victory over it.[66] Plaskow suggests that the New Testament should be seen as a source for Jewish women's history, rather than being used as evidence of a radical alternative to Jewish attitudes. This is possible precisely because of the fact that nothing is said in the New Testament about the peculiarity of Jesus' inclusive attitude towards women, which 'suggests

---

60. Jeremias 1962: 395-413. Ilan (1997: 17) calls his work 'the most fully annotated and learned study of the topic until his day' and says that 'it created the basic corpus on which many later studies relied'.

61. Swidler 1976: 167.

62. See for instance Ilan (1997: 9-25) about Jacob Neusner's radical and influential criticism of the use of Rabbinic literature as a historical source.

63. See for instance Brooten 1985: 65-91.

64. As pointed out by Brooten 1982b: 141-48 and 1985, and Plaskow 1994: 117-29. See also Kraemer 1999a.

65. Brooten (1985: 74-75) states that Swidler's 'studies of women in ancient Judaism and early Christianity have been more influential on a broad scale over the past decade than the work of any other single scholar'.

66. Plaskow 1994: 124.

that his relation to women and gender norms might not have been so different from the attitudes of his contemporaries'.[67]

This would radically change the perspectives of Swidler and Jeremias. Instead of being striking, the reference to the women who followed Jesus would simply mean that Jewish women apparently travelled and also travelled together with men. The mention of the woman at the dinner in Bethany, who is not criticized for her being there, but for her behaviour, would simply mean that Jewish women and men could be together at meals. The reference to Priscilla and Aquila, both tentmakers like Paul, being in the synagogue, listening to the learned Apollo, who was well versed in Scripture, who then took him aside to teach him, would simply mean that both Jewish women and men could have professions and both could be trained in the study of Scripture, listening and learning in the synagogue and even teaching others (Acts 18, 3.26). There is no indication that this was considered strange and nothing is said about Priscilla being inferior to Aquila. When Paul mentions them, he calls them both his fellow workers in Christ (Rom. 16.3).

Schüssler Fiorenza refers to the book of Judith as a source for the role and position of Jewish women at the time.[68] Judith is a widow who inherits the estate of her husband, which a female steward administers for her. Judith is independent and has great freedom: she refuses a second marriage, she devotes her life to prayer, asceticism and observing the Sabbath, she criticizes the elders of her city for their folly and their theologically perverse judgment; she travels with her maid and without a male escort, and is clearly not heavily veiled, but probably even unveiled because everyone notices her beauty. All this is described with approval.

Bernadette Brooten refers to Philo of Alexandria[69] as a source. In his book De Vita Contemplativa he describes the 'Therapeutai' who lived near Alexandria. This was a group of Jewish women and men who studied the Torah, who prayed, sang, and ate together and who lived in strict asceticism.[70] Philo relates that these communities existed in many other countries,[71] which could also include Palestine. These independent and learned Therapeutai women are, like Judith, favourably portrayed. They are not criticized in any way and no special attention is given to their gender. In fact, they are admired for their way of life. Brooten argues that we should reject the idea that Rabbinic opinions were all-powerful, especially during the first century.[72] The Therapeutai women studied the Torah not because they had some special Rabbinic leave to do so, but because they themselves had decided it

---

67. Plaskow 1994: 126. According to Kraemer (1999a: 39-42), both Jesus' limited speech with women and the unremarkable presence of women in public in the New Testament Gospels cannot be seen to conflict with Rabbinic restrictions.

68. Schüssler Fiorenza 1983: 116-18.

69. Brooten 1982b: 145.

70. Philo, On the Contemplative Life 2, 28, 32, 68. See also Kraemer 1989.

71. On the Contemplative Life 21.

72. Brooten (1982a: 150) cites the work of Neusner (1980), who regards as obvious the viewpoint that what the male rabbis said about women does not reflect the general attitude towards women nor the attitudes of women themselves.

to be important. Philo makes no apology for their studying the Torah, but simply states that they do so and thinks it praiseworthy.[73]

Brooten and others emphasize the great importance of non-literary documents, such as papyri (contracts or letters), inscriptions, and archaeological remains.[74] There is still much work to be done in this field, but it is already clear that women were in business and had economic resources. Documents also reveal that women had certain rights within marriage and could initiate divorce. Brooten has studied inscriptions which show that women had religious roles, for instance, within the synagogue.[75] Eileen Schuller, on the basis of what has been found at the Qumran site and one of the caves, suggests that women were members of the Qumran community, even serving as scribes and elders.[76] Ross Kraemer uses as an important source the personal papers of a Jewish woman named Babatha, which were found in a cave in the Judean desert. The papyri contain among other things marriage contracts, loan documents, guardianship papers, and land registrations.[77]

Tal Ilan made a study of all the sources that contribute to our knowledge of Jewish women in Greco-Roman Palestine, including the New Testament, the Apocrypha and Pseudepigrapha, Josephus, the Dead Sea Scrolls, funery inscriptions, and papyri and ostraca from the Judean desert. In addition, and in spite of recent discussion, she also uses Rabbinic literature as a source for the study of Jewish women's history.[78] She outlines her methodology, defending her stand that Rabbinic literature as the most extensive source concerning Jewish women available from antiquity, should not simply be labelled literary and thus dismissed as a-historical, but should instead be scrutinized with the help of historical and literary criticism to reveal the layers that might contain historical information.[79]

She shows, for instance, that in Rabbinic literature women studying the Torah is a controversial issue. Rabbi Eliezer is an especially aggressive opponent of Torah study for women. However, in more incidental remarks about women and Torah study it is clear that not only men but also women were allowed to study the Torah and other texts as well, as these quotations show: 'If a man is forbidden by vow to have any benefit from his fellow, …he may teach Scripture to his sons and daughters…' and 'Men and women who have suffered a flux, menstruants and women who have given birth are permitted to read Torah, the Prophets, and the Writings

73. Brooten 1982b: 145.
74. Brooten 1985: 88-91.
75. Brooten 1982a; Fander 1990: 215-57 and Fander 1992a: 180-85.
76. Schuller 1994; see also Ilan 1995a: 28-33.
77. Kraemer 1999b: 53.
78. Ilan 1995a.
79. Ilan 1997. Ilan 1995a and 1997 are the first and second book of a trilogy on Jewish women. Ilan regards the first book as a rather naïve attempt to master and resolve the issue of Jewish women in one single work, under traditional headings such as marriage, family, sex, childrearing, and housework. Nevertheless, it is a very useful source book. Ilan plans a third book which will consist of an incorporation of the data she found in the first two books into the framework of the main events of Greco-Roman Jewish history (Ilan 1997, preface and p. 24 n. 91).

and to learn mishnah, midrash, halakhah and aggadah…'[80] This last saying relates specifically to women handling Scripture and studying the Torah.

Ilan refers to Daniel Boyarin who has demonstrated that, although this saying was quoted literally in the Palestinian Talmud, the Babylonian Talmud changed it rather severely to exclude women: 'Men who suffer from a (veneral) discharge and (male) lepers and men who had intercourse with menstruants are permitted to read from the Torah, the Prophets and the Writings and to study mishna, gemarah, halakhot, and agadot'. The women who are conspicuously present in the earlier version are simply left out.[81] Women also used to be scribes, but their work was declared unacceptable by later rabbis, which is shown by this remark: 'They taught: …a Torah scroll, tefilin, and a mezuzah which…a woman wrote…are disqualified'.[82]

Ilan argues that reality must have been very different from even the lenient legislated ideal of the Pharisees that survived in Rabbinic literature. Jewish women did indeed go out of doors, going to the market and travelling on their own.[83] They did have professions and men and women mingled in public.[84] Women studied the Torah, questioning rabbis and receiving detailed answers.[85] Ilan attributes the discrepancy between what has been written and what was practised to the highly heterogeneous nature of Second Temple period Jewish society, and also to the fact that most of the surviving sources relate to upper-middle and aristocratic classes.[86]

Helga Melzer-Keller suggests that one should focus on contemporary opposition and renewal groups at the time of Jesus.[87] With regard to this it is interesting that Ilan researched texts which mention women supporting the Pharisees. She argues that, as an opposition group, the Pharisees accepted this support, and did not enact specific rules against women. Only later, when they came into power after the destruction of the Temple, did their misogynistic tendencies emerge.[88]

If indeed Jesus' attitudes towards women and the attitudes of women towards him are not to be considered unusual for the time but part of the pluralism of early

80.   Mishna Nedarim 4.2-3 and Tosefta Berakhot 2.12. See Ilan 1995a: 193 and 190-204. Her conclusion that women studying Scripture 'would most probably concentrate on the relative simple book of Genesis' is surprisingly meagre compared to the sources she herself refers to. Cf. for instance p. 204 and p. 193. However, Ilan (1997: 166-69) gives even more material and concludes that 'the Rabbinic world as a whole admitted to a reality…which preserved in it the possibility for women to study Torah' (p. 169).

81.   j. Berakhot 3.4, 6c and b. Berakhot 22a. Ilan 1997: 60-61.

82.   b. Menakhot 42b; see Ilan 1995a: 193.

83.   Ilan 1995a: 128-29; Ilan 1997: 171-73, 265, 268-69.

84.   Ilan 1995a: 184-90.

85.   See Ilan (1995a: 190-204) about Beruriah and Matrona and other female figures in Rabbinic literature, who apparently discuss Scripture and Halacha with knowledge and insight. See also Ilan 1997: 297-310.

86.   Ilan 1995a: esp. 226-29.

87.   Melzer-Keller (1997: 437-39), suggests that there was no gender problem in the early Jesus movement, because equal poverty and hope defined the situation of men and women alike. See also Schottroff 1980: 106.

88.   Ilan 1995b: 1-33.

Judaism, it is no longer valid to say that women especially were attracted to early Christianity because it offered them more freedom and respect. Fander concludes that the challenge is to find a different explanation of why Christianity was so appealing to women.[89] In contrast to this, Judith Lieu argues that the question in itself is wrong. According to her, the assumption that women were especially attracted to early Christianity is a mere truism, based on a naïve use of sources. Rather than asking 'what did early Christianity do for women', it is more appropriate to inquire 'what did women do to early Christianity'.[90]

In fact, the latter question was the fundamental premise of Anne Jensen who wrote a major study of early Church women in which she brings to light actual women who were missionaries, prophets, martyrs, deacons, theologians, teachers, and writers.[91] Whereas Jensen studied contemporary writings, Ute Eisen researched inscriptions and documentary papyri. She concludes that women were apostles, prophets and teachers of theology, consecrated widows, deacons, stewards, priests, and bishops.[92] Both studies are very thorough and impressive.

Thus, if we were only to rely on the studies of Jeremias and Swidler, female discipleship would, indeed, simply be inconceivable. If, however, we take into account the more recent research, it is certainly possible that women were disciples of Jesus.

2.2.5. *Markan Disciples: Women and Men.* In fact, there are early sources which call Jesus' women followers 'disciples' such as Tertullian in his book Against Marcion, and the apostles in the Didascalia Apostolorum.[93] Both mention the women in the band of Jesus' disciples: *discipulae*. The Gospel of Peter calls Mary Magdalene μαθήτρια τοῦ κυρίου (the female disciple of the Lord),[94] while the Gospel of Thomas presents Salome saying to Jesus 'I am your disciple' in Coptic using the Greek word μαθητής.[95] The Sophia of Jesus Christ and the Apocalypse of James both mention the presence of twelve male and seven female disciples.[96]

---

89. Fander 1992a: 185.
90. Lieu 1998.
91. Jensen 1992. See also Torjessen 1993.
92. Eisen 1996.
93. Against Marcion IV.19.1; Didascalia Apostolorum III.6.
94. GosPet 12.50. See Vander Stichele 1998.
95. GosThom 61.
96. SJC 90.16-18 (BG 107.4-10); 1 ApocJas 38.16-17; 42.20-24. For the twelve male and seven female disciples see also the Manichaean Psalmbook Ps. II 192.21–193.3. Marjanen (1996: 71-72) argues that the tradition of the twelve male and seven female disciples predates the early second-century Gnostic Sophia of Jesus Christ and is not necessarily Gnostic in origin. The tradition might be a good explanation to the peculiar double story about Jesus' feeding the people (Mk 6.30-44; 8.1-10), where respectively twelve and seven baskets with bread are left over. The Markan Jesus himself emphasizes the symbolic meaning of these two numbers (8.14-21). The most common interpretation is that the first feeding (twelve baskets) refers to the Jewish and the second feeding (seven baskets) refers to the Gentile mission. However, scholarly opinions differ. See Gundry (1993: 395-401), who gives a survey of opinions which 'differ wildly'. I suggest that Mark's double story might draw on the early tradition of the seven and the twelve disciples. Mk 8.14-21 underlines that the disciples do not need the leaven of the Pharisees or the leaven of Herod.

In the Gospel of Thomas and in the Sophia of Jesus Christ, Mary Magdalene's questions are about the nature of discipleship.[97]

This, however, makes it all the more striking that Mark does not explicitly call Mary Magdalene, Mary of James, Mary of Joses and Salome in Mk 15.40-41 disciples (μαθητρίαι or μαθηταί), but only refers to their role with the words following and serving. Does this perhaps reveal that Mark is ambiguous about their discipleship? On the contrary, in my opinion it supports the view that it could be a typical Markan characteristic to avoid identifying any specific individuals as disciples in order to make choosing to follow Jesus more accessible to the reader. As we showed before, the Gospel achieves this by the consistent use of the word disciples as an unspecified plural.

There is one more text in Mark which needs to be dealt with to reveal its view on the gender of Jesus' disciples. When Jesus' mother and brothers send for him, he replies:

> Who are my mother and my brothers? And looking around on those who sat about him, he said, 'Here are my mother and my brothers! Whoever does the will of God is my brother and sister and mother'. (3.33-34)

Mark calling those around Jesus his mother and his brothers suggests that the group includes women as well as men. In addition, by using the masculine plural 'brothers' (ἀδελφοί) and then splitting it up into the singular brother (ἀδελφός) and the singular sister (ἀδελφή), Mark clearly shows that the Gospel makes use of the grammatical possibility of choosing a masculine plural to mean both men and women. This strengthens the argument that Mark possibly does the same with regard to the masculine plural 'disciples'. Indeed the text strongly suggests this to be the case, because who else can the men and women sitting around Jesus, τοὺς περὶ αὐτὸν κύκλῳ καθημένους, be but Jesus' disciples?[98] This conjecture is confirmed in the following verses. In 4.10 the men and women are mentioned again as οἱ περὶ αὐτόν. They as well as the Twelve are with Jesus when he is alone. When they ask him about the parables he says:

> To you has been given the secret of the Kingdom of God, but for those outside everything is in parables. (4.10)

In 4.34 Mark explicitly calls them his disciples, even τοῖς ἰδίοις μαθηταῖς, to whom he explains everything.

I conclude, therefore, that Mark indeed wants us to visualize women as well as men when the Gospel mentions the disciples and that Mary Magdalene, Mary of James, Mary of Joses, and Salome in 15.40-41 are introduced as women belonging to the inner circle, who had followed Jesus right from the beginning of his ministry in Galilee.

Through Jesus they each individually, the twelve and the seven, male and female disciples, have their own basket of bread to share, to feed themselves (8.14-21) and to feed all the needy people (6.30-44; 8.1-10), even the non-Jewish (7.24-30).

97. GosThom 21; SJC 98.9-11; 114.8-12.

98. Cf. Mt. 12.49; see Strack and Billerbeck (1922: II, 763-64) about the custom of sitting around the teacher while being taught.

2.2.6. *Exemplifying Markan Discipleship.* Perhaps the four named female disciples, Mary Magdalene, Mary of James, Mary of Joses and Salome, at the end of Mark reflect the four named male disciples at the beginning, Simon (Peter), Andrew, James, and John, who later, just before Jesus is handed over, receive special instruction about the suffering in the near future.[99] But why does Mark introduce the women disciples only at the very end of the Gospel and not earlier? Again, some exegetes suggest that this shows Mark's ambivalence towards the disciple-ship of women.[100] In my opinion Mark is not at all ambivalent, considering that Mark clearly indicates as early as Mk 3.33-34 that women as well as men can be disciples. The Gospel consistently and characteristically uses an inviting un-specified plural to refer to the disciples. Jesus' open attitude towards women is not described as unusual and, finally, no other contemporary sources support the assumption that open attitudes of or towards women generally were to be labelled as unusual.

Mark introduces Mary Magdalene, the two other Marys, and Salome at the very end of the Gospel because only then do they play their explicit and individual part. Until then, they are implied in the larger unspecified group of Jesus' disciples: women as well as men. Yet, there may be another reason.[101]

The women are introduced immediately after the moment that Jesus died (15.33-39). At this point it is made manifest that Jesus is not a Messiah with any worldly power, but rather a suffering one, which, in fact, is the main theme of the Gospel. Similarly, in 15.40-41, it turns out that the disciples who truly understand what following Jesus means are not the specified male Twelve, who thought themselves to be the authorized followers of Jesus,[102] but who in fact betrayed him (Judas), denied him (Peter) and ran away when he was arrested.[103] Instead, until then the unknown and implied women followers at this point of Mark's story illustrate that discipleship has nothing to do with power, but with the utmost willingness to follow and to remain of service, even when it is dangerous to do so, which Mark emphasizes by situating the women looking on from afar (15.40; cf. 14.54).[104]

Thus Mary Magdalene, Mary of James, Mary of Joses and Salome exemplify Markan discipleship and by doing so they are special among the other disciples.

3. The Name 'Mary Magdalene'

It is striking that three of the four women Mark mentions by name should be called 'Mary'. Does Mark mean something special by this? Ilan demonstrated that the New Testament Gospels contain relatively more women's names than other

---

99. 1.16-20; 13.3-37; see also Schüssler Fiorenza 1983: 320 and Melzer-Keller 1997: 54.

100. As do Munro 1982: 226-29, 234-35; Melzer-Keller 1997: 54-55 and De Boer 1997: 41-44 and is opposed by Selvidge 1983.

101. In addition to Fander 1992b: 431.

102. Cf. 9.30-40; 10.32-45.

103. 14.10-11, 33-40, 43-45, 50-52, 66-72.

104. See also Schottrof 1982: 6 and Schüssler Fiorenza 1983: 320.

sources of the time in Palestine.[105] Even on funeral inscriptions in Jerusalem, where male and female bones were found equally, male names are by far the majority. Most women of the time remained anonymous and the 145 who are identified by name appear only to have 11 different names. Even more striking, almost half of these women were called Mary (or its longer version Mariamme) or Salome (or its longer version Salomezion). These names conjure up the independent time of Jewish reign of the Hasmonean line in between the periods of Greek and Roman occupation as did one-third of the male names at the time. The two female names represent two Hasmonean Queens: Queen Salomezion who reigned nine years and Queen Mariamme who, as a threat to his throne, was killed by her husband, the Nabatean Herod, who was made King of the Jews by the Romans.[106]

Mary is thus an entirely normal and much used Hebrew name. Mary Magdalene, however, is more special. Whenever the name Mary occurs in the New Testament, relatives are added to distinguish them as in the case of Mary the mother of Jesus, Mary the mother of James, Mary the mother of Joses, Mary the sister of Martha and Lazarus, and Mary of Clopas. Our Mary is not named after a father, a son, a sister, a brother, a husband, or any other relative. Perhaps her family was not known to the circle around Jesus or perhaps she was not to be defined by family relations. The research on the few women names that remain give no clues whatsoever. Only this is certain: Mary Magdalene's name, instead of referring to family, refers to a town.[107]

Magdala is the Hebrew name of a fortified mercantile town at the west shore of the Sea of Galilee, between Tiberias and Capernaum. The town was favourably located for different international trade routes and its strategic situation was also strong. The Greek name was Tarichea which refers to the drying and salting of fish. There was also trade in dyed fabrics and in a variety of agricultural products. The town was a hotbed of opposition against the Romans and a sanctuary for fugitives. It had a Hellenistic hippodrome, but also a small Jewish synagogue.[108]

In the New Testament only men have geographically fixed names such as Joseph of Arimathea (15.43), Judas Iscariot (3.18), Jesus himself (the Nazarean 10.47), and Simon of Cyrene (15.21). Mary Thompson notes that the New Testament Gospels constantly have the name of Mary Magdalene formed as proper noun + definite article + geographical name.[109] The definite article in these cases is only

105. Ilan 1989.

106. Ilan 1989: 191-92. See also Ilan 1995a: 53-55 and 174-75.

107. Some would contradict this interpretation. The Hebrew word 'migdal' means stronghold. That is why Jerome, Letters 127.5, interprets the name Magdalene symbolically as an epithet meaning 'of the tower'. According to Jerome, Mary Magdalene received this name 'because of her earnestness and ardent faith'. See Wright 1954: 451. Starbird (1998: 140-41 and 155-56) suggests a more esoteric interpretation and points to the gematria value of ἡ Μαγδαληνή which is 153 (cf. Jn 21.11). The epithet 'the Magdalene' would have been chosen to reveal that Mary Magdalene is the bride of Jesus: he represents the fish (his early Christian epithet ἰχθυς) and she the vessel of the fish. Together, as the bearers of Christianity, they bring forth many fishes (believers).

108. De Boer 1997: 21-31. See also Manns 1976: 307-337; Corbo 1976 and especially the meditations on the site by Schaberg 2002: 47-64.

109. Thompson 1995: 27-32.

used in Greek if a well-known person is to be distinguished from others with the same name.[110] She concludes:

> The evidence is clear that the form used to identify this particular disciple of Jesus was already encapsulated in a technical form by the time the Gospels were written.[111]

She argues that Mary Magdalene must have been widely known and prominent. By naming her first, not only here but also in 15.47 and 16.1, thus being the only one who is present at all three events, Mark underlines her importance. As we will see, this is in contrast to the other New Testament Gospels. Matthew first introduces many unnamed women (Mt. 27, 55), Luke introduces Mary Magdalene in 8.2 right after he mentions the Twelve, while in Lk. 23.55–24.10 she appears to be implied in a large group of unnamed women and John first mentions Jesus' mother (Jn 19.25). However, Luke and Matthew agree with Mark, in that, when they name the women, Mary Magdalene is always named first. Because of this Martin Hengel suggests that Mary Magdalene's position is comparable to the one of Peter, who is always named first when several names of male disciples are concerned.[112]

4. *Mark's Story about Mary Magdalene*

When introducing Mary Magdalene almost at the end of the Gospel, Mark encourages the readers to leaf back and visualize her, Mary of Joses, Mary of James, and Salome every time the word disciples occur. Thus Mark's story about Mary Magdalene actually starts at the beginning of the Gospel. As a disciple she is among the other disciples following and serving Jesus. Like them she shares his life. She witnesses his influence on people, his healings, the power of his teaching. Though Jesus' teaching is mostly in public the disciples receive advanced teaching when taken aside by him. Together with the Twelve and others she is one of those Jesus calls his sisters and brothers and to whom he says: 'To you has been given the secret of the Kingdom of God, but for those outside everything is in parables' (4.10).

As a disciple Mary Magdalene is amazed like the others, even shocked and terrified at what happens.[113] Like them she does not understand Jesus' words about the Son of Man who will be put to death and after three days rise again, not daring to ask anything about it (9.30-32). Like them she is at the Passover meal, sharing bread and wine, and in Gethsemane, where Jesus prays and is arrested (14.12-42). Like the other disciples she flees (14.50), but unlike them, more like Peter (14.54), she apparently takes courage and returns, since she is present at the crucifixion. At this point Mark singles her out.

---

110. Thompson 1995: 30 and p. 132 nn. 21 and 22. Blass, Debrunner and Rehkopf 1990: 268 esp. n. 1.
111. Thompson 1995: 31.
112. Hengel 1963: 243-56.
113. E.g. Mk 1.27; 4.35-41; 10.24-32.

4.1. *The Crucifixion: Looking on from Afar*

The Gospel begins with the remark that Mary Magdalene and many other women followers of Jesus are at the crucifixion scene 'looking on from afar' (ἀπο μακρόθεν θεωροῦσαι – 15.40). The women are not described wailing as one would perhaps expect of women at such a scene. Mark does not describe any activity on the part of Mary Magdalene and the other women. The soldiers are dividing Jesus' garments and are casting lots. The passersby deride him, referring to his own words about destroying the temple and rebuilding it in three days. The chief priests and the scribes and even those who are crucified with him are jeering: 'He saved others, he cannot save himself. Let the Christ, the King of Israel, come down now from the cross, that we may see and believe' (15.31-32).

Mark encourages the readers to visualize the women there for six hours, the last three hours in darkness, seeing all this happening. They hear Jesus crying loudly: 'My God, my God, why have you forsaken me?' (15.34). They note the confusion when some think he calls Elijah for help. But Elijah does not come down and after another loud cry Jesus dies.

Then, very unexpectedly for the reader, the centurion near Jesus, seeing him thus dying, says: 'Truly this man was a son of God' (15.39). Earlier the chief priests and scribes had mocked Jesus, saying 'Let the Christ, the King of the Jews come down from the cross now, so that we may see and believe' (15.32). Now for this gentile man precisely Jesus' way of dying evokes the central confession.

Mark simply portrays the women followers as looking at all of this from afar. Are they paralysed, appalled, filled with awe, fearful? Mark does not relate their emotions. Some exegetes argue that the Gospel, by using the phrase ἀπο μακρόθεν θεωροῦσαι, suggests that the women are not closely involved.[114] The women's willingness to follow and to serve Jesus would be shown by this verse to be deficient. Mark would have portrayed them over and against the Roman centurion to show the women as counter examples. These exegetes refer, among other things, to Peter who followed Jesus 'from afar' after the arrest. However, both the women and Peter had sound reasons for keeping far away, as Mark suggests when telling about the young man who tries to remain with Jesus and as a consequence is taken by the soldiers, only narrowly escaping (14.51).

Mark also uses the verb θεορέω when two of the women observe Jesus' burial (15.47) and when three of them look for the stone of the tomb, which, to their shock has been rolled away (16.4). Originally the word denotes the observance of a religious event.[115] This may also be the case here.[116] The verb indeed expresses distance, but not necessarily emotional distance. On the contrary, Mark's story portrays the women disciples in rather active roles, clearly involved with what happens.

---

114. See Brown 1993: II, 1157-1158, who refers to Ps. 38.12. See also Melzer-Keller 1997: 55-56 and Légasse 1997: 984.

115. Michaelis 1977: 318-19, 327-28, 345-46.

116. In all other instances where Mark uses the word, some religiously meaningful incident is involved: 3.11; 5.15, 38; 12.41.

4.2. *Seeing the Place where Jesus is Laid*

Mary Magdalene and Mary the mother of Joses see the place where Jesus is laid. Mark relates that Joseph of Arimathea, a respected member of the Council who also expected the Kingdom of God (cf. 12.34), arranges the burial. Raymond Brown argues that this does not mean that he was a disciple, but that he was a close observer of Jewish law and thus wanted the body to be buried before the end of the day. According to Roman law the body should not have been buried at all, but left hanging until there was nothing left of it.[117] As Mark emphasizes it took courage, even for a respected member of the Council, to ask Pilate to release the body.

Mark does not picture a lovingly performed burial, but, however, a decent one, since Joseph of Arimathea buys the linen cloth in which to wrap a body. An honorable burial would consist of the anointing of the body.

4.3. *Buying Spices and Going to the Tomb*

Very early in the morning, at sunrise, when the Sabbath is over Mary Magdalene, Mary the mother of James, and Salome buy spices to anoint Jesus. Some exegetes argue that the women's desire to anoint Jesus' body indicates their misunderstanding, since Jesus was already anointed at Bethany, which he himself interpreted to have been in preparation for his burial (14.8). Others point to the uselessness of going to balm a deteriorating body.[118] However, this is precisely why spices were used, to mask the odours from the decomposition of the body.[119] The women want to complete the burial by Joseph of Arimathea and thus to pay their respects.

The half darkness reminds the readers of the danger involved, and the courage required, to which Mark repeatedly alludes: the young man being taken by the soldiers, only narrowly escaping, the disciples running away at the arrest, the following of Peter 'from afar' and the looking on of the women 'from afar' and Joseph of Arimathea who dared to ask Pilate for Jesus' body.[120] John Donahue, describing the setting of persecution of Mark's Gospel, argues that, in the story of Peter's denial, the readers 'would inevitably hear…echoes of narratives of the trials of the various Christian martyrs, especially in Rome, where such trials characterized the persecution under Nero'.[121] This being the case the first readers would also relate to the disciples' flight at Jesus' arrest, the caution of Peter and the women keeping far off and the courage needed to draw near again.

Mary Magdalene, Mary of James and Salome run a very real danger. Jesus was not condemned for just any crime, but as 'king of the Jews', he was a supposed threat to the Roman empire. His grave was not to be visited, and those who did so

---

117. Brown 1993: 1207-1219. See also Lane (1974: 577-79), who argues that Jesus' case could be viewed as one of high treason.

118. For these opinions see Melzer-Keller 1997: 65. According to Melzer-Keller (1997: 57-59) the intention to anoint Jesus' body in Mark belongs to a redactional intervention whose aim is to combine the originally independent stories of the burial and the visit of the grave.

119. Lane 1974: 585.

120. Mk 14.50, 51, 54; 15.40, 43.

121. Donahue 1995: 19.

ran the risk of being condemned to death just as he had been.[122]

On their way to the tomb the three women disciples ask themselves who will roll the stone away. However, when they look up, they see that this has already been done.

4.4. *Entering the Tomb and Being Instructed by a Young Man*
Mary Magdalene, Mary of James and Salome enter the tomb and are quite startled when they see a young man sitting in the tomb in a white garment. He says to them:

> You seek Jesus of Nazareth, who was crucified. He has risen, he is not here; see the place where they laid him. But go, tell his disciples and Peter: 'He is going before you into Galilee'. There you will see him, as he told you. (16.6-7)[123]

Some exegetes argue that these verses make it perfectly clear that Jesus did not regard the women as disciples, since they are to tell the disciples that they will see him in Galilee.[124] They refer to the fact that Mark clearly prefers direct speech, with which I also agree. [125] The translation should not be 'Go, tell his disciples and Peter that he is going before you into Galilee' which would include the women. By using direct speech Mark seems to exclude the women on purpose. Their witness does not suffice.

The same exegetes also presume that the punctuation should be added from 'he is going' up to 'as he told you'. Another punctuation is also possible: from 'he is going' up to 'Galilee'. Then only the words 'He is going before you into Galilee' are addressed directly to the disciples, exactly the same words Jesus said to them earlier (14.28). The words 'there you will see him, as he told you' are directed to the women as a reminder and explanation of Jesus' promise. This clearly includes them.[126]

The latter would be the proper interpretation, since, as we saw, Mark in the rest of the Gospel includes both women and men in the use of the word 'disciples'. There is one new element compared to 14.28: the disciples are promised that they will see Jesus in Galilee, which would have been told earlier too. This 'seeing', Jesus appearing to people, became vital to the Christian creed.[127]

4.5. *The Unexpected End: Being Afraid and Saying Nothing*
The reaction of Mary Magdalene, Mary of James and Salome which Mark describes is quite remarkable and unexpected:

122. Schottroff 1982: 3-25 esp.7-8. Women and children were also crucified; see Josephus, Jewish War II.307.
123. The Revised Standard Version has: 'But go, tell his disciples and Peter that he is going before you into Galilee'. For the punctuation see below.
124. E.g. Schweizer 1982: esp. 298; Pesch 1977: 521, 534-35; Ernst 1981: 482, 487-88.
125. Blass, Debrunner and Rehkopf 1990: 386.1; 397.5; 470.1.
126. See also Neirynck 1969: esp. 181-82. Both he and Schottroff (1982: 3-25) point at the logic of the connection between verses 6 and 7: 'You seek Jesus, he is not here, but go…, there you will see him'. Melzer-Keller (1997: 63-64) concludes that, since in her opinion both interpretations remain possible, this is once more a sign of Mark's ambivalence towards women as disciples.
127. See 1 Cor. 15.1-8.

> And they went out and fled from the tomb; for trembling and astonishment had come upon them; and they said nothing to any one, for they were afraid. (16.8)

These sentences form the conclusion to the Gospel of Mark as we know it. However, there is a debate as to whether the Gospel originally ended with the women fleeing and keeping silent. Perhaps the real conclusion to the Gospel has been lost.[128]

A number of scholars think that in terms of narrative technique Mark could have ended very meaningfully with v. 8.[129] Mary Cotes draws attention to the fact that in all other instances in Mark fear as a result of divine manifestation does not evoke silence, but, instead, gives rise to speech.[130] She compares this to the fact that the silence of Mary Magdalene, Mary of James and Salome is in keeping with their silence in the preceding narrative. They only speak among themselves (16.3). This corresponds to the silence of the women throughout Mark and would, according to Cotes, reflect a typical image of women's behaviour in the ancient world.[131] In her view the silence and fear of the women does not need any further explanation: as women they are simply afraid of making a public declaration, since men are the speakers in the public sphere.[132] According to Cotes, Mark thus portrays the women as refusing to take on a public role. Mark would confirm the women as seers and the men as speakers: only the male disciples take up the public role of proclaiming that the crucified one is risen.[133]

An important objection to this interpretation is that the young man in white specifically instructs the women to go and speak. Cotes argues that this is ironic, and that Mark with the silent women forces the readers to focus on his words instead of on theirs. I am inclined to take the instruction more seriously in the sense that Mark suggests that it should be proper behaviour to obey the instruction, although it may be different from what women do in the rest of Mark.

Instead, I agree with Schottroff who argues that Mark puts Peter and Mary Magdalene side by side: both take courage, both fail (16.1-8; 14.66-72). In both their cases, anxiety gains the upper hand. Both are examples of the fulfillment of the prophecy of Zechariah of which Jesus reminded them shortly before his arrest when he said:

> You will all fall away; for it is written, 'I will strike the shepherd, and the sheep will be scattered'. (14.27; cf. Zech. 13.7)

128. For an account of the various views about the original conclusion, see O'Collins 1988.
129. For instance Schottroff 1982: 3-25 and Hester 1995. O'Collins discusses the views of the Badhams, Perrin, Marxsen, Pesch and Lightfoot.
130. Mk 4.41; 5.16-17; 6.49; 9.6.
131. As exceptions Cotes (1992: 159) refers to Herodias and her daughter and to the Syro-Phoenician woman, but she emphasizes that Mark situates these women in an interior (6.22-29; 7.24-30).
132. Cotes (1992: 158-60) refers to the fact that only men in Mark speak and are summoned to remain silent, not women. She also points to the vast hesitation and fear of the haemorrhaging woman to speak in public (Mk 5.25-34).
133. Cotes 1992: 166.

To the readers, both are also examples of people who have overcome their failure and their anxiety. Mary Magdalene and the women eventually did speak and Peter and the others recovered from flight and denial. Otherwise the readers would not have known about the resurrection.

However, the Gospel of Mark does not end with the overcoming of anxiety but with anxiety.[134] Donahue suggests that Mark's conclusion relates to the difficult situation of persecution faced by the first Christians. Donahue, arguing that the persecutions under Nero are involved, quotes Tacitus:

> First, then, the confessed members of the sect were arrested, next, on evidence furnished by them, a huge multitude was convicted, not so much on the count of arson as for hatred of the human race. And derision accompanied their end [deaths]: they were covered with wild beasts' skins and torn to death by dogs; or they were fastened on crosses, and, when daylight failed, were burned to serve as lamps by night. (The Annals 15.44)[135]

The conclusion of the Gospel of Mark has a literary focus precisely with respect to this situation. The Gospel shows that anxiety and failure are understandable: even Peter and Mary Magdalene were overcome by them. But the Gospel's ending shows more. There is also anxiety and failure in the face of the miracle of the resurrection.[136] However, the proclamation of the gospel depends on overcoming anxiety and failure.[137]

According to David Hester, the abrupt end of the Gospel of Mark makes a powerful impact on the readers: they are not to keep silent, but to speak.[138] And indeed they are to go to Galilee, where Jesus unfolded his teaching. He is going before them; which is the fulfillment of the promise Jesus gave the disciples before his death (14.28). Hester concludes:

> If actual readers wish to meet Jesus, they must 'return' to the ministry in Galilee and relive the story by taking his place (picking up the cross and following his example).[139]

The disciples must hold on to what Jesus taught them in Galilee: then they will see him (16.7).

However, Mark not only calls on the readers, women and men alike, to become and to remain disciples, but also, like Peter and Mary Magdalene, to overcome anxiety and failure and to become proclaimers of the suffering Messiah who was raised to life.

---

134. Schottroff 1982: 20-22.
135. Donahue 1995: 21.
136. O'Collins (1988: 499-503), following Lightfoot, interprets the fear of the women as a reaction on the revelation and the empty grave: a 'mysterium fascinans et tremendum'.
137. Schottroff 1982: 20-22.
138. Hester 1995. See also Boomershine 1981.
139. Hester 1995: 84. See also Cotes 1992: 165.

4.6. *The Second Ending: Meeting the Risen Lord*

According to the later Markan appendix (16.9-20), Mary Magdalene 'of whom he had cast seven devils', was the first to whom the risen Christ appeared (16.9). Mary Magdalene thereupon goes to those who had been with Jesus, who were mourning and weeping, to tell them that Jesus was alive and had been seen by her. However, they do not believe her. Then Jesus appears to two of them, who were walking, but when they tell it to the others they are not believed either. Finally, Jesus appears to the Eleven and reproaches them for not believing those who had seen him and summons them to preach the Gospel to every creature, which they accordingly do.

5. *Mark's Portrayal of Mary Magdalene*

5.1. *Mary Magdalene's Relation to Jesus*

By introducing Mary Magdalene, Mary the mother of James, Mary the mother of Joses and Salome almost at the end of the Gospel, as disciples who have been following Jesus from the beginning of his ministry (15.40-41), Mark encourages the readers to leaf back and visualize them every time the word disciples occurs. Thus, in Mark's portrayal Mary Magdalene from the very start of the Gospel witnesses Jesus' influence on people, his healings, and the power of his teaching. Together with the Twelve and others, Mary Magdalene is one of those whom Jesus calls his sisters and brothers and to whom he has given the secret of the Kingdom of God, in contrast to those outside who receive everything in parables (4.10).

5.2. *Mary Magdalene Among the Disciples*

Mary Magdalene, Mary the mother of James, Mary the mother of Joses and Salome at the end of the Gospel all seem to reflect the four named male disciples at the beginning: Simon, Andrew, James and John. However, in contrast to them and the other disciples, Mary Magdalene, Mary the mother of James, Mary the mother of Joses and Salome, until then the unknown and implied women disciples, are present at the crucifixion. At this point of Mark's story they exemplify the content of Markan discipleship.

In Mark, Mary Magdalene and Mary of Joses also witness the burial of Jesus. Mary Magdalene, Mary of James, and Salome see that the stone has been rolled away from the tomb and encounter the young man inside the tomb. In this way Mark makes Mary Magdalene the only witness of both circumstances: Jesus being dead and buried and Jesus no longer being in his tomb.

The young man in white instructs them to go and tell the disciples and Peter that Jesus is going before them to Galilee. This is exactly what Jesus said he would do after his resurrection, saying this to all the disciples on the night when he was captured. The sentence 'there you will see him' is new and not only directed at the other disciples, but also at Mary Magdalene, Mary of James, and Salome. However, Mary Magdalene, Mary of James, and Salome do not tell anybody and thus in the end fail Jesus like the other disciples.

5.3. *Mary Magdalene's Function in the Story*

To the readers, Mary Magdalene, Mary of Joses, Mary of James, and Salome exemplify what Markan discipleship really is. Discipleship has nothing to do with power, but with the utmost willingness to remain of service, even when it is dangerous to do so.

When we take into account that Mark encourages the reader to visualize the four women among the disciples, they are also truly Markan disciples in that they are no perfect models, but models through their failures. As Markan disciples they are amazed, shocked and terrified at what Jesus does.[140] They do not understand all his teaching (e.g. 9.30-32). Although they are at the Passover meal, sharing bread and wine, and in Gethsemane, where Jesus prays, they flee when he is arrested (14.12-50). Like Peter (14.54), Mary Magdalene and the three other women take courage and return. But, while Peter denies Jesus, Mary Magdalene, as the most important witness, fails Jesus by keeping silent.

Nevertheless in the flow of the story, Peter and Mary Magdalene, in their courage and failure, are catalysts to the readers. With Mary Magdalene Mark encourages the readers, women and men, to overcome anxiety and failure, to remain disciples and to become apostles, no matter how frightening. The courage and inspiration necessary to overcome one's fear can be found in the knowledge that the suffering Messiah was raised to life and will be seen in Galilee.

140. E.g. Mk 1.27; 4.35-41; 10.24-32.

Chapter 6

MARY MAGDALENE ACCORDING TO THE
GOSPELS OF MATTHEW AND LUKE

1. *Matthew's Introduction of Mary Magdalene*

Like Mark, Matthew introduces the women followers of Jesus at the end of the
Gospel, immediately after the death of Jesus. At first sight, it seems that Matthew
introduces Mary Magdalene the same way as Mark does. However, the sentence
construction with which Matthew introduces Mary Magdalene is strikingly different in composition. As we saw, Mark introduces the women thus:

> There were also women looking on from afar, among whom were Mary Mag-
> dalene and Mary of James the younger and the mother of Joses, and Salome, who,
> when he was in Galilee, followed him and ministered to him; and also many other
> women who came up with him to Jerusalem. (Mk 15.40-41)

Matthew, however, relates:

> There were many women there, looking on from afar, who had followed Jesus
> from Galilee to minister to him; among them were Mary Magdalene and Mary the
> mother of James and Joseph and the mother of the sons of Zebedee. (Mt. 27.55)

Whereas Mark mentions the named women before the unnamed, Matthew has it
the other way round. Furthermore, whereas Mark introduces the named women
with the words 'to follow' and 'to serve', Matthew introduces the many unnamed
women with these verbs. Moreover, Mark relates that the named women had followed (ἠκολούθουν) and served (διηκόνουν) Jesus in Galilee, while Matthew says
that the many unnamed women decided to follow (ἠκολούθησαν) Jesus from (ἀπὸ
τῆς) Galilee with the purpose of serving (διακονοῦσαι) him.[1] Last, but not least,
whereas Mark gave both the named and the unnamed women their own active
verbs, Matthew does not combine the named women with any active verbs at all.
Matthew only relates that they 'were' among the unnamed women (ἐν αἷς ἦν).

With these differences Matthew alters the Markan portrait of Mary Magdalene
in a significant way. She and the other named women, as a small group, are no
longer distinguished from the larger group of women. They have become part of it.
The named women are no longer singled out as belonging to the disciples in

---

1. ἠκολούθησαν is an aorist ingressive and διακονοῦσαι is a participle of purpose; see Blass,
Debrunner and Rehkopf 1990: 418.4.

contrast to the unnamed women who decided to join Jesus on their pilgrimage to the Passover festival. According to Matthew, the named and unnamed women not only now belong to one and the same group, but have always done so.

In this section we will go into Matthew's view on women and discipleship and on Matthean discipleship and the Twelve.

2. *Women and Discipleship in Matthew*

2.1. *One Large Group of Women Followers*
Matthew does not mention the going up to Jerusalem as Mark does. The Gospel only alludes to the pilgrimage by emphasizing that the large group of women at some point decided to follow Jesus from Galilee, thus leaving out the clear Markan pilgrimage motive of the unnamed women, and at the same time radically changing the Markan portrait of the named women as the ones who had followed and served Jesus from the beginning of his ministry in Galilee. In Matthew's view, all the women who are now at the crucifixion decided to follow Jesus when he left Galilee. They did not follow and serve him like the small group of women in Mark, but they decided to follow him with the aim of being of service. Thus their motive is not the pilgrimage to Jerusalem, as is the motive of the large group in Mark, but their motive is their decision to serve Jesus. Matthew introduces Mary Magdalene as one of a large group of women determined to serve Jesus on his journey from Galilee onward. How should we interpret this?

In any case, Matthew encourages the reader to think of the large group of women followers as being implied every time the Gospel mentions the following crowd from 19.1 onward, since this is where Jesus' journey from Galilee starts. This means that they are among the crowds in 19.2 that are healed. They hear Jesus' teaching about marriage and divorce and see him blessing the children (19.2-15). They are among the crowd rebuking two blind people when Jesus leaves Jericho (20.29-34) and spreading their garments and cutting branches from the trees when Jesus enters Jerusalem (21.1-11). The readers may visualize them speaking as the crowd shouts 'Hosanna to the son of David! Blessed be he who comes in the name of the Lord! Hosanna in the highest!' and as the crowd answers to the people in the stirred city: 'This is the prophet Jesus from Nazareth in Galilee'.

They are also among the crowd which is astonished at Jesus' teaching in the Temple (22.33): his answer to the chief priests and the elders about his authority, his parable of the two sons, of the tenants in the vineyard and of the wedding feast, his answer to the questions of the disciples of the Pharisees and of Herod's party about paying taxes, his answer to the question of the Sadducees about rising from death, his answer to the question of the Pharisees about the greatest commandment and about the Messiah, his approval of the teaching of the scribes and the Pharisees, his severe warning against their actions and his prophecy on the Temple being abandoned (21.23–24.1). Perhaps we may also visualize the women already among the crowd in Galilee, before their decision to serve Jesus upon his departure.

But what about discipleship? Does Matthew encourage the readers to think that the serving women are implied every time the Gospel uses the word disciples, as Mark does? In contrast to Mark, Matthew is rather ambivalent about this.

2.2. *Matthean Discipleship and the Twelve Disciples*
We should note that Matthew's use of the word 'disciple' differs considerably from that of Mark, who only uses it as a male plural and avoids identifying those individuals to whom it refers, not once calling the Twelve 'the twelve disciples', nor connecting the word with the name of any who belong to the Twelve, or with any other name. This is all very different in Matthew. Matthew specifically calls the male Twelve 'the twelve disciples',[2] and also uses the word in connection with their names.[3] In addition, in all those instances where Mark distinguishes between the Twelve and the disciples in general, Matthew carefully avoids doing so.[4] Furthermore, for Matthew, Peter is not a representative of the Twelve, as in Mark, but the spokesman of the disciples in general.[5]

Moreover, Matthew only connects the names of the Twelve with the word 'disciple', and not with any other name. All this suggests that the disciples in Matthew are first and foremost these twelve males. Note, for instance, the careful way in which Matthew describes Joseph of Arimathea: not as a disciple but as one who has been 'discipled' (ἐμαθητεύθη) by Jesus (27.57). Matthew says that he has 'also' (καὶ αὐτός) been 'discipled', thus referring to the serving women in 27.55-56, suggesting that they too have been 'discipled' by Jesus.[6]

Although, in Matthew's view, the disciples are first and foremost the twelve males, Matthew, nevertheless, uses the masculine plural of the word 'disciple' inclusively, meaning both men and women. Like Mark, Matthew splits the plural brothers into brother and sister. Matthew even more clearly than Mark insists that these brothers and sisters are disciples, since, whereas Mark describes the ones around Jesus as his brothers and sisters, Matthew directly calls his disciples brothers and sisters.[7]

Also significant is the importance of serving for Matthean discipleship. Some exegetes limit the ministry of the women in 27.55 to a traditional women's role of serving.[8] However, just as in Mark, the word διακονέω is used in Matthew to characterize both Jesus' ministry as well as the ministry of his disciples (Mk 10.45; Mt. 20.20). And as in Mark, the disciples in Matthew also serve in many ways, including the preparing of food and waiting at table (14.19-20; 15.36-37; 26.17). Matthew gives even more emphasis than Mark does on the importance of serving, since at the last Judgment only those who have served the Son of Man by serving

2.   10.1 and 11.1; cf. 28.16.
3.   Peter, James and John in 17.1-8 and 26.27-41. Unlike Mark, see Mk 9.2-8 and 14.33-38.
4.   Cf. Mk 4.10-12 with Mt. 13.10-11; cf. Mk 6.1-7 with Mt. 9.37–10.1; cf. Mk 6.30-35 with Mt. 14.13-15; cf. Mk 9.30-35 with Mt. 18.1-3; cf. Mk 14.16-17 with Mt. 26.19-20. The exception is Mt. 19.23-27 compared to Mk 10.23-28.
5.   E.g., Mt. 14.26-28; 15.12-15; 16.13-16; 19.25-27; 26.26-35. See, for the role of Peter in Matthew Wilkins 1988: 173-216 esp. 208-214.
6.   See Minear 1974: 37-38.
7.   Mt. 12.48-49; cf. Mk 3.33-34.
8.   See Melzer-Keller 1997: 117-19.

those who are in need, will be saved (25.31-46).[9] The serving consists of feeding
the hungry, giving the thirsty something to drink, receiving strangers, clothing the
naked, caring for the sick and visiting the prisoners. These are to be done by all of
Jesus' followers as if one did it to Jesus himself. Matthew clearly labels these
activities as *diakonia* (25.44). As such, serving is a major characteristic of Matthean discipleship, and the women followers, who consciously decided to follow
Jesus precisely with the aim of serving him, are examples of Matthean discipleship.

Moreover, in contrast to Mark, Matthew mentions one of the serving women
earlier in the Gospel than 27.55, namely the mother of the sons of Zebedee, James
and John, who are two core members of the Twelve (4.21). Matthew relates that
she, accompanied by her two sons, goes to Jesus to ask him whether her sons may
sit in his kingdom at his right and left hand (20.21). This is strikingly different than
Mark, where she is absent and the two brothers themselves ask Jesus if they may
sit with him in his kingdom.

Some exegetes argue that Matthew, in contrast to Mark, thus lays the burden of
the question on the mother's shoulders, in this way unburdening James and John.[10]
However, Matthew relates that the mother asks her question in the presence of her
sons. This suggests that, according to Matthew, she was related to the Twelve and
Jesus in such a way that she, instead of her sons, asks their question. Matthew
furthermore suggests that Jesus' answer 'You do not know what you are asking.
Are you able to drink the cup that I am to drink?' is directed to her sons as well as
to her, and that she, like them, replies firmly 'We are able'. Jesus' words 'You will
drink my cup' affirm that she is or is to be a close follower.[11]

Thus, on the one hand the disciples first and foremost seem to be the male
Twelve, but on the other hand Matthew still allows the readers to imagine women
as disciples. Elisabeth Wainwright, on the basis of a thorough examination of
the Gospel of Matthew and especially of the stories in which women function as
characters, identifies the same ambiguity. In Matthew there is a vision of inclusive
discipleship, but it is blurred by the dominant presence of male disciples in the
narrative.[12]

2.3. *Conflicting Traditions*

As we saw earlier, Mark invitingly opens up the possibility of following Jesus to
all the readers, both male and female, teaching them what discipleship really means.

---

9.   See also Ricci 1994: 170-71.

10. E.g. Melzer-Keller 1997: 139-41. I would have agreed if Matthew had pictured the sons as
not present.

11. See Wainwright 1991: 119-21 and 253-57.

12. Wainwright 1991, especially 325-39. In addition, see Wainwright 1995: 635-77 and
Melzer-Keller 1997: 104-186, according to whom Matthew's women are also less important and
more traditional than Mark's. The stories about women in Matthew are: the women in Jesus'
genealogy (1.1-17); Peter's mother-in-law (8.14-17); the woman with a flow of blood and the
daughter of Jairus (9.18-30); Herodias and her daughter (14.1-12); the Canaanite woman (15.21-
28); the mother of the sons of Zebedee (20.20-28); the believing harlots (21.31-32); the parable of
the foolish and the wise women (25.1-13); the anointing woman (26.6-16); the wife of Pilate
(27.19); the women at the crucifixion (27.55-56); Mary Magdalene and the other Mary (28.1-10).

Matthew, however, has a slightly different, more androcentric and perhaps more hierarchic point of view. Matthew is not only about being a disciple, but also about making disciples. The Gospel offers both one identified disciple, Peter, as a living and encouraging example of discipleship and, by devoting large portions to teaching on discipleship, Matthew also equips readers, as disciples, both male and female, to make others disciples.[13] In the end, however, it appears that the making of disciples is first entrusted to the Eleven (28.8, 16-20).

Already in 16.13-28 the Jesus of Matthew called Peter the rock on which the church would be built, saying to him:

> And I tell you, you are Peter, and on this rock I will build my church, and the powers of death shall not prevail against it. I will give you the keys of the kingdom of heaven, and whatever you bind on earth shall be bound in heaven, and whatever you loose on earth shall be loosed in heaven. (16.18-20; cf. Mk 8.27-33)

This is unlike Mark. However, at the same time Matthew also has the Markan passage where Peter is chastised for his bold refusal to accept Jesus' death. Though Matthew softens the scene, Jesus rebukes Peter not openly, but aside from the others, his words are virtually the same (16.22-23; cf. Mk 8.32-33). Jesus calls Peter a stumbling block and Satan, one who is not concerned with the thoughts of God but with those of men.[14] In addition, in Mt. 19.27-30, Jesus promises the Twelve 'in the regeneration' that they will sit on twelve thrones, next to the Son of Man, judging the twelve tribes of Israel, in contrast to Mk 10.28-31, where these words are absent. This seems to reveal a rather high notion of the Twelve in Matthew.

However, Matthew, unlike Mark, also reminds the disciples not to call themselves or others rabbi, father or master, for there is but one Rabbi, one Father and one Master (23.8-10), which seems to contradict such a high notion. This contradiction fits in with Wainwright's assumption that Matthew holds conflicting traditions, which destabilize and open up the predominantly patriarchal narrative world of the Gospel.

We should regard Matthew's ambiguity towards the serving women, including Mary Magdalene, in the same light. Their decision to follow Jesus with the aim of serving him exemplifies discipleship. Matthew seems to say that they have been 'discipled' like Joseph of Arimathea. They are perhaps included in the plural form of the word 'disciples' whenever it is not further specified as the male Twelve. One of them, the mother of James and John, is related to the Twelve and seems to be a close follower of Jesus. However, Matthew clearly avoids directly connecting the word 'disciples' with the serving women, whereas Matthew, unlike Mark, does not hesitate to do so in case of the Twelve.

3. *Matthew's Story about Mary Magdalene*

Matthew introduces Mary Magdalene as one of many women followers who decided to follow Jesus when he left Galilee with the aim of serving him. In this

---

13. Minear 1974: 28-44 and Wilkins 1988: esp. 172.
14. About the special place of Peter in Matthew, see Wilkins 1988: 173-216.

way Matthew encourages the reader to leaf back to 19.1 and to visualize Mary
Magdalene among the crowds which follow Jesus. Although the women in 27.55
exemplify Matthean discipleship and although Matthew's use of the word 'disciples' may refer to both women and men, as became clear in 12.48-50, the Gospel
is rather ambivalent about whether the reader should believe the women are
implied whenever the word 'disciples' is used. Matthew obviously puts the Twelve
and especially Peter to the fore.

3.1. *The Crucifixion and Graves Breaking Open*
At the crucifixion Matthew singles out Mary Magdalene. The many women
followers, among them Mary Magdalene, Mary the mother of James and Joseph,
and the mother of the sons of Zebedee, are at the crucifixion looking on from afar.
The mention of the mother of the sons of Zebedee makes the reader aware that her
sons James and John, who said they could drink Jesus' cup (20.20-23), are pain-
fully absent.[15] The disciples have all fled, just as they did in Mark (26.56).

   Matthew follows Mark closely by relating the casting of lots by the soldiers and
the people passing who insult Jesus and who make reference to his building up the
Temple in three days. Unlike Mark, Matthew's passersby and the chief priests and
the scribes also mock about Jesus being the Son of God:

> He trusts in God; let God deliver him now, if he desires it; for he said, 'I am the
> Son of God'. (27.43)

   As in Mark the whole country is covered in darkness for three hours. Then Jesus
dies as he does in Mark, crying loudly. But what happens next is very different.
The centurion and the soldiers with him see the earth shaking, the rocks splitting
apart and the graves breaking open. Terrified by this, they say: 'He really was Son
of God' (27.54), referring to the mocking of the passersby, the priests and scribes
and those who had been crucified with Jesus.

3.2. *Sitting Opposite the Tomb*
In what follows, two of the many women, Mary Magdalene and 'the other Mary'
are singled out (27.61). It is not clear who this other Mary is. Is she the same as the
Mary mentioned in 27.56? As we saw, Mark emphasizes the role of Mary
Magdalene, by portraying her in the company of different women when they see
where Jesus is buried and when they go to the tomb. In contrast to this, in Matthew's story Mary Magdalene and the other Mary are together all the time.

   Matthew does not explicitly state, as Mark does, that the women see where Jesus
is buried (27.57-61). The burial is done by Joseph of Arimathea, as in Mark, but
here he is not a member of the Council, but a rich man being 'also discipled' by
Jesus. He buries Jesus in his own tomb. Matthew ends this pericope by simply
stating:

> Mary Magdalene and the other Mary were there, sitting opposite the sepulcher.
> (27.61)

---

15. Wainwright 1991: 142; Melzer-Keller 1997: 118-19.

Matthew, thereupon, turns to the high priests and the Pharisees, who remind themselves that Jesus ('that impostor') said he would be raised after three days (27.62-67). The tomb is therefore secured and guards are put by it to make it impossible for the disciples to steal the body, and then tell the people that he indeed had risen.

Matthew gives the readers the impression that the two women have remained at the tomb, perhaps all the time, but in any case for a longer period, since the word that is used for the sitting of the women is καθήμεναι: a present tense, implying duration. Perhaps Mary Magdalene and the other Mary are sitting opposite the grave in vigil, thus showing their care and concern.[16] Or perhaps the sitting is meant as keeping guard: Matthew refers to sitting soldiers in 27.36, guarding over Jesus, during the crucifixion.[17] The vigil of the two Marys could also be an apologetic reassurance of Matthew that the tomb was not unwatched for one moment. Nobody could have stolen the body.[18]

3.3. *Going to Look at the Tomb and Witnessing its Opening*

Perhaps Matthew has another motive too. Matthew mentions the two Marys again, when they go to the tomb. They do not go to anoint the body of Jesus, as in Mark, (how could they since the tomb is sealed and guarded?), but they go to look (θεωρέω)[19] at the tomb. Why? According to Thomas Longstaff, Matthew refers to a certain custom. He argues that 'it was very likely [that] the custom in ancient Judaism [was] to watch…the tomb of a loved one until the third day after death, in order to ensure that premature burial had not taken place'.[20] In his view the two Marys go to look at the tomb to ensure that Jesus is really dead.

Other comments vary as to why the two Marys go to look at the tomb. The Marys go to look at the tomb because they simply need to find it empty from the narrator's point of view.[21] Or their going to look is a pious grave visit.[22] Some exegetes suggest that Matthew, by skipping the anointing motive, affirms the validity of the anointing at Bethany.[23] It is also suggested that the words of the

---

16. According to Gundry (1982: 582), 'they sit opposite the grave in vigil. Their vigil, too, exemplifies the care and concern for the persecuted that true discipleship requires'.

17. Wainwright (1991: 300) refers to the soldiers in 27.36 who are sitting, keeping guard over Jesus, witnessing the crucifixion and acknowledging the crucified to be the son of God. So the women who witnessed the burial will encounter the risen Christ.

18. Melzer-Keller 1997: 120. Stock (1994: 431-32) combines the three motives: 'as their final service of love at the grave, they sit in wake, by which the continuation of the narrative is assured, and the motive of security as well'.

19. Matthew does not use the word θεωρέω at the burial like Mark, but uses it in the context of the women going to look at the tomb. See also 27.55; cf. Mk 15.40, 47; 16.4.

20. Longstaff 1981: 278. He refers to Semachot 8.1, 'the classic Rabbinic text on death and mourning' (quoting Dov Zlotnick's commentary on it, Yale Judaica Series 17), and reacts to Goulder (1978: 235) according to whom Matthew's story here is rather incoherent compared to Mark. See also Longstaff 2000.

21. See Neirynck 1969: 175-76.

22. See Stock (1994: 434), who, without any references, states that the word θεωρέω is 'an apt expression for a pious grave visit'.

23. See Wainwright 1991: 143 and 302. Melzer-Keller (1997: 121) considers Matthew's story

angel 'I know that you seek Jesus who was crucified' reveal why the Marys go to look: they are looking for Jesus' dead body. By doing this Matthew shows their complete failure to believe Jesus' words that he would rise. [24] Others, however, object to this, since how could the women possibly be expected to inspect a sealed tomb?[25] Because of the Matthean story of the guards, it has also been argued that Matthew shows the faith of the women. Like the Pharisees they know what Jesus said about his resurrection and they are going to look on the first day of the week to see if anything has happened.[26]

I think it is indeed important to note the direct context in which Matthew relates that the guards are at the tomb, since the Pharisees remembered that Jesus said he would rise after three days (27.62-66). By this pericope Matthew encourages the readers to take for granted that Jesus' words about the resurrection were common knowledge (16.21; 17.23; 20.19). The two Marys are indeed aware of them, since the angel says to them: 'he is risen, as he said'. In addition, Matthew's two Marys are not struck by fear as they are in Mark. They are afraid, but at the same time rejoice greatly (28.8). We should also note that earlier in Matthew, in contrast to Mark, the women had already witnessed that, through divine intervention an earthquake caused (ἡ γῆ ἐσείσθη) graves to be opened and people to be resurrected (27.51-52). By this narrative device Matthew suggests that not only the guards, but also the two Marys, are at the tomb precisely because of Jesus' words about his resurrection.

Towards the dawn of the first day of the week, Mary Magdalene and the other Mary ignore the guards and go to look at the tomb, expecting that Jesus, whom they watched dying on the cross, will now rise, as he himself said. And indeed, there is an earthquake (σεισμός 28.1). An angel of the Lord comes down from heaven, rolls the stone away from the tomb and sits on it as if it were a throne, his appearance like lightning. He invites Mary Magdalene and the other Mary to see the empty place where Jesus has been laid. The guards are so overcome by fear that they seem to be the dead ones. But Jesus, the crucified, is gone: 'for he has risen, as he said' (28.6).

3.4. *Meeting the Risen Jesus and being Instructed by him*

Matthew, in contrast to Mark, does not relate that the women actually go into the tomb. Instead, the two Marys immediately depart from the tomb to do what the angel requires of them:

to be more logical than Mark's, since Matthew skips the paradoxical intention to anoint Jesus' body after it has been buried. Gaechter (1962: 951-52) simply harmonizes Mark, Luke and Matthew and argues that the women are going to anoint the body.

24. See Frankemölle 1994: II, 518-19. Just as the male disciples failed earlier, Matthew, in Frankemölle's view, here shows the failure of the women disciples, which consists of 'einem grundlegenden Vergessen' (p. 519).

25. See Wainwright 1991: 143.

26. See Margoliouth 1927. Also Gaechter (1962: 952) considers the women's faith as a reason to go to look at the tomb. He rejects it, however, as utterly impossible, since, whereas the Twelve could not believe the prophecy (16.21; 17.23; 20.19) the women could not have done so either.

> Then go quickly and tell his disciples: 'he has risen from the dead, and behold, he
> is going before you to Galilee; there you will see him'. Lo, I have told you. (28.7)

They are not terrified as they are in Mark where they flee and tell nobody what they
have seen and heard. In Matthew they are afraid; yet, filled with joy, they run to tell
the disciples.

Unlike Mark, it is clear here that the two Marys are not implied in the male
plural 'disciples'. They are not to see Jesus in Galilee. Instead, Jesus comes to meet
the two Marys himself. 'Rejoice (χαίρετε)', he says, and when they take hold of
his feet and worship him, he adds: 'do not be afraid' (28.9-10). The common
translation interprets χαίρετε as a familiar Greek salutation.[27] It is suggested that
this common greeting is one of the indications that Matthew is not concerned with
Jesus' appearance to the women, but only with the affirmation of the angel's
words.[28] For Wainwright, Jesus' salutation is profound irony on the part of the
evangelist, who places the same greeting, used earlier by the betraying Judas
(26.49) and the mocking soldiers (27.29), on Jesus' lips right after his death and
resurrection.[29] In my opinion, however, χαίρετε must be interpreted within the
direct context, in which the two Marys are said to be filled with fear and great joy
(μετὰ φόβου καὶ χαρᾶς μεγάλης 28.8). Jesus reacts on this with 'rejoice'
(χαίρετε) in 28.9 and 'be not afraid' (μὴ φοβεῖσθε) in 28.10.[30] In doing so Jesus
affirms the joy of Mary Magdalene and the other Mary and banishes their fear.

In the context of the persecution and death of Jesus and in the context of the
chief priests and the Pharisees who expect the disciples to steal Jesus' body and to
lie about a supposed resurrection, the encouragement to rejoice reminds the reader
of the beatitude directed to the disciples at the beginning of the Sermon on the
Mount:

> Blessed are you, when men revile you and persecute you and utter all kinds of evil
> against you falsely on my account. Rejoice (χαίρετε) and be glad, for your reward
> is great in heaven, for so men persecuted the prophets who were before you.
> (5.12)

The risen Jesus asks the two Marys to go, not to 'his disciples' as the angel said,
but to 'my brothers', in this way indicating that the disciples' flight at his arrest has
not changed their relationship (cf. 12.49-50).[31] It is unclear whether in this case the
male plural 'brothers' implies the sisters as it did in 12.48-50.

3.5. *The End: Mission Charge to the Eleven Disciples*
The Gospel does not relate the meeting of the two women and the others, but
clearly what they say is accepted as true. However, not all the disciples, men and
women, go to Galilee; only the Eleven do. They even appear to have a special

---

27. Buchanan (1996: 1021) translates: 'Jesus met them, saying, "Hi!", which is the most
modern version of Jesus' greeting'.
28. Melzer-Keller (1997: 123) regards it as 'äusserst banal'.
29. Wainwright 1991: 310.
30. See also Zahn 1910: 718 n. 4.
31. See also Zahn 1910: 719.

appointment, since they go to a specific hill as Jesus had instructed them. There they worship Jesus, as the two women did, however, some disciples doubt the appearance. Coming closer, Jesus says to them:

> Go therefore and make disciples of all nations, baptizing them in the name of the Father and of the Son and of the holy Spirit, teaching them to observe all that I have commanded you; and lo, I am with you always, to the close of the age. (28.19-20).

The difference with Mark is significant. In Mark the readers, women and men, are encouraged to proclaim the gospel and to overcome their anxiety as Mary Magdalene and Peter eventually did. In Matthew it is the Eleven, and especially Peter as is clear from the Gospel as a whole, where the reader is first and foremost encouraged to look to, not to become like them, but, on the contrary, to be guided, to be 'discipled', to be baptized and to be taught.

4. Matthew's Portrayal of Mary Magdalene

4.1. Mary Magdalene's Relation to Jesus
Matthew introduces Mary Magdalene as one of many women followers who decided to follow Jesus on his leaving Galilee. Their aim is to serve him. As such Matthew encourages the readers to leaf back to 19.1 and to see Mary Magdalene among the crowds which follow Jesus. As such she experiences Jesus' healings, his teaching and his triumphant entry into Jerusalem (19.1–21.11). She also witnesses his teaching in the Temple, his parables on the end of times and his answers on questions about controversial political issues such as paying taxes, rising from death, the greatest commandment, the Messiah, the difference of the teaching of the scribes and Pharisees and their actions, and the prophecy on the Temple being abandoned (21.23–23.39).

Between this moment and the arrest of Jesus only his disciples are with him (24.1–26.19). Only the Twelve seem to be present at the Last Supper (26.20).

Mary Magdalene emerges from the crowds and is present again at the crucifixion. She and the other Mary are portrayed as courageous and trustworthy followers of Jesus, 'discipled' by him as were the other women who came from Galilee. Mary Magdalene and the other Mary sit in vigil opposite the tomb and go to look at it on the first day of the week, expecting Jesus to rise as he promised. And indeed they meet the risen Jesus and touch him and worship him. According to Matthew, the risen Lord spoke to Mary Magdalene and the other Mary and authorized them to instruct the disciples, who once again may be called his brothers, to go to Galilee.

4.2. Mary Magdalene among the Disciples
Although the women in 27.55 by their emphasis on service exemplify Matthean discipleship and although Matthew's use of the word 'disciples' may refer to both women and men, as became clear in 12.48-50, the Gospel is rather ambivalent about whether the readers should believe the women are implied whenever the

word 'disciples' is used. Matthew emphasizes the presence of the Twelve as disciples and especially puts Peter to the fore. Nothing is said of the women who followed Jesus from Galilee, but Matthew assures the readers that they are there to serve Jesus.

In contrast to Mark, Matthew does not single out Mary Magdalene; she is constantly in the company of the other Mary. In Matthew the readers are to hold Mary Magdalene and the other Mary in high esteem. Their faith in the resurrection and their courage to follow Jesus, even remaining near him near the tomb, in spite of the guards, make them inspiring examples. As such they are special compared to the other women following Jesus from Galilee. They also stand out from the twelve disciples who have all fled and especially Judas who betrayed him and Peter who denied him. Furthermore, in contrast to some of the remaining eleven disciples who later in the story doubt when they see the risen Jesus, Mary Magdalene and the other Mary worship him without hesitation.

Nevertheless, it is clear that Jesus does not encourage Mary Magdalene and the other Mary, as he does the eleven disciples, to go and bring the gospel to all nations. They are not to be apostles in general. Their apostleship is confined to a certain moment and limited to the 'brothers'.

4.3. *Mary Magdalene's Function in the Story*

In Matthew, Mary Magdalene exemplifies Matthean discipleship, as one among many women who decided to follow Jesus with the aim of serving him. In Matthew, Mary Magdalene and the other Mary are important as the only witnesses of the angel of the Lord descending from heaven, rolling away the stone from before the sealed tomb, where Jesus had been laid. In contrast to Mark Mary Magdalene and the other Mary are not to see Jesus in Galilee. They see him on their way to go and tell the disciples, as the angel commissioned them to do.

Matthew suggests that Mary Magdalene and the other Mary fulfil an intermediary role between Jesus and his remaining eleven disciples. Their mission is to send the disciples to Galilee to see the risen Jesus and to assure them that Jesus still considers them as his brothers in spite of their flight. Furthermore, Mary Magdalene and the other Mary can also testify that the risen Jesus himself encouraged them to rejoice without fear.

To the reader, Mary Magdalene and the other Mary are inspiring examples of serving, faith, courage, and stability, but it is the Eleven and especially Peter they are to look to, to be guided, to be 'discipled', to be baptized, and to be taught.

5. *Luke's Introduction of Mary Magdalene*

In contrast to the Gospels of Mark and Matthew, Luke introduces Mary Magdalene not at the end of the Gospel after Jesus has died, but rather at the beginning of his ministry, in the third of the summaries of Jesus' activities. In the first summary, covering the period after the forty days of temptation in the wilderness, Luke relates:

> And Jesus returned in the power of the Spirit into Galilee, and a report concerning
> him went out through all the surrounding country. And he taught in their syna-
> gogues glorified by all. (4.14)

In the second summary when people in Capernaum try to keep him from
leaving, Luke's Jesus himself explains his purpose:

> I must preach the good news of the kingdom of God to the other cities also; for I
> was sent for this purpose. (4.43)

Luke then adds that 'he was preaching in the synagogues of Judea' (4.44). Back
in Galilee, he appears to have gathered a great crowd of disciples from which he
chooses twelve, naming them 'apostles' (6.12-17). When Luke for the third time
summarizes Jesus' activities, Mary Magdalene is mentioned:

> Soon afterward he went through cities and villages, preaching and bringing the
> good news of the kingdom of God. And the twelve were with him, and also some
> women who had been healed of evil spirits and infirmities: Mary called Mag-
> dalene, from whom seven demons had gone out, and Joanna the wife of Chuza,
> Herod's steward, and Susanna, and many others, who provided for them[32] out of
> their means. (8.1-3)

Luke's introduction of Mary Magdalene in a summarizing pericope of Jesus' early
ministry is strikingly different from the late and sudden introductions in Mk 15.40-
41 and Mt. 27.55-56. Another difference is that the Markan and Matthean ministry
to Jesus in Luke has become a support for Jesus and his followers provided out of
the women's means. Also notably different is the mentioning of the Twelve as well
as Joanna and Susanna. An entirely new feature is the statement that the women
had been healed. In fact, the only similarity between Mark and Matthew on the one
hand and Luke on the other is the large group of women being divided into named
and unnamed persons. What is the significance of all this for the Lukan portrayal of
Mary Magdalene?

6. *Women and Discipleship in Luke*

6.1. *Typically Women's Roles?*
Some scholars argue that Luke portrays the women in 8.1-3 as having typically
women's roles which are distinguished from male ones. According to C.F. Evans,
for example, Lk. 8.1-3 explains how Jesus could have been able to travel extensively. He states:

---

32. Some texts read 'him'. See Bieberstein (1998: 33-35) for a discussion of the two possibilities. However, the singular looks like a harmonization with Mk 15.41 or Mt. 27.55. See for
instance Fitzmyer 1981: 698; Seim 1994: 58 and Bieberstein 1998: 34-35. This is in contrast to
Schürmann 1969: 444 and 447, Ricci 1994: 156-58 and Karris 1994: 6-7, who argue in favour of
the singular 'him'. Collins (1990: 245-46) interprets the 'them' as a specific Lukan trait to avoid
stating 'that ministrations at table were directed exclusively at the Lord' (p.246). The shift is rather
to the Lord who breaks the bread, who refreshes and satisfies. Cf. Lk. 12.37; 13.29; 22.16, 24-30;
24.29-31.

This is the only explicit explanation (Mk 14.50f. is only implicit) of how Jesus and his immediate companions were able to travel so extensively, especially in Luke's account, without working to support themselves. It also establishes the function of women disciples as material care and not preaching and healing.[33]

According to Josef Ernst, Jesus' allowing women to follow him shows his open attitude towards them, but in a specific way. He writes about 8.1-3:

> Lk sieht wie Jesus in der Frau das Kind Gottes, allerdings in einer angepassten gesellschaftlichen Position (die dienende Frau).[34]

Ben Witherington, who was the first to devote a whole article on Lk. 8.1-3,[35] is enthusiastic about the distinct position of the women, since it shows that Jesus gave typical women's roles significance and importance. He concludes:

> This meant something unique... Being Jesus' disciple did not lead these women to abandon their traditional roles in regard to preparing food, serving etc. Rather it gave these roles significance and importance, for now they could be used to serve the Master and the family... Luke admirably preserves the tension between the old and the new in regard to women roles in the Christian community.[36]

Is this the case? Does Luke, in sharp contrast to Mark, divide the followers of Jesus in two gender-specified categories, portraying the women followers in a typically women's role of providing material care, whereas the male followers are portrayed as spiritually concerned? A close look at 8.1-3 within the context of the Gospel of Luke as a whole gives quite another, more nuanced view on the role of the women in this text.

6.2. *Being with Jesus and Learning from Him*

By mentioning Mary Magdalene and the other women in this early summarizing statement, Luke makes the women followers of Jesus more visible and present than they are in Mark and Matthew. We do not need to leaf back from the crucifixion narrative and assume their presence when the words 'crowds' or 'disciples' appear. We are rather encouraged to take as given that they are everywhere Jesus goes. They are 'with him' (σὺν αὐτῷ 8.1) like the Twelve. What does this mean?

Lk. 8.1 relates what Jesus is doing while the Twelve, Mary Magdalene, Joanna, Susanna, and many other women are with him. He travels through the area (διώδευεν) from city to village preaching (κατὰ πόλιν καὶ κώμην κηρύσσων) and bringing the good news of the Kingdom of God (καὶ εὐαγγελιζόμενος τὴν βασιλείαν τοῦ θεοῦ). Being with Jesus means that the Twelve, Mary Magdalene, Joanna, Susanna, and many other women travel around with him and witness him preaching. In this way the Twelve and the named and unnamed women have the

---

33. Evans 1990: 366-67.

34. Ernst 1993: 202. Translation: Like Jesus, Luke sees God's child in the woman, to be sure, in an adjusted social position (the serving woman).

35. Witherington (1979) introduces his article with the words: 'Luke 8:1-3 has the dubious honour of being a New Testament pericope that has not been studied in any of the specialist reviews for the last hundred years' (p. 243). See also Ricci 1994: 29-50.

36. Witherington 1979: 247.

same role. They all travel with Jesus, they all witness him preaching from city to village and they all learn from him the good news of the Kingdom of God.

Being with Jesus may also mean that the Twelve, Mary Magdalene, Joanna, Susanna, and the many unnamed women, preach and evangelize themselves. However, with the use of αὐτός (8.1), Luke perhaps indicates that at this stage this is done only by Jesus himself. Luke might include the women in the mission of the Seventy sent out two by two (10.1), but this seems not very likely. Paul relates that the apostles take women with them on their mission, especially mentioning the brothers of the Lord and Cephas (1 Cor. 9.5). He himself mentions Euodia and Syntyche as women who were on mission with him and Clement and others preaching the gospel (Phil. 4.2-3). Luke, however, mentions only one mission couple, Priscilla and Aquila, who are wife and husband (Acts 18.2, 26). Luke gives no further indication of mixed couples or of women couples. The other mission couples in Acts are exclusively male.[37]

Although the women do not specifically appear again until the crucifixion, Luke assures the reader that Mary Magdalene, Joanna, Susanna, and many other women have been following Jesus the entire time. The Gospel makes this clear at the end, when it relates that all Jesus' acquaintances are watching the crucifixion, including the women who followed him from Galilee onwards (23.49).[38] They later appear to be the same women who had already followed Jesus in Galilee (23.55; 24.1, 6, 10). Thus Luke shows that the women followed Jesus from the beginning of his ministry until the end.

Luke does not allow the reader simply to visualize Jesus and the Twelve surrounded by women who are there to serve them. This is also evident from the story about Martha and Mary where Jesus points to Mary's learning as an example to Martha, who reminds him that Mary's duty is, instead, to help her to serve. Elsewhere in Luke's Gospel, hearing the word of God and doing it, with regard to women, is also more highly valued than gender-specified duties and privileges (cf. 8.21; 11.27-28).

At the end of the Gospel, Luke shows that the women followers from Galilee indeed listened to Jesus' words and remembered them. Having found Jesus' tomb empty, they are asked by the 'men' at the tomb to remember what Jesus said about the Son of Man being delivered into the hands of sinful men, crucified, and on the third day rising again (24.6-7). Luke then states: 'And they remembered his words' (24.8). Luke thus emphasizes that not only the men, but also the women following Jesus did so first and foremost to learn from him. In this way the Twelve, Mary Magdalene, Joanna, Susanna, and many other women who are with Jesus in 8.1-3 are all disciples.

---

37. Acts 11.30; 15.22, 39, 40; 16.3; 18.5.
38. Note the difference with Matthew. The women did not decide to follow Jesus when he left Galilee (ἠκολούθησαν ingressive aorist), as in Mt. 27.55 but here in Lk. 23.49 they have been following him from Galilee onwards (συνακολουθοῦσαι present indicative).

6.3. *Two Groups of Women Disciples*

Lk. 8.1-3 is not about males and females as such, but about specific men and women: the Twelve apostles, some named women and many unnamed. Mark and Matthew also divide the group of women in some named and many unnamed. We saw that Mark distinguishes between two groups of women: a large group of unnamed women who followed Jesus in his pilgrimage to Jerusalem and a small group of women disciples, Mary Magdalene, Mary of Joses, Mary of James, and Salome who followed Jesus right from the start of his ministry. We also saw that Matthew portrays the named and unnamed women as belonging to one group: they all followed Jesus from Galilee onwards. In addition, Matthew is ambivalent in portraying them as disciples. Luke, on the one hand, treats the group of women as a unity. In his account of the resurrection he refers to them as the women 'who followed him from Galilee' (αἵτινες ἦσαν συνεληλυθυῖαι ἐκ τῆς Γαλιλαίας 23.55). A few verses later this group is called: Mary Magdalene, Joanna, Mary of James, 'and the others who were with them' (αἱ λοιπαὶ σύν αὐταῖς 24.10). This is a parallel to the Eleven and all the others in 24.9. This suggests that Luke distinguishes between two groups of women: an inner and an outer circle.

The long sentence construction of 8.1-3 is also somewhat ambiguous. The sentence, having four subjects – Jesus, the Twelve, some named women, and many others unnamed – could be divided in two parts: Jesus and the Twelve on the one hand, and the named and unnamed women on the other. This would imply that all the women serve all the men. The sentence can also be interpreted as an inclusion: providing the frame are Jesus and the unnamed women, each with their own active verbs; enclosed are the Twelve and the named women, who have no active verbs of their own but like the others are said to be 'with him'. The many unnamed women in this configuration provide for Jesus and the Twelve as well as for Mary Magdalene, Joanna, and Susanna.

Lk. 8.1-3 thus allows two quite different answers to the question of who serves whom: either all the women serve all the men, or the many unnamed women serve Jesus, the Twelve, and Mary Magdalene, Joanna, and Susanna.[39] The latter interpretation would mean that, according to Luke, the women following Jesus did not all have the same role.

This interpretation seems the more appropriate one,[40] since Luke's story about Martha and Mary actually shows different types of women's behaviour in relation to Jesus: Mary listens to Jesus' teaching and Martha serves (10.38-42). The story also very realistically reveals the conflict inherent with regard to gender roles: Martha urges Jesus to command Mary to help her.

---

39. No other author seems to make a point of this. Without any argument αὐτοῖς in 8.3 is supposed to refer exclusively to the men. See Zahn 1913: 339-40; Fitzmyer 1981: 698; Heine 1986: 69; Seim 1994: 57; Reid 1996: 126; Melzer-Keller 1997: 195.

40. I do not follow the view of Karris (1994: 9) that the women in 8.1-3 used their resources to go on mission for Jesus (which is one of the meanings of 'diakonia' suggested by Collins (1990) in his major philological study of the word), since, in my interpretation this would mean that the unnamed women went on mission for Jesus as well as for the Twelve and Mary Magdalene, Joanna, and Susanna. However, the suggestion remains intriguing.

Luke's long sentence construction also raises another question concerning the number of healed women. Are all the women healed or only the three women mentioned by name: Mary called the Magdalene, Joanna, and Susanna? If the words καὶ ἕτεραι πολλαί are to be interpreted as grammatically subordinate to γυναῖκές τινες and are read in one breath with the three named women, the implication is that both the named and unnamed women would have been healed. However, καὶ ἕτεραι πολλαί may also be interpreted as coordinative to γυναῖκές τινες, Jesus, and the Twelve, meaning that only the three named women were healed.[41] I opt for the latter interpretation, since the idea that some women would consist of three named persons together with many others is very unlikely.[42]

Thus, Lk. 8.1-3 distinguishes between two groups of women: first, a large group of unnamed women disciples who serve Jesus, the Twelve and the named women and, secondly, a small group of named women disciples who have been healed by Jesus.

6.4. *The Large Group of Women Disciples*

6.4.1. *Lukan Discipleship and the Meaning of Serving.* Luke's use of the verb διακονέω differs from that of Mark and Matthew. In Luke's context the verb means the preparing of food and waiting at table.[43] This is done by women and slaves. The women in Lk. 8.3, moreover, serve not only Jesus as in Mark and Matthew, but also serve others with him, including the Twelve. Does this mean that the women's serving is typical for them as women and has nothing to do with discipleship?

With respect to this we should note Luke's story about Martha: Jesus insists she should not be absorbed by her serving and encourages her to take time and learn from him (10.38-42). Furthermore, the dutiful and unrewarded serving carried out by slaves is presented as a positive example to Jesus' followers (17.7-10), and Jesus promises that the Lord will invite all who served, and will serve them at his table (12.35-37). Indeed, the preparing of food and waiting at table in this gospel is also done by the male disciples. As in Mark and Matthew's accounts, the disciples distribute the food when Jesus is feeding the people (9.14-15) and Peter and John prepare the Passover meal themselves (22.7-13). Serving in the Lukan sense of preparing food and waiting at table is obviously not a role reserved only for women. It is a discipleship role for all.

---

41. Most authors do not discuss these two possibilities. Either all women being healed is taken for granted (Fitzmyer 1981: 697; Seim 1994: 39) or only three women being healed (Zahn 1913: 339; Schürmann 1969: 445).

42. With Ricci 1994: 127 and Bieberstein 1998: 37-38, and against Melzer-Keller 1997: 195 n. 27, who argues, referring to Blass, Debrunner and Rehkopf (1990: 306.2), that 'many others' must enhance the list of cured women. However, there is no reference to Lk. 8.1-3, but to Mt. 15.30, ἑτέρους πολλούς not being preceded by τινες. Indeed, ἕτερος must refer to the other within a unity: however, the unity here need not be only the cured women, but may also be the group of women as a whole.

43. 10.40; 12.37; 17-7-10; 22.26-30 are clear examples. Perhaps because of this we should also interpret the serving of Simon's mother-in-law in 4.39 as preparing food.

Luke relates that the women who follow Jesus are serving out of their means (8.3).[44] This does not necessarily mean that the women are rich.[45] Luke's point is that the women use what they themselves own for the benefit of all. They thus personify an important Lukan ideal: distributing their means in order to provide for those in need (Acts 4.32-35).[46]

In other words, when one reads 8.1-3 within the context of the Gospel of Luke as a whole, it becomes apparent that Luke is portraying the many serving women in a discipleship role which is exemplary to all who follow Jesus.

6.4.2. Lukan Discipleship and the Twelve Apostles. We concluded that the many serving women are disciples like the Twelve and the named women in Lk. 8.1-3 in that they follow Jesus and learn from him about the Kingdom of God. We also saw that serving others out of one's own means is a Lukan ideal for all Jesus' followers. In this way the women would exemplify Lukan discipleship. But would Luke call the many women disciples?

Luke does not identify the disciples as the Twelve as Matthew does. Lk. 6.12-19 tells that Jesus on a mountain chooses his twelve apostles from his disciples, whom he called to him. When these apostles and the remaining disciples go down from the mountain, these disciples appear to be a great crowd (ὄχλος πολὺς μαθητῶν 6.17). Thus, the many women could easily be part of them. In Luke the group of disciples is not small as in Mark and Matthew, but there is a large crowd of disciples (cf. 19.37; Acts 6.2).

In Acts, Luke's use of the word 'disciples' is not restricted to those people who followed Jesus in his earthly lifetime, but is used for all believers. Paul, for instance, has become a disciple (Acts 9.26) and makes disciples (e.g. Acts 14.21). There are the disciples of Damascus (Acts 9.20), of Joppe (Acts 9.38), of Derbe, Lystra, Iconium, and Antioch (Acts 14.20-22), of Achaje (Acts 18.27), of Ephesus (Acts 19.30; 20.1), of Tyre (Acts 21.3-4), Cyprus, and of Caesarea (21.16). In Acts, Luke, with his use of the word 'disciples', seems to exclude women, since Acts 21.5 relates that all disciples with their wives and children say goodbye to Paul.

---

44. For an extensive review of scholarly interpretations see Bieberstein 1998: 53-69. For Sim (1989: 55-60), Lk. 8.1-3 gives no information whatsoever about the day-to-day role of the women followers. In his opinion it only says that they donated their money: their role as disciples is not being described. On the basis of 10.38-42 Sim concludes that they apparently were expected 'to be faithful and attentive students' (p. 60). On the basis of the same pericope, however, I conclude that the providing consisted of more than donating money and could have been a highly regarded, significant role (cf. Acts 6.1-4). Bieberstein (1998: 64-65) also refers to Acts 19.22.

45. Sim (1989: 52-53) suggests that they were not wealthy, wealth and discipleship being incompatible. He suggests that they 'combined their monetary resources to make a common fund'. According to him this is 'the most logical explanation for the early church's "experiment in communism" (Acts 2.44-45; 4.32; 5.1-11). The Jerusalem church simply adopted the economic system which operated at the time of Jesus' ministry'.

46. In contrast to Bieberstein (1998: 68), who argues that Luke presents the women as economically independent who apparently still hold on to their possessions instead of leaving everything behind. In this way Luke would contradict his portrayal of women wandering with Jesus.

This must, however, be an androcentric way of speaking, since Luke, in contrast to Mark and Matthew uses the female word for μαθητής, namely μαθήτρια (Acts 9.36). This disciple is Tabitha, a woman who did many good works. When she dies the widows stand weeping, showing the coats and garments that she made.

Luke seems to include women within the masculine plural 'disciples'. This is also clear from the Galilean women in 24.6-8 who remember Jesus' words about his suffering and resurrection. Only as disciples could they be aware of these words, since they are spoken by Jesus, when he is alone with his disciples, commanding them to tell no one about his pronouncement (9.21).[47]

However, when Luke's Jesus describes the cost of discipleship he seems, in contrast to Mark and Matthew, to aim exclusively at men:

> If any one comes to me and does not hate his own father and mother and wife and children and brothers and sisters, yes, even his own life, he cannot be my disciple. (14.26; cf. Mk 10.28-30 and Mt. 10.37-40)

The disciples are to hate their wives and children: the husband is strikingly absent (see also 18.29). Is this simply an androcentric way of putting things or does this indicate that only men can be disciples? The same question may be posed in regard to 8.21, where Luke omits the Markan and Matthean splitting of the 'brothers' into 'sister' and 'brother' (cf. Mk 3.33-35 and Mt. 12.48-49). Nevertheless, Luke, unlike Mark and Matthew, does not hesitate to use the singular female noun μαθήτρια (Acts 9.36). Perhaps in Luke's view women are not supposed to hate their husbands and to take the initiative to abandon them to lead ascetic lives. Seim, referring to the wholly male-oriented Lukan language when marriage, divorce, and remarriage are concerned (16.18; 20.37-38), suggests that for Luke the women disciples either remained married, or did not have a husband, for instance being widows. Perhaps they were divorced, single, or abandoned women.[48]

With respect to this, it is noteworthy that some of the women are said to have been healed from evil spirits and infirmities. This may indicate that they were not women who were held in great esteem. The mention of Joanna being the wife of Chuza, Herod's steward, strengthens this view, since already 3.19-20 makes clear that Herod is notorious for his evil deeds. In fact, this connection to the Herodian court gives Joanna a dubious status comparable to that of a tax collector.[49]

6.5. *The Small Group of Women Disciples*

6.5.1. *Healed Women Disciples.* Compared to Mark and Matthew's accounts, Luke's emphasis on the named women as having been ill is unique, as is the mention of their being healed. Seim suggests that the healing of women throughout Luke demonstrates their restoration to the community: they are 'daughters of Abraham'

---

47. See also Bieberstein 1998: 247-48.
48. Seim 1995: 755-61. See for instance also Sim (1989: 53-55), who argues that the women followers generally must have been non-married women being less restricted in first-century Palestinian society.
49. Seim 1994: 37; see also her n. 39.

(13.16; cf. 8.48) and thus share in God's promise of blessing.[50] In addition, in contrast to Mark and Matthew, Luke demonstrates Jesus' miraculous power at the beginning of his ministry, before he has any disciples (4.34-41);[51] the first three disciples – Peter, James and John – decide to follow Jesus after they, having followed his instructions, catch an astonishing quantity of fish. Luke thus emphasizes Jesus' power and relates the experience of it to the discipleship of the three core disciples of the male Twelve.

However, Luke not only relates the three women's experience of Jesus' power in the sense that they are cured by him, but, in contrast to the men, Luke thus also underlines their need to be cured.[52] Scholars argue that, according to Luke, whereas the Twelve are called to their discipleship (6.12-19), the women follow Jesus out of gratitude.[53]

Sabine Bieberstein points to the direct relation between healings and the coming of the Kingdom of God in Luke.[54] She understands the healed women as visible marks of the power of the Kingdom of God. Mary Magdalene, Joanna, and Salome, in her view, forcibly experienced the dawn of the Kingdom of God in their own lives. She suggests that as the Twelve may be understood as representing the twelve tribes of Israel, the three healed women following Jesus could be understood as representing the realization of the coming Kingdom of God. They represent the human experience of being made whole by Jesus.[55]

Perhaps another view underlies the unique Lukan description of the three healed women as well. At that time it was thought that women, because of their womanly nature, were more vulnerable to diseases than men. Philo, for instance, states:

> The soul has, as it were, a dwelling, partly men's quarters, partly women's quarters. Now for the men there is a place where properly dwell the masculine thoughts (that are) wise, sound, just, prudent, pious, filled with freedom and boldness, and kin to wisdom. And the women's quarters are a place where womanly opinions go about and dwell, being followers of the female sex. And the female sex is irrational and akin to bestial passions, fear, sorrow, pleasure and desire, from which ensue incurable weaknesses and indescribable sicknesses. He who is conquered by these is unhappy, while he who controls them is happy. And longing for and desiring this happiness, and seizing a certain time to be able to escape from terrible and unbearable sorrow, which is (what is meant by) 'there ceased to be the ways of women' – this clearly belongs to minds full of the Law, which resemble the male sex and overcome passions and rise above all sense-pleasure and desire and are without sorrow and fear and, if one must speak the truth, without passion, not zealously practising apathy, for this would be

50. See Seim (1994: 43-57) about the term 'daughter of Abraham'.

51. According to Luke, in contrast to Mark and Matthew, Peter's mother-in-law is cured before he becomes a disciple (4.38-39).

52. So also Bieberstein 1998: 65.

53. Ernst 1993: 201; Reid 1996: 132; Melzer-Keller 1997: 198-99; De Boer 1997: 50-51; cf. Bovon 1989: 398.

54. Bieberstein (1998: 42-45) refers to Lk. 4.18-19, 40-44; 6.17-19; 7.22; 10.9, 11, 20; 13.10-21.

55. Bieberstein 1998: 45.

ungrateful and shameless and akin to arrogance and reckless boldness, but that which is consistent with the argument given, (namely) cutting the mind off from disturbing and confusing passions. (Questions and Answers on Genesis IV.15)[56]

Philo uses the terms 'male' and 'female' in a metaphorical sense; at the same time they relate to real men and women.[57] Man is the symbol of reason and woman of perception through the senses. Thus men are 'manly' by disposition just as women are 'womanly'. Yet women can be made 'manly' and men can degenerate into 'womanliness', since, just as men should rule over women, so the manly should dominate the womanly in every person: understanding must regulate sensual perception, among both men and women.[58] As Philo states, only 'spirits full of the law' can control the womanly impulse. If that does not happen, then illnesses develop and women are obviously more vulnerable to these illnesses than men. Luke's addition may thus reveal an apologetic touch: the three are not 'womanly' women anymore; they have become 'manly' since Jesus banished the evil spirits and the sicknesses that were part of their womanly weakness. However, this remains a conjecture, since Luke does not give any hint that such thoughts would be at the background of Lk. 8.2.

6.5.2. The Seven Demons of Mary Magdalene. Luke describes only the illness of Mary Magdalene: not just one demon has gone out of her, nor a legion, but precisely seven (cf. 4.33; 8.30; 9.42). Most exegetes suggest that the number seven indicates totality (cf. 11.21-26), meaning that Mary Magdalene would have been totally possessed and subsequently completely healed.[59] As Ricci phrases it: Mary Magdalene was 'dispossessed of herself' and through Jesus could 'return to self'.[60]

The seven demons also coincide with the Stoic view of the soul as having seven parts difficult to control: the capacities to feel, to hear, to touch, to taste, to see, to desire, and to speak. The eighth part of the soul is the 'commander': it has the task of keeping these different capacities in check and giving direction.[61] To achieve a life in harmony with the Divine, one should free oneself from the claims of the seven, more sensual parts.[62] If this is the context of Mary's seven demons, Jesus, apparently, successfully taught her to control them.[63]

56. See for the translation Marcus 1953: I, 288-89. This is Philo's interpretation of Gen. 18.11: There ceased to be to Sarah the ways of women.

57. That this was generally done, is shown by Petersen 1999: 309-334.

58. See for this: Questions and Answers on Genesis II.49 and IV.15, 148.

59. E.g. Rengstorff 1976a: esp. 629-31.

60. Ricci 1994: 133-39 esp. 137 and 139; see also n. 35.

61. Pohlenz 1948: 87-88. See also Long and Sedley (1987: I, 315) who quote Calcidius 220. According to Pohlenz (1948: 363-64), Stoic philosophy was part of the general knowledge of the Roman period.

62. When the 'commander' is not healthy, he fails to recognize bad influences (Pohlenz 1948: 141). Zenon distinguished three powers in this 'hegemonikon': image, drive, and reasoning (logos). The logos is to be the one who rules (Pohlenz 1948: 90).

63. GosThom log. 114 has preserved a tradition which pictures Mary Magdalene as being made 'male' by Jesus. 1 ApocJas 38.22-23 describes Jesus' seven women followers as powerless vessels who have become strong by a perception which is in them.

But Luke is far from clear. The seven demons of Mary Magdalene and the illnesses of Joanna and Susanna raise many questions, especially since Luke does not hesitate to specify the ailments of other women.[64] Luke simply gives no clues to enable us to find definitive explanations concerning the conditions of these three women.

6.5.3. *Like and Unlike the Twelve Apostles*. In the same way that Luke does not specify their illnesses, he also does not specify the role of Mary Magdalene, Joanna, and Susanna: like the Twelve they are not connected to active verbs. Later in the Gospel, the Twelve receive instruction: Jesus calls them together, gives them power and authority over all demons and diseases, and sends them out to preach the Kingdom of God and to heal (9.1-2). Nothing special is said about the women, although we might perhaps assume that they, and also the other women, could be included in the mission of the Seventy, sent out two by two (10.1; cf. 1 Cor. 9.5; Phil. 4.2-3).[65]

Although Mary Magdalene, Joanna, and Susanna in 8.1-3 seem to be closely connected to the Twelve and are provided for like them, Luke does not give them the same function. Luke affirms this when all the women, named and unnamed, appear as a group over and against the Twelve (23.55–24.10).

Except for the fact that the Twelve are chosen as apostles, the difference between the three women and the Twelve is not immediately evident, since it is not based on the act of providing. Mary Magdalene, Joanna, and Susanna as well as the Twelve are served by the many women. The Twelve and all the women are also on an equal footing with regard to learning from Jesus. As disciples they all learn from him. Furthermore, Luke's description of them as groups is the same: the Twelve appear to have three core disciples and so do the women.[66] Only at the beginning of Acts does the difference between them become clear. The Twelve, as men, have leadership roles, the women do not (Acts 1.20-22; cf. 6.3).

When the apostles want to replace the twelfth apostle, Luke summarizes the criteria of being an apostle. It must be one of the men who were with the apostles (δεῖ οὖν τῶν συνελθόντων ἡμῖν ἀνδρῶν Acts 1.21) from the baptism of John until the day that Jesus was taken away. Why one of the men? What about the women who were with Jesus and the apostles?

6.6. *Luke's Narrative Technique of Silencing Women*

Luke, not only in 8.1-3, but throughout the Gospel, and more so than Mark and Matthew, describes women playing a prominent part. Luke is especially known for his peculiar Lukan 'gender pairs': parallel stories with, respectively, a woman and a man as subject (e.g. the shepherd with his lost sheep and the woman with her lost coin 15.3-7, 8-10).[67] Luke seems to be consciously aiming at an audience of both

---

64. High fever (4.38-39), flow of blood (8.43-48), sick to death (8.40-56), and unable to stand upright (13.10-17).

65. But this is not very likely, see Chapter 6, section 6.2.

66. Peter, James, and John (5.9-11; 8.51; 9.28) and Mary Magdalene, Joanna, and Susanna or Mary of James (8.1-3; 24.10).

67. See Seim 1994: 11-24. She mentions Zechariah and Mary (1.11-20/26-38; 46-55/67-79),

men and women, although Tal Ilan, referring to Jewish parallels, suggests that the gender pairs are a literary convention of the time that indicate the story-teller's perception of what is typical of women and of men.[68] Turid Karlsen Seim, who supports the view that Luke consciously addresses both women and men, concludes:

> At the same time, he conveys a picture of a world divided by gender, of a culture and a mediation of tradition in which men and women, within the same community, nevertheless, keep each to their own sphere of life.[69]

Seim draws attention to the fact that, although Luke has several stories about women not found in Mark and Matthew,[70] the story of the Syro-Phoenician/ Canaanite woman who boldly questions Jesus' rejecting attitude towards non-Jews and is praised for her faith, is strikingly absent.[71] In addition, Mary D'Angelo points to the significant fact that the woman prophet who anoints Jesus in Mark and Matthew has become a repentant sinner in Luke.

Last, but not least, the silent and receiving Mary, sister of Martha, is referred to as a role model (10.38-42). As Jane Schaberg notes, learning is often done in dialogues (e.g. 5.1-11; 8.4-15; 9.10-11), but Mary's study is not described as such. What she learns remains private and is evidently not meant to instruct the community as a whole.[72] Luke indeed speaks favourably of women when their strength and perseverance are concerned in hearing the word of God, and doing it in prayer and in the sharing of possessions.[73] Yet, as Seim rightly concludes, 'the rest is silence'.[74] D'Angelo concludes about the women in Luke:

Simeon and Anna (2.25-35/36-38), Naaman and the widow in Zarephta (4.27/25-26), Jairus's daughter and the widow's son (8.40-56/7.11-17), Jairus and the woman with the issue of blood (8.40-41, 49-56/43-48), the men of Nineveh and the queen of the South (11.32/31), a man healed on Sabbath and a woman healed on Sabbath (14.1-6/13.10-17), Abraham's son and Abraham's daughter (19.9/13.16), a man who sowed a seed and a woman who hid yeast (13.18-19/20-21), a shepherd with sheep and a woman with coins (15.3-7/8-10), men sleeping and women grinding (17.34/35), Peter at the tomb and women at the tomb (24.12/1-11), Aeneas and Tabitha (Acts 9.32-35/36-42). See Seim 1994: 15. See also the more extensive survey of D'Angelo 1999c: 182-84.

68. Ilan 1997: 269-73.

69. Seim 1994: 24.

70. The women stories unique to Luke are: Elizabeth, Mary and Anna (1.5–7, 24-66; 2.36-52), the widow at Nain (7.11-17), the woman sinner (7.36-50); Mary Magdalene, Joanna and Susanna and many other women following Jesus (8.1-3), Martha and Mary (10.38-42), the woman from the crowd (11.27-28), the woman who could not stand upright (13.10-17), the woman with the coins (15.8-10), the widow and the judge (18.1-8), the women wailing (23.27-31).

71. Seim 1994: 56; Seim 1995: 738, 747-48. One may object that Luke's Jesus in contrast to Mark and Matthew only mixes with Jews. However, Luke does relate Matthew's story about Jesus and the Roman centurion, simply by adding Jews who act on his behalf (7.5; cf. Mt. 8.5-6). Why did Luke not alter the story of the Syro-Phoenician/Canaanite woman in the same way, by adding Jews who act on her behalf? The inclusion of the story of the Roman centurion in Luke makes the absence of the story of the Syro-Phoenician/Canaanite woman even more striking: the two stories together would have formed a good Lukan gender pair.

72. Schaberg 1992: 288-89.

73. Lk. 2.36-38; 18.1-8; cf. Acts 1.14//21.4-6 and Acts 9.36-39.

74. Seim 1994: 745.

Luke's multiplication of representations of women is accompanied by a cor-
responding limitation of their roles. Luke is concerned not with changing the
status of women, but with the appropriate deployment of gender.[75]

Luke thus addresses the issue of gender more directly than Mark and Matthew.[76]

What does appropriate women's behaviour contain according to Luke? Remaining silent in public seems to be an important virtue. Seim analysed the stories in
Luke concerning women's healings.[77] She concludes that Luke describes these
women primarily as passive recipients and not as active persons taking the initiative.[78] In the one account where a woman does actively seek her cure (8.43-48),
Luke omits the Markan and Matthean verse in which she herself explains her
action (8.44; cf. Mk 5.28-29; Mt. 9.21-22). Similarly, Luke regularly introduces
women whom the reader is supposed to imagine speaking, but who at the same
time are silenced, since Luke grants them no actual voice.[79] The major exceptions
are Elizabeth and Mary in the infancy stories, who praise God among themselves
and in a domestic situation (1.24-60).[80] As we will see, at the end of the Gospel,
Luke, unlike Mark and Matthew, makes it clear that Mary Magdalene and the other
women are not to go and tell about the crucified Lord being raised. The women are
to remember what they experienced among themselves.

7. *Luke's Story about Mary Magdalene*

Luke's story about Mary Magdalene begins in 8.1-3. The readers are encouraged to
visualize her, together with the Twelve, Joanna and Susanna and many other
women, everywhere Jesus goes. They travel with Jesus on his journeying in Galilee
(4.14–9.50), they follow him on his way to Jerusalem (9.51–19.27) and stay with
him, until the crucifixion. This is a major difference between Mark and Matthew
and Luke. In Luke the disciples do not flee at the arrest of Jesus, as they do in Mark
and Matthew. Not only do the women followers watch the crucifixion, but all who
knew Jesus. Even the crowds are watching and, when he dies, beat their breasts in
sorrow (23.48). On his way to the cross Jesus encounters women already wailing
for him, whom he addresses as 'daughters of Jerusalem' and whom he tells not to
cry for him, but for themselves. 'For, if they do this to the green wood, what shall
be done with the dry?' (23.31).

What the Galilean women see at the crucifixion differs significantly from the
events described by Mark and Matthew. The darkness is there, but Luke explains it
as a solar eclipse and relates no other special signs of nature. As in Mark and
Matthew, the curtain of the Temple is torn in two, but the centurion does not

---

75. D'Angelo 1999c: 187.
76. D'Angelo 1999c: 190.
77. Lk. 4.38-39; 7.11-17; 8.43-48; 8.40-56; 13.10-17.
78. Seim 1994: 39-57. See also Melzer-Keller 1997: 278-300.
79. For instance Lk. 2.36-38; 8.47; 13.13; 23.27; 24.9-10; Acts 1.14; 9.39; 12.13-15; 18.26;
21.9.
80. Reid (1996: 52), concludes that apart from the infancy narratives 'women who speak in the
rest of the Gospel are reprimanded by Jesus or are disbelieved'.

declare Jesus to be Son of God. Instead he emphasizes Jesus' innocence by calling him righteous. As in Mark and Matthew, Jesus is mocked by the Jewish leaders, but in Luke, although the crowds are present, they do not mock him. Instead the soldiers do. In contrast to Matthew and Mark, only one of the two criminals crucified with Jesus derides him, and he, in turn, is rebuked by the other who asks Jesus to remember him when he comes into his kingdom (23.39-43).

Luke also portrays Jesus differently. He is not the man who cries out 'My God, my God, why did you abandon me', but while he is crucified he says 'Father, forgive them, for they know not what they do' (23.34).[81] And to one of those crucified with him he says 'Verily, I say to you, today you will be with me in Paradise' (23.43). When he is dying in Mark and Matthew he only shouts, but in Luke he cries out loudly, 'Father, into your hands I commend my spirit' (23.46).

7.1. *Watching the Burial, Preparing Spices and Going to the Tomb*

Only after the crucifixion does Luke single out the Galilean women. In contrast to Mark and Matthew they all are present at the burial of Jesus by Joseph of Arimathea. Luke relates that, after they all returned, they also prepare spices and ointments together (23.55-56). They then rest on the Sabbath, according to the commandment. Luke gives the same reason as Mark does for the visit to the tomb: the women go to the tomb to anoint the body of Jesus (24.1). In contrast to Mark and Matthew's accounts, however, these women are not Mary Magdalene and one or two others. For Luke they initially are those women 'who had come with Jesus from Galilee' (23.55). Only at the end of Luke's story the women are identified as Mary Magdalene, Joanna, Mary of James, and those who were with them.

7.2. *Meeting Two Men and Remembering Jesus' Words*

The women are perplexed when they find the tomb empty. Two men in shining garments encourage them to remember how Jesus himself, while he was in Galilee, had said that he had to suffer and rise (9.18-22). At this point Luke declares: 'And they remembered his words' (24.8). Some scholars argue that the women remember the words, but without understanding. R.J. Dillon, for instance, argues that the women's witness has the purpose 'of building a total experience bereft of understanding and belief, so that faith's inception should prove to be the independent gift of the risen Lord'.[82]

The major scholarly objection to the interpretation that the women understand the remembered words is formulated by M.D. Goulder, who states:

> Being women, the receivers of this message do not presume to rise to faith before the apostles, but limit themselves to remembering his 'sayings' (a Lucanism), and scuttling off to the Eleven. For all his feeling for women, Luke comes from a world of male chauvinists.[83]

---

81. However, this text is missing in various early and important manuscripts. See Fitzmyer 1981: II, 1503-1504.

82. Dillon 1978: 56.

83. Goulder 1989: 775.

Remembering Jesus' words, however, is important according to Luke. Seim refers to two instances where Peter, upon remembering the words of the Lord, comes to understand what is happening to him in the present. First, after his denial, Peter remembers Jesus' prediction that this would happen, which causes him to realize what he has done (22.61-62). Second, in Acts 11.16-18, Peter relates, that upon remembering the words of the Lord 'John baptized with water, you shall be baptized by the holy Spirit', he understood that, since the Holy Spirit had also been poured out on the Gentiles (Acts 10.44-48), he was not to hinder their baptism. In the same way, the Galilean women in Lk. 24.8 remember Jesus' words about his death and resurrection, and as a result they understand why the tomb, in which they had seen Jesus' body interred, is now empty.[84]

7.3. *'They Had Seen a Vision of Angels'*

Luke, in contrast to Mark and Matthew, does not depict the women as commissioned to speak to the others. They receive no charge. Instead, the women go to the Eleven and all the others of their own accord and tell them everything.

Luke does not record their exact words, but later the two disciples going to Emmaus repeat to Jesus what the women said. According to them, when the women did not find the body, they came to the others and announced that they had seen a vision of angels who said that he was alive (24.23). The word for vision is ὀπτασία, which primarily and neutrally means 'appearing'. However, one may ask what Luke intends with this word. If it rather denotes 'vision' here,[85] could it signify that Luke wants to downplay what the women experienced at the empty tomb as only a vision? This is not likely, since Luke uses the same word for Zecharia's encounter in the Jerusalem temple (1.22) and for Paul's experience on his way to Damascus (Acts 26.19), both of which events are taken very seriously.

The equivalent words, ὅρασις (sight, appearance, vision) and ὅραμα ('what is to be seen', appearance, vision), as well as ὀπτασία itself most frequently occur in Luke and Acts and very rarely in other canonical New Testament writings.[86] In every instance, the experience causes the one who sees the vision to do something, even something which may be quite overwhelming. No story about a vision in Luke or Acts has the connotation of 'only a vision'.[87]

---

84. See also Perkins 1984: 155; Karris 1994: 14-15. For additional arguments see Seim 1994: 150-55 and also Bock 1996: 1895-1896.

85. See Michaelis 1977: 372. He states that the angelophany here cannot be called a 'vision', since the sense 'visionary appearance' would not have been 'firmly established'.

86. See Michaelis 1976: 370-73. The word ὅρασις occurs in Revelation (4.3; 9.17) and in Acts 2.17. The word ὅραμα occurs in Mt. 17.9 and in Acts 7.31; 9.10, 12; 10.3, 17, 19; 11.5; 12.9; 16.9-10; 18.9. The word ὀπτασία occurs in 2 Cor. 12.1 and in Lk. 1.22; 24.23; Acts 26.19. Here I use the English word 'vision' in the widest sense of the word.

87. There is one instance in Luke–Acts where the question 'reality or vision' is at stake. The author of Acts relates that, when Peter followed the angel who freed him from prison, he did not know whether what was happening with the angel's help was real. Peter thought that he saw a vision (Acts 12.9). However, the reality of the appearance of the angel is not at stake here. Peter actually saw the angel, which is also the case in a vision, but was uncertain about the reality of what was happening to him at that moment.

Zechariah has a vision in which he is told that his barren wife will bear a son and is instructed to call him John. When Zechariah asks for a sign, his speech is taken from him, since he doubted. According to Stephen, Moses' experience with the thorn bush is a vision in which God summons Moses, at that time no more than a shepherd, to free his people from mighty Pharaoh. He obeys (Acts 7.31). The Christian Ananias has a vision in which he is told to go to the persecutor, Paul. He obeys (Acts 9.10-16). Paul has visions in which he is told to convert to the Christian faith (Acts 26.19), to receive Ananias (Acts 9.12), and to keep preaching the Gospel (Acts 18.9), even as far as Macedonia (Acts 16.9). He obeys. The Roman centurion has a vision in which he is told to listen to the unknown Jew, Peter (Acts 10.3). Peter has a vision in which he learns to reverse his insistence on Levitical purity laws, to go to Cornelius and to baptize Gentiles (Acts 16.9-10). Both Peter and Cornelius obey their visions.

In this light, the fact that the Galilean women at the empty tomb, in their vision, according to Luke, only receive the charge to remember and are not summoned to do anything, is even more striking.

7.4. *Being Silenced*

Nevertheless, on their own initiative the Galilean women go to tell the disciples. At this point in the story the name of Mary Magdalene occurs again, as one of three named women[88] among the unnamed (24.10).[89] This seems odd, for in contrast to Mark and Matthew's accounts, here she is no longer special. Further, the role of the Galilean women is in and of itself not important to anyone other than to themselves. Luke relates that they are not believed and at the same time shows that they do not need to be believed, since what they have to relate is not unique. Others also found the tomb empty (24.12; 24.24)[90] and when Cleopas and his unnamed companion return from Emmaus, ready to share their experiences, they are told before they are allowed to speak: 'The Lord has risen indeed, and has appeared to Simon!' (24.34). In Luke's story, not only the women but also Peter and others witnessed the empty tomb and, according to the disciples, Simon is the first to whom the risen Lord appeared, although Luke does not describe the event.

Why did Luke not describe Jesus' appearance to Peter? Could it be that there was no such story available? Or is Luke engaging in irony by depicting Peter as being believed while the women are doubted although a clear story underlines their truthfulness? Luke differs significantly from Mark and Matthew and also from

88. Compared to 8.1-3 the names are changed though. Luke leaves Susanna out and adds Mary of James.

89. By a difference in punctuation this verse is interpreted in two ways in subsequent editions of Nestle and Aland. In the 25th edition, it is suggested that only the other women and not the three who are named relate everything to the apostles, in which case Luke silences them radically. In the 26th edition, it is suggested that both the named three and the other women convey the news to the apostles. The latter seems the more appropriate interpretation since it parallels the phrase 'the eleven and the others' in 24.9.

90. The verse 24.12 has been interpreted as a later insertion, but scholarly opinion has changed on this point because of new text-critical evidence and the Lukan terms which are used; see Bock 1996: 1902.

John. In Matthew and John's resurrection accounts, Mary Magdalene is the first to see Jesus. In Mark, both Peter and Mary Magdalene, and all the other disciples are promised that they will see him. Luke also differs significantly from the Markan appendix and the non-canonical Epistula Apostolorum, where, when the disciples do not believe the women, Jesus reproaches them.[91] Luke relates no rebuke from Jesus for disbelieving the women.

According to Luke, Mary Magdalene and the other women are on their own. They are not believed and need not be believed. Their testimony is not important in the flow of the story. They stand in sharp contrast to Peter, whose words immediately evoke sincere belief, since his testimony prompts all the others to exclaim: 'The Lord has risen indeed'! (24.34). Thus Luke not only downplays the role of the Galilean women and Mary Magdalene as one of them, but also firmly establishes the importance of Peter's role.

Luke does portray Mary Magdalene and the other women as trustworthy and understanding witnesses.[92] They simply lack authority and the authority is not given to them, as in other texts, by any of the male disciples, or by Jesus himself or by the angels. Although they keep repeating what has happened,[93] their words cause confusion rather than belief (24.11, 22). As Seim states:

> Their own immediate attempt to break through the boundaries shows how still-born this is. Men's lack of confidence in women makes it useless.[94]

7.5. *The End: Receiving an Open Mind, Being Witnesses and Being Blessed*
The risen Lord appears to the two disciples on the Emmaus road. When they come back they are told that the Lord appeared to Simon. While they are together, the Lord appears to them all: to the eleven and those who were with them. He opens their minds so that they can understand the scriptures, and says:

> Thus it is written, that the Christ should suffer and on the third day rise from the dead, and that repentance and forgiveness of sins should be preached in his name to all nations, beginning from Jerusalem. You are witnesses to these things. And behold, I send the promise of my Father upon you; but stay in the city, until you are clothed with power from on high. (24.46-49)

In Matthew the mission charge 'to all nations' is addressed to the eleven disciples; in Luke the statement 'you are witnesses to these things' (24.48) is addressed to the Eleven 'and those who were with them' (24.33). On the basis of Lk. 8.1-3 we may assume that Mary Magdalene and the other women were also 'with them'. However, if we look within the direct context, Mary Magdalene, Joanna, and Mary of James are distinct from the Eleven and all the others (24.9-10). Nevertheless, the

---

91. Mk 16.14; EpAp 20-22.
92. Seim 1994: 156-57.
93. ἔλεγον past continuous (24.10).
94. Seim 1994: 163. Karris (1994: 16-17) argues that Luke is 'equating the women's confession with the community's christological creed and with Jesus' self revelation of his resurrection after an ignominious death' (p. 16), comparing 24.22-24 to 24.19-20 (see also Acts 2.22-24; 10.38-39) and 24.25-27.

ones who went to Emmaus called them: 'certain women also of our company' (24.22). Moreover, we may assume that the women are with the Eleven, since Jesus calls them 'witnesses to these things' (24.48) and indeed they have witnessed all his activities and teaching throughout the Gospel.[95] After promising them the power from on high, Jesus leads them out as far as Bethany, blesses them and is carried up into heaven.

7.6. *The Difference between Luke and Acts*

When Luke's story resumes in Acts 1.1-11, only the apostles are present.[96] Yet, women appear to be with them in Jerusalem and to receive the Holy Spirit as they do (Acts 1.14; 2.1, 17). Are they to witness as the apostles do (1.8)? In Acts 13.31 Paul assures his hearers that the risen Lord appeared for many days to 'those who came up with him from Galilee to Jerusalem and who are now his witnesses unto the people'. Would they not include the women from Galilee?[97]

It is very strange that these women in Acts 1.14 are only referred to and that Mary the mother of Jesus and his brothers are mentioned, although they play no discipleship role in the Gospel.[98] One would have expected at least the name of Mary Magdalene to occur again, but this is not the case. Throughout Acts she is not mentioned; also absent is the name of any other woman Luke mentioned in his Gospel. They play no role in Luke's story about the beginnings of the Church.

This can mean one of two things: either the author of Luke is not the same as the author of Acts,[99] or that Luke in his second book deliberately remains silent about Mary Magdalene and the others. It appears that Luke seeks to limit the role of the Galilean women to Jesus' lifetime. They are history. The Church can do without them, since the Church relies on the male Twelve and on the males who receive their blessing. Nevertheless, Seim observes:

> The masculinisation which dominates Acts, however, does not cover the whole of Luke's story cloaking women in silence and invisibility... By means of the narrative sequence and of the positioning of the gospel as a 'first volume', the traditions from Jesus' life, that is the life and voice of Jesus, lack the strong historical transparency of Mark and Matthew. They are located in the past and given the character of remembrance. The same is true of the examples of women and the stories about them. But this does not bring them to silence... On the

---

95. Perkins 1984: 167; Karris 1994: 13-19; Melzer-Keller 1997: 271-73; Bieberstein 1998: 267-69 indeed argue that the women as part of the group receive the mission charge and witness the ascension.

96. See also Melzer-Keller 1997: 273-75.

97. See Ryan 1985: 58; Schüssler Fiorenza 1983: 321; Melzer-Keller 1997: 272-73.

98. See also Bieberstein 1998: 274.

99. For the theory of various sources, see Boismard and Lamouille 1990. They do, however, defend the original unity of a proto Luke and what they call Act I, which already concentrated on Peter and Paul. According to their source theory, Act I uses Peter to show that Jesus is the Messianic King who, like a new Elijah, has ascended to heaven from whence he will come again. Act I uses Paul to show that, although this message was taken from synagogue to synagogue, it was refused. Act I warns against a possible ruin of Jerusalem as a consequence of this blindness (Boismard and Lamouille 1990: 26-30).

contrary, Luke's own employment of the motive of 'memory' shows that it is precisely in the remembrance of this past story that the key to critical insight and to a new evaluation and a new understanding is to be found.[100]

Luke's story of the emerging Church in The Acts of the Apostles omits the contribution of the Galilean women, concentrating especially on Peter, and then on Paul. This does not mean, however, that the Galilean women and others did not play their part. It means that Luke does not focus on the emerging Church as a whole, but mainly on the contribution to it by these two apostles. Very rightly, the publishers of the recent commentary on Acts in the series Études Bibliques did not choose the commonly used canonical[101] title The Acts of the Apostles for their book. Instead, they decided for the more accurate title: The Acts of the Two Apostles.[102]

8. Luke's Portrayal of Mary Magdalene

What does all this mean for the Lukan portrayal of Mary Magdalene? What is her relation to Jesus? What is her role among the disciples? What is her function in the story and to the readers?

8.1. *Mary Magdalene's Relation to Jesus*

Luke's portrayal of Mary Magdalene's relation to Jesus is special in that Jesus has freed her from seven evil spirits, as also occurred in the Markan appendix. To Luke, Mary Magdalene is one of the Galilean women who are disciples among the Gospel's use of the grammatically masculine plural of disciples (24.6-7; cf. 9.18-22). As disciples they know and remember Jesus' words, even those words about the suffering and resurrection of the Son of Man which he only told in private. They follow Jesus as disciples like the Twelve.

Like the Twelve, Mary Magdalene, Joanna, and Susanna are with Jesus, being provided for by many unnamed women disciples. They follow Jesus right from the start until the very end. However, although the specific roles of the Twelve and the unnamed women disciples during their following Jesus become clear (the Twelve are apostles and the unnamed women use their resources for the benefit of all), nothing is said about the role of Mary Magdalene, Joanna, and Susanna. Luke emphasizes instead their specific status as healed ones, and explicitly mentions Mary Magdalene's healing from seven demons.

---

100. Seim 1994: 259-60.

101. As Metzger (1987: 301-304) shows, in antiquity titles were commonly added later. As early as the end of the second century the Canon Muratori asserts that by Luke 'the acts of all the apostles were written in one book'. At the same time, however, the author concludes that Luke only 'compiled the individual events that took place in his presence', since he apparently skipped Peter's martyrdom and Paul's journey to Spain (Canon Muratori 34-39). Metzger (1987: 196) suggests that the statement of the Muratorian author about 'all the apostles' while mentioning only Peter and Paul 'may be directed against Marcion, who identified Paul as the apostle. Or may be directed against the growing number of apocryphal books of acts of apostles'.

102. Boismard and Lamouille 1990: Les Actes des Deux Apôtres.

8.2. *Mary Magdalene among the Disciples*
Unlike Mark and Matthew, in Luke Mary Magdalene has no special function among the disciples. Luke's story about Mary Magdalene begins in 8.1-3. The readers are encouraged to visualize her everywhere Jesus goes, together with the Twelve, Joanna, Susanna and many other women. They, women and men, travel with him and learn from him in Galilee (4.14–9.50), on his way to Jerusalem (9.51–19.27) and stay with him, until the crucifixion. This is a major difference from the other Synoptics. In Luke's Gospel the disciples do not flee at the arrest of Jesus, as they do in Mark and Matthew. Not only the women followers watch the crucifixion, but all who knew Jesus. Even the crowds are watching and when he dies beat their breasts in sorrow.

Compared to Mark, Luke de-emphasizes the role of Mary Magdalene, and the other women followers in favour of Peter and other male followers. Not only the women, but he and others as well are witnesses to the empty tomb (24.12, 24). On his words that he saw the Lord, the disciples all cry out 'The Lord has risen indeed' (24.34), whereas Mary Magdalene and the other Galilean women are not believed.

Nevertheless the readers are encouraged to value Mary Magdalene, as well as the other Galilean women, as trustworthy and capable witnesses to Jesus: to his healing and teaching, to his death, burial, resurrection, and ascension. When Jesus opens the minds of his disciples to enable them to understand the Scriptures, he opens Mary Magdalene's and the other women's minds too. By this Luke suggests that Mary Magdalene and the other Galilean women must have played their part in the rise of the early Church. However, they have a specific task. They are first and foremost to remember Jesus' words among themselves, rather than going and speaking about them, since, in spite of their trustworthiness as witnesses they lack the authority to do the latter.

8.3. *Mary Magdalene's Function in the Story*
In Luke, Mary Magdalene is a disciple, like the other Galilean women, knowing also those words Jesus said only in private. Like the Markan and Matthean women, the Lukan women exemplify what Lukan discipleship means, since they provide for Jesus and his disciples out of their own means. However, Mary Magdalene, Joanna, and Susanna are special among them, since they belong to the small group of healed women who are with Jesus, and, as the Twelve, are being provided for, instead of providing themselves.

Although the Galilean women, Mary Magdalene among them, are trustworthy and capable witnesses, their testimony is not asked for, nor needed. They simply lack authority, causing confusion rather than belief. The women readers are thus encouraged by the role of the Galilean women, excluding Mary Magdalene, Joanna, and Susanna, to use their goods for the benefit of all and by the role of the Galilean women, Mary Magdalene and Joanna (and Mary of James) included, to remember Jesus' teaching and the revelation they experienced among themselves.

Chapter 7

MARY MAGDALENE ACCORDING TO THE GOSPEL OF JOHN

1. *John's Introduction of Mary Magdalene*

Like Mark and Matthew, but unlike Luke, John introduces Mary Magdalene at the scene of the crucifixion. However, Jesus has not yet died and Mary Magdalene is not introduced as watching from afar. We find her close to the cross, within speaking distance. While the soldiers divide Jesus' garments into four parts and are casting lots for his seamless tunic, John relates:

> So the soldiers did this; but standing by the cross of Jesus were his mother and his mother's sister, Mary of Clopas and Mary Magdalene. When Jesus saw his mother, and the disciple whom he loved standing near, he said to his mother, 'Woman, behold your son!' Then he said to the disciple, 'Behold your mother!' And from that hour the disciple took her to his own home. (19.25-27)

John's introduction of Mary Magdalene is strikingly different from those in Mark, Matthew and Luke, the most important difference being the complete absence of any allusion to her having followed Jesus and having ministered to him. Another important difference is the absence of the many unnamed women. Instead, John portrays Mary Magdalene as part of a small group of Jesus' near relatives. What does this mean for John's portrayal of Mary Magdalene?

2. *Women and Discipleship in John*

2.1. *In the Company of Jesus' Mother*
As in Luke, the sentence in which John introduces Mary Magdalene (19.25) is difficult to interpret. In addition, in John, the specific connection with the next two verses (19.26-27) is rather unclear. Scholars wonder about the number of women standing under the cross, about how the names of the women differ from those that occur in the Synoptic Gospels and about the sudden presence of an anonymous male disciple. Why does John not mention this disciple in verse 25? And why mention Mary Magdalene, Mary of Clopas, and Jesus' mother's sister in verse 25, when Mary of Clopas, and Jesus' mother's sister play no role whatsoever in the next verse, in the scene between Jesus, his mother and the disciple he loved, nor in the rest of John?

Various solutions have been offered which presuppose the redaction of the text and the copying of the list of women from tradition.[1] Because of the incongruity between 19.25 and 19.26-27 most scholars conclude that the presence of the anonymous disciple is due to a redaction of the text. It is John's supplement to the tradition.[2] That this is generally believed is shown by the thorough study of the disciple Jesus loved by James H. Charlesworth, who presents seven pages of questions about 19.25-27, but does not even mention the question of the relation between 19.25 and 19.26-27.[3]

Today the common interpretation is that there are four women standing under the cross: Jesus' mother, her sister, Mary of Clopas, and Mary Magdalene. This is seen to agree with Mk 15.41 and to form counterpart to the four soldiers in 19.23 who are dividing Jesus' clothing.[4] Earlier the interpretation which presupposed three women under the cross was popular: Jesus' mother, her sister called Mary of Clopas, and Mary Magdalene.[5] This agrees with the number of named women in Mk 16.1, Mt. 27.56 and Lk. 8.2-3; 24.10. The mysterious disciple in this case could be the fourth person to contrast with the soldiers. Both interpretations depict Mary Magdalene in the same way. John portrays her within a small group of women, two of them having close family ties to Jesus.

A third interpretation of 19.25 would introduce Mary Magdalene as a relative herself. When the verse is viewed as a parallelism John introduces Mary Magdalene as the sister of Jesus' mother:

> his mother and his mother's sister
> –Mary of Clopas and Mary Magdalene–

Some exegetes mention the option of two women, but do not really discuss the possibility.[6] The interpretation of two women is, for the most part, not regarded as a serious option, since the two sisters would have the same name.[7] However, ἀδελφή may also be interpreted in a wider sense as a kinswoman, for instance as a 'sister-in-law' or 'niece'[8] and, as we have seen, the name 'Mary' was

1.   For a comparison with the lists of synoptic women, see Brown 1970: 904-906 and Brown 1994: II, 1013-1019.

2.   Brown 1970: 922.

3.   Charlesworth 1995: 57-64.

4.   E.g. Hoskyns 1947: 530.

5.   See Klauck 1992: 2347-51. Bauckham (1992: 231-55) is a recent example of a scholar, who defends the view that there are three women under the cross.

6.   Charlesworth does not mention the option. Klauck (1992) thinks the possibility should be taken more seriously. In his view: 'Die nahezu reflexhafte Ablehnung der Zweierlösung ist konditioniert durch das fest umrissene Bild von den Familienverhältnissen Jesu, das wir durch Harmonisierung und Kombination verschiedener Daten gewonnen haben. Auch wenn das Johannesevangelium die einschlägigen synoptischen Stoffe kennen sollte, steht damit immer noch nicht fest, wie es sie selbst verstanden hat und aus seiner Sicht verstanden wissen wollte' (p. 2346).

7.   E.g. Westcott 1902: 275; Wikenhauser 1961: 332; Brown 1970: 904 and Brown 1994: II, 1014. Schackenburg (1975: 321) has yet another reason to object to the parallelism: the option of two women 'scheidet aus sachlichen Gründen aus; Maria von Magdala wäre dann die Schwester der Mutter Jesu!'

8.   Liddell and Scott 1968: 20; sister, kinswoman. See also Bauckham 1992: 233.

very common at the time.[9]

The third interpretation would also imply that, according to John, the name of Jesus' mother is Mary of Clopas, Clopas' wife, his daughter, or his mother: Mary the daughter of Clopas perhaps being the most probable.[10] Could this really be John's intention? An objection against the conjecture that John identifies Clopas as the father of Jesus' mother could be that later tradition generally identifies the father of Jesus' mother as Joachim. This is, however, not the objection of Richard Bauckham, in his article on Jn 19.25. He states:

> It is really inconceivable that Mary the mother of Jesus, who could always and most obviously be distinguished from other women called Mary by calling her the mother of Jesus, could ever have been known in the early church as Mary of Clopas.[11]

His main objection is that Mary in the early Church would generally have been known by reference to her famous son, rather than to her father. Some other exegetes would object, since in their view one of the peculiarities of John is leaving Jesus' mother unnamed. By not naming her, John emphasizes her being a mother. As mother of Jesus she would symbolize the Church.[12]

However, if John really wanted to emphasize the motherhood of Jesus' mother, why would John's Jesus, when he speaks to her in 2.4, address her in such an uncommon way as 'woman'? There is no other son in Greco-Roman and Hebrew sources who addresses his mother in such a manner.[13] The only other instance where Jesus addresses his mother, he also addresses her as 'woman' (19.26). At the beginning of John, Jesus' mother asks him to intervene at the wedding of Cana, but he rejects this saying 'what is there between you and me, woman' (2.4). Her motherhood apparently allows her no particular claim on him.[14]

The second time Jesus addresses his mother is here, at the end of his work, where again her motherhood is the object of his remark. I would like to argue that John mentions her name precisely here, because Jesus' mother is on the verge of losing her identity as 'his mother'. She is on the verge of having to live a life without him, no longer being known, and knowing herself, as 'his mother', but becoming 'Mary of Clopas' again. Jesus' words to her are precisely about the fact that she is going to lose her identity as 'his mother', opening up a new way of belonging and relating.

Another important consideration is that John's description of two women fits with a peculiar Johannine trait discerned by William Watty: the Gospel's 'massive

---

9.   See Chapter 5, section 3.

10.   See also Bauckham 1992: 232: according to Matthew and Luke, Mary's husband would be Joseph and no brother of Jesus called Clopas is known. Bauckham (1992: 235-36), on the basis of epigraphical evidence from Jewish Palestine, mentions cases in which a married woman is designated by reference to her father.

11.   Bauckham 1992: 232.

12.   For instance Hoskyns 1947: 530 and Brown 1970: 98, 107-109.

13.   Brown 1966: 99.

14.   See also Seim 1987: 60 and Schüssler Fiorenza 1983: 327. Cf. Mk 3.31-35; Mt. 12.46-50; Lk. 8.19-21; 11.27-28.

effort at precision' when introducing places or persons, not only giving names as such, but also several connections with other places or persons. John relates, for instance, that Simon, also named Peter, is the son of John (1.14; 21.15-17) and that Philip is of Bethsaida in Galilee, the birthplace also of Andrew and Peter (1.44; 12.21).[15]

We must, however, simply conclude that John's sentence construction is not clear. Jn 19.25 leaves three options open: there are either two women at the cross, or three, or four. This led Thomas Brodie to an unusual interpretation, not choosing between the three possibilities, but respecting them from the point of view of the reader. In his view:

> within the reader there is a process of shifting from one combination to another, a process which in some ways is unsettling but one which corresponds to what is in question – the changing shape of God's people, the unsettling but fruitful process of moving towards a people that is one and universal.[16]

According to Brodie, the two women represent the Judaism which seeks to believe (the mother) and the Judaism which does not (Mary Magdalene). The three women represent the Judaism that does not believe (Mary Magdalene), together with the Church's Jewish and Gentile components (the sisters). The four women, as counterpart to the four soldiers, evoke 'the emerging universalism'.[17]

Most scholars, however, choose one of the interpretations. I opt for two women, not only because of the above-mentioned arguments, but also because in the case of two women John would not introduce a sister of Jesus' mother or Mary of Clopas in 19.25 without referring to them again. The two women, Jesus' mother named Mary of Clopas and Mary Magdalene, do have their roles after Jn 19.25: Jesus' mother has her role under the cross and Mary Magdalene appears in John's account of the resurrection.[18]

Yet, it must be admitted that the other options are also credible. This leaves us with the conclusion that, in any case, John introduces Mary Magdalene at the cross, within speaking distance either in the company of several relatives of Jesus, among them his mother, or with his mother alone. This is strikingly different from the introductions in Mark, Matthew, and Luke, where Mary Magdalene is presented looking on from afar and in the company of many women followers of Jesus. What is the implication of this for John's portrayal of Mary Magdalene? Should we regard her as belonging to a small circle of close relatives?

If so, it may be possible to visualize her in the train of Jesus' followers which is described in 2.12, where John first mentions Jesus' mother, then his brothers (and sisters) or in a broader sense his relatives (οἱ ἀδελφοί), and, finally, his disciples. In contrast to the Synoptics, Jesus' relatives do have a role in John. His mother urges him to intervene at the wedding in Cana and speaks to the servants on his

---

15. Watty (1979: 209-210) gives numerous examples. However, Watty does not mention 19.25. In his view Jesus' mother remains anonymous.

16. Brodie 1993: 549.

17. Brodie 1993: 547-49.

18. Bauckham 1992.

behalf (2.1-11). She and other relatives are near the cross. His relatives, after he has lost many disciples in Galilee following his discourse on his flesh and blood giving eternal life (6.66), recommend that he go to Judea, to show his disciples his works (7.3). John adds that even his relatives did not believe in him (7.5). Is Mary Magdalene part of this group?

2.2. *Mary Magdalene as Disciple*

What exactly is Mary Magdalene's relation to Jesus and what about discipleship? In John's account of her we find some clues. In 20.14-17 Jesus appears to her, calling her by name (20.16). This is the only instance in John where Jesus addresses a woman by her name. He addresses his mother, the Samaritan woman, the adulteress[19] and Mary Magdalene as 'woman'.[20] The fact that Jesus calls her by name in 20.16 reminds one of John's account of Jesus, comparing his 'own' to sheep who recognize his voice as that of the good shepherd, when he calls them by name, and who are guided by him to seek good pastures (10.1-10). This would imply that Mary Magdalene, since she recognizes Jesus' voice when he calls her by name and is guided by him, belongs to Jesus' own. This coincides with the circumstance that Jesus calls his disciples his 'own' (13.1, 34; cf. 15.9-17; and 17.6-12).[21]

Mary Magdalene in turn addresses Jesus with 'Rabbouni', which John explains as the Hebrew word for teacher (διδάσκαλε 20.16). This reminds one of the two disciples of John the Baptist who decide to follow Jesus instead and thus call Jesus 'Rabbi' (1.35-40),[22] which the Gospel again translates as teacher (διδάσκαλε 1.38).[23] Jesus' question is also similar. He asks the two first disciples 'what do you seek' (τί ζητεῖτε 1.38) and Mary Magdalene 'whom do you seek' (τίνα ζητεῖς 20.15).[24] Raymond Brown argues that these questions reflect a theology of discipleship.[25] He states: 'If the training of the disciples begins when they *go* to Jesus to *see* where he is staying and *stay* on with him, it will be completed when they *see* his glory and *believe* in him'.[26] The first two disciples seek where Jesus is staying, whereas Mary Magdalene first seeks his body in order to stay with it and finally sees the risen Jesus and believes in him, which is clear when she tells the disciples that she has seen the Lord (20.18).

---

19. See Hoskyns (1947: 563-66), for a detailed text-critical and linguistic analysis of this rather early story. In various manuscripts it is missing. In others it is found at different places: after Lk. 21.38, after Jn 7.36 or 7.44, or directly after the Gospel of John as a whole. Most commonly, the story is understood to belong in or near John.

20. Seim (1987: 56-73), draws attention to the instances where John's Jesus addresses women as γύναι: 2.4; 4.21; 19.26; 20.13-15, thus emphasizing their womanhood and otherness.

21. See also Brown 1970: 1009-1010.

22. Cf. Nathanael in 1.50; the disciples in 11.8 call Jesus Rabbi too.

23. See also Ruschmann 2002: 153-56.

24. See also Ruschmann 2002: 151-53.

25. Brown 1966: 74. For the conjecture that the verb 'to seek' indicates discipleship see also Schüssler Fiorenza (1983: 333) and M.C. De Boer (1992: 226-27) who refers to Jn 4.27. To Ruschmann (2002: 151-52), the verb to seek especially denotes the human search for Jesus. She points to Jesus' question τίνα ζητεῖτε to the soldiers in 18.4, 7.

26. Brown 1966: 79. Italics original.

In addition, Susanne Ruschmann draws attention to two additional similarities between the first disciples and Mary Magdalene. In 1.38 Jesus turns around to the disciples, whereas in 20.16 Mary Magdalene turns around to Jesus.[27] As Andrew in 1.41 and Philip in 1.45, now Mary Magdalene in 20.18 goes to others to tell about whom she found.[28] All this would imply that John in 20.16 depicts the relation between Mary Magdalene and Jesus as one between a pupil and her teacher, as is the case with the first disciples in 1.35-51.

This raises two questions. First, when John portrays Mary Magdalene as disciple, is it possible that John, like Mark, encourages the readers to visualize Mary Magdalene every time the word 'disciples' occurs, being anonymously present from the very start of Jesus' ministry? And secondly, when considering the close connection between 1.35-40 and 20.15-18 and the fact that of the first two disciples only one is named (Andrew in Jn 1.40) and the other remains anonymous in a context of other explicitly named male disciples: could it be possible that John means to suggest that this disciple is Mary Magdalene?[29]

2.3. *Johannine Discipleship and the Twelve*

In John, Jesus has many disciples, at least in the beginning of his ministry. In 6.66, John relates that many of his disciples leave Jesus and Jesus asks the Twelve whether they also want to leave him (6.67). Simon Peter answers on behalf of the Twelve and they stay. It is reasonable to assume that, as in Mark and Luke, also in John the group of remaining disciples is not limited to the Twelve, since Joseph of Arimathea is a disciple too (19.38).

In contrast to the Synoptics, in John the Twelve play no further role, except that Judas and Thomas are identified as belonging to the group (6.71; 20.24). In contrast to the Synoptics, John also favours other disciples than those favoured in the Synoptics: Peter, John and James. In John, Peter speaks on behalf of the Twelve (6.68), he refuses to allow Jesus to wash his feet (13.8), he denies Jesus (18.25-27), he, against Jesus' wish, draws his sword at Jesus' arrest (18.10-11), he witnesses the grave to be empty (20.6) and Jesus asks him whether he truly loves him, giving him the authority to care for Jesus' followers like a shepherd for his sheep (21.15-17). This is very different from Matthew's view of Peter, who is, according to this Gospel, the rock on which the Church is to be built and the one who receives the keys to the Kingdom of Heaven (Mt. 16.18-20). In contrast to the Synoptics, Peter recognizes Jesus as the holy one of God (6.69) and not as the Christ the Son of the living God.[30] Instead, Nathanael confesses him as the Son of God the king of Israel while Martha confesses Jesus as the Christ Son of God, who

---

27. Ruschmann 2002: 150-51. She explains Mary Magdalene's turning around in 20.14 as part of the process of seeking. To others, Mary Magdalene's turning around twice towards Jesus (20.14, 16) is one of the notions that has led to various theories about the composition of Jn 20.1-18; see Brown 1970: 995-1004.

28. Ruschmann 2002: 145, 212.

29. As is suggested by Schaberg 2002: 342.

30. Cf. Mk 8.29; Mt. 16.16; Lk. 9.20.

would come to the world, which is also the confession of the author of John.[31]

The sons of Zebedee, James and John, who are prominent in the Synoptics, do not occur in John until perhaps in 21.2 and then only very vaguely as 'those of Zebedee'. Instead Andrew, Philip, Nathanael, Thomas, and Judas (not Iskarioth), play a prominent role (e.g. 1.35-52 and 13.1–14.24). In contrast to the Synoptics, John does not mention the names of the Twelve[32] and only Philip is found and called as disciple by Jesus himself (1.44). Andrew, another disciple, Simon Peter, and Natanael follow him on their own initiative, respectively recommended to do this by John the Baptist, Andrew, and Philip (1.35-52).

John's view on discipleship is also different from that of the Synoptics. In John, the disciples follow and serve Jesus as they do in Mark, Matthew, and Luke, but the specific Johannine criteria of discipleship are remaining in Jesus' words (8.31), showing love to one another (13.35), and bearing much fruit (15.8). Hating one's father and mother, one's wife, sons and daughters and brothers and sisters is not required, nor is leaving everything behind.[33] The crucial message of the Gospel, formulated in the prologue, says that Jesus has come, so that all those who accept him, who believe in his name, will receive from him the strength to become children of God by being born anew (1.12-13). John uses the inclusive word τέκνα for children and not the more masculine word 'sons', which Matthew uses when Jesus says that those who love their enemies and those who make peace will be children of God (υἱοί Mt. 5.9, 45). However, the disciples are called 'sons' (υἱοί) of light in Jn 12.36.

Since the disciples in John are not limited to the Twelve, Johannine discipleship does not necessarily depend on breaking family ties, and John's prologue and the criteria of discipleship seem inclusive, we can assume that John includes women as well as men when the Gospel uses the masculine plural disciples.[34] However, two objections must be made against this conjecture. First, whereas John specifically calls Andrew, Judas Iskarioth, and Joseph of Arimathea disciples (6.8; 12.4; 19.38), not one of the prominent women is identified as such. Secondly, whereas Mary Magdalene in 20.18 goes to 'the disciples' to tell them whom she has seen, in 20.25 'the other disciples' tell Thomas what they have seen, thus suggesting that Thomas belongs to the disciples and Mary does not belong to them. Are these androcentric slips of the pen, or is there more behind this?

2.4. *John's Attitude towards Women*

2.4.1. *Conservative Boundaries.* Some scholars emphasize John's positive attitude towards women and women's experience and refer to the theological importance of the women portrayed in the Gospel.[35] Others are more sceptical about this.[36]

---

31. Jn 1.50; 11.27, cf. 20.31.
32. Cf. Mk 3.13-19; Mt. 10.1-4; Lk. 6.12-16.
33. Cf. Mt. 10.37-39; Lk. 14.26 and also Mk 10.28-31; Mt. 19.27-30; Lk. 18.28-30.
34. See for instance Schüssler Fiorenza 1983: 323-27 and M.C. De Boer 1992: 210, 228-29.
35. See Brown 1975 (reprinted in Brown 1979); Schneiders 1982; Schüssler Fiorenza 1983: 323-34; O'Day 1992; Reinhartz 1994: esp. 594-95; Beirne 2003.
36. E.g. Seim 1987 and van Tilborg 1993: 169-208. Fehribach (1998) extensively discusses the

Although John indeed depicts remarkable women, the Gospel also relates circumstances which disclose a repressive attitude towards women. There are hints of an awareness of being seen and spoken to primarily as 'woman', or as 'other'[37] and being in a suspect situation when acting as a person, without regard for maleness and femaleness (4.27; cf. 4.9). In addition, the story of the adulteress (8.1-11), although it would or did not originally belong to the Gospel,[38] reflects the female awareness of being vulnerable as a woman at the mercy of male power.

In contrast to the Synoptics, in John, the women whom Jesus addresses are either his relatives (his mother) or in the company of his mother (Mary Magdalene), or are already acquainted with him, being in the company of a male relative of their own who is Jesus' friend (Martha and Mary as sisters of Lazarus). Only the Samaritan woman is a complete stranger to Jesus.[39]

Furthermore, the women Jesus relates to in John are in their domestic situations or fulfilling domestic tasks. The Samaritan woman is drawing water near her own town (4.4-42) and Martha and Mary are in their own Bethany, caring for their brother (11.1-44; 12.1-8). In view of this, Mary Magdalene seems to be the exception, since she appears rather unexpectedly in Jerusalem, instead of in a domestic situation in Magdala. Moreover, she is in the company of the mother of Jesus, the only woman clearly mentioned to be travelling. John, however, depicts the mother of Jesus travelling in the company of her family (2.12), which also suggests a conservative view on gender roles.[40]

This is all very different from the Synoptic Gospels, in which Jesus addresses women freely. The Synoptic Gospels do not portray them as his relatives or as relatives of male friends. Moreover Mark, Matthew, and Luke all speak of 'many women' who followed Jesus, travelling with him and learning from him. In John, Jesus apparently moves within the boundaries of more conservative attitudes towards women than he does in the Synoptic Gospels.

John, instead, depicts a certain ambiguity towards women on the part of the disciples and Jesus. This becomes clear in the story about Jesus and the Samaritan woman, with whom he is not acquainted. Jesus addresses her briefly which according to Rabbinic texts befits a man talking to a strange woman. According to Rabbinic texts, women outside the circle of family and friends should especially be addressed as briefly as possible.[41] Indeed Jesus uses only the necessary words, δός μοι πεῖν and even omits γύναι from his address (4.7).[42] The woman thereupon

patriarchal and androcentric traits of the women's portrayals in John. Maccini (1996), however, argues against any conclusion about John's attitude towards women. In his view John does not focus on gender but on individuals (e.g. p. 244).

37. Seim (1987), rightly draws attention to the instances where John's Jesus addresses women as γύναι: 2.4; 4.21; 19.26; 20.13-15, thus emphasizing their womanhood and otherness.

38. See note 16.

39. In the remaining encounter with an unknown woman in 8.1-11, the woman is presented to Jesus by the Pharisees. The contact with Jesus is not her or his initiative.

40. We may visualize her among the οἱ ἀδελφοι, if we do not interpret the word as brothers and sisters, but in the wider sense as relatives (2.12).

41. Ilan 1995a: 126-27.

42. Kraemer (1999a: 39-41) argues that the New Testament portrayal of Jesus' conversation

starts the dialogue (4.9).[43] Furthermore, when she asks to be given the living water, Jesus wants her to fetch her husband (4.16). The disciples, returning from their shopping, marvel that Jesus is talking with a woman (4.27). In a way the story builds up like the story of the Syro-Phoenician/Canaanite woman in Mark and Matthew: not only the Samaritan woman, but also Jesus is learning, and so are the disciples and the readers.

Ilan refers to a passage about the Jewish woman Beruriah, which is quite interesting with regard to our story:

> R. Yose the Galilean was once on a journey when he met Beruriah. By what road, he asked her, do we go to Lod? Galilean fool, she replied, did not the sages say this 'Talk not much with womankind?' You should have asked: By which to Lod? (b. Erubin 53b)[44]

Ilan comments that R. Yose, ironically, already avoiding all polite formality, is now drawn against his own will into a conversation by a woman exactly about how to address women to avoid conversation with them.

The same happens to Jesus. He uses only the words he really needs, thus avoiding conversation with the woman, but she finds enough reason to question him about them. The great difference between the Beruriah story and the one about Jesus and the Samaritan woman is that the Samaritan woman does not linger on the behaviour of males towards females, like Beruriah, but focuses on the behaviour of Jews towards Samaritans. Whereas Jesus' attitude reveals that he is focused on his maleness and her femaleness, the Samaritan woman is more concerned by the fact that he is a Jew and she is a Samaritan.

The Johannine story of the Samaritan woman illustrates that women are able to be partners in theological discourse and of having their share in mission (quite successfully too), even on their own initiative as their response to Jesus' self-revelation that he is the Messiah. The story also shows that Jesus himself becomes aware that women may be also sowers of the seed, and that the disciples need not be afraid, or need not stop them, but may rejoice with them, reaping the harvest (4.27-38).

According to Martinus de Boer, the Johannine Jesus tradition as attested in the narrative portions of John is thoroughly androcentric, but the marvelling disciples in 4.27 would reflect 'the growing and developing faith of Johannine Christianity away from an androcentric understanding of discipleship and mission to one emphasizing and recognizing the equality of women to men in Christian life and praxis'.[45]

with women in general fits easily within the Rabbinic notion of limited speech with women. Of the few narratives where Jesus is portrayed speaking more than five words or engages in actual dialogue, two involve non-Jewish women: the Syro-Phoenician/Canaanite woman and the Samaritan woman.

43. I do not agree with Seim (1987: 59), who argues that Jesus takes the initiative: Jesus only wants water.
44. Ilan 1995a: 127.
45. De Boer 1992: 228.

2.4.2. Speaking Women. Apparently there is a conservative attitude from John's Jesus and his disciples, which would imply that the attitude within the Johannine community is conservative too. The Johannine Jesus and his disciples approach women carefully.

However, although John portrays women in their domestic situations, or in the company of Jesus' relatives or male friends and thus keeping them in conservative boundaries, the Gospel within these boundaries depicts them as self-confidently speaking women even when they are in dialogue with Jesus and in theological discourse. John's narratives where women speak freely are in sharp contrast to Luke's narrative technique of silencing women.

John portrays women as speaking far more than Mark, Matthew, and Luke. In Mark only five instances of women speaking are recorded,[46] in Matthew women speak nine times[47] and in Luke eleven times,[48] only four of which occur in stories about Jesus as a grown man.[49] In contrast to the Synoptics, John records 22 instances of women speaking.[50]

When one considers the words of women spoken in dialogue with Jesus the difference is even more obvious. In Mark and Matthew only the Syrophoenician/ Canaanite woman speaks with Jesus (one in Mark; three times in Matthew),[51] and in Luke only his mother, Martha, and the woman from the crowd (each one time), all three of whom are rebuked by Jesus.[52] In John, however, all the women, except the doorkeeper of the court of the high Priest, are portrayed in a self-confident dialogue with Jesus: his mother speaks once, the Samaritan woman six times, Martha, and Mary together once, Martha alone four times, her sister Mary once, and Mary Magdalene twice.[53]

Both Martha and Mary are prominent in John. Peter's confession in the Synoptics that Jesus is the Christ is in John ascribed to Martha (11.27). The balming of Jesus' feet is done by Mary (12.3), a gesture which is followed by Jesus as an example for his disciples, when he washes their feet (13.1-20). Martha calls her sister Mary to Jesus as Andrew called his brother, Simon Peter, and Philip called Nathanael. It is strikingly different, however, that her call is said to be in secret. After she confessed Jesus to be the Christ, the Son of God, the one coming into the world, John relates:

> When she had said this, she went and called Mary her sister secretly, saying, The Teacher is here and is calling for you. (11.28)[54]

46.   Mk 5.28; 7.28; 14.67, 69; 16.3.

47.   Mt. 14.8; 15.22, 26, 27; 25.8, 9, 11; 26.69, 71.

48.   Lk. 1.25, 34, 38, 42-45, 46-55, 60; 2.48; 10.40; 11.27; 18.3; 22.56.

49.   Lk. 10.40; 11.27; 18.3; 22.56.

50.   Jn 2.3, 5; 4.9, 11-12, 15, 17, 19-20, 25, 29, 39; 11.3, 21-22, 24, 27, 28, 32, 39; 18.17; 20.2, 13, 15, 16.

51.   Mk 7.28; Mt. 15.22, 26, 27. Although she is rather bold, Jesus praises her faith in both Mark and Matthew.

52.   Lk. 2.48-49; 10.40-42; 11.27-28.

53.   2.3; 4.9, 11-12, 15, 17, 19-20, 25; 11.3, 21-22, 24, 27, 32, 39; 20.15, 16.

54.   Revised Standard Version: '…called her sister Mary, saying quietly…'

In response to Martha's call, Mary rises quickly and goes to him.

The remaining six times that women speak to someone other than Jesus are in a self-confident context too. The mother of Jesus, at the wedding of Cana, tells the servants to do whatever Jesus asks them to do (2.5). The Samaritan woman evangelizes the citizens of her hometown Sychar (4.29, 39). The woman doorkeeper at the court of the high Priest takes the initiative of identifying Peter to be one of Jesus' disciples (18.17). Last, but not least, Mary Magdalene summons Peter and the other disciple Jesus loved to come to the empty tomb (20.2), where she, after they have gone, addresses the angels to find out where Jesus' body has been taken (20.13).

2.4.3. *Implicit Women's Discipleship.* Adeline Fehribach, in her extensive study on the women in John, states that it is a modern interpretation to see Jesus' mother, the Samaritan woman, Martha and Mary and Mary Magdalene as disciples. Although she admits that there are good reasons for doing so, it would not reflect the interpretation of first-century readers of John. As she argues, by comparing the Johannine stories about women with literary and social conventions of the time, first-century readers would interpret the women in a far more androcentric context.

In Fehribach's interpretation, a first-century reader would recognize the mother of Jesus as the mother of an important son, who in the story supports the portrayal of Jesus as the messianic Bridegroom. The Samaritan woman, Martha, Mary, and Mary Magdalene, subsequently, function as the betrothed or a bride. Jesus provides the seed for them to bring about children from above. Thus, they symbolize various communities of faith. The Samaritan woman does this on behalf of the Samaritan people, Mary of Bethany on behalf of the Jews (Martha is an example of Jewish faith) and Mary Magdalene on behalf of the entire community.

However, would the first-century reader of the Johannine community not recognize that John depicts Jesus' mother, the Samaritan woman, Martha and Mary, and Mary Magdalene in discipleship roles? Jesus' mother, the Samaritan woman, Martha and Mary Magdalene are taught by him. They express their belief in him and they evangelize. Mary the sister of Martha is an example of service Jesus asks of his disciples. Indeed, the Samaritan woman, Martha, and Mary are disciples in domestic situations and Mary Magdalene belongs to the company of Jesus' mother. Within these conservative boundaries, however, John portrays the women in self-confident and theologically relevant dialogue with Jesus.

In addition, John does not mention the many women who, according to the Synoptics, followed Jesus during his ministry. Should we assume that this feature of tradition was unknown to John or does this difference emphasize John's conservative attitude towards women? If John's use of the masculine plural of disciples refers to women as well as men, which is reasonable to assume, John keeps the women disciples who follow Jesus and travel with him in the shadows. They remain invisible.

Although John's women are depicted in prominent roles as disciples, their names are not specifically combined with the word disciple, as are the names of

Andrew, Judas Iskariot, and Joseph of Arimathea. If identified as disciples, women
remain invisible behind the masculine plural of disciples. Because of the marked
similarities between 20.15-18 and 1.38-40, we assumed earlier that John perhaps
suggests that the unnamed disciple who together with Andrew began to follow
Jesus in 1.35-41 is Mary Magdalene. Does John leave this disciple unnamed, in
contrast to Andrew and in contrast to all other first followers of Jesus in 1.35-52,
because she is a woman?

John depicts other anonymous single disciples, who are, however, mostly identified as one disciple: the disciple Jesus loved. We will return to this in an excursus
below.

3. *John's Story about Mary Magdalene*

3.1. *Standing by the Cross*

John begins the story about Mary Magdalene at the end of the Gospel, beneath the
cross, just before Jesus dies. Mary Magdalene is standing by the cross with a small
group of women closely related to Jesus (19.25). If we think of two women being
present, Mary Magdalene is introduced as the niece or sister-in-law of Jesus'
mother. On the cross is the title: Jesus of Nazareth, the King of the Jews. Soldiers
are casting lots for his coat (19.24). Jesus sees his mother and the disciple he loved
standing by and talks to them (19.26-27). John states that after this he knows that
all is accomplished, he receives the vinegar and he says: 'It is finished' (19.30).

Mary Magdalene is thus introduced at a very important moment in John. This is
Jesus' hour. She witnesses the Son of Man being lifted up and glorified (cf. 3.14;
12.23): the shepherd giving his life in defence of his sheep (cf. 10.11; 15.13), the
grain falling in the earth in order to bring forth many fruits (12.24-25). In addition,
she witnesses the constitution of the new community. In 19.26-27 Jesus declares
that his mother and the disciple he loved are to act as a mother and a son, which
implies that this disciple from this hour on also stands in a fraternal relation to
Jesus. Mary Magdalene thus stands at the threshold between an earthly belonging
to Jesus and a spiritual one.[55]

In contrast to the Synoptics, no women attend the burial of Jesus. Instead, it is
Joseph of Arimathea, who buries Jesus together with Nicodemus. They bury him in
a markedly honourable manner, as a true King would have been buried. They wind
the body in linen cloths with spices, which Nicodemus brought with him: a
hundred pounds of myrrh and aloe. Then they lay Jesus' body in a new tomb in a
garden (19.38-42).[56]

3.2. *Seeking Jesus' Dead Body*

In John, Mary Magdalene is alone when she goes to the tomb of Jesus. Nothing is
said about the purpose of her visit. While, according to Mark and Luke, Mary

55. See also Ruschmann 2002: 106-107.
56. See Brown 1994: II, 1258-71 for a survey of several interpretations of the meaning of this
burial. Brown suggests that the huge amount of spices and the tomb being in a garden is a symbolic
honouring of Jesus as King of the Jews and Son of David.

Magdalene and the other women are going to anoint Jesus' body and, according to Matthew, Mary Magdalene and the other Mary are going to have a look, John relates nothing of the sort. In John, Jesus is anointed already and quite sufficiently too. And there is no context of suspense awaiting the moment of the third day, as in Matthew.

Another difference is the circumstance that, when Mary Magdalene discovers the grave to be empty, she immediately goes to tell Simon Peter and the other disciple Jesus loved. Peter and the other disciple Jesus loved react to Mary Magdalene's message by running to the grave, the other disciple outrunning Peter, both finding the body not to be there, as Mary Magdalene said.

The author then comments that the anonymous disciple sees and believes. Believes what? That Mary Magdalene is right?[57] Or believing that Jesus has now gone up, as he said he would? Perhaps like Elijah, whose body could not be found again either (2 Kgs 2.1-18)? John does not explain. The reader here is reminded of the words of Jesus which he twice spoke to others and at the Last Supper repeated to his disciples:

> Yet a little while I am with you. You will seek me: and as I said to the Jews, so now I say to you 'Where I am going you cannot come'. (Jn 13.33; cf. 7.33-36; 8.21-22)[58]

Mary Magdalene is seeking Jesus and confides in Peter and the other disciple Jesus loved that Jesus' body is not there. They cannot come where he is going.

The believing of the disciple is contrasted to knowing the scripture, as the author explains:

> For as yet they [all three] did not know the scripture, that he must rise from the dead. (Jn 20.9)

After this the two return, each to their own things. Mary Magdalene is alone again. The readers are held in suspense.

In Mark, Matthew and Luke there is no such story. The women at the empty tomb in the Synoptics do not fetch anyone. They do, or do not, talk about the revelation they received. They ask no other person to go to the tomb and there is no distinguishing between Peter who 'sees' and the other disciple Jesus loved who 'sees and believes', both of them returning 'to their own things'. In Luke in the Emmaus story there is an allusion to other persons who went to the tomb, one of the two disciples saying:

> Some of those who were with us went to the tomb, and found it just as the women had said; but him they did not see. (Lk. 24.24)

---

57. Brown (1970: 987) refers to no one less than Augustine for this interpretation (without an exact reference). However, according to Brown and others, the disciple Jesus loved is the first to believe in the risen Jesus.

58. See also Ruschmann 2002: 195.

In Lk. 24.12 Peter alone runs to the tomb to find it empty.[59] Peter and the other disciple in John are witnesses to the empty tomb too. In the case of Mary Magdalene all the emphasis is on the significance of the body of Jesus not being there.

One may ask if the other disciple Jesus loved already grasped this significance. Some exegetes suggest that the disciple who 'saw and believed' is the first in the Gospel to believe in the living Jesus.[60] This disciple's faith is lauded, with reference to Jesus' words to Thomas:

> Have you believed because you have seen me? Blessed are those who have not seen and yet believe. (20.29)

David Beck assumes that the other disciple Jesus loved, thus, compared to Peter, Mary Magdalene, and Thomas, is the only one who gives an 'appropriate response' to Jesus, which he defines as 'an active faith response to Jesus' word without a sign or the need to "see" and bearing witness to the efficacy of Jesus' words to others'.[61] In Beck's view John invites the readers to identify with the anonymous disciple and to reject the ways in which Peter, Mary Magdalene, and Thomas react to Jesus.

Brown refutes this kind of reasoning, since, as he rightly argues:

> the praise of those who believe without having seen Jesus by no means implies a lesser beatitude on those who have seen and have believed.[62]

Dodd concludes that faith in John always is a 'form of vision'.[63] He states:

> When Christ was on earth, to have faith was to 'see His glory' – to apprehend and acknowledge the deity through the veil of humanity. Now that he is no longer visible to the bodily eye, faith remains the capacity of seeing His glory.[64]

It is this 'seeing' which is at stake in our pericope. John does not invite the readers to accept or reject ways of reacting to Jesus; rather the Gospel takes the readers cautiously by the hand to enable them to really understand what is going on.

3.3. *Seeing, but What Exactly?*
John, as in a thriller movie, gradually heightens the suspense by disclosing more and more of what there is actually to be seen. Mary Magdalene sees that the stone has been taken from the tomb (20.1). The anonymous other disciple sees the linen cloths (20.5). Simon Peter, going into the tomb, observes the linen cloths and the napkin 'not lying with the linen cloths but rolled up in a place by itself' (20.6-7). The other disciple, going into the tomb sees and believes: 'for as yet they did not know the scripture, that he must rise from the dead' (20.8-9). This remark

---

59. This verse has been interpreted as a later insertion, but Bock (1994: 1902) and others on the basis of text-critical and literary arguments advocate the stand that the verse originally belongs to the text.
60. Brown 1970: 987.
61. Beck 1997: 121-36, esp. 133.
62. Brown 1970: 1005.
63. Dodd 1953: 177-86.
64. Dodd 1953: 186.

heightens the suspense even more. What is going to happen? What more is there to be seen? When Mary Magdalene, alone again, looks into the tomb she 'observes two angels in white, sitting where the body of Jesus had lain, one at the head and one at the feet' (20.12). Later she even 'caught sight of Jesus standing', but she thinks he is the gardener (20.14). Verbs of seeing are used six times, βλέπειν, θεωρεῖν and ἰδεῖν but still it is not clear what there is actually to be seen.[65]

3.4. *Determined to Take Hold of Jesus' Body*

It is striking that, in contrast to the stories of Mark, Matthew and Luke, in John there are no heavenly figures who, immediately, give their knowledge to Mary Magdalene. In John, the two angels in the empty tomb only ask a question. In addition, in John, as in Matthew, Mary Magdalene actually meets the resurrected Jesus, but while in Matthew he encourages her and the other Mary to rejoice without any fear, in John he, just like the angels, asks a question. Mary Magdalene in John is gradually coming to a full understanding, whereas in Mark, Matthew and Luke she and the woman or women in her company, at once, almost as soon as they discover the grave to be empty, receive a revelatory message.

By this, John not only takes the readers by the hand to enable them to unravel the significance of the body of Jesus not being there, but also, in contrast to the other three Gospels, describes Mary Magdalene as one who is persistently seeking for an answer. Mary Magdalene speaks three times; each time she expresses her forlornness. She says to Simon Peter and the other disciple Jesus loved:

> They have taken away the Lord out of the tomb, and we know not where they have laid him. (20.2)

When they leave and she herself goes into the tomb, and sees the angels at the head and the feet of the place where Jesus' body should have been, she answers their question 'Woman, why do you weep?' by saying:

> Because they have taken away my Lord and I do not know where they have laid him. (20.13)

Then, when she turns around and sees Jesus whom she does not recognize, thinking him to be the gardener, she answers his question 'Woman, why do you weep? Whom do you seek?' saying:

> Sir, if you have carried him away, tell me where you have laid him, and I will take him away. (20.15)

Three times she expresses the great loss she feels, because she cannot find the dead body of Jesus. The third time when she speaks, she reveals why she wants to know where he is: tell me where you have laid him and I will take him away (20.15).

---

65. The translations to see, observe and catch sight are from Brown 1970: 979. Some exegetes argue that βλέπειν refers to material sight, θεωρεῖν to sight with concentration and intensity and ἰδεῖν, to sight accompanied by understanding. Brown (1966: 501-503) argues that the verbs sometimes seem to have these specific meanings, but not always and not in the case of Jn 20.1-18. See also Brown 1970: 986.

This sheds light on why she came: to be with Jesus' dead body, almost to keep him to herself, seeking comfort in his physical proximity.

3.5. Seeing the Lord and being Instructed by Him

The sense of loss is overwhelmingly present in this part of the story. Mary Magdalene experiences the distress that had been prophesied to the disciples in Jesus' farewell speech (14.1, 27; 16.20).[66] As John emphasizes in 20.1, it is still dark. But then, when Jesus calls her by name, she suddenly realizes who this gardener is. 'Rabbouni!' she exclaims.[67] In John, no heavenly figures, but Jesus himself reveals to Mary Magdalene what is happening, saying:

> Do not hold me, for I have not yet ascended to the Father; but go to my brothers (and sisters) and say to them, I am ascending to my Father and your Father, to my God and your God. (20.17)

Mary Magdalene thereupon goes to Jesus' disciples, and not to Jesus' relatives.[68] John reports that she repeats Jesus' words to her and adds: 'I have seen the Lord!' (20.18).

3.5.1. 'Do not hold me'. Jesus does not only ask Mary Magdalene to 'go' (πορεύου) and 'say' (εἰπέ), two positive imperatives, but also directs a negative imperative unto her: μή μου ἅπτου (20.17). This negative imperative has received much attention throughout the ages.[69] It has often been seen as a problem that Mary Magdalene is not allowed to touch Jesus, whereas he invites Thomas to do so (20.27). On the one hand, it is important to note that the imperative has the notion of stopping a present action.[70] This means that we have to ask ourselves what action is taking place. On the other hand, the verb may have not only a literal but also a more figurative meaning.[71]

Literally it would mean: 'Stop touching me' in a physical way. In this case the readers must assume that Mary Magdalene indeed touched Jesus, as in Matthew, where she and the other Mary held Jesus' feet, thus worshipping him (Mt. 28.9). This may be the case; however, John does not actually relate that Mary Magdalene touched or worshipped Jesus.

The negative imperative may also be interpreted more figuratively as 'stop touching me' in a psychological way, assuming that Jesus was moved by Mary Magdalene's forlornness and her weeping. This would be more plausible, since,

66. Also Ruschmann 2002: 195. She interprets the narrative of 20.1, 2, 11-18 in the context of 13.31–14.31 (pp. 165-209). Brown (1970: 1013) does the same with respect to Jn 20.17.

67. See Brown (1970: 991-92) for a survey of several interpretations. Rabbouni in later Rabbinic literature is used to address God. It may also mean 'my dear rabbi'. Brown argues we should follow John, who explains the word as meaning 'teacher' (20.16).

68. See section 3.5.2, below.

69. See Brown (1970: 992-94) for several interpretations.

70. Present imperative Blass, Debrunner and Rehkopf 1990: 336.2c note 4. Cf. for instance Lk. 8.52.

71. Liddell and Scott 1968: 231: literally it would mean to grasp, metaphorically it would mean take hold of, and more psychologically it would mean to touch, to affect.

when Lazarus has died, John relates that Jesus 'was deeply moved in spirit and troubled' (11.30), when he saw Mary, the sister of Lazarus, and others weeping. In my view, the more accurate (figurative) interpretation would be 'stop grasping me'. This would refer to what John indeed relates: Mary's persistently seeking Jesus' dead body, her wish to have it and to take hold of it.[72]

With the negative imperative Jesus wants Mary Magdalene (and John wants its readers) to finally understand what is going on. Jesus is no object, no spiritless body. There is no point in her looking for him like that. She has to stop her search. He is not lying somewhere, but standing before her. He explains: he has to go his way to the Father and she is to go her way to his brothers (and sisters).

Ruschmann compares this negative imperative to Mary with Jesus' answer to Peter in 13.36-38, when Peter asks 'Lord where are you going?': 'Where I am going, you cannot follow me now; but you will follow later'. The present way of relating to Jesus must be relinquished.[73] Ruschmann states that, to the reader, Mary Magdalene thus models the way towards the experience of the risen Jesus: she is 'eine Vermittlerin zwischen den Zeiten'.[74] Through Mary Magdalene the readers can find the way from the earthly relationship with Jesus towards the spiritual relation with the risen one.

Ruschmann specifically studied Jn 14.18-24 as a commentary on the narrative of 20.14-18.[75] The narrative of 20.14-18 is a fulfilment of 14.21-23, in which the promise of Jesus' revelation is given to those who love him. According to Ruschmann, Mary Magdalene is portrayed as the one who loves Jesus by various references to the Song of Songs.[76]

Ruschmann also argues that Mary Magdalene in her encounter with the risen Lord experiences the fulfilment of 14.18-20, where Jesus says:

> I will not leave you orphans; I will come to you. Yet a little while, and the world will see me no more, but you will see me. Because I live, you will live also. In that day you will know that I am in my Father, and you in me, and I in you. (Jn 14.18-20)

According to Ruschmann, Mary, in hearing her name and recognizing Jesus, experiences that she is not left behind as an orphan by him (14.18). She also experiences the words: 'You will see me, because I live' (14.19). In addition, through Jesus' words in 20.17, she understands and remembers that Jesus' going to his Father is meant to make a lasting relationship possible (14.2-3) and that that day will reveal to the disciples what exactly this new relationship is about: 'I am in my Father, and you in me, and I in you'. She understands that this day has now

---

72. This is in contrast to Brown (1970: 1012 and 1014). In his view, Mary Magdalene thinks the risen Jesus has already fulfilled all he promised and now has come to continue their earthly relationship.

73. Ruschmann 2002: 196.

74. Ruschmann 2002: 245-49. Quotation p. 245.

75. Ruschmann 2002: 190.

76. Ruschmann 2002: 201-205. She mentions e.g. Song of Songs 7.1 – Jn 20.14, 16; Song of Songs 3.4 – Jn 20.15; Song of Songs 2.16 and 6.2 – Jn 20.17. The whole narrative can be interpreted from Song of Songs 8.6: stronger than death and Hades is love.

come, since she indeed stops holding on to the earthly Jesus and brings the message about the new relationship, which will be completed in the narrative of the evening of the same day (20.18-23).[77]

3.5.2. *Go to my Brothers (and Sisters) and Say to Them.* Mary Magdalene does not go to Jesus' brothers (and sisters), as Jesus instructed her to do, but to the disciples. When one thinks of the Synoptics this seems quite logical: in these gospels Jesus calls his disciples his brothers and sisters.[78] One may suggest that John copied Jesus' reference to his brothers from tradition, since it also appears in the resurrection story of Matthew, when Jesus instructs Mary Magdalene and the other Mary (Mt. 28.10).

In John, however, Jesus nowhere calls his disciples his brothers (and sisters) as he does in Mark, Matthew, and Luke. In contrast to the Synoptics in John, Jesus' earthly brothers (and sisters) actually play a role in following him. In addition, in John, Jesus always refers to God as 'my Father' or 'the Father' and never, when addressing his disciples, to 'your Father' or 'our Father' as in the Synoptic Gospels.[79] John, in contrast to Matthew and Luke, does not mention the Lord's prayer which Jesus teaches to his disciples. The disciples, according to the Matthean and Lukan Jesus, are to begin their prayer with the words 'our Father' in Matthew (6.9) or 'Father' in Luke (11.2). Instead in John, when some Jews, in discussion with Jesus, call God their Father (8.40-41), Jesus answers that the devil is their Father, since 'if God were your Father, you would love me, for I proceeded forth and came from God; neither came I of myself, but he sent me' (8.42).

Notwithstanding this specific Johannine trait, John does not suggest that Mary Magdalene is mistaken by going to Jesus' disciples, instead of to his brothers (and sisters).[80] What does this mean? Brown suggests that John's Jesus in 20.17 refers to the disciples as brothers in anticipation.[81] As is clear from the prologue and the dialogue with Nicodemus, the disciples will be set in the same relationship to the Father as Jesus: as new creations, being born from God, through the Spirit (1.12–13.17-18; 3.5).

Brown argues that in Johannine theology the ascension of the Son of Man and the giving of the Spirit are intimately connected. The Spirit can only be given when Jesus is glorified (7.39), which means when he has returned to his Father (16.7, 17). In the introductory verse to the passion narrative John describes Jesus' hour as the hour to pass from this world to the Father (13.1). This theme re-occurs several

77. Ruschmann 2002: 198-200. For the interpretation that that day in 14.20 and elsewhere refers to the day described in 20.1-29 see for instance Grundmann 1961: 219, 221 and Brown 1970: 1016.

78. Mk 3.31-35; Mt. 12.46-50; Lk. 8.19-21.

79. 'Your Father' occurs 17 times in Matthew: 5.16, 48; 6.1, 4, 6, 8, 14, 15, 18, 26, 32; 7.11, 21; 10.20, 29; 18.14; 23.9. 'Your Father' occurs two times in Mark (11.25, 26) and four times in Luke (6.36; 11.13; 12.30, 32). 'Our Father' and 'their father' both only occur once (Mt. 6.9; 13.43), the latter referring to the righteous.

80. Some scholars suggest that she misunderstands Jesus' instruction and should indeed have gone to Jesus' relatives: e.g. Dodd 1953: 147.

81. Brown 1970: 1016.

times in the farewell discourse.[82] This way upwards to the Father in Johannine theology consists of crucifixion, resurrection and ascension. As Brown states:

> If John reinterprets the crucifixion so that it becomes part of Jesus' glorification, he dramatizes the resurrection so that it is obviously part of the ascension. Jesus is lifted up on the cross; he is raised up from the dead; and he goes to the Father – all as part of one action and one 'hour'.[83]

To Brown, Mary Magdalene is the vehicle for the Johannine reinterpretation of the resurrection.[84] She is the one to go to the brothers (and sisters) to declare that Jesus' resurrection is part of the ascension (ἀναβαίνω present tense: I am going upwards to the Father)[85] and that through Jesus' ascension his Father will become the Father of his disciples and by implication his brothers (and sisters).[86]

Brown emphasizes the great importance of Jesus' solemn declaration in Jn 20.17: 'I am ascending to my Father and your Father, to my God and your God'. It is covenantal language, reminding one of Ruth who says to Naomi: 'Your people shall be my people and your God shall be my God' (Ruth 1.16). It also reminds of God's promise of a new covenant in Jeremiah: 'I will be their God and they shall be my people' (Jer. 31.33).[87] Through Jesus' resurrection/ascension a new relationship will be established for the disciples.

According to Walter Grundmann, Jn 20.17 constitutes the decisive pronouncement of a new way of discipleship after Jesus' resurrection. In his view it must be seen in relation to Jesus' words to the disciples that he will no longer call them his slaves, 'for a slave does not know what his master does', but his friends, 'since', as he explains, 'all things that I have heard from my Father, I have made known unto you' (15.15).[88] In 20.17 Jesus declares that the disciples are his brothers (and sisters): his Father is now their father. This new relationship is what John is all about, as is summarized in the prologue:

> To his own he came; yet his own people did not accept him. But all those who did accept him he empowered to become God's children. (Jn 1.11-12)

To Grundmann, Jn 1.19–4.42 is about Jesus' coming to his own; 4.43–12.50 is about those who do not accept him, whereas 13.1–20.29 is about those who do accept him and whom he subsequently empowers to become children of God.[89] Jn 20.17 pronounces the completion of Jesus' work as mentioned in the prologue, thus enclosing the whole gospel[90] and fulfilling what was said before in the farewell

82. Jn 14.12, 28; 16.5, 10, 28.
83. Brown 1970: 1013-1014.
84. Brown 1970: 1014.
85. Brown 1970: 994: 'The present tense here means that Jesus is already in the process of ascending but has not yet reached his destination'. For this use of the present tense see also Blass, Debrunner and Rehkopf 1990: 323.3.
86. Brown 1970: 1016.
87. Brown 1970: 1016-1017. He refers to Feuillet 1963.
88. Grundmann 1961: 213-14.
89. Grundmann 1961: 214.
90. Grundmann 1961: 215.

discourses in 13.1–14.31 and 15–16: Jesus makes possible the access to the Father, by his returning to him.[91]

Grundmann recognizes the same theme not only in the Letters of John, but also in New Testament theology in general, for instance in Paul's letter to the Romans in which Paul characterizes the risen Jesus as 'the first born among many brothers' (Rom. 8.29). Grundmann also refers to the letter to the Hebrews which declares that Jesus 'brought many sons to glory' (Heb. 2.9-10) and to Ephesians, which states: 'Through Jesus we have access in one Spirit to the Father' (Eph. 2.18). He concludes that in 20.17 John shows a confession that especially in more Hellenistic communities would have been common: that Jesus provides access to his own to his Father, brings him to them and establishes the genuine relationship of a Father to his children.[92]

What does all this mean for John's portrayal of Mary Magdalene? Grundmann does not even mention her.[93] Brown calls her a 'vehicle' for Johannine interpretation of the resurrection. In the flow of John's story, however, Mary Magdalene seems to be more than that. Indeed, she is the one who interprets the brothers (and sisters) Jesus sends her to as the disciples. In John's picture of Mary Magdalene this going to the disciples, instead of going to Jesus' actual family, means that John portrays her as independently interpreting Jesus' words. Only by both Jesus' words and Mary Magdalene's interpretation of them are the readers reminded of the purpose of Jesus' work as is phrased in John's prologue.

In John it is Mary Magdalene alone who at this point of the story, between death and implicit ascension, is the sole witness of Jesus going upwards and the sole witness to his final revelation: my Father – your Father, my God – your God. This is in sharp contrast to Mark, Matthew, and Luke in which the heavenly figures, when speaking to Mary Magdalene and other women, only refer to something that Jesus had already revealed before his death to all the disciples.

Grundmann and Brown very impressively show the importance and meaning of Jn 20.17, but they both fail to see the role John subsequently chooses to give to Mary Magdalene. John gives Mary Magdalene the role of interpreting the meaning of and proclaiming the final message of the gospel. Both Mary Magdalene's interpretation and proclamation, apparently, became authoritative to the Johannine community and constitutive to the Gospel of John.

3.6. *The End: Proclaiming, Receiving the Holy Spirit and being Sent as Jesus was*
Mary Magdalene, according to John, has her own understanding and initiative. This is also apparent since she is not described as literally repeating Jesus' words to the disciples. She adds her own experience to it: 'she told the disciples that she had seen the Lord' (20.18). This is similar to the way in which all the disciples in John tell of their contact with the risen Lord (20.20, 25). At the same time, these words of Mary Magdalene also form the apotheosis of what is to be seen in John's

---

91. Grundmann 1961: 218-22.
92. Grundmann 1961: 229.
93. Although Grundmann (1960: 144) does mention Mary Magdalene's message to the disciples, he does not draw any conclusion with regard to John's portrayal of her.

story of the empty tomb.[94] After recording six instances of seeing by three different persons, this seventh time John finally discloses what is actually to be seen: the Lord.

This seeing the Lord is also important outside John, as is clear from Mk 16.7; Mt. 28.7; Lk. 24.34 and Acts 1.3. In 1 Cor. 9.1 seeing the Lord is the basis of Paul's apostleship. Seeing the risen Christ forms one of the elements of the Christian core confession that Paul received and which accordingly is central to his preaching (1 Cor. 15.5-8).

John relates that Mary Magdalene went to the disciples to bring the news that she had seen the Lord and that he had told her these things. By this John suggests that she said: I have seen the Lord and this is what he told me: 'Go to my brothers (and sisters) and say to them, I am ascending to my Father and your Father, to my God and your God'.

John does not actually depict Mary Magdalene doing this, allowing her only indirect speech. The readers must remain without an account of Mary Magdalene's encounter with her brothers (and sisters) and also later in the story John does not disclose any reaction or reference to her words.

Instead, John's next verses are about the disciples being together on the same evening in a place where the doors are closed because of their fear of the Jews. It is uncertain whether Mary Magdalene is present (20.19). Yet, we may assume this to be the case, since 20.18 describes Mary Magdalene going to the disciples. The same day on which Jesus revealed his purpose of going up to his Father to Mary Magdalene, he returns and sends his disciples and Mary Magdalene as he himself was sent (cf. 8.42), giving to them the authority to forgive and blowing the Holy Spirit on them, which he promised he would do a short time after he ascended to his Father (20.21-23; cf. 16.7, 16).[95]

4. *John's Portrayal of Mary Magdalene*

4.1. *Mary Magdalene's Relation to Jesus*
According to John, Mary Magdalene belongs to the group of relatives to Jesus. Perhaps she is introduced as a relative of his mother. She is portrayed in a discipleship role. As we have seen, Jesus loved all his disciples, calling them 'his own', being those who recognize his voice when he calls them by name, and who listen to his words. In John's story about Mary Magdalene she indeed recognizes his voice when Jesus calls her by name (20.16). She listens to his words and goes to the disciples, saying what he asked her to say (20.18). In addition, she calls Jesus Rabbouni. This would suggest that Mary Magdalene belongs to Jesus' own and that she thus is a disciple, loved by him.

Their relation is such that she persistently seeks his dead body, wishing to have

94. Beck (1997: 133) who, as we saw earlier, values the emphasis on 'seeing' as 'inappropriate response to Jesus', argues that Mary Magdalene by adding these words herself obviously shows that she misunderstood what Jesus said to her.

95. Brown 1970: 1016.

it and to take hold of it, seeking comfort in his physical proximity. Yet, she meets the risen Jesus, is instructed by him and authorized by him to tell his brothers (and sisters) about his ascending and the new relationship between him, his Father and them. She independently interprets his words and understands that she has to go to his disciples instead of to his relatives. Jesus explains to her that they have to go their separate ways, but that they are bound by the same God and the same Father.

4.2. *Mary Magdalene among the Disciples*
In John, Mary Magdalene may perhaps be implied in the masculine plural of he word disciples. If she is the anonymous disciple among the first disciples of Jesus, then she is present throughout John, but perhaps more specifically she belongs in the company of Jesus' mother. Because John portrays her as understanding Jesus' words in 20.17, since she goes to the disciples and not to Jesus' relatives, Mary Magdalene must be considered included among the disciples which are present during the farewell discourse in 13.1–16.33 and perhaps Jesus' prayer in John 17, both of which would have prepared her for such an understanding. Mary Magdalene is on such footing with Peter and the other disciple Jesus loved that they are the first to whom she turns when she finds the tomb empty.

In John, Mary Magdalene is the only one to see Jesus between his death and implicit ascension. She alone receives Jesus' proclamation that the disciples' direct access to the Father, which according to the prologue to John became vital to the Johannine community, has now been completed.

It is not evident what this means for her position among the disciples, since, if she is present in the further story, she is present invisibly among the other disciples. John does not depict the disciples reacting to Mary Magdalene's words, nor are her words discussed by the others.

4.3. *Mary Magdalene's Function in the Story*
In John, Mary Magdalene functions as a disciple who first witnesses Jesus after his burial. Her function is to pass on her knowledge. Mary Magdalene is portrayed as an independent interpreter of Jesus' words spoken to her between his death and ascension. Although her interpretation and her testimony of the meaning of Jesus' death became vital to the Johannine community, John does not depict anyone receiving her message or reacting on it.

To the reader, Mary Magdalene not only proclaims but also models the way from the earthly relationship with Jesus towards the spiritual relationship with the ascended one, who through his ascension provides direct access to the Father for all who recognize and love him.

EXCURSUS: THE DISCIPLE JESUS LOVED

Ramon K. Jusino, in his article 'Mary Magdalene: Author of the Fourth Gospel?' argues in favour of the possibility that Mary Magdalene could be the disciple Jesus loved in the Gospel of John. In his view, Mary Magdalene, who is called the disciple most loved by Jesus in the Gospel of Philip and the Gospel of Mary,[96] is in the Gospel of John, after first being mentioned by name in an earlier version of the Gospel, deliberately turned into the anonymous and male Beloved Disciple. According to Jusino, in the two instances where Mary Magdalene's name could not be avoided, in Jn 19.25-27 and 20.1-11, the redactor added the Beloved Disciple to be sure that Mary Magdalene and he would be interpreted as two different people. To strengthen this argument Jusino refers to the inconsistencies most exegetes see in Jn 19.25-27 and 20.1-11: the sudden presence of the male disciple in 19.26 and the text about Peter and the disciple Jesus loved in 20.2-10, which seems to have been added later.[97]

Jusino suggests, on the basis of Brown's widely respected research on the Johannine community,[98] that this was done as part of a later process.[99] Jusino distinguishes three stages in the process: 50–80 the community is led by Mary Magdalene; 80–90 after the death of Mary Magdalene the community is divided by a Christological schism; 90–100 one faction, fearful of persecution, seeks amalgamation with the emerging institutional Church, the other holds on to the community's tradition and cites Mary Magdalene as the Beloved Disciple of Jesus, which is reflected in the Gospel of Mary and the Gospel of Philip.

According to Jusino, the female beloved disciple is made anonymous and male to be acceptable to mainstream ideology. Brown argues that the Johaninne community in a very early stage became divided because of a Christological argument. The more heterodox believers defended a very high Christology, whereas the more orthodox believers wanted to be part of the mainstream emerging Church which defended Jesus' corporeality. To those wanting to take part in the growing institutional Church, Jusino argues, 'the claim that a female disciple of Jesus had been their community's first leader and hero quickly becomes an embarrassment'.[100] According to him, the other, more heterodox believers of the community held on to their tradition. This is the reason why Mary Magdalene in various heterodox writings is depicted as the one loved most by Jesus.

In this excursus I, like Jusino, want to argue that Mary Magdalene may be concealed in the male anonymous disciple, but, unlike Jusino, my argument does not draw on the Gospel of Mary or the Gospel of Philip nor on textual inconsistencies in Jn 19.25-27 and 20.1-18 or Brown's research on the Johannine community. My argument is based on the Gospel of John considered as a meaningful unity, on the importance of 20.17, on the parallels between 1.35-40 and 20.15-18 and on John's conservative, but also affirmative, attitude towards women as disciples and apostles.

96. GosPhil 64.1-5; GosMar 18.14-15.
97. Jusino 1998: 9-18.
98. Brown 1979.
99. Jusino 1998: 5.
100. Jusino 1998: 5.

Anonymous Disciples

In John there are several instances where individual disciples remain anonymous. The first passage concerns one of two disciples, who is a former disciple of John the Baptist and one of the first two disciples to follow Jesus (1.37-42). This disciple remains unnamed in a section in which John explicitly mentions all others who decide to follow Jesus by name.[101]

The second is to 'another disciple' (ἄλλος μαθητής 18.15). This disciple is said to be acquainted with the high Priest and as such able to enter the court of the high Priest and to bring Peter in (18.15-16).

The anonymous disciple Jesus loved (ὁ μαθητὴς ὃν ἠγάπα) occurs for the first time at Jesus' bosom during the Last Supper, prompted by Peter to ask Jesus who will betray him (13.23-26). This disciple also appears to be under the cross with Jesus' mother, where the disciple is instructed to act as her son and to regard her as a mother (19.26-27). The disciple Jesus loved again occurs in the company of Peter in a boat when the disciples are fishing. The disciple reveals to Peter that the one who tells them where to cast their net is Jesus (21.7). The disciple Jesus loved also occurs at the close of John, expressly identified as the one who was at Jesus' bosom earlier. John explains that rumour says Jesus stated that this disciple would not die, but John denies that this was the meaning of Jesus' words (21.20-24). This disciple is furthermore identified as the one who is the witness behind the Gospel of John and the one who wrote things down (21.24).

Another anonymous disciple appears in the resurrection story of 20.1-18. This disciple is called: the other disciple Jesus loved (τὸν ἄλλον μαθητὴν ὃν ἐφίλει 20.2). Mary fetches this disciple when she finds the tomb empty. This disciple features further in the story: the other disciple (ὁ ἄλλος μαθητής 20.2, 3). This disciple outruns Peter, enters the tomb after Peter and sees and believes (20.2-10).

'Two others of his disciples' (ἄλλοι ἐκ τῶν μαθητῶν αὐτοῦ δύο) are mentioned in 21.2, when after the resurrection the disciples join Simon Peter and go fishing. The two are in the company of Thomas called the Twin, Nathanael of Cana in Galilee and those of Zebedee (21.2).

Why does John leave these disciples explicitly anonymous? I suggest that the reason could be that they are women, since John does not name women as disciples, and only allows the named women to have discipleship roles within conservative boundaries. At the same time, however, although John does not identify these named women as disciples, the Gospel gives them prominent roles.

Oral or written tradition may have included names in those instances where John suggests an anonymous disciple who acts outside the Gospel's conservative boundaries. This is especially probable, since the other disciples in the company of the anonymous disciples are named. Perhaps John's grammar concerning these disciples is masculine, since feminine grammar would disclose their gender. I will defend this conjecture below.

---

101. Jn 1.35-52: Andrew, Simon Peter, Philip and Nathanael.

The Disciple Jesus Loved

Scholars from all over the world have addressed the problem of the individual anonymous disciples in John. Especially the identity of the disciple Jesus loved has been the subject of many thorough studies. Various hypotheses as to the identity of this disciple have been suggested, among them Andrew, Lazarus, Apollos, Paul, a Paulinist, Benjamin, Judas Iskariot, Philip, Nathanael, Judas Jesus' brother, John Mark, John the son of Zebedee, John the Elder, Matthias, a disciple of the Baptist, Thomas, an Essene monk from Jerusalem. It has also been suggested that the disciple Jesus loved is a symbolic figure representing the Johannine community, the Hellenistic brand of the Church, or the ideal Christian disciple.[102]

The name John comes from Church tradition and is the most common solution to the problem of the identity of the disciple Jesus loved. The raised Lazarus is proposed because of Jesus' love for him (11.5) and because of the rumour that the disciple Jesus loved would not die (21.23). The option for Andrew was recently propounded by Klaus Berger.[103] In his thorough monograph about the disciple Jesus loved, Charlesworth studies most of the options that have been suggested and presents an exegesis of all the Johannine passages that are relevant to the topic. He specifically investigates the suggestion of Hans Martin Schenke who studied beloved disciples in the Nag Hammadi manuscripts – Mary Magdalene, James, and Judas Thomas – and assumes that Judas Thomas could be the identity of the disciple Jesus loved in John. Charlesworth agrees with Schenke's theory.[104]

It has, however, also been suggested that the disciple Jesus loved is a redactional fiction used to present the Gospel as having been based on the testimony of an eyewitness.[105] The modern interpretation that the disciple Jesus loved is anonymous as a character for the reader to identify with is defended by several scholars.[106] Watty, for instance, states:

> As long as the disciple remains unnamed, any disciple, however recent, however late, may be the disciple whom Jesus loved, who reclined on his breast at the Supper and who may be still alive when he comes.[107]

Scholars distinguish either five passages about the disciple Jesus loved (13.23-26; 19.26-27; 20.2-10; 21.7, 20-24), or six (plus 18.15-16) or seven (plus 1.37-42). The other disciple Jesus loved in 20.2-10 is interpreted in a descriptive way as 'the other disciple, the one whom Jesus loved'. This allows scholars to include this passage and the passages mentioning 'another disciple' (1.37-42; 18.6) in their investigation of the disciple Jesus loved. Thus John's reference to anonymous

102. For various options and their arguments see Brown 1966: xcii-xcviii; Schenke 1986: 114-19 and especially Charlesworth 1995: 127-218.
103. Berger 1997: 96-109.
104. Schenke 1986: 120-25.
105. See also the survey of Schenke 1986: 114-19.
106. E.g. Watty 1979; Beck 1997.
107. Watty 1979: 212.

disciples would almost all refer to one disciple.[108] The passage about an anonymous person whose testimony is recorded in 19.35 is also frequently included. This
person witnessed Jesus' side being pierced by a spear and saw blood and water
pouring out of his side.

This one disciple has become such a fixed identity that scholars call him the
Beloved Disciple, or abbreviated: BD. Others, in my view rightly, keep to the
original expression 'the disciple Jesus loved', since the title the Beloved Disciple
does not do enough justice to the narrated anonymity. Moreover the title the
Beloved Disciple, more than the expression 'the disciple Jesus loved', suggests a
sense of being loved most.[109]

In John not only one disciple is mentioned as being loved by Jesus. Jesus also
loved Lazarus, Martha, and Mary (11.5). He loved all his disciples, calling them
'his own' (13.1, 34; cf. 15.9-17 and 17.6-12), even loving those disciples who are
yet to come (10.16; 14.21; 17.20-26). Jesus compares 'his own' with sheep who
recognize his voice, as that of the good shepherd, when he calls them by name, and
who are guided by him to seek good pastures (10.1-10). That Mary Magdalene is
also considered one of 'his own', as we already noticed, emerges from John's story
about her in which she recognizes Jesus' voice when he calls her by name, and
listens to his words (20.16-18).[110] In addition, she calls him 'Rabbouni', which
means 'my teacher' (20.16). She is thus implicitly one of the disciples Jesus loved.

In 20.2 the Greek expression for the disciple Jesus loved is different from that
used in 13.23-26; 19.26-27 and 21.7, 20-24. In the latter instances ὃν ἠγάπα is
used, whereas the expression in 20.2 reads ὃν ἐφίλει. This difference is not
necessarily of great importance, but it is striking that it occurs exactly here, where
the disciple is also specifically called 'the other disciple Jesus loved'. No other
author, however, seems to interpret the Greek expression in 20.2 as 'the other
disciple Jesus loved'. This passage is commonly translated as 'the other disciple,
the one whom Jesus loved', thus suggesting that this disciple (ὃν ἐφίλει) is to be
identified with the disciple referred to as ὃν ἠγάπα. Since John describes other
disciples as being loved by Jesus, the possibility that there are two different beloved disciples deserves to be taken seriously.

This is also probable when looking at the disciple's presence in the story at the
end of the Gospel of John. The disciple Jesus loved (ὃν ἠγάπα) recognizes Jesus
on the shore and tells Peter (21.7). When Jesus later asks Peter to follow him,
Peter, turning, sees that the disciple Jesus loved indeed follows (21.20-23). John
here emphasizes that the disciple Jesus loved (ὃν ἠγάπα) is the same one who was
at Jesus' chest at the Last Supper (21.20). Does John here specifically clarify the
expression 'the disciple Jesus loved' as the one who was at Jesus' chest, because
John distinguishes more disciples loved by Jesus? This would strengthen the
assumption that the reference to the other disciple Jesus loved in 20.2 is indeed
about another person. Continuing this line of argument it could be possible that

108. Brown (1966: xciv; 1979: 31-34), like many exegetes, argues for the latter interpretation.
See also Charlesworth 1995: 326-59. But Charlesworth leaves out 18.15-16.

109. See also Beck 1997: 110-11.

110. Brown 1970: 1009-1010.

'the disciple Jesus loved' (ὅν ἠγάπα 21.7, 20-23) together with the 'other disciple Jesus loved' (ὅν ἐφίλει 20.2) are the two unnamed 'others' of his disciples in 21.2.[111]

Mary Magdalene as the Disciple Jesus Loved

In Jn 20.2 Mary Magdalene does not fetch Peter and 'the disciple whom Jesus loved' (ὁ μαθητὴς ὅν ἠγάπα) but John very precisely describes the disciple being with Peter as 'the other disciple Jesus loved' (τὸν ἄλλον μαθητὴν ὅν ἐφίλει). Theoretically, the presence of this other beloved disciple leaves the option open that either Mary Magdalene or Peter could be the disciple Jesus loved (ὁ μαθητὴς ὅν ἠγάπα), who is mentioned earlier in 19.25-27. In most of the pericopes where John uses the expression, 'the disciple Jesus loved', however, is in the company of Peter.[112] Thus it cannot be Peter. This implies that Mary Magdalene could be an option: Mary Magdalene as the disciple Jesus loved (ὅν ἠγάπα), when she discovers the tomb to be empty, fetches Simon Peter and the other disciple Jesus loved (ὅν ἐφίλει).

The scene under the cross may also be understood in such a way that it points to Mary Magdalene as the disciple Jesus loved, the same one who rested at the bosom of Jesus at the Last Supper. In the scene under the cross Jn 19.26 describes Jesus seeing two people: his mother and the disciple he loved. John's description of the women standing under the cross in 19.25 leaves three possibilities: there are either four, three or two women. I suggested earlier that two women seems the most reasonable interpretation.[113] In 19.25 Jesus' mother and her sister-in-law or niece Mary Magdalene stand under the cross. No sister of Jesus' mother or Mary of Clopas would be mentioned here without referring to them or her again.

This leaves us with two women under the cross in 19.25 – Jesus' mother who is named Mary of Clopas and her sister-in-law or niece Mary Magdalene – and the two people Jesus sees in 19.26: Jesus' mother and the disciple Jesus loved. Does John in this pericope both reveal the identity of Jesus' mother as Mary of Clopas and the identity of the disciple Jesus loved as Mary Magdalene?

Objections

There are important objections to be made. First, scholars argue that both 19.25-27 and 20.1-18 are the result of redaction. Secondly, the solutions scholars offer to the identity of the disciple Jesus loved exclusively point to men, because the grammar

---

111. According to Westcott (1902: 300), the two are disciples in a wider sense than the Twelve. Brown (1970: 1068), suggests as possible candidates for the two Philip and Andrew (6.7-8; 12.22) or Andrew and Levi (referring to the Gospel of Peter). Schnackenburg (1975: 419-20), argues that the seven disciples together represent the future Church. The two anonymous disciples allow the inclusion of the disciple Jesus loved. Morris (1995: 760), concludes that the author has 'reasons of his own' not to identify the two.

112. Jn 19.25-27 being the one exception.

113. See section 2.1, above.

concerning this disciple is masculine, and because Jesus presents him as a son to his mother (19.27).

Martin Hengel gives a survey of the various scholarly opinions on the unity of the Gospel of John as a whole, ranging from the view that the unity 'is lost beyond saving' (E. Schwartz) to the view that the Gospel is like the 'seamless robe of Christ' (D.F. Strauss).[114] Hengel himself argues for a 'relative unity', since three recently found Johannine papyri dating from the second century give no evidence of alleged primal forms of the Gospel. A second important argument is the unity in language and style and the coherence of the narrative (he refers to studies of E. Schweizer, E. Ruckstuhl, R. Kieffer, B. Olsson, R.A. Culpepper, G. van Belle). In Hengel's view the Gospel is a 'relative' unity due to the fact that it has been written over a long period of time, based on oral teaching, and that the Gospel was completed after the author's death by his pupils.[115] There is, however, one dominant creative and theological unity behind the Gospel. Thus, when we treat John as a unity, there are scholars who would agree.

The second objection concerns the maleness of the disciple Jesus loved, which is assumed because of the exclusively masculine grammar John uses. This is no doubt an important objection. Yet, if anonymity in the case of the disciple Jesus loved (and other anonymous disciples) was so important to the author of John, would the use of masculine grammar not guarantee the anonymity in a better way than the use of feminine grammar, which would obviously reveal to the readers at least one important feature of the disciple, namely that she is a woman?[116]

Moreover, a woman being referred to as male was not so strange at the time, as it would be to us now. Grace M. Jantzen has shown that spirituality in early Christianity gradually became identified with maleness.[117] She gives several examples of the fact that 'women whose spirituality was beyond question were described as honorary males'.[118] She also gives examples of cases of cross-dressing. And, indeed, with regard to Mary Magdalene there is a tradition which speaks of her maleness. In the Gospel of Thomas Jesus promises Peter that he will lead Mary Magdalene in order to make her male 'so that she too may become a living spirit resembling you males. For every woman who will make herself male will enter the Kingdom of Heaven'.[119] In the Acts of Philip the Saviour praises Mary Magdalene for her manly character. Because of this he gives her the task of joining the weaker Philip on his mission journey. But she is not to join him as a woman. 'As for you, Mary', he says, 'change your clothing and your outward appearance: reject everything which from the outside suggests a woman'.[120]

114. Hengel 1989: 83-96.
115. Hengel 1989: 96-108.
116. Cf. Chapter 4, section 3.2.
117. Jantzen 1995: 43-58.
118. Jantzen 1995: 51.
119. GosThom 114; see Meyer (1985), who comments on this logion and shows, that to castigate femaleness and to recommend the transformation to maleness is by no means rare in the ancient world.
120. Acts of Philip 95; see Bovon 1984: 57-58.

Charlesworth, in his impressive monograph on the disciple Jesus loved, leaves open the possibility that this figure could be a woman, perhaps Mary, Martha, or Mary Magdalene, in spite of the masculine grammar.[121] For him, the final proof that the disciple must be male, is not the grammar, but the circumstance that the disciple is called 'son'.[122]

This is, however, not the case. Jesus does not address the disciple as 'son' in 19.26, and uses no other masculine formal address, which would have completed the parallelism:

> He said to his mother:
> 'Woman, behold your son'.
> Then he said to the disciple
> 'Behold your mother'.

By leaving out any masculine formal address, and by only saying 'Behold your mother', Jesus declares the disciple to represent him as a son. This representation does not necessarily mean that the disciple has to be male. That a woman may fulfil the function of a son to a mother is clear from the story of Ruth and Naomi. The female neighbours praise the way Ruth cared for her mother-in-law, by mentioning her to Naomi as: 'she, who has been more to you than seven sons' (Ruth 4.15).

But, more important, I would like to argue that the word 'son' in Jn 19.26 does not primarily refer to the disciple Jesus loved, but rather refers to Jesus himself. For the reader who does not know the flow of the story beforehand, the word 'son' directed to the mother of Jesus designates her own son: the dying crucified Jesus. The reader is focused on Mary, thoroughly relating with her, when hearing Jesus' words towards her: 'Woman, behold your son'. It is only after Jesus' words to the disciple 'behold your mother' that the reader suddenly turns to this second person. Turning to the disciple Jesus loved, and hearing those words 'behold your mother' the reader is reminded of earlier farewell words of Jesus:

> I will not leave you orphans; I will come to you. Yet a little while, and the world will see me no more, but you will see me. Because I live, you will live also. In that day you will know that I am in my Father, and you in me, and I in you. He who has heard my commandments and keeps them, he it is who loves me; and he who loves me will be loved by my Father, and I will love him and manifest myself to him. (Jn 14.18-21)

Obviously, after Jesus died, he can be found in those who keep his words and as a consequence are loved by him. His father and he himself will come to them and live in them (14.23).

The ultimate importance of the scene in 19.26-27 lies in Jesus' invitation to his mother to look away from her dying son to find him, alive, in the disciple he loved. At the same time Jesus' words are a solemn declaration to this disciple: he (or she) may act on Jesus' behalf, as if he (or she) were Jesus himself. To the reader, who

---

121. Charlesworth (1995: xiv) gives no arguments why the grammatically male disciple may be female. For about two pages Charlesworth refers to the anonymous disciple as 'he or she'. However, from page xvi onwards, without any comment, the disciple becomes 'he' again.

122. Charlesworth 1995: 5-6.

remembers Jesus' prayer to his Father for all those who followed him, and who in their turn will attract new followers – 'that the love with which thou has loved me, may be in them, and I in them' (17.26) – , the disciple Jesus loved is the first of a vast number of those disciples yet to come.

Both Jesus' mother and the disciple react to Jesus' words, the disciple by taking Jesus' mother to him (or her) and the mother by accepting this. Jesus' words to his mother and the disciple he loved, together with their reaction to them, constitute the beginning of the growing *koinonia* of those who follow Jesus.[123]

In this interpretation of 19.26-27 the word 'son' in 19.26 does not point to the gender of the disciple Jesus loved. The 'son' is the dying Jesus, who, alive, can be found in the disciple he loved as the one who may represent him.

Criteria

Charlesworth, on the basis of a detailed exegesis of the passages in which the disciple Jesus loved occurs, developed eight criteria to judge the various attempts to identify this person.[124]

1. The love Jesus felt for the disciple must be demonstrable.
2. A clear reason for the anonymity must be given.
3. The closeness of exactly this disciple to Jesus, and his or her authority over The others, should be adequately explained.
4. An explanation is needed for the fact that the disciple occurs relatively late in the Gospel.
5. An explanation must be given for the scene at the cross.
6. The emphasis of the validity of the testimony should be explained.
7. The fear, that is caused by the prospect of the death of the disciple, must be explained.
8. And the almost polemic rivalry between the disciple and Peter should be clarified.

These criteria can be used to investigate the option for Mary Magdalene as the disciple Jesus loved in more detail.[125]

As we have seen, Jesus loved all his disciples, calling them 'his own', being those who recognize his voice when he calls them by name, and who listen to his words. In John's story about Mary Magdalene she indeed recognizes his voice, when Jesus calls her by name, and she listens to his words, going to the disciples, saying what he asked her to say (20.16, 18). This would suggest that Mary Magdalene is one of Jesus' own and that she thus, implicitly, is a disciple, loved by

---

123. As far as I could find, no interpretation of 19.25-27 emphasizes that 'son' in 19.26 may refer to Jesus himself. For a survey of several interpretations of 19.25-27 see Brown 1994: II, 1019-1026. They range from the filial duty of Jesus, caring for his mother even at his own crucifixion, to various symbolic interpretations of the Church being born.

124. Charlesworth 1995: xiv-xviii.

125. Charlesworth (1995: 428-31) uses these criteria to show that Thomas could be the disciple Jesus loved.

him. Also the three criteria of Johannine discipleship apply to her. She remains in Jesus' words (20.18; cf. 8.31), she shows love to the mother of Jesus (19.27; cf. 13.35), and as the witness to the significance of the resurrection (20.17; cf. 1.12), she bears much fruit (15.8). In addition, she recognizes Jesus as Rabbouni (20.16) and understands his teaching which has been prepared for in the farewell discourse (20.17-18).[126]

The anonymity of Mary Magdalene as the disciple Jesus loved (the second criterion), as argued earlier, may be explained by the fact that she is a female disciple. Testimony from a female disciple, one who followed the teacher like the male disciples, would have been difficult to accept, not only for those outside the Johannine community, but, as I have shown, also for the Johannine community itself.[127]

Mary Magdalene's special authority (the third criterion) is evident from the fact that she is the sole witness to the precise meaning of Jesus' resurrection, which Jesus reveals only to her. Jesus appears to Mary Magdalene alone before he has ascended to his Father. She alone is the witness and proclaimer of the new bond Jesus initiates at that very moment: 'my Father – your Father, my God – your God' (20.17). Jesus urges her to go and tell this to his brothers (and sisters). Mary Magdalene independently interprets this request in the light of the farewell discourse and does not go to Jesus' relatives, but to the disciples. Earlier at the Last Supper Jesus said to his disciples, his 'own' (13.1), as such also Mary Magdalene, Martha and Mary and perhaps other women too, that he would no longer call them slaves, but friends, since he had revealed everything to them (15.15), but now they have become his brothers and sisters, he and they are all children of the one Father. The reader understands that Mary Magdalene's interpretation has become authoritative to the Johannine community, since it is the crucial message of the Gospel, formulated in the prologue, which says that Jesus indeed has come, so that all those who accept him, who believe in his name, will receive from him the strength to become children of God, by being born anew (1.12-13).[128] This will be done through the Spirit (3.5), Jesus' ascension to the Father making the gift of the Spirit finally possible (16.5-7).[129]

But how should we explain Mary Magdalene's closeness to Jesus at the Last Supper (the second clause of the third criterion), where she is 'reclining on Jesus' bosom', which means sitting/lying next to him, Peter motioning to her to ask Jesus who will betray him? Why this special position? In Hellenism a 'favourite pupil' was quite common. Sjef van Tilborg gives examples of favourites who succeeded their teachers. According to him the love of Jesus for the anonymous disciple reflects the love of the Father for Jesus.[130]

But why would Mary Magdalene be at the bosom of Jesus? On the one hand this could be explained by the circumstance that Mary Magdalene in our interpretation

126. See Chapter 7, section 2.2 and Chapter 7, 3.2.5.
127. See the Chapter 4, section 3.2.1 and Chapter 7, section 2.4.
128. Here indeed the inclusive word τέκνα has been used.
129. See also Brown 1970: 1014-1017.
130. Van Tilborg 1993: 77-91.

is a family member: the niece or the sister-in-law of his mother (19.25). And if not, she is obviously in the company of Jesus' mother. In contrast to the Synoptics, Jesus' relatives do have a role in John. When in 2.12 the train of his followers is described, his mother is mentioned first, then his brothers and sisters and, finally, his disciples (2.12).

The 'reclining on Jesus' bosom' may also be understood metaphorically. The metaphor of the bosom in Judaism symbolizes the handing over of authoritative tradition.[131] The disciple Jesus loved being at Jesus' bosom represents the receiving of tradition and authority especially now, when Jesus' end is near. If indeed there are two women under the cross and the disciple Jesus loved is one of them, Mary Magdalene is this disciple to whom Jesus refers his mother, as the one in whom he himself can be found, declaring this disciple to be the one who may represent him (19.25-27). But, more important, the prologue and Jn 20.17 indeed suggest that Mary Magdalene's teaching have become authoritative for the Johannine community.

Why does the disciple Jesus loved, if she is to be identified as Mary Magdalene, occur so late in the Gospel (Charlesworth's fourth criterion)? Indeed, John introduces the expression 'the disciple Jesus loved' relatively late in 13.23. This might be because chapter 13 forms the beginning of the farewell discourse which ends in chapter 17. Jesus, as the one loved by God, now passes his authoritative knowledge on to the one he loved. The anonymous disciple may have been present right from the start as one of Jesus' first two disciples in 1.35, a former disciple of John the Baptist.[132] As we already noted earlier, the parallels between Jn 20.15-18 and 1.35-40 suggest that John perhaps identifies this anonymous disciple as Mary Magdalene.[133]

According to Brown, the anonymous disciple is distinguished as the loved one at the Last Supper and not earlier, since only in this Christological context of 'the hour', the identity as the loved one, close to Jesus, plays a role.[134] This coincides with the fact that in Mark and Matthew, Mary Magdalene is also anonymously present from Galilee onwards, being specifically mentioned only late in the Gospel story, at the time of the suffering, death, and resurrection of Jesus. Even in Luke, although her name is mentioned earlier, she only plays her part at the end of the Gospel.

An explanation of the scene at the cross, the fifth criterion of Charlesworth, has already partly been given. Jesus solemnly declares Mary Magdalene to represent him and to act on his behalf, while he invites his mother to find him in Mary

---

131. Berger 1997: 99, 109.

132. Brown (1979: 33) argues that the disciple Jesus loved is a former disciple of John the Baptist. In his view the disciple in 1.35-40 is not called the disciple Jesus loved, since in the beginning of the Gospel story he has not yet achieved this closeness to Jesus.

133. See section 2.2, above.

134. Brown (1979: 33) states: 'During his lifetime…the Beloved Disciple lived through the same growth in christological perception that the Johannine community went through, and it was this growth that made it possible for the community to identify him as the one whom Jesus particularly loved'.

Magdalene. By reacting positively to this, together they represent the growing *koinonia* of those who follow Jesus in the near and distant future. Yet something else happens after Jesus has died. His side is pierced by a spear and is testified to by an eyewitness. This is the second half of Charlesworth's fifth criterion. Why could this witness be Mary Magdalene? In my opinion everyone who was under the cross could be this witness. Even one of the soldiers. But, since John expressly emphasizes the trustworthiness of this witness and this person remains anonymous, it might be a woman. John presents this witness to the insight that Jesus' death indeed procured not only blood, as a symbol of his gift of love (cf. 10.11-15) but also water, as a symbol of the Holy Spirit (cf. 1 Jn 5.6-8; Jn 7.37-39).[135] A similar emphasis on the truthfulness of a particular witness occurs again in 21.24. This verse refers to the disciple Jesus loved in 21.20. The similar emphasis in both 21.24 and 19.35 could indicate that the anonymous witness of 19.35 is to be identified as the disciple Jesus loved. Mary Magdalene is an option, since she is present under the cross and in our interpretation John portrays no other named persons present under the cross except Jesus' mother.

Testing Mary Magdalene against Charlesworth's sixth criterion we are to explain why the validity of her testimony should be emphasized. As I already suggested, this emphasis is due to the fact that at least the we-group in Jn 21.24 knows that the disciple Jesus loved is a woman. The conservative attitude towards women in John and the negative attitude of the time towards women claiming authority, shows that especially the testimony of a woman could have been easily doubted or rejected.[136]

Charlesworth's seventh criterion is based on his interpretation of 21.21-23. He suggests that the community feared the death of the disciple Jesus loved. Apparently a rumour circulated which had its origin in what Jesus himself said, that the disciple he loved would not die (21.21-23). The community, who found its identity in the testimony of the disciple Jesus loved, could have feared the death of Mary Magdalene (or could have been traumatized by the death of Mary Magdalene), since she is the only one to whom Jesus revealed the meaning of his resurrection and her testimony and interpretation became vital to the creed of the community (1.12).

Concerning the eighth criterion we have to remember that we choose to interpret the other disciple that outruns Peter as another (female) disciple (perhaps to symbolize the gender difficulties in the community?), rather than the disciple Jesus loved who stood beneath the cross. Charlesworth's idea that any rivalry between Peter and the disciple Jesus loved derives for the most part from the disciple outrunning Peter. Nevertheless, it is obvious that Peter recognizes the fact that the disciple Jesus loved is closer to Jesus than he himself (13.23-24 and 21.7, 20-23). In the Synoptics there is no disciple closer to Jesus than Peter. In the later non-canonical sources, such as the Gospel of Thomas, the Gospel of Mary and Pistis Sophia, Peter and Mary Magdalene appear together, Peter denying rather than

135. For a survey of several interpretations see Brown 1970: 946-56.
136. See Chapter 4, section 3.2.1.

recognizing Mary Magdalene's closeness to Jesus.[137] In these writings Mary Magdalene indeed has a special position. In the Gospel of Philip and the Gospel of Mary she is the only person to whom the other disciples refer to as the one loved by Jesus more than the others and as the one who has a greater insight.[138] In the Gospel of John the two are held in balance, Peter receiving the authority to care for Jesus' followers in a pastoral way (21.15-19),[139] whereas Mary Magdalene receives and understands the crucial message of the Gospel (20.17; cf. 1.12).

Mary Magdalene as One of the Options

This excursus does not pretend to offer a final solution to the problem of the identity of the anonymous disciple Jesus loved. It is presented as one possibility among others and is meant to contribute to the ongoing debate. Taking into account the numerous and very different scholarly hypotheses that have been offered thus far, one can only conclude that, if, indeed, the Gospel of John wanted the disciple Jesus loved to remain anonymous, at least to outsiders, the author has proved to be quite successful.

If we look upon Mary Magdalene as concealed in the grammatically male anonymous disciple Jesus loved, this will affect our perspective on her as well as on the Gospel of John. Not only Mary Magdalene's testimony about the meaning of the Lord's resurrection would have been important to the Johannine community, as we concluded earlier, but Mary Magdalene would also have had disciples, who preserved her accounts of Jesus' life and teachings, which later received the title the Gospel of John. Moreover, through the canonization of the Gospel of John, Mary Magdalene's accounts of Jesus would have been canonized and taught through the ages, and spread over the world.

---

137. GosThom log. 114; GosMar 17.16-23; PS 36; 72.

138. GosPhil 64.1-5; GosMar 18.14-15.

139. This is very different from Matthew's view on Peter, who is, according to this Gospel, the rock on which the Church is to be built and the one who receives the keys to the Kingdom of Heaven (Mt. 16.18-20).

Chapter 8

THE NEW TESTAMENT GOSPELS AND THE
GOSPEL OF MARY ABOUT MARY MAGDALENE

To be able to investigate the background of the portrayal of Mary Magdalene in the Gospel of Mary we turned to the New Testament Gospels, since they contain the earliest written material on Mary Magdalene that has survived. To what extent can the portrayal of Mary Magdalene in the Gospel of Mary be understood from the New Testament Gospels? In addition, we will examine what the different New Testament portrayals of Mary Magdalene reveal about their use of first-century Mary Magdalene traditions.

1. *Common Themes*

This section compares Mary Magdalene's portrayal in the Gospel of Mary with those in the New Testament Gospels by considering Mary Magdalene's relation to Jesus, her role among the disciples and her function in the Gospel stories.

1.1. *Mary Magdalene's Relation to Jesus*

1.1.1. *Having been Taught by Jesus Alone.* In Mark, Mary Magdalene is taught by Jesus as a disciple belonging to the small circle of Jesus' disciples. Though Jesus' teaching is mostly in public she and the other disciples are taken aside to receive advanced teaching from him. Together with the Twelve and others she is one of the inner group to whom Jesus has given the secret of the Kingdom of God, in contrast to those outside who receive everything in parables. In Matthew, Mary Magdalene is among the crowds who are taught by Jesus and together with the other Mary when the risen Jesus speaks to them. In Luke, Mary Magdalene has been taught by Jesus, being with him all the time. John, in contrast to the Synoptics, actually describes Jesus teaching Mary Magdalene alone. Thus, the Gospel of Mary in portraying Mary Magdalene as having been taught by Jesus alone is closest to the Gospel of John.

1.1.2. *Being Loved by Jesus.* Mark, Matthew and Luke do not mention Jesus' love for Mary Magdalene. According to John, Jesus loved all his disciples, even loving those who are yet to come, calling them 'his own'. John compares Jesus' love to the relationship between a good shepherd and his sheep. The sheep recognize his voice and are guided by him to seek good pastures. Mary Magdalene implicitly belongs to these loved ones, since she recognizes his voice, listens to him and calls him Rabbouni. She may also be concealed in the anonymous disciple called 'the disciple Jesus loved': the one who is the witness behind the Gospel of John and the one who wrote things down.

In the Gospel of Mary, Peter explicitly states that Jesus loved Mary more than the rest of the women. That is the reason why he assumes that she knows things that the other disciples do not. According to Levi, Jesus loved her more than the other disciples, because he knows her thoroughly. The author's opinion remains unclear. The Gospel of John and Mary are close in that both relate Jesus' love to knowing his words and being known by him.

1.1.3. *Being Authorized and Prepared to Proclaim the Gospel.* In Mark, the young man in white authorizes Mary Magdalene to go and tell the disciples and Peter that the risen Jesus is going before them into Galilee and will be seen there by them. In Matthew, the risen Lord himself authorizes Mary Magdalene and the other Mary to instruct his brothers (and sisters) that he will go before them to Galilee, but he instructs the Eleven to preach the gospel to the nations.

Luke implicitly includes Mary Magdalene when relating that Jesus opened the minds of the apostles and those who were with them. In Luke this happens so they can understand the Scriptures. With them she also receives Jesus' blessing and the promise that she will be clothed with power from on high. Luke, however, also suggests that, although the women from Galilee are able to understand the gospel, they should not preach it, because of the confusion they cause.

In John, the risen Jesus himself authorizes Mary Magdalene to tell his brothers (and sisters) about his way upwards and the new relationship between his Father and his disciples. In addition, implicitly, as one of the disciples, Mary Magdalene receives the Holy Spirit and is sent by Jesus as he was sent by the Father. In the Gospel of Mary, Mary Magdalene's extra knowledge and Peter's request authorize Mary to instruct the disciples. The Saviour authorized and prepared her as well as the others to go to the nations and preach the gospel of the Kingdom of the Son of Man and made her true Human Being like the other disciples. With respect to being authorized and prepared to proclaim the gospel, the Gospel of Mary is thus again closest to the Gospel of John.

1.1.4. *A Teaching Mary Magdalene.* Mark ends with the information that Mary Magdalene, Mary of James, and Salome do not instruct the disciples, but suggests that they must have done this at some point. The second ending of Mark relates that Mary Magdalene tells the disciples that the risen Lord has appeared to her and the narrator confirms that she indeed did so, but those who had been with Jesus did not believe what she said.

Matthew relates that Mary Magdalene and the other Mary are on their way to tell the disciples to go to Galilee and that the Eleven indeed go there, but to a certain mountain to which Jesus himself apparently had directed them. Luke relates that Mary Magdalene, Joanna and Mary of James and the other women with them instructed the apostles. The women's words seem idle tales to them and are not believed. The two followers of Jesus going to Emmaus relate that the women had confused them. Instead, Peter's story evokes immediate belief.

John relates that Mary Magdalene instructed the disciples about what the risen Jesus told her alone and shows a specific regard for Mary Magdalene's teaching, since its content is the central confession in the prologue. The Gospel of Mary shows that Mary's teaching turns the disciples' hearts inwards to the Good One and confirms that her teaching indeed consists of the words of the Saviour that he told her alone. The Gospel of John and the Gospel of Mary are thus similar in that the author declares that Mary Magdalene's teaching is both trustworthy and of consequence.

1.1.5. *Not his Suffering, but his Greatness*. In the New Testament Gospels, Mary Magdalene is portrayed as having seen Jesus dying on the cross, as having found his tomb empty and as receiving the revelation about Jesus being alive. In each New Testament Gospel, Mary Magdalene is thus associated with Jesus' suffering and with his transcending his suffering. In the Gospel of Mary, Mary encourages the disciples to focus on the greatness of the Son of Man instead of on his suffering. With respect to this the Gospel of Mary is close to all the New Testament Gospels.

1.2. *Mary Magdalene among the Disciples*

1.2.1 *Mary Magdalene as a Sister among the Brothers (and Sisters)*. In Mark, as well as in Matthew, the disciples are portrayed as brothers and sisters of Jesus. In Mark, Mary Magdalene is included in the masculine plural of disciples. Mark invites the readers to identify with them, whereas it criticizes the Twelve. In contrast to this, in Matthew, Mary Magdalene is portrayed, on the one hand, as a disciple and is included in the masculine plural of disciples, brothers and sisters, but, on the other hand, Matthew puts the twelve disciples to the fore. Mary Magdalene belongs more specifically to a large group of women followers. Matthew presents Mary Magdalene in the company of the mother of James and Joseph and the mother of the sons of Zebedee. The latter is the mother of two of the three core disciples of the twelve: Peter, James and John. In this way Mary Magdalene is closely connected to the twelve disciples.

In Luke, Jesus calls all those who do the will of God 'my mother and my brothers'. Luke distinguishes between the twelve apostles and the many disciples. Mary Magdalene is included in the masculine plural of disciples and belongs in particular to the group of women disciples who followed Jesus in and from Galilee. Together with Joanna and Susanna she belongs to an inner circle of three healed women, who, like the Twelve, are with Jesus wherever he goes and who are served by the many women disciples.

In John, Mary Magdalene is portrayed as a disciple, but it remains unclear whether she is included in the masculine plural of disciples. She may, however, be concealed in the anonymous 'disciple Jesus loved'. Her relation to Peter and the other disciple Jesus loved is such, that she fetches them the moment she finds the tomb empty. In John, Mary Magdalene proclaims the central message of the Gospel of John: thanks to Jesus' crucifixion, resurrection and ascension the disciples become his brothers and sisters and children of God.

In the Gospel of Mary, Peter calls Mary Magdalene 'sister', and she calls him 'my brother'. With respect to this the Gospel of Mary is close to Mark, Matthew, and John in that looking upon Jesus' disciples as brothers and sisters also occurs in Jesus' earthly lifetime in Mark and Matthew and, as a result of Jesus' ascension to his Father, also in John. The New Testament Gospels and the Gospel of Mary all agree that Mary Magdalene belongs to the disciples and as such is related to the Twelve.

1.2.2. *Knowing More than the Others*. In Mark, Mary Magdalene appears to be the only witness of Jesus' burial as well as of the tomb being empty. The second ending of Mark portrays Mary Magdalene relating that she has seen the Lord. In Matthew, Mary Magdalene and the other Mary together are the first to see the risen Jesus, who affirms their joy and banishes their fear. In Luke, Mary Magdalene is one of many women witnessing the tomb being empty and remembering words of the Saviour which are told earlier in the Gospel to the disciples in general.

In John, the specific knowledge of Mary Magdalene consists of having seen the Lord between his death and his ascension and of being told by him about the new bond between his Father and his disciples and their new identity. The content of this instruction is only conveyed earlier in the prologue of John. Although the disciples are prepared for this teaching through Jesus' farewell discourse, in the flow of the story, the specific content of Mary Magdalene's teaching is new to them.

In the Gospel of Mary, Peter and Levi state that Mary Magdalene knows more than the other disciples, which she herself confirms. In the Gospel of Mary, Mary's new knowledge consists of having seen the Lord in a vision, of the specific nature of the disciples' new identity, and of the way upwards to the Divine. Thus, the Gospel of Mary, as in Mark, the second ending of Mark, and John suggest that Mary knows more than the other disciples. But the themes of Mary's new teaching in the Gospel of Mary especially parallel those of the Gospel of John.

1.2.3. *Mary Magdalene and Peter*. In Mark, Mary Magdalene and Peter both are courageous and both fail. However, it is not the Twelve with Peter as their representative who exemplify Markan discipleship, but, instead, Mary Magdalene, Mary of Joses, Mary of James, and Salome.

In Matthew, Peter is to the readers the spokesman of the disciples in general. Throughout Matthew, Peter is an encouraging example of the practice of discipleship both in his belief and his failure. As disciples, Mary Magdalene and the other Mary are models of service, faith, courage and stability, but in order to be made disciples, to be baptized and taught, the readers must turn to the remaining eleven disciples.

In Luke, Peter belongs to the twelve apostles, whereas Mary Magdalene is a disciple healed by Jesus from seven evil spirits. Both are present at the crucifixion, like all Jesus' acquaintances. Both witness the tomb being empty, but the witness of Mary Magdalene and the other Galilean women is not believed, whereas all readily accept that the Lord is risen when he is said to be seen by Simon (Peter).

In John, Peter comes to the empty tomb on Mary Magdalene's initiative. Jesus is seen by her. She receives the message which is crucial to the Gospel of John. Peter receives the responsibility of the pastoral care for the believers. In the Gospel of Mary, Mary Magdalene and Peter both, as disciples, have been made true Human Being by the Son of Man and have been prepared to bring the gospel of his Kingdom. But, whereas Mary Magdalene encourages the weeping disciples and shows them the way to stability, Peter allows the power of Wrath to take over and rejects Mary's teaching because she is a woman. Thus, the portrayals of Mary Magdalene and Peter in the New Testament Gospels and the Gospel of Mary all seem to reflect a certain rivalry or hierarchy as if the views on the roles of Mary Magdalene and Peter are interdependent.[1] When Peter's role is crucial, Mary Magdalene's is not (Matthew and Luke). When Mary Magdalene's role is crucial, Peter's role is not (Mark and John), but in none of the New Testament Gospels is the contrast between Mary Magdalene and Peter so striking as in the Gospel of Mary.

1.3. *Mary Magdalene's Function in the Story*

Through Mary Magdalene's example, Mark encourages the readers to overcome anxiety and failure, to remain disciples and to become apostles, no matter how frightening this may be. The courage and inspiration necessary can be found in the knowledge that the suffering Messiah was raised to life and will be seen in Galilee to which Mary Magdalene, Mary of James, and Salome are witnesses. In the second ending of Mark, Mary Magdalene is to the readers an example of faithfulness. She proclaims to the weeping disciples that she has seen the Lord. The risen Jesus rebukes the Eleven when they do not believe her.

In Matthew, Mary Magdalene and the other Mary are inspiring examples of serving Jesus, of having faith in him, of courage and of stability, but they are not to preach the gospel. In Luke, Mary Magdalene functions as a trustworthy and capable witness and at the same time as a warning that a woman's witness may be confusing. As their witness is apparently not asked for and not needed, women should be satisfied with remembering Jesus' words among themselves, as the two men in shining garments advised Mary Magdalene and the other women.

With Mary Magdalene the readers of John are invited to stop focusing on and go beyond the death of Jesus. Jesus can still be seen and heard, he is still calling his disciples by their names and they can still answer his call. The readers also recognize that Mary Magdalene is the disciple who alone received Jesus' instruction about their new identity, which according to the prologue is crucial to the message of the Gospel of John.

With Mary Magdalene in the Gospel of Mary the readers are encouraged to

---

1. This is also the case in other early Christian texts. On the basis of her study of Peter and Mary Magdalene in early Christian literature, Brock (2003: 162) concludes: 'in no text do both Mary Magdalene and Peter enjoy the same status as witnesses. Indeed, this study has shown that as one of the two figures gains prominence, the status of the other often declines'.

proclaim the Gospel of the Kingdom of the Son of Man, in spite of their fear of his suffering. Although Andrew and Peter object to Mary's trustworthiness as a woman teaching, the readers are invited to believe Mary's instruction. A similar function of Mary Magdalene as in the Gospel of Mary is found in Mark and John while Matthew and Luke limit her role. In both Mark and John, however, Mary Magdalene's importance is implied and not brought to the fore as in the Gospel of Mary.

1.4. *Conclusion*

In one way or another most of the aspects of Mary Magdalene's portrayal in the Gospel of Mary are present in the New Testament Gospels as well. The New Testament Gospels and the Gospel of Mary all portray Mary Magdalene as a disciple: a sister among the brothers (and sisters). She is associated with Jesus' suffering and with transcending this. She is a woman who teaches the other disciples since she knows more. There is the implicit suggestion that she proclaims the gospel.

But we can say more: certain themes in the Gospel of Mary appear to be especially close to the Gospel of John. The Gospel of John and the Gospel of Mary refer to Jesus' love for her which they both relate to being known by him and knowing his words. The Gospel of Mary is close to the Gospel of John in portraying Mary Magdalene as having been taught by Jesus alone as well as in the content of this teaching. They both contain the themes of having seen the Lord, of the new identity of the disciples and of the way upwards to the Divine. With respect to being prepared to proclaim the gospel, the Gospel of Mary is also closest to the Gospel of John. Furthermore, the Gospel of John and the Gospel of Mary are similar in that the author declares that Mary Magdalene's teaching is trustworthy and of particular consequence.

2. *Different Choices*

A comparison between the Gospel of Mary's portrayal of Mary Magdalene and those of the New Testament Gospels also shows that they decided to colour her portrait in their own ways. Especially in four respects the portrayals appear to be evidence of different choices. In contrast to the New Testament Gospels, in the extant pages of the Gospel of Mary, Mary Magdalene has a role after the final departure of the Saviour and not only between Jesus' crucifixion and his final departure as in the New Testament Gospels.

A second difference is that the Gospel of Mary specifically depicts Mary Magdalene instructing the disciples, whereas the New Testament Gospels relate that she does, but do not describe her actually doing it. John is the exception by granting her one sentence of (indirect) speech, whereas the Gospel of Mary grants her several pages of (direct) speech.

A third difference is that the Gospel of Mary openly portrays the male disciples' difficulty with Mary Magdalene being a woman and a disciple to be listened to, whereas the New Testament Gospels suggest that they feel the same problem, but leave the topic vague. A fourth difference is that to the author of the Gospel of

Mary, Mary Magdalene has the leading part, whereas the New Testament Gospels mainly focus on the male disciples.

It is clear that the New Testament Gospels show traces of a high esteem of Mary Magdalene, but they also show traces of a choice to reduce the importance of her role. Mark suggests that all is lost, when Mary Magdalene, Mary of James, and Salome do not speak. No one will go to Galilee and actually see the risen Jesus. By this open ending the readers are strongly invited to speak themselves, knowing that Mary Magdalene and the others eventually must have spoken too, since they are reading their story. The readers are encouraged to overcome their fear just like Mary Magdalene, Mary of James, and Salome apparently must have done.

Compared to Mark, Matthew puts Mary Magdalene in a golden cage. She is no longer the important witness of Mark, on whom the impact of Jesus' work depends. She is the faithful and courageous model disciple who experiences the opening of the tomb, meets the risen Jesus and joyfully obeys him, but the impact of Jesus' work depends on himself and on the eleven disciples.

Compared to Matthew, Luke takes a different view. In Luke, Mary Magdalene is also special as in Matthew, not because of her belief and courage, however, but because she has been healed from seven evil spirits. Her account of the revelation at the empty tomb is not believed, but instead causes confusion and is deemed superfluous, whereas the word that the Lord is seen by Simon is readily believed.

Although Matthew and Luke go very different ways, both are similar, compared to Mark, in that they introduce male disciples to de-emphasize the importance of the Markan Mary Magdalene. Both suggest that the impact of Jesus' work rests solely on the shoulders of the male Eleven, instead of on the shoulders of the Markan Mary Magdalene and the women accompanying her. On the basis of this observation we must conclude that one of the reasons why Matthew and Luke limit the role of the Markan Mary Magdalene is that she is a woman. This is affirmed by the exclusion of women as one of the criteria of apostleship in the Lukan account at the beginning of Acts.

With respect to this, another observation is important as well. Although the Synoptics differ considerably in their portrayals of Mary Magdalene, they are similar in that the main content of Mary Magdalene's instruction is not new to the disciples. In the Synoptics Mary Magdalene and the other women first and foremost have a role of reminding the disciples of certain words Jesus already spoke when still being among them. In contrast to the Synoptic accounts, in the account of John the main content of the instruction which is entrusted to Mary Magdalene is new to the disciples. In addition, Mary Magdalene on her own accord interprets Jesus' instruction in a certain way, which on the basis of the prologue the readers know to be the right one.

With respect to women, John, apparently, made other choices than the Synoptics. In contrast to them, for instance, John does not hesitate to depict women being in relevant dialogue with Jesus. At the same time, however, the Gospel of John and the Synoptic Gospels remain androcentric in a similar way. In the Synoptic Gospels many women are said to follow Jesus, but these women are not depicted in dialogue with him. In John, women are in dialogue with Jesus, but John portrays women within conservative boundaries and does not picture women travelling with Jesus. If they are, they are made invisible in the masculine plural of the word disciples or in the single anonymous disciples.

In the Gospel of Mary the teaching of Mary Magdalene is openly discussed. Is she to be relied on? Do her words really come from the Saviour? Are the disciples to believe that the Saviour would have taught a woman alone and that the disciples should listen to her? This kind of discussion is not openly dealt with in the New Testament Gospels. In the New Testament Gospels, a discussion about the position of Mary Magdalene is, instead, implicitly present. The outcome of this discussion is very different: whereas the Gospel of Mary chooses to depict Mary Magdalene as a disciple to whom one should listen carefully, the New Testament Gospels show ambiguity and reservation with regard to her role as well as to the roles of other women disciples.

3. *First-Century Traditions and the New Testament Gospels*

In the introduction to Chapter 4 I suggested that, compared to other writings, it is extraordinary that the author of the Gospel of Mary gives Mary Magdalene such an explicit role. At the end of this chapter I wonder whether I should say, is it not extraordinary that the New Testament Gospels take so much trouble to limit her role? The New Testament Gospels apparently have different reasons for keeping Mary Magdalene silent. Mark and Matthew do so because of the purpose of their Gospels. Luke and John both seem to address the issue of gender, but in very different ways: Luke by actually silencing women and John by carefully bringing them to speech in a conservative context.

The common themes about Mary Magdalene in the New Testament Gospels are evidence of a first-century main tradition about her. But, when she was generally known as a disciple of Jesus and closely related to the circumstances that led to the core confession of the first Christians, then we can imagine that there must have been stories not only about her presence at Jesus' crucifixion and his grave, but also about what she learnt from him and the content of her gospel.

Perhaps Mark made use of these stories, but we do not know, since Mark has its own theological device. Mark only identifies the twelve apostles by name, but does not directly identify any disciple, consistently using an inviting unspecified plural to refer to the disciples. Mark portrays Mary Magdalene, the other two Marys and Salome at the end of the Gospel, contrasting them to the Twelve, to reveal what discipleship actually means. In addition, their portrayal as remaining silent has a literary focus, challenging the readers to overcome their own silence.

In the Gospel of Matthew no explicit role of Mary Magdalene as a disciple is required, since the author presents Jesus' disciples first and foremost as the twelve males. To them the readers should turn, to be made disciples, to be baptized and to be taught.

The Gospel of Luke, although implicitly, seems to actually address the issue of gender. Luke's gender pairs convey a picture of a world divided by gender. Luke speaks favourably of women when their strength and perseverance are concerned in hearing the word of God and doing it, in prayer, and the sharing of possessions, but also uses the narrative technique of silencing them. The witness of the Galilean women, Mary Magdalene among them, is not important other than to remember among themselves.

The Gospel of John shows quite the reverse motive. According to the author, Mary Magdalene's interpretation and proclamation of the meaning of Jesus' death, resurrection and ascension is authoritative to the Johannine community and constitutive to the Gospel of John. In addition, other teaching of her as an eyewitness may also be present in John. However, there are conservative boundaries to be dealt with. In the Gospel of John, even Jesus himself only gradually comes to the understanding that women may be sowers of the seed, and that the disciples need not be afraid, or need to stop them, but may rejoice with them, reaping the harvest.

Chapter 9

SUMMARY AND CONCLUSION

As we saw in Chapter 1, the scholarly debate about the Gnostic Mary concentrates on the origin of the Gnostic portrait of Mary Magdalene and on its evaluation. Concerning its origin, two basic viewpoints can be distinguished: (1) Gnostic authors have constructed a Gnostic Mary Magdalene using the New Testament portrait of her as a vehicle for Gnostic teaching, and (2) New Testament authors neglected the important role of Mary Magdalene, evidence of which is preserved in Gnostic writings. Subsequently, on the one hand the Gnostic Mary is regarded as a specific Gnostic construct, and, on the other hand the conjecture is defended that the Gnostic portrayal of Mary Magdalene has a solid historical core.

The evaluations of the Gnostic portrayal of Mary Magdalene also vary widely. The Gnostic Mary is valued as the feminine counterpart of Jesus, as a female apostolic leader, as a prophetess, as an advocate of female leadership, of egalitarian discipleship and of a non-hierarchical and charismatic way of being the church in contrast to Peter who represents a male-oriented and hierarchically structured church. The Gnostic Mary is also valued as an important representative of Gnostic insights. Other scholars, however, point to the specific dualism, and the subsequently negative female imagery in Gnostic writings.

In addition, Marjanen and Mohri have shown that the Gnostic writings represent different Gnostic evaluations of Mary Magdalene. In Marjanen's view, for instance, it is only in the Gospel of Mary that the conflict between Mary and Peter symbolizes a conflict between Gnostic and non-Gnostic orthodox Christians. Petersen, on the basis of the Gnostic portrayal of Mary Magdalene and other women disciples, concluded that women only could join the Christian Gnostic community on the condition that they put aside their feminine nature and became male.

To be able to evaluate these viewpoints on the Gnostic Mary Magdalene, the present study focused on the Gospel of Mary, which is considered to be the most important early witness to the esteem of Mary Magdalene in Gnostic circles. I raised four questions:

1. Is the dualism involved in the Gospel of Mary a Gnostic dualism and does it contain a negative use of female imagery?
2. What is the specific content of Mary's teaching in the Gospel of Mary?
3. Does the Gospel of Mary's view on Mary Magdalene advocate the apostolic leadership of women, an egalitarian discipleship and a non-hierarchical way

of being the church?

4. To what extent can the portrayal of Mary Magdalene in the Gospel of Mary, her relation to the Saviour, her position among the disciples, and her function in the story, be understood from the New Testament Gospels?

This chapter will try to answer these questions and take a position with regard to the Gospel of Mary and the debate about the Gnostic Mary Magdalene.

1. *Dualism and Female Imagery in the Gospel of Mary*

1.1. *The Specific Dualism in the Gospel of Mary*

After having introduced the Gospel of Mary in Chapter 2, in Chapter 3 we studied the specific dualism in the gospel. The Gospel of Mary contains a dualistic view of this world and another world and of body and soul. The dualism in the Gospel of Mary is mostly interpreted as a radical dualism, which belongs to a Gnostic context: the material world is a fall from the spiritual world and should not have come into existence; it originates from an inferior Demiurge, who created the world according to his own image. The dualism of this world and another world and of body and soul, however, may also belong to contexts other than a Gnostic one. The dualism could belong to a Jewish and Christian context: the material world originates directly from the spiritual world, or could belong to a more Platonic setting: the material world originates from a Demiurge, a lower deity, who created the world according to models, which belong to the spiritual world.

Perkins who studied the genre of Gnostic dialogue, to which most scholars believe the Gospel of Mary belongs, concluded that the most characteristic trait of Gnostic belief is the view that God is radically transcendent and has nothing to do with the cosmos. This marks the importance of the question about the specific dualism in the Gospel of Mary. If it is not a Gnostic dualism, then the Gospel of Mary lacks the trait that makes Gnosticism in the second century so different from other views of the divine and must be interpreted in the broader context of pluriform Christianity. In addition, Williams warns against the view that a clearly defined Gnostic movement really existed. Like Perkins, he considers the dualism in creation the most characteristic trait of the 'Gnostic' belief, but he argues that the label should only be used as a modern way to categorize certain late antique writings in order to understand them better.

When we tried to understand the dualism involved in the Gospel of Mary we concluded that there are two difficulties in the current interpretation of the remarks on cosmology in GosMar 7.1–8.10. The expression 'all nature' (ⲫⲩⲥⲓⲥ ⲛⲓⲙ) is interpreted in a contradictory way: on the one hand as referring to the material world and on the other hand as referring to the spiritual world (GosMar 7.3, 18). In addition, matter is seen as something contrary to nature (GosMar 8.2-4). In order to find an interpretation which would solve these contradictions we turned to Stoic philosophy and to the Jewish exegete Philo of Alexandria who made use of dualistic (Platonic) as well as Stoic categories, to express the deeper meaning of Jewish Scripture.

We concluded that the dualism of the Gospel of Mary is a moderate one and belongs to a Jewish-Christian context in which the material world directly derives from the spiritual one. The world is not created by an inferior Demiurge, but is created by God himself through his Nature. The creation is divine in origin, but somehow something went wrong. In the language of Genesis, the snake tempted the woman to sin. In Jesus' parable of the sower and his enemy, it is the enemy who sows weeds. In the language of Philo the cause of evil is the existence of two opposing powers; the salutary and beneficent power and the opposite one, the unbounded and destructive. In the language used in the Gospel of Mary, Nature is originally rooted into the Divine, but has become mixed with a power contrary to Nature. Both Nature and this power contrary to Nature act upon (passive) matter, as do the sower and his enemy in Jesus' parable and the two powers in Philo.

The particular language of the Gospel of Mary, however, belongs to a more specifically Stoic context, in which matter is a thought construct and matter and Nature are intertwined. This means that the material world as such is not to be avoided, as would be the case in a Gnostic dualistic view, but that one should be careful not to be ruled by the power contrary to Nature.

1.2. *Female Imagery in the Gospel of Mary*

As we have seen in the debate about the Gnostic Mary Magdalene, scholars such as Maisch, Petersen, and Marjanen point to Gnostic radical dualistic thought and the subsequent negative use of female imagery. Petersen, however, also showed that such views not only occur in a Gnostic, but also in a more orthodox Christian context. In her view, Christian texts of antiquity show a fatal alternative: either women become men, or, as women, they are to be submissive to men. We saw the latter opinion to be true when looking to the use of New Testament texts about the creation and the submissiveness of women. We also noticed that Philo uses dualistic categories of maleness and femaleness. Therefore, not only the radical Gnostic dualism, but also the moderate dualism that belongs to a Jewish and Christian context can give rise to a repressive attitude towards women.

What about female imagery in the context of the dualism in the Gospel of Mary? The negative power contrary to Nature is feminine (ⲡⲁⲣⲁⲫⲩⲥⲓⲥ), but the positive power of Nature is feminine too (ⲫⲩⲥⲓⲥ).[1] Matter is feminine (ϩⲩⲗⲏ), but is labelled neither positively nor negatively.[2] Matter bringing forth passion contains the female imagery of giving birth (ϫⲡⲟ), but at the same time the disciples being able to bring forth peace contains the same imagery.[3] The soul is feminine (ⲯⲩⲭⲏ), but is not particularly depicted as the seat of perceptions, as emotion, but also as the seat of the mind, as reasoning, which is a positive category.

The Son of Man and the mind are masculine (ⲡϣⲏⲣⲉ ⲙⲡⲣⲱⲙⲉ and ⲡⲛⲟⲩⲥ), but they are inside male as well as female followers.[4] Nothing is said of females who would have to become male: both men and women have been made true Human

1. GosMar 8.4 and GosMar 7.3, 7, 8, 18; 8.10.
2. GosMar 7.1, 7; 8.2.
3. GosMar 8.2 and 8.15.
4. GosMar 8.18-19; 10.21.

Being by the Son of Man. The only indication of a negative use of female imagery is the fact that three of the four powers of passion are feminine: Desire (ⲧⲉⲡⲓⲑⲩⲙⲓⲁ), Ignorance (ⲧⲙⲛⲧⲁⲧⲥⲟⲟⲩⲛ), and Wrath (ⲧⲟⲣⲅⲏ).[5] And only two of the seven appearances of Wrath are masculine: Darkness (ⲡⲕⲁⲕⲉ) and the Jealousy of Death (ⲡⲕⲱϩ ⲙ̄ⲡⲙⲟⲩ).[6] However, the goal of the soul's ascent is again described with female imagery: the Rest in Silence (ⲧⲁⲛⲁⲡⲁⲩⲥⲓⲥ ϩⲛ̄ ⲛⲟⲩⲕⲁⲣⲱϥ).[7] Moreover, when the author of the Gospel of Mary describes the salvation of the soul no imagery is used that could suggest that masculinity saves from the evils of femininity. Instead, the author only uses masculine words. The soul says: 'From a world (ⲕⲟⲥⲙⲟⲥ) I am unloosened through a world and from a model (ⲧⲩⲡⲟⲥ) through a model which is from the side of Heaven'.[8]

When we thus consider the use of female imagery in the Gospel of Mary no dualistic use is made of male and female imagery and female imagery does not specifically occur in a negative context alone. On the contrary, the fact that Mary is called blessed because of her stability, whereas the brothers (and sisters) are pictured as unstable right after the departure of the Saviour, turns the current views of male and female behaviour upside down.[9]

2. *The Content of Mary's Teaching in the Gospel of Mary*

2.1. *Mary's Teaching*

In the extant pages of the Gospel of Mary, Mary's teaching concerns three subjects. These are the greatness of the Son of Man (GosMar 9.14-20), the importance of the mind (GosMar 10.7-23) and the way upwards to the Rest in Silence (GosMar 15.1–17.7).

The disciples feel far from assured and prepared to bring the Gospel of the Kingdom of the Son of Man after the Saviour has departed. They fear that they will suffer as the Son of Man did. In this situation Mary encourages them (GosMar 9.14-20). In Mary's words, the disciples are in 'two minds ' (ϩⲏⲧ ⲥⲛⲁⲩ GosMar 9.15-16). On the basis of our interpretation of GosMar 7 and 8 we concluded this to mean that the disciples' minds are not only directed towards Nature, but also towards what is contrary to Nature. What the Saviour warned against is happening to the disciples. They are allowing themselves to become 'persuaded' by what is contrary to Nature (GosMar 8.8). Their hearts are torn and inwardly divided. They are confused by the suffering of the Son of Man and fear their own. Mary instead calls on the disciples to remember and praise the Son of Man's greatness. She reminds them of his re-creating them into true Human Being and thus of their being prepared.

The words of the Saviour, which are still unknown to the disciples, and which Mary at Peter's request recalls in GosMar 10.7-23, help them to understand in a

---

5.   GosMar 15.1, 12; 16.13.
6.   GosMar 16.6, 8.
7.   GosMar 17.5-7. Rest is feminine and silence is masculine.
8.   GosMar 16.21–17.3.
9.   GosMar 10.14-15 and GosMar 9.5-12.

more profound way the teaching of the Saviour about the Son of Man being within, who is to be followed, sought after and found. By recalling words of the Saviour that she knows and the others do not, Mary explains the way out of the disciples' wavering. The disciples do not depend on their soul's senses, nor do they need to wait for divine inspiration from outside. The Saviour has explained to Mary that there are not two categories, soul and spirit, but three, the third one being the mind. Their soul's mind which has the spirit of the Son of Man blown into it enables them, first, to see the Lord's greatness; second, to become stable; and third, to experience bliss.

In GosMar 15.1–17.7 Mary recalls the theme of the ascent of the soul to reveal to the disciples what the Saviour had taught to her alone about the significance of following the Son of Man, being made true Human Being, and living in accordance with one's renewed mind. Mary identifies the adversaries on the way upwards as Darkness, Desire, Ignorance, and Wrath with its seven appearances and shows the wavering disciples the way stability can be experienced. On this way it is important to be able to identify false reasoning with the help of Divine reason. Divine reason consists of the conviction that the soul has been freed from the world she lived in by a heavenly world: the power opposite to Nature has been made powerless. This enables one to overcome the powers that try to keep the soul from drawing near to the Divine.

Mary, last but not least, through the words which the Saviour taught her, also shows that the soul's way to the Rest in Silence is not a road of suffering, but one of victory and joy. Her knowledge about this is perhaps behind her earlier words in GosMar 9.14-20 where she encourages the weeping disciples to praise the greatness of the Son of Man, instead of fearing his suffering.

2.2. *Hermeneutical Tools: Philo, Paul and John*
We first checked whether Mary's teaching on the three subjects outlined above could be seen as related to Gnostic writings, but we saw that this did not bring us any further.[10] Gnostic thoughts on suffering, on primordial Man, on being stable and on the post-mortem ascent past archontic powers offered no help in interpreting the content of Mary's teaching in the Gospel of Mary. Instead, Philo's writings, the Pauline letters and the Gospel of John appeared to be illuminating when searching for the meaning of Mary's teaching. The Pauline letters and the Gospel of John were useful for the metaphor of the Son of Man being inside and clothing oneself with him and for the view that one, as a follower of the Son of Man, is re-created. The writings of Philo appeared to be instructive for the meaning of being made true Human Being, for the importance of the mind and for the relation between seeing the Divine, stability, vices that try to stop the soul by reasoning and Divine reason which enables the soul to continue her way to the Rest in Silence.

This strengthens the view that not only the dualism in the Gospel of Mary, but also the interpretation of Mary's teaching in the Gospel of Mary, should not be limited to a specific Gnostic context, but should be situated in the broader context of first and partly second-century pluriform Christianity. Not only the words of the

---

10. See Chapter 4, section 2.

Saviour before his departure, but also Mary's teaching after his departure are more closely related to a broader Christian context than a Gnostic one, and are rooted in similar ground as Philonic, Pauline, and Johannine thought.

3. *The Gospel of Mary and the Apostolic Leadership of Women*

3.1. *Male Opinions on Mary's Teaching*
First of all it can be noted that the debate about Mary's teaching takes place solely among the men: there is no debate with Mary, but only a debate about her.[11] Although Mary at one point breaks into the male evaluation of her teaching, she receives no answer.[12] These are most important elements in a debate about women leadership.

The Gospel of Mary offers four male opinions on Mary's teaching:

1. She knows more than the brothers (and sisters) because she is a woman and the Saviour loved her more than the rest of women (Peter, GosMar 10.1-6).
2. Her teaching must be rejected, since she tells things that seem to differ from those that the brothers (and sisters) already know (Andrew, GosMar 17.11-15).
3. Her teaching must be rejected, since the Saviour, as a man, would never have told her, as a woman, things that the males should listen to (Peter, GosMar 17.18-22).
4. She knows more than the brothers (and sisters) because the Saviour made her worthy, knowing her thoroughly and subsequently loving her more than the other disciples (Levi, GosMar 18.7-15).

In this debate the author or early copier of the Gospel of Mary takes a clear stand by dedicating the gospel to a woman: the Gospel of Mary.[13] In the Gospel of Mary, the male opinions about Mary's teaching are contradicted through the development of the plot.[14] Peter's first opinion (1) is contradicted by Levi (4). Peter's later opinion is contrary to his first (1 against 3). In addition, the narrator contradicts the opinion that Mary's teaching should be rejected (2 and 3).[15] Moreover, Peter's first opinion is contradictory to Andrew's (1 against 2). Andrew's words are also shown to be inconsistent by the author, since Mary's teaching is demonstrably related to the Saviour's teaching earlier in the Gospel of Mary. Last but not least, Levi's opinion is contradicted by Mary herself, when she taught earlier that the Son of Man made 'us' true Human Being, and not herself alone.

I suggest that it is more accurate to conclude that the Gospel of Mary refutes those who reject Mary's teaching because she is a woman, rather than that the Gospel of Mary specifically advocates the apostolic leadership of women. The

11. GosMar 17.10–18.21. See Chapter 4, section 1.
12. GosMar 18.1-6.
13. See Chapter 4, section 3.2.
14. See Chapter 4, sections 3.1 and 3.3.
15. GosMar 17.7-9.

Gospel of Mary seems instead to advocate the apostolic leadership of all those who can shed light on the words of the Saviour: women and men. In addition, the Gospel of Mary advocates egalitarian discipleship in the sense that all disciples have been made true Human Being and all received the instruction to preach the gospel.

3.2. *No Rules and Laws*

By introducing the theme of making rules and laws, the author gives a clue to how he or she regards the behaviour of Peter and Andrew. The Saviour in the Gospel of Mary, before departing, warns the disciples against making rules and laws, other than the one rule he gave to them, which may be the one rule of love (GosMar 8.22–9.3). The reactions of Andrew and Peter show that they also adhere to other rules. Andrew's rule contains the conviction that only the words of the Saviour that the brothers (and sisters) regard as a canon determine the truth-content of what others contribute to their knowledge of the Saviour (GosMar 17.10-15). Peter, apparently, adheres to rules about the roles of women and men. According to Peter a man is not to listen to a woman, a man must not speak to a woman alone and a woman disciple is never above male disciples (GosMar 17.18-22).

These objections to Mary's teaching do not seem to reflect a specific option in favour of a hierarchically structured church. This conjecture coincides with the fact that Peter and Andrew do not object to the Saviour's warning not to make additional rules and laws. If this warning suggests a more charismatic way of being the church, then Peter and Andrew seem to agree with it.

Andrew's objection shows the belief that until then words of the Saviour must be in harmony with the teaching already known, which is a common opinion in both hierarchical and more charismatic contexts, and one, as we have seen, that is shared by the author of the Gospel of Mary. The author is also clear that Andrew's words reflect a male bias against a woman's role of authority, but disguised in a seemingly rational objection against the context of Mary's words. I suggest that the author of the Gospel of Mary through the Saviour's warning against additional rules and laws and through Andrew's and Peter's extra rules, instead of stating something about hierarchy or charisma, emphasizes that the emerging rules concerning gender roles are not evidence of obedience, but of obvious disobedience to the Saviour.

The Saviour in the Gospel of Mary, before he departs, warns the disciples that adhering to other rules than the one he gave will imprison them (GosMar 8.22–9.4). And indeed, Andrew and Peter, through their extra rules, are no longer free to really listen to what the Saviour teaches them through Mary. They are no longer able to discuss the content of the Saviour's words, as they did before, but instead turn to accusing Mary of deceit.

4. *The Origin of the Gospel of Mary's Portrayal of Mary Magdalene*

The Gospel of Mary is the earliest remaining testimony of an open attitude towards the teaching of a woman disciple of Jesus. To be able to investigate the background of the portrayal of Mary Magdalene in the Gospel of Mary, we turned to the New

Testament Gospels, since they contain the earliest written material on Mary Magdalene.[16] We studied their various portraits with respect to Mary Magdalene's relation to Jesus, her role among the disciples and her function in the Gospel stories. We concluded that the basic traits of the Gospel of Mary's portrayal of Mary Magdalene are also present in the New Testament Gospels, especially in the Gospel of John.[17] Does this mean that the author devised the Gospel of Mary inspired by the New Testament Gospels? Or did the author's esteem of Mary Magdalene stem from a broad stream of earlier written and oral tradition about her of which the New Testament Gospels are the only testimonies that survived?

The common themes about Mary Magdalene in the New Testament Gospels are evidence of a first-century main tradition about her. But, when she was generally known as a disciple of Jesus and closely related to the circumstances that led to the core confession of the first Christians, then we can imagine that there must have been stories not only about her presence at Jesus' crucifixion and his grave, but also about what she learnt from him and the content of her gospel. It is quite plausible that there were traditions that focused especially on Mary Magdalene.

In addition, we noticed that the New Testament Gospels show both traces of a sincere esteem for Mary Magdalene as well as traces of a choice to reduce her role. Moreover, we saw that each of the New Testament Gospels had their own particular reasons to keep Mary Magdalene silent. Therefore it seems less likely that the author's esteem of Mary Magdalene derives from the New Testament Gospels, than that it is rooted in a broader stream of first-century written and oral tradition about her. This first-century evidence which specifically focused on Mary Magdalene has not survived, but is reflected in the Gospel of Mary and less explicitly in the Gospel of John.

5. *The Present Study's Contribution*

The purpose of the present study was to evaluate the different viewpoints on the Gnostic Mary Magdalene by studying the Gospel of Mary which is considered to be the most important early witness to the esteem for Mary Magdalene in Gnostic circles. First of all, a significant conclusion of this study is that the Gospel of Mary is not to be categorized as a Gnostic writing and that Mary in the Gospel of Mary is not promoting Gnostic teaching. This means that the Gospel of Mary cannot be seen as evidence of an early esteem of Mary Magdalene in Gnostic circles. Thus the Gospel of Mary is not at home in the reconstruction of a Gnostic portrayal of Mary Magdalene. This conclusion calls for a new evaluation of the Gnostic portrayal of Mary Magdalene.

A second conclusion concerns the more specific traits of the portrayal of Mary Magdalene in the Gospel of Mary. These are closest to the evaluation of her as an apostolic leader. The author of the Gospel of Mary presents Mary Magdalene as a disciple of the Saviour to whom one should listen. The author considers Mary

16. See Chapters 5, 6, and 7.
17. See Chapter 8.

Magdalene's contribution especially relevant in a situation of fear to go and proclaim the gospel, since she has been taught by the Saviour about the identity of the adversaries the disciples are to meet. In the author's view, Mary Magdalene's words, when heard, can empower the disciples to take courage and become stable.

A third conclusion concerns the role of gender in the Gospel of Mary. The Gospel of Mary contains no dualistic use of male and female imagery. On the contrary, the Divine is described with feminine words: Nature, Root, and Rest in Silence. Furthermore, the insight in the identity of the adversaries sheds a specific light on the gender difficulties which especially Peter experiences. They are a result of the power of Wrath, and do not stem from the Divine, but instead, hinder one from finding the way upwards to the Divine. In addition, the author of the Gospel of Mary emphasizes that rules concerning gender roles are evidence of disobedience rather than of obedience to the Saviour.

A fourth conclusion of the present study concerns the origin of the portrayal of Mary Magdalene in the Gospel of Mary. On the basis of the examination of the different portrayals of Mary Magdalene in the New Testament Gospels we concluded that the portrayal of Mary Magdalene in the Gospel of Mary most likely does not depend on the New Testament Gospels, but rather on earlier tradition about Mary Magdalene.

The Gospel of Mary is thus plain evidence against the conjecture that early Christian texts present a fatal alternative: either women become men or, as women they are to be submissive to men. The Gospel of Mary is significant proof of an early Christian view which considered (at least) Mary Magdalene to be on an equal footing with her brothers (and sisters) in the sense that they all have been made true Human Being and that they all are prepared to preach the gospel of the Kingdom of the Son of Man. According to the Gospel of Mary, Mary Magdalene's additional knowledge is vital to be able to fulfil this task. As a consequence, the Gospel of Mary contradicts all those who reject Mary Magdalene's teaching, simply because she is a woman.

6. *Further Study*

In Chapter 7, solely on the basis of the Gospel of John itself, it was suggested that the theory that Mary Magdalene is concealed in the anonymous disciple Jesus loved cannot be dismissed out of hand and merits further investigation.[18] At the end of this study it was concluded that the portrayal of Mary Magdalene in the Gospel of Mary is close to that in the Gospel of John. We also noted that the Gospel of John proved to be helpful in understanding Mary's teaching in the Gospel of Mary. This calls for a further examination of the relationship of the Gospel of John and the Gospel of Mary and a deeper study of Mary Magdalene and the anonymous disciple in the Gospel of John in relation to Mary Magdalene in the Gospel of Mary.

18. See the excursus at the end of Chapter 7.

BIBLIOGRAPHY

Primary Sources and their Translations

Aland, K., and E. Nestle (eds.)
    1975   *Novum Testamentum Graece XXV* (Stuttgart: Deutsche Bibelstiftung).
    1981   *Novum Testamentum Graece XXVI* (Stuttgart: Deutsche Bibelstiftung).
    1993   *Novum Testamentum Graece XXVII* (Stuttgart: Deutsche Bibelstiftung).
Allberry, C.R.C.
    1938   *A Manichaean Psalm-Book. Part II* (Manichaean Manuscripts in the Chester Beatty Collection, 2; Stuttgart: W. Kohlhammer).
Arnim, H. von (ed.)
    1968   *Stoicorum Veterum Fragmenta (SVF)* (4 vols.; Stuttgart: B.G. Teubner).
Attridge, H.W. (ed.)
    1985   *Nag Hammadi Codex I (The Jung Codex). Vol. I: Introduction, Texts, Translations, Indices. Vol. II: Notes* (NHS, 23; Leiden: E.J. Brill).
Attridge, G.W., and G.W. MacRae
    1988   'The Gospel of Truth', in J.M. Robinson (ed.), *The Nag Hammadi Library in English* (Leiden: E.J. Brill, 3rd rev. edn): 38-51.
Böhlig, A., and F. Wisse (eds.)
    1975   *Nag Hammadi Codices III,2 and IV,2. The Gospel of the Egyptians (The Holy Book of the Great Invisible Spirit)* (edited with translation and commentary, in cooperation with P. Labib; NHS, 4; Leiden: E.J. Brill).
Brashler, J., and D.M. Parrott
    1979   'The Act of Peter. BG 4.128,1-141,7', in D.M. Parrott, *Nag Hammadi Codices V,2-5 and VI with Papyrus Berolinensis 8502,1 and 4* (NHS, 11; Leiden: E.J. Brill): 473-93.
Budge, E.A.Th.
    1898   *The Earliest Known Coptic Psalter* (London: Kegan Paul, Trench, Trubner).
Colson, F.H., and G.H. Whitaker
    1929–62   *Philo in Ten Volumes* (LCL; London: William Heinemann).
Connolly, R.H.
    1929   *Didascalia Apostolorum: The Syriac version Translated and Accompanied by the Verona Latin Fragments* (Oxford: Clarendon Press).
Emmel, S. (ed.)
    1984   *Nag Hammadi Codices III,5. The Dialogue of the Savior* (NHMS, 26; Leiden: E.J. Brill).
Evans, E.
    1972   *Adversus Marcionem / Tertullian* (Oxford: Clarendon Press).
Ficker, G.
    1905   'Widerlegung eines Montanisten', *ZKG* 26: 447-63.

Grenfell, B.P., and A.S. Hunt
1898–   *The Oxyrhynchus Papyri* (London: Egypt Exploration Fund).
Grese, W.C.
1979   *Corpus Hermeticum XIII and early Christian literature.* Studia ad Corpus
           Hellenisticum Novi Testamenti V (Leiden: E.J. Brill).
Horner, G.
1969   *The Coptic Version of the New Testament in the southern dialect otherwise
           called Sahidic and Thebaic* (repr. of the edition 1911–24; 7 vols.;
           Osnabrück: Otto Zeller).
Jenkins, C.
1909   'Origen on I Corinthians', *JTS* 9: 231-47, 253-372, 500-514; 10: 270-75.
King, K.L.
1992   'The Gospel of Mary', in R.J. Miller (ed.), *The Complete Gospels* (Sonoma,
           CA: Polebridge Press): 361-66.
Layton, B. (ed.)
1989   *Nag Hammadi Codex II,2-7 together with XIII, 2* Brit. Lib. Or. 4926(1) and
           P. Oxy. 1, 654, 655. Vol. I. Gospel according to Thomas, Gospel according
           to Philip, Hypostasis of the Archons, Indexes. Vol. II. On the Origin of the
           World, Expository Treatise on the Soul, Book of Thomas the Contender*
           (NHMS, 20-21; Leiden: E.J. Brill).
Long, A.A., and D.N. Sedley
1987   *The Hellenistic Philosophers. I. Translations of the Principal Sources with
           Philosophical Commentary. II. Greek and Latin Texts with Notes and
           Bibliography* (Cambridge: Cambridge University Press).
Lührmann, D.
1988   'Die griechischen Fragmente des Mariaevangeliums P Ox 3525 und P Ryl
           463', *NovT* 30: 321-38.
Luttikhuizen, G.P.
1986   *Gnostische geschriften I. Het Evangelie naar Maria; Het Evangelie naar
           Filpppus; De brief van Petrus aan Filippus. Uit het Koptisch vertaald,
           ingeleid en toegelicht* (Kampen: J.H. Kok).
Mara, M.G.
1973   *Évangile de Pierre. Introduction, texte critique, traduction, commentaire*
           (Sources chrétiennes, 202; Paris: Éditions du Cerf).
Marcus, R.
1953   *Philo: Supplement* (LCL; 2 vols.; London: William Heinemann).
Marcovich, M. (ed.)
1986   *Hippolytus Romanus, Refutatio omnium haeresium* (Patristische Texte und
           Studien, 25; Berlin: Walter de Gruyter).
Ménard, J.-E.
1972   *L'Évangile de Vérité* (NHS, 2; Leiden: E.J. Brill).
Miller, R.J. (ed.)
1992   *The Complete Gospels* (Sonoma, CA: Polebridge Press).
Parrott, D.M. (ed.)
1991   *Nag Hammadi Codices III,3-4 and V,1 with Papyrus Berolinensis 8502,3
           and Oxyrhynchus Papyrus 1081. Eugnostos and the Sophia of Jesus Christ*
           (NHMS, 27; Leiden: E.J. Brill).

Parsons, P.J.
1983   '3525. Gospel of Mary', in B.P. Grenfell and A.S. Hunt (eds.), *The Oxyrhynchus Papyri*, vol. L (London: British Academy): 12-14.

Pasquier, A.
1983   *L'Évangile selon Marie (BG 1): texte établi et présenté* (Bibliothèque Copte de Nag Hammadi, sections 'Textes' 10; Québec: Les Preses de l'Université Laval).

Pearson, B.A. (ed.)
1981   *Nag Hammadi Codices IX and X* (NHS, 15; Leiden: E.J. Brill).
1996   *Nag Hammadi Codex VII* (NHMS, 30; Leiden: E.J. Brill).

Puech, H.-Ch.
1959   'Gnostische Evangelien und verwandte Dokumente', in E. Hennecke and W. Schneemelcher (eds.), *Neutestamentliche Apokryphen in deutscher Übersetzung. I. Band: Evangelien* (3 vols.; Tübingen: J.C.B. Mohr [Paul Siebeck]): 158-271.

Rader, R.
1981   'Perpetua', in P. Wilson-Kastner, *A Lost Tradition: Women Writers of the Early Church* (Lanham, NY and London: University Press of America): 1-32.

Roberts, C.H.
1938   *Catalogue of the Greek and Latin Papyri in the John Rylands Library*, III (Manchester: Manchester University Press).

Robinson, J.M. (ed.)
1972–84 *The Facsimile Edition of the Nag Hammadi Codices* (11 vols.; Leiden: E.J. Brill).
1988   *The Nag Hammadi Library in English* (Leiden: E.J. Brill, 3rd rev. edn).

Rousseau, A.
1969   *Irenée de Lyon. Contre les Hérésies Livre V* (Sources Chrétiennes, 153; Paris: Éditions du Cerf).

Schmidt, C. (ed.)
1978   *The Books of Jeu and the untitled text in the Bruce Codex. Translation and notes by V. MacDermot* (NHS, 13; Leiden: E.J. Brill).
1978   *Pistis Sophia* (translation and notes by V. MacDermot; NHS, 9; Leiden: E.J. Brill).

Schneemelcher, W. and E. Hennecke
1990   *Neutestamentliche Apokryphen in deutscher Übersetzung* (Tübingen: J.C.B. Mohr [Paul Siebeck]).

Schulz-Flugel, E., and P. Mattei
1997   *Tertullien. Le voile des vierges* (Sources Chrétiennes, 424; Paris: Éditions du Cerf).

Schüssler, K.
1995–   *Die Koptischen Bibeltexte* (Wiesbaden: Harassowitz).

Scopello, M.
1985   *L'exégèse de l'âme. Nag Hammadi Codex II,6. Introduction, traduction et commentaire* (NHMS, 27; Leiden: E.J. Brill).

Sieber, J.H. (ed.)
1991   *Nag Hammadi Codex VIII* (NHMS, 31; Leiden: E.J. Brill).

Till, W.C., and H.-M. Schenke
    1972   *Die gnostischen Schriften des koptischen Papyrus Berolinensis 8502* (Texte
                und Untersuchungen zur Geschichte der altchristlichen Literatur, 60; Berlin:
                Akademie-Verlag).
Todd, R.B.
    1976   *Alexander of Aphrodisias on Stoic Physics: A Study of De Mixtione with
                Preliminary Essays, Texts, Translation and Commentary* (Philosophia
                Antiqha, 28; Leiden: E.J. Brill).
Williams, F.
    1987   *The Panarion of Epiphanius of Salamis. Book I (Sects 1-46)* (NHMS, 35;
                Leiden: E.J. Brill).
    1994   *The Panarion of Epiphanius of Salamis. Books II and III (Sects 47-80, De
                Fide)* (NHMS, 36; Leiden: E.J. Brill).
Wilson, R. Mcl., and G.W. MacRae
    1979   'The Gospel according to Mary', in D.M. Parrott (ed.), *Nag Hammadi
                Codices V,2-5 and VI with Papyrus Berolinensis 8502,1 and 4* (NHS, 11;
                Leiden: E.J. Brill): 453-71.
Wisse, F., and M. Waldstein (eds.)
    1988   'The Apocryphon of John (II,1, IV,1 and BG 8502,2)', in J.M. Robinson
                (ed.), *The Nag Hammadi Library in English* (Leiden: E.J. Brill, 3rd rev.
                edn): 104-123.
    1995   *The Apocryphon of John. Synopsis of Nag Hammadi Codices II,1; III,1; IV,1
                with BG 8502,2* (NHMS, 33; Leiden: E.J. Brill).
Wright, F.A.
    1954   *Select Letters of St. Jerome, with an English translation* (London: William
                Heinemann; Cambridge, MA: Harvard University Press).

                            Secondary Literature

Anstett-Janssen, M.
    1961   *Maria Magdalena in der abendländischen Kunst. Ikonographie der Heiligen
                von den Anfängen bis ins 16. Jahrhundert* (Inaugural dissertation, Freiburg
                in Breisgau).
    1974   'Maria Magdalena', in E. Kirschbaum SJ and W. Braunfells (eds.), *Lexikon
                der christlichen Ikonographie*, VII (Freiburg: Herder): 516-41.
Atwood, R.
    1993   *Mary Magdalene in the New Testament Gospels and Early Tradition* (New
                York: Peter Lang).
Baarda, Tj.
    1975   *The Gospel Quotations of Aphrahat the Persian Sage. I. Aphrahat's Text of
                the Fourth Gospel* (2 vols.; Amsterdam: Vrije Universiteit).
Baert, B.
    2002   *Maria Magdalena. Zondares van de Mideleeuwen tot vandaag* (Museum
                voor Schone Kunsten Gent / Cahier 4; Sabam: Belgium).
Bauckham, R.
    1992   'Mary of Clopas (John 19.25)', in G.J. Brooke (ed.), *Women in the Biblical
                Tradition* (Studies in Women and Religion, 31; Lewiston: Edwin Mellen
                Press): 231-56.

Bauer, W.
1909   *Das Leben Jesu im Zeitalter der neutestamentlichen Apokryphen* (Tübingen: Mohr).

Bauer, W., K. Aland and A. Aland (eds.)
1988   *Griechisch-deutsches Wörterbuch zu den Schriften des Neuen Testaments und der frühchristlichen Literatur, 6. völlig neu bearbeitete Auflage* (Berlin: Walter de Gruyter).

Beck, D.R.
1997   *The Discipleship Paradigm: Readers and Anonymous Characters in the Fourth Gospel* (Biblical Interpretation Series, 27; Leiden: E.J. Brill).

Beirne, M.M.
2003   *Women and Men in the Forth Gospel, A Genuine Discipleship of Equals* (JSNTSup, 242; London/New York: Sheffield Academic Press).

Berger, K.
1997   *Im Anfang war Johannes. Datierung und Theologie des vierten Evangeliums* (Stuttgart: Quell Verlag).

Beyer, H.W.
1976   'διακονέω, διακονία, διάκονος', in *TDNT*, II: 81-93.

Bieberstein, S.
1998   *Verschwiegene Jüngerinnen – vergessene Zeuginnen. Gebrochene Konzepte im Lukasevangelium* (Novum Testamentum Orbis Antiquus, 38; Göttingen: Vandenhoeck & Ruprecht).

Blass, F., A. Debrunner and F. Rehkopf
1990   *Grammatik des neutestamentlichen Griechisch* (Göttingen: Vandenhoeck & Ruprecht).

Bock, D.L.
1994   *Luke. Volume 1: 1.–9.50* (Baker Exegetical Commentary on the New Testament, 3a; Grand Rapids, MI: Baker Books).
1996   *Luke. Volume 2: 9.51–24.53* (Baker Exegetical Commentary on the New Testament, 3b; Grand Rapids, MI: Baker Books).

Boismard, M.-É., and A. Lamouille
1990   *Les Actes des deux Apôtres. I. Introduction – Textes* (Paris: Librairie Lecoffre).

Boomershine, T.E.
1981   'Mark 16.8 and the Apostolic Commission', *JBL* 100: 225-39.

Bormann, C. *et al.*
1972   'Form und Materie', in J. Ritter (ed.), *Historisches Wörterbuch der Philosophie*, II (Darmstadt: Wissenschaftliche Buchgesellschaft): 977-1030.

Bovon, F.
1984   'Le privilège Pascal de Marie Madeleine', *NTS* 30: 50-62.
1989   *Das Evangelium nach Lukas* (EKKNT, 3; Zürich: Benziger Verlag; Neukirchen-Vluyn: Neukirchener Verlag).

Brashler J. and D.M. Parrott
1988   'The Act of Peter' in J.M. Robinson (ed.), *The Nag Hammadi Library in English* (Third Completely Revised Edition; Leiden: E.J. Brill): 528-31.

Brock, A.
2002   'Setting the Record Straight–The Politics of Identification', in F. Stanley Jones (ed.), *Which Mary? The Marys of Early Christian Tradition* (Symposium Series, 19; Atlanta: Society of Biblical Literature): 43-52.

2003   *Mary Magdalene, the First Apostle. The Struggle for Authority* (Harvard Theological Studies, 51; Cambridge, MA: Harvard University Press).

Brodie, T.L.
1993   *The Gospel According to John: A Literary and Theological Commentary* (New York: Oxford University Press).

Brooten, B.J.
1982a   *Women Leaders in the Ancient Synagogue: Inscriptional Evidence and Background Issues* (BJS, 36; Chico, CA: Scholars Press).
1982b   'Jüdinnen zur Zeit Jesu', in B. Brooten and N. Greinacher (eds.), *Frauen in der Männerkirche* (Grünewald: Kaiser): 141-48.
1985   'Early Christian Women and their Cultural Context: Issues of Method in Historical Reconstruction', in A.Y. Collins (ed.), *Feminist Perspectives on Biblical Scholarship in North America* 10 (Chico, CA: Scholars Press): 65-91.

Brown, P.
1989   *The Body and Society: Men, Women and Sexual Renunciation in Early Christianity* (London: Faber and Faber).

Brown, R.E.
1966   *The Gospel According to John. Introduction, Translation and Notes. Part One (John I-XII)* (AB, 29; Garden City, NY: Doubleday).
1970   *The Gospel According to John. Introduction, Translation and Notes. Part Two (John XIII-XXI)* (AB, 29A; Garden City, NY: Doubleday).
1975   'Roles of Women in the Fourth Gospel', *TS* 36: 688-99 (reprinted in his *The Community of the Beloved Disciple* [New York: Doubleday, 1979]: 183-98).
1979   *The Community of the Beloved Disciple: The Life, Loves and Hates of an Individual Church in New Testament Times* (New York: Doubleday).
1994   *The Death of the Messiah. From Gethsemane to the Grave: A Commentary on the Passion Narratives in the Four Gospels* (2 vols.; New York: Doubleday).

Buchanan, G.W.
1996   *The Gospel of Matthew* (New Testament Series, I/2; Mellen Biblical Commentary; Leviston: Mellen Biblical Press).

Bultmann, R,
1961   *Die Geschichte der synoptischen Tradition* (Göttingen: Vandenhoeck & Ruprecht).

Charlesworth, J.H.
1995   *The Beloved Disciple: Whose Witness Validates the Gospel of John?* (Valley Forge: Trinity Press International).

Colish, M.L.
1985   *The Stoic Tradition from Antiquity to the Early Middle Ages* (2 vols.; Leiden: E.J. Brill).

Collins, J.J.
1979   *Apocalypse: The Morphology of a Genre* (Semeia, 14; Missoula: University of Montana).

Collins, J.N.
1990   *Diakonia: Re-interpreting Ancient Sources* (New York and Oxford: Oxford University Press).

Colpe, C.
1967   'Die Himmelsreise der Seele ausserhalb und innerhalb der Gnosis', in U.
            Bianchi (ed.), *Le origini dello gnosticismo, Colloquia di Messina 13-18
            aprile 1966* (Studies in the History of Religion, 12; Leiden: E.J. Brill): 429-
            47.
Comfort, W.P.
1992   *The Quest for the Original Text of the New Testament* (Grand Rapids, MI:
            Baker Book House).
Corbo, V.
1976   'La città Romana di Magdala', *Studia Hierosolymitana* 1: 356-78.
Cotes, M.
1992   'Women, Silence and Fear (Mark 16.8)', in G.J. Brooke (ed.), *Women in the
            Biblical Tradition* (Studies in Women and Religion, 31; Lewiston: Edwin
            Mellen Press): 150-66.
Crum, W.E.
1939   *A Coptic Dictionary* (Oxford: Clarendon Press).
Culianu, I.P.
1983   *Psychanodia I: A Survey of the Evidence Concerning the Ascension of the
            Soul and its Relevance* (Études preliminaries aux religions orientales dans
            l'Empire Romain, 99; Leiden: E.J. Brill).
1984   'The Gnostic Revenge: Gnosticism and Romantic Literature', in J. Taubes
            (ed.), *Religionstheorie und Politische Theologie, Band 2: Gnosis und Politik*
            (Munich: Wilhelm Fink/Ferdinand Schöningh).
D'Angelo, M.R.
1999a   'Reconstructing "Real" Women in Gospel Literature: The Case of Mary
            Magdalene', in R.S. Kraemer and M.R. D'Angelo (eds.), *Women and
            Christian Origins* (New York and Oxford: Oxford University Press): 105-
            128.
1999b   '(Re)Presentations of Women in the Gospels: John and Mark', in R.S.
            Kraemer and M.R. D'Angelo (eds.), *Women and Christian Origins* (New
            York and Oxford: Oxford University Press): 129-49.
1999c   '(Re)Presentations of Women in the Gospel of Matthew and Luke–Acts', in
            R.S. Kraemer and M.R. D'Angelo (eds.), *Women and Christian Origins*
            (New York and Oxford: Oxford University Press): 171-98.
Dannemann, I.
1996   *Aus dem Rahmen fallen. Frauen im Markusevangelium. Eine feministische
            Re-vision* (Berlin: Alektor-Verlag).
Davies, W.D.
1964   *The Setting of the Sermon on the Mount* (Cambridge: Cambridge University
            Press).
De Boer, E.A.
1988   'Maria van Magdala en haar Evangelie', in G. Quispel (ed.), *Gnosis. De
            derde component van de Europese cultuurtraditie* (Utrecht: Hes Uitgevers):
            85-98.
1997   *Mary Magdalene: Beyond the Myth* (trans. John Bowden; Harrisburg:
            Trinity Press International).
2000a   'Discipleship of Equals and Historical "Reality" ', in K. Biezeveld *et al.*
            (eds.), *Proeven van Vrouwenstudies Theologie* 6 (IIMO Research Publica-
            tion, 53; Zoetermeer: Meinema): 99-122.

2000b	'Mary Magdalene and the Disciple Jesus Loved', *Lectio Difficilior. European Electronic Journal for Feminist Exegesis* 1: 1-20. http://www. lectio.unibe.ch
2002	'The Lukan Mary Magdalene and the Other Women Following Jesus', in A.J. Levine and M. Blickenstaff (eds.), *A Feminist Companion to Luke* (Sheffield: Sheffield Academic Press): 147-68.
2004	'A Gnostic Mary in the Gospel of Mary?', in J. van der Vliet (ed.), *Proceedings of the Seventh International Congress of Coptic Studies* (Orientalia Lovaniensia Analecta; Louvain: Peeters, forthcoming).

De Boer, M.C.
1992	'John 4.27 – Women (and Men) in the Gospel and Community of John', in G.J. Brooke (ed.), *Women in the Biblical Tradition* (Studies in Women and Religion, 31; Lewiston: Edwin Mellen Press): 208-230.

Dean-Otting, M.
1984	*Heavenly Journeys: A Study of the Motif in Hellenistic Jewish Literature* (Judentum und Umwelt, 8; Frankfurt am Main: Peter Lang).

Dillon, J.M.
1977	*The Middle Platonists: A Study of Platonism 80 B.C. to A.D. 220* (London: Duckworth).

Dillon, R.J.
1978	*From Eye-witness to Ministers of the Word: Tradition and Composition in Luke 24* (Analecta Biblica, 82; Rome: Biblical Institute Press).

Dodd, C.H.
1953	*The Interpretation of the Fourth Gospel* (Cambridge: Cambridge University Press).

Donahue, J.R.
1995	'Windows and Mirrors: The Setting of Mark's Gospel', *CBQ* 57: 1-26.

Dörrie, H.
1976	*Platonica minora* (Studia antiqua, 8; München: Fink).

Duperray, E.
1989	*Marie Madeleine dans la mystique, les arts et les lettres* (Actes du Colloque International; Avignon 20-22 July 1988; Paris: Beauchesne).

Eisen, U.E.
1996	*Amtsträgerinnen im frühen Christentum. Epigraphische und literarische Studien* (Forschungen zur Kirchen- und Dogmengeschichte, 61; Göttingen: Vandenhoeck & Ruprecht).

Ernst, J.
1981	*Das Evangelium nach Markus* (RNT; Regensburg: Verlag Friedrich Pustet Regensburg).
1993	*Das Evangelium nach Lukas* (RNT; Regensburg: Verlag Friedrich Pustet Regensburg).

Evans, C.F.
1990	*Saint Luke* (TPI New Testament Commentaries; London: SCM Press; Philadelphia: Trinity Press International).

Evans, G.A., R.L. Webb and R.A. Wiebe
1993	*Nag Hammadi Texts and the Bible: A Synopsis and Index* (New Testament Tools and Studies, 18; Leiden: E.J. Brill).

Fander, M.

1990   *Die Stellung der Frau im Markusevangelium. Unter besonderer Berücksichtigung kultur- und religionsgeschichtlicher Hintergründe* (Münsteraner Theologische Abhandlungen, 8; Altenberge: Telos-Verlag).

1992a   'Frauen im Urchristentum am Beispiel Palästinas', in H.C. Brennecke (ed.), *Volk Gottes, Gemeinde und Gesellschaft* (Jahrbuch für Biblische Theologie, 7; Neukirchen-Vluyn: Neukirchener Verlag): 165-85.

1992b   'Frauen in der Nachfolge Jesu. Die Rolle der Frau im Markusevangelium', *EvT* 52: 413-32.

Fee, G.D.

1994   *God's Empowering Presence: The Holy Spirit in the Letters of Paul* (Peabody, MA: Hendrickson).

Fehribach, A.

1998   *The Women in the Life of the Bridegroom: A Feminist Historical-Literary Analysis of the Female Characters in the Fourth Gospel* (Collegeville, MN: Liturgical Press).

Feuillet, A.

1963   'La recherche du Christ dans la nouvelle Alliance d'après la Christophanie de Jo. 20.11-18 Comparaison avec Cant. 3,1-4 et l'épisode des Pèlerins d'Emmäus', in M.H. Lubac (ed.), *L'Homme devant Dieu. Exégèse et Patristique* (Paris: Aubier): 93-112.

1975   'Les deux onctions faites sur Jésus, et Marie-Madeleine. Contribution à l'étude des rapports entre les Synoptiques et le quatrième évangile', *Revue Thomas* 75: 357-94.

Fitzmyer, J.A.

1981   *The Gospel According to Luke* (AB, 28; 2 vols.; New York: Doubleday).

Flashar, H. (ed.)

1994   *Die Philosophie der Antike Band 4: Die Hellenistische Philosophie* (Basel: Schwabe & Ag Verlag).

Frankemölle, H.

1994   *Matthäus; Kommentar* (2 vols.; Düsseldorf: Patmos).

Fredriksson, M.

1999   *According to Mary Magdalene* (English translation by Joanne Tate; Charlottesville: Hampton Roads Publishing Company). Original Swedish title: *Enlight Maria Magdalena* (Stockholm: Wahlström & Widstrand, 1997).

Gaechter, S.J.

1962   *Das Matthäus Evangelium. Ein Kommentar* (Innsbruck: Tyrolia Verlag).

Garland, D.E.

1984   *One Hundred Years of Study on the Passion Narratives* (Bibliographic Series, 3; National Association of Baptist Professors of Religion; Macon, GA: Mercer University Press).

Gerhardsson, B.

1989   'Mark and the Female Witnesses', in H. Behrens *et al.* (eds.), *DUMU-E2-DUB-BA-A. Studies in Honor of Ake Sjöberg* (Philadelphia: Occasional Publications of the Samuel Noah Kramer Fund): 217-26.

Goulder, M.D.

1978   'Mark XVI.1-8 and Parallels', *NTS* 24: 235-40.

1989   *Luke. A New Paradigm* (JSNTSup, 20; 2 vols.; Worcester: Billing & Sons).

Grese, W.C.
1979   *Corpus Hermeticum XIII and Early Christian Literature* (Studia ad Corpus Hellenisticum Novi Testamenti, 5; Leiden: E.J. Brill).

Grundmann, W.
1960   'Verständnis und Bewegung des Glaubens im Johannes-Evangelium', *Kerygma und Dogma* 6: 131-54.
1961   'Zur Rede Jesu vom Vater im Johannes-Evangelium. Eine Redaktions- und bekenntnisgeschichtliche Untersuchung zu Joh 20, 17 und seiner Vorbereit-ung', *ZNW* 52: 213-30.

Gryson, R.
1972   *Le ministère des femmes dans l'Église ancienne* (Recherches et synthèses, section d'histoire; Gembloux: Éditions J. Duculot, SA).

Gundry, R.H.
1982   *Matthew: A Commentary on His Literary and Theological Art* (Grand Rapids, MI: Eerdmans).
1993   *Mark: A Commentary on His Apology for the Cross* (Grand Rapids, MI: Eerdmans).

Harnack, A. von
1931   *Lehrbuch der Dogmengeschichte* I (Tübingen: J.C.B. Mohr).

Hartenstein, J.
2000   *Die Zweite Lehre. Erscheinungen des Auferstandenen als Rahmenerzählun-gen frühchristlicher Dialoge* (TU, 146; Berlin: Akademie Verlag).

Hartenstein, J., and S. Petersen
1998   'Das Evangelium nach Maria', in L.S. Schottroff and M.Th. Wacker (eds.), *Kompendium. Feministische Bibelauslegung* (Gütersloh: Kaiser, Gütersloher Verlag Haus).

Haskins, S.
1993   *Mary Magdalen: Myth and Metaphor* (London: HarperCollins).

Heiler, F.
1977   *Die Frau in den Religionen der Menschheit* (Berlin: Walter de Gruyter).

Heine, S.
1986   *Frauen der frühen Christenheit. Zur historischen Kritik einer feministischen Theologie* (Göttingen: Vandenhoeck & Ruprecht).
1989   'Eine Person von Rang und Namen. Historische Kontouren der Mag-dalenerin', in D.A. Koch, G. Sellin and A. Lindemann (eds.), *Jesu Rede von Gott und ihre Nachgeschichte im frühen Christentum. Festschrift für Willi Marxsen* (Gütersloh: Gütersloher Verlagshaus Gerd Mohn): 179-95.

Helderman, J.
1984   *Die Anapausis im Evangelium Veritatis. Eine vergleichende Untersuchung des valentinianisch-gnostischen Heilsgutes der Ruhe im Evangelium Veritatis und in anderen Schriften der Nag Hammadi-Bibliothek* (NHS, 18; Leiden: E.J. Brill).

Hengel, M.
1963   'Maria Magdalena und die Frauen als Zeugen', in O. Betz (ed.), *Abraham unser Vater. Festschrift für Otto Michel* (Leiden: E.J. Brill): 243-56.
1973   *Judentum und Hellenismus. Studien zur ihrer Begegnung unter besonderer Berücksichtigung Palästinas bis zur Mitte des 2. Jh.s v. Chr* (Tübingen: J.C.B. Mohr [Paul Siebeck]).

1989	*The Johannine Question* (trans. John Bowden; London: SCM Press).

Hester, J.D.
1995	'Dramatic Inconclusion: Irony and the Narrative Rhetoric Ending of Mark', *JSNT* 57: 61-86.

Himmelfarb, M.
1993	*Ascent to Heaven in Jewish and Christian Apocalypses* (New York and Oxford: Oxford University Press).

Holzmeister, U.
1922	'Die Magdalenenfrage in der kirchlichen Überlieferung', *ZKT* 46: 402-422, 556-84.

Hoskyns, E.C.
1947	*The Fourth Gospel* (ed. F.N. Davey; London: Faber and Faber).

Ilan, T.
1989	'Notes on the Distribution of Jewish Women's Names in Palestine in the Second Temple and Mishnaic Periods', *JJS* 40: 186-200.
1995a	*Jewish Women in Greco-Roman Palestine: An Inquiry into Image and Status* (Texte und Studien zum Antiken Judentum, 44; Tübingen: J.C.B. Mohr [Paul Siebeck]).
1995b	'The Attraction of Aristocratic Women to Pharisaism During the Second Temple Period', *HTR* 88: 1-33.
1997	*Mine and Yours are Hers: Retrieving Women's History from Rabbinic Literature* (Leiden: E.J. Brill).

Jansen, K.L.
2000	*The Making of the Magdalen: Preaching and Popular Devotion in the Later Middle Ages* (Princeton, NJ: Princeton University Press).

Jantzen, G.M.
1997	*Power, Gender and Christian Mysticism* (Cambridge Studies in Ideology and Religion, 8; Cambridge: Cambridge University Press).

Jastrow, M.
1982	*A Dictionary of the Targumim, the Talmud Babli and Yerushalmi, and the Midrashic Literature* (New York: The Judaic Press).

Jensen, A.
1992	*Gottes selbstbewusste Töchter. Frauenemanzipation im frühen Christentum?* (Freiburg: Herder Verlag).

Jeremias, J.
1962	*Jerusalem zur Zeit Jesu. Eine kulturgeschichtliche Untersuchung zur neutestamentlichen Zeitgeschichte* (Göttingen: Vandenhoeck & Ruprecht).

Jusino, R.K.
1998	'Mary Magdalene: Author of the Fourth Gospel?', http://www.Beloved Disciple.org

Karris, R.J.
1994	'Women and Discipleship in Luke', *CBQ* 56: 1-20.

Ketter, P.
1935	*The Magdalene Question* (trans. Revd H.C. Koehler; Milwaukee: The Bruce Publishing Company).

Kidd, I.G.
1971	'Posidonius on Emotions', in A.A. Long (ed.), *Problems in Stoicism* (London: Athlone): 200-215.

King, K.L.

1995 'The Gospel of Mary', in E. Schüssler Fiorenza (ed.), *Searching the Scriptures. II: A Feminist Commentary* (London: SCM Press): 601-634.

1998a 'Heiligverklaring en marginalisering: Maria Magdalena', *Concilium* 34/3: 35-43.

1998b 'Prophetic Power and Women's Authority: The Case of the *Gospel of Mary* (Magdalene)', in B.M. Kienzle and P.J. Walker (eds.), *Women Preachers and Prophets through Two Millennia of Christianity* (Berkeley: University of California Press): 21-41.

2002 'Why All the Controversy? Mary in the *Gospel of Mary*', in F. Stanley Jones (ed.), *Which Mary? The Marys of Early Christian Tradition* (Symposium Series, 19; Atlanta: Society of Biblical Literature): 53-74.

2003a *What is Gnosticism?* (Cambridge, MA and London: The Belknap Press of Harvard University).

2003b *The Gospel of Mary of Magdala: Jesus and the First Woman Apostle* (Sonoma, CA: Polebridge Press).

King, K.L. (ed.)

1988 *Images of the Feminine in Gnosticism* (Studies in Antiquity and Christianity, 3; Philadelphia: Fortress Press).

Kittel, G. (ed.)

1976 *Theological Dictionary of the New Testament* (trans. and ed. G.W. Bromily; Grand Rapids, MI: Eerdmans).

Klauck, H.-J.

1992 'Die dreifache Maria. Zur Rezeption von Joh 19,25 in EvPhil 32', in F. Van Segbroeck *et al.* (eds.), *The Four Gospels 1992. Festschrift Frans Neirynck III* (Leuven: Leuven University Press): 2343-57.

Koivunen, H.

1994 *The Woman Who Understood Completely: A Semiotic Analysis of the Mary Magdalene Myth in the Gnostic Gospel of Mary* (Acta Semiotica Fennica, 3; Helsinki: Imatra).

Kraemer, R.S.

1989 'Monastic Jewish Women in Greco-Roman Egypt: Philo on the Therapeutrides', *Signs* 4: 342-70.

1999a 'Jewish Women and Christian Origins: Some Caveats', in R.S. Kraemer and M.R. D'Angelo (eds.), *Women and Christian Origins* (New York and Oxford: Oxford University Press): 35-49.

1999b 'Jewish Women and Women's Judaism(s) at the Beginning of Christianity', in R.S. Kraemer and M.R. D'Angelo (eds.), *Women and Christian Origins* (New York and Oxford: Oxford University Press): 50-79.

Kühlewein, J.

1984 '*znh* huren', in E. Jenni and C. Westermann (eds.), *Theologisches Handwörterbuch zum Alten Testament. Band 1* (München: Chr. Kaiser Verlag): 518-20.

Lampe, G.W.H.

1961 *A Patristic Greek Lexikon* (Oxford: Clarendon Press).

Lane, W.L.

1974 *The Gospel According to Mark* (London: Marshall, Morgan & Scott).

Légasse, S.
    1997   *L'Évangile de Marc* (Lectio Divina Commentaires, 5; Paris: Éditions du Cerf).

Leisegang, H.
    1967   *Der heilige Geist. Das Wesen und Werden der mystisch-intuitive Erkenntnis in der Philosophie und Religion der Griechen. Band 1: Die vorchristlichen Anschauungen und Lehren vom Pneuma und der mystisch-intuitiven Erkenntnis* (Stuttgart: Teubner).

Liddell, H.G., and R. Scott (eds.)
    1968   *A Greek English Lexicon* (Oxford: Clarendon Press).

Lieu, J.M.
    1998   'The "Attraction of Women" in/to Early Judaism and Christianity: Gender and the Politics of Conversion', *JSNT* 72: 5-22.

Livingstone, E.A. (ed.)
    1977   *The Concise Oxford Dictionary of the Christian Church* (Oxford and New York: Oxford University Press).

Long, A.A.
    1968   'The Stoic Concept of Evil', *The Philosophical Quarterly* 18: 329-43.
    1974   *Hellenistic Philosophy: Stoics, Epicureans, Sceptics* (New York: Charles Scribner's Sons).

Longstaff, R.W.
    1981   'The Women at the Tomb: Matthew 28.1 Re-examined', *NTS* 27: 277-82.
    2000   'What Are Those Women Doing at the Tomb of Jesus? Perspectives on Matthew 28,1', in A.J. Levine and M. Blickenstaff (eds.), *A Feminist Companion to Matthew* (Sheffield: Sheffield Academic Press): 196-204.

Lucchesi, E.
    1985   'Évangile selon Marie ou Évangile selon Marie-Madeleine?', *Analecta Bollandiana* 103: 366.

Luttikhuizen, G.P.
    1988   'The Evaluation of the Teaching of Jesus in Christian Gnostic Revelation Dialogues', *NovT* 30: 158-68.

Maccini, R.G.
    1996   *Her Testimony is True: Women as Witnesses according to John* (JSNTSup, 125; Sheffield: Sheffield Academic Press).

MacLennon, H.
    1968   *Oxyrhynchus: An Economic and Social Study* (Amsterdam: Adolf M. Hakkert).

Maisch, I.
    1996   *Maria Magdalena. Zwischen Verachtung und Verehrung. Das Bild einer Frau im Spiegel der Jahrhunderte* (Freiburg: Herder Verlag).

Malbon, E.S.
    1986   'Disciples / Crowds / Whoever: Markan Characters and Readers', *NovT* 28: 104-130.

Malvern, M.
    1975   *Venus in Sackcloth: The Magdalen's Origins and Metamorphoses* (Carbondale and Edwardsville: Southern Illinois University Press).

Manns, F.
    1976   'Magdala dans les sources littéraires', in *Studia Hierosolymitana. In onore*

del P. Bagatti. I Studi Archeologici (Studium Biblicum Franciscanum, Collectio Maior; Jerusalem: Franciscan Printing Press): 307-37.

Margoliouth, D.S.
1927   'The Visit to the Tomb', *ExpTim* 28: 278-80.

Marjanen, A.
1996   *The Woman Jesus Loved: Mary Magdalene in the Nag Hammadi Library and Related Documents* (NHMS, 40; Leiden: E.J. Brill).
2002   'The Mother of Jesus or the Magdalene? The Identity of Mary in the So-Called Gnostic Christian Texts', in F. Stanley Jones (ed.), *Which Mary? The Marys of Early Christian Tradition* (Symposium Series, 19; Atlanta: Society of Biblical Literature): 31-42.

Maurer, C.
1977   'ῥίζα, ῥιζόω, ἐκριζόω', in *TDNT*, IV: 985-90.

Mayor, J.B.
1906   'Mary', in J. Hastings (ed.), *A Dictionary of the Bible Dealing with its Language, Literature and Contents Including the Biblical Theology* III (Edinburgh: T. & T. Clark): 278-86.

Melzer-Keller, H.
1997   *Jesus und die Frauen. Eine Verhältnisbestimmung nach den synoptischen Überlieferungen* (Herders biblische Studien, 14; Freiburg: Herder Verlag).

Metzger, B.M.
1987   *The Canon of the New Testament: Its Origin, Development, and Significance* (Oxford: Clarendon Press).

Meyer, M.W.
1985   ' "Male" and "Female" in the Gospel of Thomas', *NTS* 31: 554-70.

Michaelis, W.
1977   'ὁράω', in *TDNT*, V: 315-82.

Minear, S.
1974   'The Disciples and the Crowds in the Gospel of Matthew', *ATR*, Supplementary Series 3.

Mohri, E.
2000   *Maria Magdalena. Fraunbilder in Evangelientexten des 1. bis 3. Jahrhunderts* (Marburger Theologische Studien, 63; Marburg: N.G. Elwert Verlag).

Moltmann-Wendel, E.
1980   *Ein eigener Mensch werden. Frauen um Jesus* (Gütersloh: Gütersloher Verlagshaus Gerd Mohn).

Montandon, A. (ed.)
1999   *Marie-Madeleine. Figure mythique dans la littérature et les arts* (Clermont-Ferrand: Presses Universitaires Blaise Pascal).

Morard, F.
2001   'L'Évangile de Marie, un message ascétique', *Apocrypha* 12: 155-71.

Morris, J.
1987   'The Jewish Philosopher Philo', in E. Schürer (ed.), *The History of the Jewish People in the Age of Jesus Christ (175 B.C.-A.D. 135).* Volume III, part 2 (ed. Geza Vermes, Fergus Miller and Martin Goodman; Edinburgh: T. & T. Clark): 809-889.

Morris, L.

1995   *The Gospel According to John* (The New International Commentary on the New Testament; Grand Rapids, MI: Eerdmans, rev. edn).

Mosco, M. (ed.)

1986   *La Maddalena tra sacro e profano* (Milan: Mondadori).

Munro, W.

1982   'Women Disciples in Mark?', *CBQ* 44: 225-41.

Murray, R.

1975   *Symbols of Church and Kingdom: A Study in Early Syriac Tradition* (Cambridge: Cambridge University Press).

Neusner, J.

1980   *A History of the Mishnaic Law of Women* (Studies in Late Antiquity, 33; Leiden: E.J. Brill).

Newsom, C.A., and S.H. Ringe (eds.)

1992   *The Women's Bible Commentary* (Louisville, KY: Westminster/John Knox Press).

Neyrinck, F.

1969   'Les Femmes au Tombeau: Étude de la rédaction Matthéenne (Mat. XXVIII.1-10)', *NTS* 15: 168-90.

O'Collins, G.

1988   'The Fearful Silence of Three Women (Mark 16.8c)', *Gregorianum* 69: 489-503.

O'Day, G.R.

1992   'John', in C.A. Newsom and S.H. Ringe (eds.), *The Women's Bible Commentary* (Louisville, KY: Westminster/John Knox Press): 293-304.

Pagels, E.

1978   'Visions, Appearances and Apostolic Authority: Gnostic and Orthodox Traditions', in B. Aland (ed.), *Festschrift für Hans Jonas* (Göttingen: Vandenhoeck und Ruprecht): 415-30.

1981   *The Gnostic Gospels* (New York: Vintage Books).

Pasquier, A.

1981   'L'Eschatologie dans l'Évangile selon Marie: étude des notions de nature et d'image', in B. Barc (ed.), *Colloque International sur les textes de Nag Hammadi (Québec 22/8-25/8 1978)*. (Bibliothèque Copte de Nag Hammadi, section 'Études' 1; Québec: Les Presses de l'Université Laval).

1983   *L'Évangile selon Marie: texte établi et présenté* (Bibliothèque Copte de Nag Hammadi, sections 'Textes' 10; Québec: Les Presses de l'Université Laval).

Passcher, J.

1931   *Η ΒΑΣΙΛΙΚΗ ΟΔΟΣ. Der Königsweg zu Wiedergeburt und Vergottung bei Philon von Alexandreia* (Paderborn: Verlag Ferdinand Schöningh).

Perkins, P.

1980   *The Gnostic Dialogue: The Early Church and the Crisis of Gnosticism* (New York: Paulist Press).

1984   *Resurrection: New Testament Witness and Contemporary Reflection* (Garden City, NY: Doubleday).

Pesch, R.

1977   *Das Markusevangelium* (HTKNT, 2; Freiburg: Herder Verlag).

Petersen, S.
1999   *'Zerstört die Werke der Weiblichkeit!': Maria Magdalena, Salome & andere Jüngerinnen Jesu in christlich-gnostischen Schriften* (NHMS, 48; Leiden: E.J. Brill).
Pierre-Marie (Frère)
1995   'Marie-Madeleine', in Fraternités Monastiques de Jérusalem (ed.), *Vézelay* (Paris: Sources Vives): 7-22.
Pinto-Mathieu, E.
1997   *Marie-Madeleine dans la Littérature du Moyen Age* (Paris: Beauchesne).
Plaskow, J.
1994   'Anti-Judaism in Feminist Christian Interpretation', in E. Schüssler Fiorenza (ed.), *Searching the Scriptures. I: A Feminist Introduction* (London: SCM Press): 117-29.
Pohlenz, M.
1948   *Die Stoa. Geschichte einer geistigen Bewegung* (Göttingen: Vandenhoeck & Ruprecht).
Price, R.
1990   'Mary Magdalene: Gnostic Apostle?', *Grail* 6: 54-76.
Quispel, G.
1988   'De vrouw en de gnosis', in G. Quispel (ed.), *Gnosis: De derde component van de Europese cultuurtraditie* (Utrecht: Hes Uitgevers): 71-84.
Quispel, G. (ed.)
1988   *Gnosis: De derde component van de Europese cultuurtraditie* (Utrecht: Hes Uitgevers).
Reid, B.E.
1996   *Choosing the Better Part? Women in the Gospel of Luke* (Collegeville, MN: The Liturgical Press).
Reinhartz, A.
1994   'The Gospel of John', in E. Schüssler Fiorenza (ed.), *Searching the Scriptures. II: A Feminist Commentary* (London: SCM Press), pp. 561-600.
Rengstorf, K.
1976a   'ἑπτά', in *TDNT*, II: 627-35.
1976b   'διδάσκω', in *TDNT*, II: 135-65.
1977   'μανθάνω', in *TDNT*, IV: 390-461.
Ricci, C.
1994   *Mary Magdalene and Many Others: Women Who Followed Jesus* (trans. Paul Burns; Minneapolis: Fortress Press).
Roberts, C.H.
1979   *Manuscript, Society and Belief in Early Christian Egypt* (London: Oxford University Press).
Roloff, J.
1965   *Apostolat – Verkündigung – Kirche. Ursprung, Inhalt und Funktion des kirchlichen Apostelamtes nach Paulus, Lukas und den Pastoralbriefen* (Gütersloh: Gütersloher Verlagshaus Gerd Mohn).
Roukema, R.
1996   *De uitleg van Paulus' eerste brief aan de Corinthiërs in de tweede en derde eeuw* (Kampen: Kok).

1999   *Gnosis and Faith in Early Christianity: An Introduction to Gnosticism*
     (London: SCM Press).

2004   'Les anges attendant les âmes des défunts: une comparaison entre Origène et
     quelques gnostiques', in L. Perrone, P. Bernardini and D. Marchini (eds.),
     Origeniana Octava (Louvain: University Press, forthcoming): 367-74.

Rudolph, K.

1990   *Die Gnosis. Wesen und Geschichte einer Spätantiken Religion* (Dritte durch-
     gesehene und ergänzte Auflage; Göttingen: Vandenhoeck & Ruprecht).

1996   'Gnostische Reisen. Im Diesseits und im Jenseits', in K. Rudolph, *Gnosis
     und Spätantike Religionsgeschichte. Gesammelte Aufsätze* (NHMS, 42;
     Leiden: E.J. Brill): 244-55.

Runia, D.T.

1983   *Philo of Alexandria and the Timaeus of Plato* (Amsterdam: VU Boek-
     handel). Revised edition *Philo of Alexandria and the Timaeus of Plato*
     (Philosophia Antiqua, 44; Leiden: E.J. Brill, 1986).

1990   *Exegesis and Philosophy: Studies on Philo of Alexandria* (Collected Studies
     Series, 332; Hampshire: Variorum).

Ruschmann, S.

2002   *Maria von Magdala im Johannesevangelium* (Neutestamentliche Ab-
     handlungen, 40; Münster: Aschendorf).

Ryan, R.

1985   'The Women from Galilee and Discipleship in Luke', *BTB* 15: 56-59.

Safrai, C.

1991   *Women and the Temple: The Status and Role of Women in the Second
     Temple of Jerusalem* (Amsterdam: n.p.).

Sandbach, F.H.

1975   *The Stoics* (London: Chatto & Windus).

Sanders, E.P.

1993   *The Historical Figure of Jesus* (Harmondsworth: Penguin Press).

Saxer, V.

1959   *Le culte de Marie Madeleine en Occident. Des origines à la fin du Moyen
     Âge* (Cahiers d'archéologie et d'histoire, 3; Auxerre: Societé des Fouilles
     Archéologiques des Monuments Historiques de l'Yonne).

Schaberg, J.D.

1992   'Luke', in C.A. Newsom and S.H. Ringe (eds.), *The Women's Bible
     Commentary* (Louisville, KY: Westminster/John Knox Press): 275-92.

2002   *Resurrection of Mary Magdalen: Legends, Apocrypha, and the Christian
     Testament* (London: Continuum).

Schenke, H.-M.

1986   'The Function and Background of the Beloved Disciple in the Gospel of
     John', in C.W. Hedrick and R. Hodgson Jr (eds.), *Nag Hammadi,
     Gnosticism and Early Christianity* (Peabody, MA: Hendrickson): 111-25.

Schmid, R.

1990   *Maria Magdalena in Gnostischen Schriften* (München: Arbeitsgemeinschaft
     für Religions- und Weltanschauungsfragen).

Schnackenburg, R.

1965   'Der Menschensohn im Johannesevangelium', *NTS* 11: 123-37.

1975   *Das Johannesevangelium* (HTKNT, 4; Freiburg: Herder Verlag).

Schneiders, S.

1982   'Women in the Fourth Gospel and the Role of Women in the Contemporary Church', *BTB* 12: 35-45.

Scholer, D.M.

1971   *Nag Hammadi Bibliography 1948–1969* (NHS, 1; Leiden: E.J. Brill).

1997   *Nag Hammadi Bibliography 1970–1994* (NHS, 32; Leiden: E.J. Brill).

Schottroff, L.

1980   'Frauen in der Nachfolge Jesu in neutestamentlicher Zeit', in W. Schottroff and W. Stegemann (eds.), *Traditionen der Befreiung. Sozialgeschichtliche Bibelauslegungen. Band 2 Frauen in der Bibel* (München: Chr. Kaiser Verlag): 91-133 (repr. in L. Schottroff, *Befreiungserfahrungen. Studien zur Sozialgeschichte des frühen Christentums* [München: Chr. Kaiser Verlag, 1990]: 96-133).

1982   'Maria Magdalena und die Frauen am Grabe Jesu', *EvT* 42: 3-25 (repr. in L. Schottroff, *Befreiungserfahrungen. Studien zur Sozialgeschichte des frühen Christentums* [München: Chr. Kaiser Verlag, 1990]: 134-59).

Schottroff, L.S., and M.Th. Wacker (eds.)

1998   *Kompendium. Feministische Bibelauslegung* (Güterloh: Kaiser, Gütersloher Verlag Haus).

Schröter, J.

1999   'Zur Menschensohnvorstellung im Evangelium nach Maria', in S. Emmel *et al.* (eds.), *Ägypten und Nubien in spätantiker und christlicher Zeit. Akten des 6. Internationalen Koptologenkongresses Münster, 20-26. Juli 1996, Band 2 Schrifttum, Sprache und Gedankenwelt* (Wiesbaden: Reichert Verlag): 178-88.

Schuller, E.M.

1994   'Women in the Dead Sea Scrolls', in M.O. Wisse *et al.* (eds.), *Methods of Investigation of the Dead Sea Scrolls and the Khirbet of Qumran Site: Present Realities and Future Prospects* (Annals of the New York Academy of Science, 722; New York: New York Acadamy of Sciences): 115-31.

Schürmann, H.

1969   *Das Lukasevangelium* (HTKNT, 3; 2 vols.; Freiburg: Herder Verlag).

Schüssler Fiorenza, E.

1983   *In Memory of Her: A Feminist Theological Reconstruction of Christian Origins* (London: SCM Press).

1992   *But She Said: Feminist Practices of Biblical Interpretation* (Boston: Beacon Press).

Schüssler Fiorenza, E. (ed.)

1994   *Searching the Scriptures 1: A Feminist Introduction* (London: SCM Press).

1995   *Searching the Scriptures 2: A Feminist Commentary* (London: SCM Press).

Schweizer, E.

1982   'Scheidungsrecht der jüdische Frau? Weibliche Jünger Jesu?' *EvT* 42(3): 294-300.

Seim, T.K.

1987   'Roles of Women in the Gospel of John', in L. Hartman and B. Olsson (eds.), *Aspects on the Johannine Literature. Papers Presented at a Conference of Scandinavian New Testament Exegetes at Uppsala, June 16-19* (ConBNT, 18; Stockholm: Almquist & Wiksell), pp. 56-73.

1994   *The Double Message. Patterns of Gender in Luke-Acts, Studies of the New Testament and its World* (trans. Brian McNeil; Edinburgh: T&T Clark).

1995   'The Gospel of Luke', in E. Schüssler Fiorenza (ed.), *Searching the Scriptures: A Feminist Commentary* (London: SCM Press): 728-62.

Selvidge, M.J.

1983   'And Those Who Followed Feared. Mk. 10.32', *CBQ* 45: 396-400.

Shoemaker, S.J.

2001   'Rethinking the "Gnostic Mary": Mary of Nazareth and Mary of Magdala in Early Christian Tradition', *Journal of Early Christian Studies* 9.4: 555-95.

2002   'A Case of Mistaken Identity? Naming the Gnostic Mary', in F. Stanley Jones (ed.), *Which Mary? The Marys of Early Christian Tradition* (Symposium Series, 19; Atlanta: Society of Biblical Literature): 5-30.

Sickenberger, J.

1926   'Ist die Magdalenen-Frage wirklich unlösbar?' *BZ* 17: 63-74.

Siegert, F.

1982   *Nag-Hammadi-Register. Wörterbuch zur Erfassung der Begriffe in den koptisch-gnostischen Schriften von Nag-Hammadi* (WUNT, 26; Tübingen: J.C.B. Mohr [Paul Siebeck]).

Sim, D.C.

1989   'The Women Followers of Jesus: The Implications of Luke 8.1-3', *HeyJ* 30: 51-62.

Spanneut, M.

1957   *Le Stoïcisme des Pères de l'Église: de Clément de Rome à Clément d'Alexandrie* (Paris: Éditions du Seuil).

Stanley Jones, F. (ed.)

2002   *Which Mary? The Marys of Early Christian Tradition* (Symposium Series, 19; Atlanta: Society of Biblical Literature).

Starbird, M.

1993   *The Woman with the Alabaster Jar, Mary Magdalen and the Holy Grail* (Santa Fé, New Mexico: Bear & Co.).

1998   *The Goddess in the Gospels: Reclaiming the Sacred Feminine* (Santa Fé, New Mexico: Bear & Co.).

Steinmetz, P.

1994   *Die Stoa. Band 4*, in H. Flashar (ed.), *Die Hellenistische Philosophie. Die Philosophie der Antike. Grundriss der Geschichte der Philosophie begründet von F. Ueberweg* (2 vols.; Basel: Schwabe & A.G. Verlag).

Stock, A.S.

1994   *The Method and Message of Matthew* (A Michael Glazier Book; Collegeville, MN: The Liturgical Press).

Strack, H.L., and P. Billerbeck

1922   *Kommentar zum Neuen Testament aus Talmud und Midrasch* (München: Oskar Beck).

Stricker, B.H.

1990   *De Hemelvaart des Konings* (Mededelingen en verhandelingen van het Voorariatisch-Egyptisch Genootschap 'Ex Oriente Lux' XXVII) (Leiden: Ex Oriente Lux).

Swidler, L.

1976   *Women in Judaism: The Status of Women in Formative Judaism* (Metuchen, NJ: Scarecrow Press).

Synek, E.M.
    1995   'Die andere Maria. Zum Bild der Maria von Magdala in den östlichen
                    Kirchentraditionen', *Oriens Christianus* 79: 181-96.
Tardieu, M.
    1984   *Écrits Gnostiques: Codex de Berlin* (Sources gnostiques et manichéennes, 1;
                    Paris: Éditions du Cerf).
Tardieu, M., and J.-D. Dubois
    1986   *Introduction à la littérature gnostique. I: Collections retrouvées avant 1945*
                    (Paris: Éditions du Cerf).
Thimmes, P.
    1998   'Memory and Revision: Mary Magdalene Research since 1975', *Currents in
                    Research: Biblical Studies* 6: 193-226.
Thompson, M.R.
    1995   *Mary of Magdala: Apostle and Leader* (New York: Paulist Press).
Till, W.C.
    1978   *Koptische Grammatik (Saïdischer Dialekt). Mit Bibliographie, Lesestücken
                    und Wörterverzeichnissen* (Leipzig: VEB Verlag Enzyklopädie Leipzig).
Torjessen, K.J.
    1993   *When Women were Priests: Women's Leadership in the Early Church and
                    the Scandal of their Subordination in the Rise of Christianity* (San
                    Francisco: Harper).
Turner, E.G.
    1952   'Roman Oxyrhynchus', *Journal of Egyptian Archeology* 38: 78-93.
Van den Broek, R.
    1996   *Studies in Gnosticism and Alexandrian Christianity* (NHMS, 39; Leiden:
                    E.J. Brill).
Vander Stichele, C.
    1998   'Maria Magdalena und ihre Freundinnen', in L.S. Schottroff and M.Th.
                    Wacker (eds.), *Kompendium. Feministische Bibelauslegung* (Güterloh:
                    Kaiser, Gütersloher Verlag Haus): 789-94.
Van Haelst, J.
    1976   *Catalogue des papyrus littéraires juifs et chrétiens* (Université de Paris IV,
                    Serie Papyrologie –1; Paris: Publications de la Sorbonne).
Van Kooten, G.H.
    2001   *The Pauline Debate on the Cosmos: Graeco-Roman Cosmology and Jewish
                    Eschatology in Paul and the Pseudo-Pauline Letters to the Colossians and
                    the Ephesians* (Leiden: n.p.).
Van Tilborg, J.
    1993   *Imaginative Love in John* (Biblical Interpretation Series, 2; Leiden: E.J.
                    Brill).
Wainwright, E.M.
    1991   *Towards a Feminist Critical Reading of the Gospel according to Matthew*
                    (BZNW, 60; Berlin: Walter de Gruyter).
    1995   'The Gospel of Matthew', in E. Schüssler Fiorenza (ed.), *Searching the
                    Scriptures, volume 2: A Feminist Commentary* (London: SCM Press): 635-
                    77.
Warner, M.
    1985   *Alone of All Her Sex: The Myth and Cult of the Virgin Mary* (London: Pan
                    Books).

Watty, W.W.
1979   'The Significance of Anonymity in the Fourth Gospel', *ExpTim* 90: 209-212.
Westcott, B.F.
1902   *The Gospel According to St. John* (London: John Murray).
Wikenhauser, A.
1961   *Das Evangelium nach Johannes* (RNT, 4; Regensburg: Verlag Friedriech Pustet).
Wilkins, M.J.
1988   *The Concept of Disciple in Matthew's Gospel. As Reflected in the Use of the Term* μαθητης (NovTSup, 59; Leiden: E.J. Brill).
Williams, M.A.
1985   *The Immovable Race: A Gnostic Designation and the Theme of Stability in Late Antiquity* (NHS, 29; Leiden: E.J. Brill).
1988   'Variety in Gnostic Perspectives on Gender', in K.L. King (ed.), *Images of the Feminine in Gnosticism* (Studies in Antiquity and Christianity; Philadelphia: Fortress Press): 2-22.
1996   *Rethinking 'Gnosticism': An Argument for Dismantling a Dubious Category* (Princeton, NJ: Princeton University Press).
Wilson, R. McL.
1957   'The New Testament in the Gnostic Gospel of Mary', *NTS* 3: 236-43.
Wisse, F.
1988   'Flee Femininity: Antifemininity in Gnostic Texts and the Question of Social Milieu', in K.L. King (ed.), *Images of the Feminine in Gnosticism* (Studies in Antiquity and Christianity; Philadelphia: Fortress Press): 297-307.
Witherington, B. III
1979   'On the Road with Mary Magdalene, Joanna, Susanna and other Disciples – Luke 8.1-3', *ZNW* 70: 243-48.
1990   *Women and the Genesis of Christianity* (Cambridge: Cambridge University Press).
Zahn, Th.
1910   *Das Evangelium des Matthäus* (Kommentar zum Neuen Testamen, 1; Leipzig: A. Deichert).
1913   *Das Evangelium des Lucas* (Kommentar zum Neuen Testament, 3; Leipzig: A. Deichert).

INDEXES

INDEX OF REFERENCES

BIBLE

INDEX OF AUTHORS